COMMUNISM
AND THE
SPANISH CIVIL WAR

COMMUNISM
AND THE
SPANISH CIVIL WAR

BY

DAVID T. CATTELL

NEW YORK

RUSSELL & RUSSELL · INC

1965

FIRST PUBLISHED IN 1955
REISSUED, 1965, BY RUSSELL & RUSSELL, INC.
BY ARRANGEMENT WITH THE UNIVERSITY OF CALIFORNIA PRESS
L.C. CATALOG CARD NO: 65—17881

IN MEMORIAM

JOHN C. TREDWELL

PREFACE

AT THE BEGINNING of the Spanish Civil War, the Soviet Union was hailed by the Loyalists as their savior. In the face of Italian and German intervention in favor of General Franco, Russia violated her pledge of non-intervention and sent military aid to Republican Spain. She was the only great power willing to risk helping the Republicans. But two and a half years later, when the Republic had gone down in defeat, many Loyalist supporters considered the Soviet Union and the Communist Party of Spain not only the cause of their defeat but an enemy to be feared as much as Franco. Other participants and observers, however, reported it was only because of Soviet aid and advice that the Loyalists were able to hold out as long as they did. Which of these conflicting views on the Communists' role in Spain is the more valid? One of the purposes of this study is to examine the evidence in an effort to answer this question.

The Soviet Union's entrance into the League of Nations in 1934, and the signing of the defense pact with France in 1935, marked a sharp change in the Communists' interpretation of their relationship to other countries. Before 1934 the Soviet Union had viewed the world generally as split into two hostile camps—the Communists and the non-Communists. In 1934 this policy was revised providing for the temporary alliance of all anti-Fascists against fascism. This revised interpretation found its reflection not only in a change in Russian foreign policy but in the program of the Communist International. The Seventh Congress of the Comintern in 1935, defined this new policy of the United Front. The Spanish conflict, beginning in July, 1936, was the first real opportunity for the Comintern to put the United Front tactics into practical operation. This study will attempt to determine the success of the United Front policy in its first test case in Spain.

Several hypotheses have been advanced as to why the government of the Soviet Union intervened in Spain. The Fascist states, Catholic, and conservative elements throughout the world claimed that Russia's purpose was simply to set up a Soviet Republic. The pro-Communist interpretation, supported by much of the liberal opinion of the time, was that Russia was stopping the spread of fascism, upholding collective security, and protecting her ally, France, from encirclement by the Fascist powers. Those more skeptical of the Communists' motives thought that the Soviet Union was trying to involve Germany and the Western democracies in a war in the west in order to alleviate German pressure to the east. Finally, after the German-Soviet Pact in 1939, many declared that the Spanish adventure had merely been a build-up for the pact. Spain was to be used as a concession to Hitler in the negotiations and would serve to show Germany that Russia was a power of some consequence.

A complete discussion of these hypotheses requires a study both of the internal events within Spain itself and of the diplomacy of the Soviet Union and Western European powers in relation to the Civil War. Consequently, I have chosen to divide my analysis into two separate volumes. This volume will discuss internal events in Spain and the extent to which Communist policy was motivated by the desire to spread Communist hegemony. The second volume will analyze how Spain fitted into Russia's foreign policy and in what way, if any, she intended to use Spain to stop Hitler.

In spite of the emphasis placed on the international aspects of the Spanish Civil War by most writers, it is my contention that the Civil War was primarily caused by the outburst of a long accumulation of internal conflicts rather than by the action of a foreign power. It seems particularly fitting, therefore, that this first study should confine itself mainly to the internal phases since they are basic to all the issues involved.

Although this purports to be a study of only the Communist party in the Civil War it is manifestly impossible to lift the activities of the Communists out of their intricate relationships with all the other groups of Loyalist Spain. If this had been done a neat bundle of supposed facts could be set down to present a compact, clear picture which would have greatly simplified the problems. The results, however, could only have been half truths and distortions since the activities of the Communists are not meaningful without establishing their relationships to the Anarchists, Socialists, and Republicans, to the course of the fighting, and even to the personalities of the individuals involved.

I should like to express my gratitude to the various libraries and institutes which were helpful in the collection of material for this study. The Royal Institute of International Affairs, the Division of Historical Policy Research in the Department of State, and the International Institute of Social History in Amsterdam were particularly helpful in supplying material on Soviet participation in the Spanish Civil War. Miss Margaret Cleeve and Mrs. Jane Degras of the Royal Institute gave freely of their time. I am also especially indebted to Dr. E. Taylor Parks in the State Department for collecting pertinent information for me from State Department archives and from Italian documents. It was the excellent collection and the free use I was allowed to make of the Anarchist, Socialist, and Communist material in the International Institute of Social History in Amsterdam that gave me my clearest insight into the policies of the various factions of the Left in Spain during the Civil War. The helpful coöperation of all the members of the Institute has been greatly appreciated.

I am also profoundly grateful to the Social Science Research Council for the fellowship which they awarded me. This grant made it possible for me to travel to the libraries and archives in Europe and the United States and permitted me to spend full time on my research.

To Professor Philip E. Mosely, Director of the Russian Institute at Columbia University, I am indeed indebted, and grateful for his direction of this study as my doctoral dissertation. His encouragement and help in every conceivable way smoothed out many of the more difficult problems which I had to face. His advice was invaluable.

In conclusion it need hardly be said that without the long patient hours which my wife, Nancy, spent in helping me in every phase of the work this book would never have been completed.

D. T. C.

CONTENTS

CHAPTER   PAGE

I. The Origins of the Civil War 1
Social and Economic Backgrounds of the Civil War—The Problem
of Autonomy—The Political Organizations of the Left—The
Character of Spanish Politics.

II. The Second Republic 10
The Constituent Cortes—The Reaction—The Victory of the
Popular Front.

III. Communist Influence in Spain 19
Responsibility for the Civil War—Communist Strength Before
February, 1936—The Comintern and Spain—The Popular Front
in Spain—Growth of Communism After February, 1936.

IV. Responsibility for the Insurrection 35
The Nationalists Accuse—The "Red Menace"—A Fascist Plot—
A Domestic Problem.

V. The Generals Revolt 46
The Attempted Army Coup—The Communists and the Army
Coup—Communist Analysis of the Causes.

VI. The Communist Program 53
Spain and the United Front—A Democratic Revolution—The
Agrarian Policy of the Communists—Industry—The Church—
Autonomy.

VII. Formation of the Popular Front Government 65

VIII. Soviet Aid 69
Supplies from Russia—The Support of Non-Communist Groups—
Spanish Gold—The International Brigade.

IX. The Communist Leadership—Discipline and Unity . . 84
The Effect of Soviet Aid in Spain—A Regular Army—Discipline
in Industry—A New Type of Democracy—The Communist Party
Organization.

X. Infiltration 98
The Struggle for Power—The Siege of Madrid—Communist
Influence over the Government—The Soviet Advisers—The Power
of Soviet Aid—Communist Influence in the Cabinet—Communist
Infiltration of the Army—Communist Front Organizations—The
Activities of the *GPU* in Spain.

XI. A Plea for a Single Party of the Proletariat 120
The Communists and Largo Caballero's Leadership—A Single
Proletarian Party—The Communists' Changing Attitude toward
the Anarchists—Trade-union Unity.

[xi]

CHAPTER   PAGE

XII. The Kleber Incident 130

XIII. A Change in Communist Methods 132
The End of the Communist-Caballero Alliance—Terror against
the Anarchists—"The Trotskyite Traitors"—The Communists
and the Bourgeoisie—Reasons for the *Cheka* Terror.

XIV. The May Crisis. 141
"The Barcelona Revolt"—The Anarchists Accuse—An Anti-
Communist Plot?—The Allies of the Communists—The
Consequences of the Barcelona Revolt—The Reaction of the
Anarchists—Communist Propaganda in Catalonia.

XV. The Resignation of Largo Caballero. 153
The Communists *vs.* Largo Caballero—A Cabinet Crisis—The
Government of Negrín—Communist Aims.

XVI. The Aftermath of the Cabinet Crisis 164
The Anarchists Strike Back—The Communists Attempt to
Reassert the Popular Front.

XVII. The Elimination of the Opposition 169
The Activities and Character of the New Cabinet—The Opposition
—The End of the *POUM*—A Schism in the *UGT*.

XVIII. The Communists and the Right Socialists 179
Negotiations for a United Front—The Dissident Socialist Youth—
Anti-Communist Activities.

XIX. The Renewal of the Popular Front 187

XX. The Removal of Prieto 191
Prieto and the Communists—Another Cabinet Crisis.

XXI. The Last Days 200
The Policies of the New Negrín Cabinet—The Fall of Catalonia—
The Overthrow of Negrín and the Communists.

XXII. Conclusions 208
Communist Responsibility—The Lessons of Spain.

Notes 215

Bibliography 251

Index 271

CHAPTER I

THE ORIGINS OF THE CIVIL WAR

SOCIAL AND ECONOMIC BACKGROUNDS OF THE CIVIL WAR

A STUDY OF the problems posed by the Civil War must of necessity begin with some discussion of recent Spanish history. The hostilities in Spain from 1936 to 1939 had their roots primarily in the domestic situation of Spain itself. The revolution was the outcome of problems indigenous to Spain with very little relation to the events of the rest of Europe. During the past hundred years the most striking feature to the foreign traveler in Spain has been its isolation from the rest of Europe. The Pyrenees seem largely to have cut off this peninsular country from the civilization of Western Europe whose dynamic force invaded all the continents of the world but seemed to have passed over Spain. Although some sections of the intelligentsia and upper classes had absorbed some of the ideas of the French Revolution and of modern Western Europe, these conceptions had not affected the vast majority of Spaniards.

Many analysts, both Spanish and non-Spanish, have overlooked the isolation of Spain and have considered the Civil War only in its international context without any relation to the internal factors. Both sides in the conflict tended to support an international viewpoint in their propaganda, compressing all the issues simply into those of a world war. The very terms "Red" and "Fascist" which they called each other connote a world conflict between communism and the Axis. The propagandists, in stressing the international role of the Civil War, were motivated by several factors. Most armies, no matter how bloodthirsty and aroused, are not anxious to kill their fellow countrymen, particularly on such a wide scale and over so long a period as the Spanish Civil War. Consequently, propagandists on both sides tried to create the idea that the opponent was an alien element invading the homeland against whom most Spaniards could fight without compunction. Furthermore, since the Civil War was pictured as an international conflict, the Spanish soldier felt he was saving not only Spain but the whole world from the menace of communism or fascism. Finally, the international aspects of the war were stressed to develop allies abroad to help in the internal struggle. This attempt to categorize the other side as a foreign invader has tended to obscure the basic issues causing the war, which were peculiarly Spanish and had little connection with the over-all European conflict of this time.[1]

Ever since Spain was pushed from the apex of her power during the era of discovery by Great Britain, Spanish prosperity has been on the decline with only an occasional respite. Her decay was particularly marked in the nineteenth century. She had always based her wealth on the exploitation of her colonies, but as these fell away, Spain failed to replace her colonial sources with home industries and agriculture. The atmosphere of a constantly unstable political situation in Spain militated particularly against modernization and industrialization. Only on the fringes, in Barcelona and the Basque country, did the industrial revolution penetrate.

Except for the border areas the economy of Spain remained agricultural, based on a system of absentee landlords and large estates. The landowners were generally of the middle and upper classes who lived in the cities and seldom visited their land. Rent was normally a fixed payment of money, which, in the semiarid lands of a large part of Spain with their recurring droughts and the general uncertainty of crops, was often impossible to meet. The result was that most of the peasants had to borrow extensively. The lack of agricultural credit agencies forced the peasants to rely on the private moneylender who charged high rates of interest. In the areas of large estates in southern Spain, where most of the work was done by hired labor, the position of the peasant was even worse. The wages were only about thirty cents a day and rarely was a worker employed for the whole year—usually he was unemployed for four or five months of the year. The Catalonian and Basque farmers, however, were an exception to the general rule. Many owned their own farms, and those who rented were generally on good terms with their landlords, who usually lived close by.

The condition of the industrial proletariat was closely related to that of the peasants; as long as there were large pools of unemployed peasants to draw from, it was impossible for the factory workers to improve their standard of living. In the Basque provinces, however, which were separated from the large pools of unemployed agricultural workers of southern Spain, the lot of the workers was much better. The labor force was well organized into unions, and factory owners were usually willing to bargain with them.

Because of their low standard of living, verging on starvation, it is little wonder that the proletariat and peasantry resorted to violence and favored utopian schemes, such as anarchism, which offered them liberty and equalization of the vast differences between themselves and the landowners. Half-starved and with a bitter hatred for his superiors, the peasant in particular, once aroused, was revengeful and destroyed everything in his path. Peasant uprisings, which were frequent, left a path of carnage and pillage in their wake. Usually they were unorganized so that the whole countryside rarely rose at one time, thus permitting the government easily to suppress them.

Agricultural reform had been talked of and debated for over a century in Spain as the solution to peasant unrest. All but the most reactionary groups realized the necessity of reform. All the talk, however, came to nothing. Some feeble attempts were made by several regimes but the end results were negligible. The only real step taken to solve the problem was expropriation of the Church lands in the 1830's by the Liberals. The Church had been one of the largest landowners in Spain with about twelve million acres, approximately one-third of the tilled land. The Liberals, being imitators of the bourgeoisie of Western Europe and strong proponents of *laissez faire*, decided to sell the Church lands on the open market. Since the peasants needed land but did not have the money with which to purchase it, the lands were bought up by the rich landowners and the middle class who continued the policy of absentee landlordism. Thus the Liberal reform only tended to aggravate the agrarian problem.

By 1900 agriculture in Spain had reached such a state that any reform which would do substantial good required a long era of political stability, careful planning, the coöperation of all concerned, and money to establish the necessary irrigation projects and to improve the soil. No government which came to power had these necessary prerequisites. The instability of the governments in Spain was notorious. The average government in the 1900's lasted little over a year. Only during the dictatorship of Primo de Rivera (1923–1930) was there the necessary time and stability to start the tremendous task of reform. Primo de Rivera, however, had little interest in such a move and his only effort in this direction was to improve the irrigation system. His supporters of the Right and the King had even less interest in changes.

The lack of ability within the government bureaucracy to plan and carry out the necessary reforms was even more apparent. The bureaucracy was overcrowded with government employees of no ability: a modern competitive civil service was unknown. Employees got their positions as rewards for political services and they looked on them not as duties but as positions of exploitation. The government workers were so numerous it was impossible to pay large salaries, so that the bureaucrats used their positions to extort money by bribery and graft. Such a group was certainly not interested in carrying out an agricultural reform.

Coöperation by either the landowners or peasantry was also not forthcoming. The landowners, who controlled the government until 1931 except for a few short periods, resisted reforms.[2] They were only interested in solidifying their position against the growing enmity of the Left. The peasants, on the other hand, although interested in reform, would not wait until it could be carried out in an orderly fashion. Once in a dominating position, they destroyed everything that was the landowners' and then took over the land without the necessary tools or planning required to cultivate it with any success. The government also lacked the money to carry out any plans. It would have necessitated careful budgeting over a number of years in as poor a country as Spain to gain the funds to modernize agriculture. But the budget was never established with a view to economy or public improvement. Primo de Rivera, in his dictatorship, made some attempt at public improvement, aided by the boom of the 1920's. The projects, however, were the sources of widespread graft and soon ran the country into debt.

Although the agrarian problem in Spain was the prime disintegrating factor, other factors also made for unsettled conditions. The Church in Spain, which had once been the most vigorous branch of the Church in Europe, disintegrated with the empire. Changing from its earlier position of looking out for the welfare of the masses, the Church went into league with the landowners. With the loss of the Church lands in the 1830's, the Catholic hierarchy took less and less interest in the peasants. It became obsessed with the building of a fortune by industrial and commercial investment in order to have power to fight anticlericalism, which threatened to reduce its influence in the country as it had done in France. Only the village priest remained in contact with the people, but since he often had an income little better than that of his parishioners, poverty plus poor education made his task a hopeless one.[3] For the peasant, the Church, which had once given him solace, hope, and charity, and which he would support with his life as he had done in 1808 against Napoleon, had failed him and gone over to the enemy.[4] He turned against it with all his vengeance and throughout the nineteenth and twentieth centuries when the peasants rose and shed blood, the blood of the Church was shed too. Church burnings and shootings of priests became common during this period. With the growth of atheism and the opening of a religious void, socialism, and especially anarchism, found an easy path into the passions of the workers and peasants.

THE PROBLEM OF AUTONOMY

The antagonism based on class lines was made more complex by rivalry on geographic lines. In Spain the province of Castile occupies the central position. It had the largest population and for the previous three hundred years had dominated the country. It was, however, one of the most backward sections of Spain, whereas Catalonia and the Basque country during the industrial revolution assumed the aspect of modern industrial regions. The middle classes of these border areas resented the domination by more backward Castile. Furthermore, the Basques and Catalonians were interested in programs of public endeavor in their regions for better education, irrigation, more and better railroads and roads, but they were unlikely to get help from the corrupt regime in Madrid and, if they did so, it would come only at a very high cost. This feeling of resentment soon developed into a movement for greater autonomy. It never produced a separatist movement because the industries of these regions needed the protected markets of Spain as an outlet for their goods. They stood little chance of competing against the larger industrial countries. This autonomy movement was also in keeping with the strong local loyalties among all the peoples of Spain. Most Spaniards were loyal first to their own village or town and second to Spain.[5]

The movement for autonomy in the nineteenth and twentieth centuries among the Basques and Catalonians had a very difficult history. The final result was that by the time of Primo de Rivera they had made little headway against the jealous domination of the Castilians. With the dictatorship, even this little was taken away. But the pressure and desire for autonomy, in spite of frustration, had not lessened over these years, but only increased so that by 1931 the problem of autonomy had become acute.

THE POLITICAL ORGANIZATIONS OF THE LEFT

The growing antagonism of the peasants and workers against the ruling circles in Spain organized itself primarily into two groups—moderate Marxian Socialists and Anarchists.[6] The development of socialism followed very closely the pattern of growth in other countries of Western Europe, relying for its main strength on a strong federation of trade-unions, the *Unión General de Trabajadores (UGT)*, founded in 1888. The growth of the *UGT* was steady, with some fluctuations as strikes called by the union succeeded or failed, until in 1931 it had almost one million members. It was centered largely around Madrid. Spanish socialism, which, compared with anarchism, has authoritarian and centralistic tendencies, appealed to the Castilian workers. The *UGT*, together with the Catholic unions, also was strong in the industrial centers of the north because of its moderation and absence of terroristic methods.

The policy of the Socialist unions and party was moderate, relying on parliamentary tactics, bargaining, and peaceful strikes to gain their ends. Pablo Iglesias, long the leader of both the *UGT* and the Socialist party, had urged restraint and had influenced the party not to adhere to the Third International in 1921. But moderation and parliamentarianism in Spain, where all elections were made through a system of caciques, or political bosses, and rule was by force, could not expect to get very far. Consequently, the mild program of the Socialists, in their attempt to follow the democratic pattern in a revolutionary situation, turned many of the workers away from it into the hands of the more revolutionary party of anarchism. But as violence became more and more the order of the day in the 1930's the Socialists, under the influence of Largo Caballero, the Secretary-General of the *UGT*, became more and more revolutionary in their outlook and adopted the general strike and revolution as necessary tools to their ends.[7] This change in the attitude of the Socialist party had a very important effect on the events of the Republic after 1931. It meant that the Anarchists and the Socialists were moving closer together to a point where they could coöperate in gaining their ends. It is the coöperation of these two forces of the Left which turned the balance of power against the upper classes in favor of the masses and ultimately produced the Civil War in 1936.

The other channel of leftist activity was the Anarchist movement, which, like the Socialist movement, was closely allied with its trade-union organization, the *Confederación Nacional del Trabajo (CNT)*. The Anarchist political and revolutionary leadership was under the *Federación Anarquista Ibérica (FAI)*, founded in 1927. The *FAI* was composed in general of the leaders of the various syndicates of the *CNT* and was the sole unifying factor of the Anarchist movement in respect to doctrine and revolutionary activity.[8] Except for the *FAI* the Anarcho-Syndicalist organization was just a loose band of trade-unions without any common program of action or leadership. One of the distinguishing features of the Anarcho-Syndicalists, in comparison with the Socialists, was this decentralization and stress on localism. No union could be compelled from above to call a strike or take up revolutionary activity. Since all action had to come spontaneously from below it seldom happened that all the unions of the *CNT* came out on strike together or resorted to concerted violence.

The Anarchist movement was essentially a reaction against force from above and authoritarianism. Anarchism, with its dream of life without a state, with every individual living in coöperative companionship with other men without compulsion, has had little appeal to the practical trade-unions of the industrial states of Western Europe. Likewise, the use of excessive violence in the destruction of the state and the bourgeoisie has made little headway in the rest of Western Europe. Only to a small degree in Italy, and more extensively in Spain, has this ideology found any satisfaction. The elements which turned the workers of Germany, England, and France away from anarchism were those which most appealed to the Spanish masses. Their quick Latin anger, which often led to bloodshed; their revulsion against the excesses of the state and the landowners; their religious zeal, which had once found its expression in the reconquest of Spain for Christianity, in the spreading of Catholicism in the New World, and in the Inquisition, found realization in the latter part of the nineteenth century in the violence and utopianism of anarchism.[9]

The spread of anarchism was mostly through the south of Spain and in the turbulent city of Barcelona, which depended for its labor supply largely on the poor agricultural regions of southern Spain. There were also a few *CNT* enclaves of anarchism in Madrid and Asturias. The numerical strength of the *CNT* was somewhat larger than that of the *UGT*, running to well over a million in 1931.

The Character of Spanish Politics

The Civil War or Revolution, which broke out in 1936, was by no means the first outbreak of unrest in Spain. Nor was the generals' insurrection of July 19, 1936, the first military coup ever to be attempted in Spain. From the period of the Napoleonic Wars military revolts and government by generals were common: the army always stood ready to take advantage of troubled times.

In 1808 the Spanish masses, having shaken off their usual lethargy as they were to do again in 1936, arose and fought to rid themselves of Napoleon. The defeat of Napoleon did not, however, bring Spain the sought-for peace, but plunged her deep into a half century of civil war during which the army took the opportunity to stage several coups. The struggle was a prolonged rivalry between the Liberals, who wanted to introduce a new bourgeois-type state, and the Conservatives, led at first by the Carlists, who wanted to restore the Inquisition and return to the old days. In these first years the Conservatives were allied with the Church and had a large following in the northern part of Spain, whereas the Liberals, on their side, had most of the middle class and the army. The masses of the south remained apathetic.

With the final defeat of the Carlists in 1874, and with the growth of political consciousness in the forms of anarchism and socialism among the peasants and especially the industrial workers at the end of the nineteenth century, the alignment of forces changed. The Conservatives and the Liberals became indistinguishable. Though the Liberals still formally maintained an anticlerical policy, their main aim was to share with the Conservatives the spoils of office and maintain the *status quo* against the lower classes. The two parties, by a gentleman's agreement, alternated in ruling the country. The army by this time had gone over to the Conservative side with the Liberals. The Church also, in a desire for power and wealth, had become allied with the upper classes and had lost most of its popular support. During the latter part of the nineteenth century this alliance of Liberals, Conservatives, Church, and army had little difficulty in controlling the country. By the system of caciques they were able, through coercion, to achieve any electoral outcome they desired. Election results could even be published days in advance.

As the political articulation and organization of the masses expanded, the system of controlled elections became more and more difficult. The caciques found it was necessary to use ever increasing force to gain the desired results, and sometimes even forceful methods were not enough against the resistance of the people. At the turn of the century the superiority of the forces of the Right and those for the *status quo* was rapidly diminishing. Their cause was not helped by the intrigues and games of King Alfonso XIII, and by their own resistance to all regional movements, which alienated a large section of the Catalonians and the Basques who tended to be religious and conservative regardless of class. The Conservatives and Liberals chose rather to rule by repression, which allowed the Left to make more and more converts and arouse the people to action, particularly in Catalonia.

In Barcelona, the struggle in the early part of the twentieth century assumed a state of semi-civil war. Gangs of *pistoleros*, representing the police and *CNT*, were in almost open warfare against each other, throwing bombs and carrying out assassinations. Three prime ministers were eliminated within less than two years as reprisals against the assassination or execution of Anarchists.

In the long period of unrest, from about 1820 to 1874, when the antagonistic Liberals and Conservatives had been nearly equal, and neither side was able to force a decision on the other, the army had stood as the balancing factor and often stepped in and established a military government. By the early 1920's the same set of circumstances had again developed. The forces of the Left were not yet powerful enough to take command, and the bureaucratic government of the Right was no longer strong enough or competent enough to hold the revolutionary forces in check; as a result the army took charge in the person of General Primo de Rivera. Although Primo de Rivera was not a direct candidate of the army, he depended upon it for his major support along with the conservative elements of the country.

Like many a military dictatorship, Primo de Rivera's regime was greeted with great enthusiasm as a desired change, but soon proved disappointing. It turned out to be only the lull before the storm. The factions of the Right and Left were too bitter and uncompromising ever to come to a peaceful settlement, and too strong to refrain from open force for long.

The only real accomplishment of Primo de Rivera's rule was the successful conclusion of the Moroccan War with the help of the French. He also gave Spain a modern system of roads and more irrigation and electricity. These, however, were purchased at an excessive cost and large budget deficits so that the 1929 collapse hit Spain an extra hard blow. It was the apprehension of both sides, and the boom of the 1920's, that kept Primo de Rivera in office so long. By 1929 Primo de Rivera had lost all his support; the army, the Conservatives, and the Church had all deserted him. He proved to be merely a figurehead. When Alfonso XIII asked him to resign in 1930, his house of cards fell apart and he quietly retired to Paris and died.

Unfortunately for Alfonso, the fall of Primo de Rivera had taken his prestige along with it, since he had been associated so closely with the dictatorship. He tried desperately to separate himself from this disgrace, but to no avail. The King, in the face of overwhelming odds, reluctantly called for elections, starting first with municipal elections and hoping to hold off the issue as long as possible in order to try to reëstablish the old system of controlled voting. But matters had gone too far for any return to the past, and the municipal elections by themselves proved fatal. The elections showed a strong Republican sentiment, though not as strong as at first appeared. The King, failing to win even the support of the army, left the country for good and immediately a Republic was proclaimed.

CHAPTER II

THE SECOND REPUBLIC

The Constituent Cortes

THE REPUBLIC had been proclaimed without bloodshed or the excesses that usually come with the overthrow of the *status quo*. The forces of the Left and Center had won without a struggle. But such a superficial interpretation of events was all too deceiving. The municipal election returns themselves proved that in the country districts, at least, the Right was able to maintain its control, whether through apathy, force, or genuine support.[1] Disregarding voting strength, the military and economic power of the Right was far from having been sheared: it was caught temporarily unorganized and unprepared. The eight years of comparatively mild dictatorship of Primo de Rivera had lulled the Right into a feeling of complacency, but had by no means lessened its potential power.

The July, 1931 election to the Cortes, the national parliament, came two months after the municipal elections and resulted in a strong Left victory, particularly for the moderate Left. In a country which had been polarizing for the last fifty years, this appearance of a strong vote for moderation was surprising. Below is the approximate division of seats:

PARTY	DEPUTIES
Socialists	116
Left Republicans	160
Right Republicans	110
Right	60[2]

The strong Left Republican vote, however, was by no means a true indication of the degree of fundamental support among the people. The popularity of the Republicans had reached a peak at this time because of the ease with which they had brought about the Republic. Since the first step had been so simple there was buoyant optimism concerning the Republicans' ability to bring about reforms without bloodshed, but this confidence was soon to lapse when they began to face the difficult and complex problems of trying to carry out a revolution peacefully. The seeming vitality of the Republican movement is proven even more false when the support of the Anarchists is examined. The *CNT* and the *FAI*, true to their ideology of having nothing to do with the state, refused to put up candidates for the Cortes. But over the question of whether they should go to the polls and vote, there was sharp division among the Anarchists. Enthusiasm for the Republic, however, brought most of the

[10]

Anarchists out to vote, but only a minority remained rigidly doctrinaire. Because of close rivalry, the Anarchist vote was not generally in favor of the Socialists whose program was nearest to their own. They chose rather to vote for the Republicans, thereby swelling the ranks of the Republicans in the Cortes by their ballots.

The Republic, in spite of the hope it inspired, was born under the ill-fated star of world depression. Unemployment, the flight of capital, the falling value of the peseta, and the closing down of industries supplied a backdrop for the Republican play which was to end in tragedy.

The Constitution which the new Cortes created had nothing in it that, under other circumstances, might not have suited a democracy well. For Spain in 1931 it was utopian. The Constitution itself was generally not a factor in the collapse of the Republic but stood outside it, not affecting the situation either way. Salvador de Madariaga has suggested, however, that the lack of a senate acting as a moderating second chamber was important. But it is doubtful whether such a moderating influence could have been of much use in the violence of the next years.

The only elements of the Constitution which seem to have been outright mistakes and contributed appreciably to the fire under the caldron were the clauses on the Church. The Church had been a strong supporter of the monarchy and the dictatorship and had attempted to associate all Republicans with Moscow and atheistic communism. The members of the Constituent Cortes, as a result, let their passions control when it came time to legislate in respect to the Church, determined to break the chief supporter of reaction. They voted for the disbandment of the Jesuits, the closing of all convents and religious schools (except seminaries), and rescinded the annual state grant to the clergy. In closing the religious schools in a fit of anger, the new government was able to do little about supplying the twenty-seven hundred state schools needed to replace them. Such a project required time to educate teachers and build facilities. The cutting of the Church subsidy was even more foolish since the village clergy already was poor and usually suffered the same lot as the parishioners. The majority of the village priests had long been isolated from the Church hierarchy and very often were strong supporters of the Republican cause. Cutting off their salary could but alienate them from the new regime and force them over to the side of the Right. The Cortes, which had passed most of the Constitution with little debate, split on the Church issues. The Basque deputies and several others walked out of the assembly, weakening the Republican cause even further.

The problem of regionalism was solved quite easily. Except for the grumblings of some Castilians, statutes of local autonomy were being worked out. On September 9, 1931, the Cortes passed the Catalan statute with only a few modifications. The internal divisions between the Basques and Navarrese slowed up their statute, and autonomy was not granted by the Cortes before the reaction to the Right in 1933.

The agrarian problem presented a much more serious difficulty. The law was delayed for a year before it finally secured passage in two parts in July and September, 1932. The problems which stood in the way of successful completion of this reform were insurmountable. There was first of all a basic difference between the Socialists and Republicans as to the type of reform needed. The Socialists wanted a collectivist solution, whereas the Republicans wanted the establishment of individual farms. Furthermore, collapse of the world market during the depression put the whole farm problem in chaos. Added to this were the growing impatience and uneasiness of the peasantry and the obstinacy of the landowners. Against these difficulties the Institute of Agrarian Reform set up by the Statute of 1932 was able to make little progress before the reaction of 1933.

Before the Constitution had even been settled, unrest spread across the country. The Republic had not brought the immediate relief many had expected, and the growth of unemployment made the situation perilous. The Republic found itself helpless against these forces. In January, 1932, there was an Anarchist uprising in the Llobregat Valley, followed by periodic risings throughout Spain, especially in the south and in Barcelona, including a *Putsch* by the Right. The government met these rebellious actions with force, quelling them in the same fashion that they had always been suppressed—by the use of troops and imprisonment—thus bringing further discredit to the regime. One suppression in the small town of Casa Viejas was particularly brutal and indignation was widespread. The government was finally forced to make a full investigation. A long series of strikes and gang warfare added further to the unrest, until the situation approached that of the black days of 1917–1920, just before the dictatorship of Primo de Rivera.

THE REACTION

When the old Cortes was dissolved and new elections were called in November and December, 1933, the Republican government was at a low ebb of popularity. It had become discredited and the pendulum had swung sharply to the Right. Following is a breakdown of the election results:

PARTY	NUMBER OF DEPUTIES	
	1931	1933
Socialists.................................	116	59*
Left Republicans..........................	160	40
Right Republicans.........................	110	167
Right.....................................	60	207[3]

*Includes one Communist deputy

The movement to the Right was by no means as sharp as the composition of the Cortes indicated. In the first place the election law of the Cortes favored large parties or a coalition of parties. The majority of the seats in a district (thirteen out of seventeen in Madrid) went to the party with the highest number of votes no matter what the minority parties might poll, even though combined they obtained an overwhelming majority of votes. The parties of the Right had taken advantage of the electoral law and combined, but the parties of the Left refused to ally. Secondly, the Right had by this time awakened to the danger of the Left and had brought their full force and organization to bear on the elections. The enfranchisement of women may also have made the vote more conservative. Even more significant to the outcome was the attitude of the Anarchists. In 1931 the majority had gone to the polls, but the repression of Anarchist uprisings by the Left Republican governments had confirmed the Anarchists in their doctrine of having nothing to do with the state. The Anarchists this time carried on an extensive campaign of *no votad*, which kept most of their followers away from the polls. The factors above, however, cannot account for the complete swing to the Right. This can only be explained by the failure and discredit ascribed to the Republican forces during their term in office.

The government of the Right proved to be only an attempt to annul the decisions of the Left and to return to the past. The leadership of the Right was under José María Gil Robles, who was the head of the largest element within the Right—the *Confederación Española de Derechos Autónomos (CEDA)*. Although pressure from the Left and the enmity of the moderate Republican President Alcalá Zamora kept Gil Robles from being actual prime minister, he effectively controlled the destinies of the government from outside. Most of the legislation improving labor conditions passed by the Constituent Cortes was revoked. Church legislation was allowed to lapse or go unheeded, and the lands expropriated under the agrarian reform were returned to their original owners. More unrest and uprisings were the answers of the people to the new government. As early as December 8, 1933, the Anarchists in Aragon broke out in revolt, and church burnings and strikes became more and more frequent throughout Spain.

Before long the government also came into conflict with Catalonia and the Basque provinces. They refused to pass the autonomy statute of the Basques, and in protest the municipal councillors in the Basque towns resigned. In Catalonia the government of the Generalitat had set up its own agricultural reform law but it was revoked by the Madrid government. The Generalitat promulgated it in defiance anyway.

The crisis came in October, 1934, when Gil Robles withdrew his support from the government of the Right Center led by the Radical party, and demanded the majority of the posts in the next cabinet for his coalition, the *CEDA*. Such an act, the Left stated, would mean a declaration of war. President Alcalá Zamora, in an effort to compromise and adhere to the Constitution, allowed the *CEDA* to be given three minor positions in the next cabinet. The Socialists refused to accept this and declared a general strike on October 5. The strike, which soon took on the character of an armed rebellion, revealed three centers: Asturias, Madrid, and Barcelona. The rebellion in Barcelona was quickly doomed to failure without the support of the *CNT*, which refused to participate. Catalonia lost her autonomy as a result of her participation. The Madrid rising was also a fiasco because the Socialists lacked the necessary arms, and because the army in Madrid was too strong. Only in Asturias did the rebellion reach significant proportions, but because they received no help from the other parts of Spain there was no chance of success. The Asturian miners lashed out and gained control of the area around Oviedo, including Gijón, but the government, with the help of Moorish troops and the Foreign Legion, forced the miners to surrender on October 17. The whole center of Oviedo was destroyed and it has been estimated that some 3,000 were killed and 7,000 wounded in the struggle, mostly workers. Approximately 70,000 laborers had risen.

Though the Asturias revolt had failed, it struck terror into the hearts of the Right and showed clearly the bitterness beneath the conflict between the Right and Left. On the side of the Left the working masses of Spain were aroused, and the miners became heroes. The use of the Moors and the Foreign Legion, considered foreigners by Spaniards, especially aroused the ire of the people. But more important to the Left was the lesson it taught: in the Asturias uprising for the first time the *CNT* and the *UGT*, along with some Communists, had united in their struggle against the Right, and only there had the rebellion reached the proportions of a real revolt. The lesson was obvious, and was quickly learned.

Gil Robles had won his seats in the cabinet at a high price. From October, 1934, to 1936, the Right ruled unopposed. The situation in the country did not improve. The mass reprisals after the revolt, continued unemployment, and the fall of wages made conditions very serious. The landowners, having learned nothing, went right back to doing what they had always done, squeezing the workers for the lowest possible wages and leaving large areas uncultivated. In spite of the warning signs, Gil Robles was riding high. The *CEDA* had a mushroom growth among the alarmed bourgeoisie and Gil Robles went so far as to demand a complete reform of the Constitution. Gil Robles, however, even with his increased following, was not able to give his government stability, and it remained ineffective and weak with its composition constantly changing. The threat of the Left, in spite of the 1934 repression, was still strong. Gil Robles was forced to postpone indefinitely constitutional changes because the revolutionary parties threatened renewal of armed revolt. Furthermore, the government was unable to straighten out the finances. The public debt continued to rise and the economic condition of the country was rapidly growing worse. The Finance Secretary, Don Joaquín Chapaprieta, tried, to no avail, to carry out reforms against the pressure of the Conservatives. This unstable state of affairs came to an end when President Alcalá Zamora, who still refused to allow the premiership to Gil Robles, could no longer find a cabinet and granted a decree of dissolution of the Cortes on January 7, 1936.

THE VICTORY OF THE POPULAR FRONT

The revolutionary forces had been only temporarily defeated at Asturias and the repression of participants in the uprising was used effectively by the Left to gain prestige. At the same time they prepared for future rounds by strengthening their organizations. With the dissolution of the Cortes, the parties of the Left combined their electioneering in order to take advantage of the election law. The Anarchists refused, as usual, to take part in developing a slate of candidates. On January 15, 1936, however, the other parties of the Left joined in the Popular Front. This included the Socialists, Left Republicans, Union Republicans (a dissident branch of the Radicals), the Syndicalist party, the National Federation of Socialist Youth, the Communist party, and the *POUM* (*Partido Obrero de Unificación Marxista*). The Anarchists, although not signing the pact of the Popular Front, supported it. In 1933 they had learned the danger of abstaining. Furthermore, the promise of amnesty to all political prisoners won their sanction, since large numbers of their leaders were in prison.

The alliance was only an election alliance although a common program was set up as a basis for campaigning. The program was extremely mild and asked only for the return to pre-1933. It refrained from demanding nationalization of land, industry, or even the Bank of Spain, and there was to be no further persecution of the Church. The agricultural reform was to continue, but there was no mention of mass expropriation and, generally, the program aimed to improve the economic and educational standards of the country.[4] In a revolutionary atmosphere such a mild program was astounding, and shows the strength of Manuel Azaña, leader of the moderate elements, and the Left Republicans.

In the elections of February, the Right and Left were competing on even ground. In spite of the intensity of passions the day of election itself was very calm and few incidents occurred. The Popular Front won an overwhelming number of seats. Following is the approximate division of seats among the important groups:

PARTY	DEPUTIES
Popular Front	256
Right Republican or Center	55
Right	143

Supplementary elections were held on March 1, and altered the above figures slightly in favor of the Popular Front.[5]

The popular vote, on the other hand, did not show an overwhelmingly strong Left vote. The results were very close and, depending on the source of figures, the Left and Right were each credited with the absolute majority. The outstanding feature of the election was the weakening of the Right Republicans from 167 to 55 seats. Their popular vote showed a similar decline. The actual strength of the Left Republicans cannot be surmised because they were part of the Popular Front and the division of seats within this group was on the basis of a prearranged percentage. The weakening of the Right Center was due primarily to its failure as a government from 1933. Its rule had been discredited by its weakness and the repressions, particularly after the Asturias revolt. Its decline was furthermore an indication of growing polarity of opinion throughout the country. The bourgeoisie in particular had abandoned the Center for the Right, in fear of an open rebellion of the Left.

The next five months, after February, 1936, showed a weakening of the forces of moderation and a rapid disintegration of civil order. The role of the Cortes became less important as it was used more and more for the endless polemics and acrimony of both sides. The only important act of the Cortes was the removal of Alcalá Zamora as President and the election of Manuel Azaña in his place.

The struggle in the streets and country on the other hand was taking on serious proportions. The countryside had been in a state of turmoil for a number of years and these five months saw a crescendo in its intensity. Burning of convents, the seizure of land, and the burning of the landowners' homes and fields became everyday occurrences. In the cities, assassinations and gang warfare went on almost continuously. The main perpetrators of these crimes were the extreme Right and revolutionary Left. The Fascist Falange, which grew rapidly in these months, and the terrorist groups of Socialists and particularly the Anarchists were both responsible. Gil Robles, defending a motion of the Right demanding government measures for the restoration of order, informed the Cortes on June 16, of the recent damage to property and bloodshed: 160 churches destroyed; 251 churches damaged; 269 people killed; 1,287 wounded; 381 buildings attacked or damaged; 113 strikes; 228 partial strikes; 43 newspaper offices attacked or destroyed; and 146 bombs thrown. His figures went unchallenged. It would be difficult to prove these figures but most authorities, Right and Left, agree that they are near to being correct. It would be wrong, however, to assume, as Gil Robles indicated, that the crimes had been perpetrated by the Left only. These figures are an indication of the growing anarchy throughout the country and the inability of the government to do anything about it.[6] Mass demonstrations were an everyday occurrence. At the same time the economic situation was worsening. Unemployment was ever on the increase and factories continued to shut down. The peseta was further devaluated as a result of the heavy flow of capital abroad—most of it being sent by the middle and upper classes, who feared the consequences of a Left government.

A marked tendency throughout this period was the weakening of the forces for moderation. Manuel Azaña, the voice of moderation, lost his prestige, whereas Largo Caballero, as the head of the revolutionary section of socialism, became the popular hero. During this period of uneasiness Largo Caballero, who had originally "collaborated" with the dictatorship of Primo de Rivera, began giving speeches demanding the immediate inauguration of socialism. His speeches calling for a collectivist utopia and a government of peasants and workers caused a further spread of alarm among the Right, and also kept the Left from seeing the developing insurrection on the part of the Right. His demagoguery made even the moderate elements uneasy. Manuel Irujo, a Basque Nationalist, who became a minister in the Republican government during the Civil

War, declared in a speech to the Cortes on April 18, that the danger to the government was more from the Left than from the Right.[7] Caballero resisted all attempts at moderation. Azaña wanted to replace the weak government of Left Republicans under Casares Quiroga by a Popular Front government under Prieto, but Largo Caballero refused to give his permission.

The government, which was so weak it could not stop street brawls and the continuous excesses by gangs of both sides, was in no position to deal with a well-organized coup. The preparation for a military coup was known to almost everyone. Yet the government chose to ignore it and remained optimistic about the future, until it was too late.

Largo Caballero's only action to defend the Republic was to ask that arms be distributed among the workers. Such an act of abdication of power could hardly be expected of even a weak government.

The climax of the atrocities came with the murder of Lieutenant Castillo of the government shock troops,[8] and later the assassination of Calvo Sotelo, leader of the Monarchists. Three days following this last event, on July 16, the troops in Morocco revolted, followed by garrisons all over Spain. Late on July 18, arms were distributed among the people by the government. The Civil War had begun.

CHAPTER III

COMMUNIST INFLUENCE IN SPAIN

RESPONSIBILITY FOR THE CIVIL WAR

FROM THE EVIDENCE presented thus far it would seem that the Civil War beginning in 1936 was exclusively an internal matter with the roots of the conflict going back a hundred years and more into the domestic problems of Spain. This brief summary of Spanish history for the hundred years up to 1936 shows, above all, the importance of the internal situation in any study of the Civil War, and that, irrespective of the foreign politics which can be proved to be involved, the domestic issues played a paramount role. To overlook them would be to present a false picture.

On the other hand, it is impossible to disregard the reiterated claim that the Civil War was a Communist or Fascist plot instigated from abroad. To what extent were these accusations true, or were they merely propaganda devices? How far were the Comintern and the Fascist states of Italy and Germany desirous or able to impose their aims and wishes on the highly volatile situation in Spain?

The Nationalists, from the very beginning, claimed that they were saving Spain from communism and that their military plot was merely a move to forestall a Communist coup. This conception of Communist intrigues leading to a Soviet state in Spain became accepted not only by the Fascist states but by conservative elements all over the world. The Catholic Church outside allied with the Catholic Church in Spain to condemn the Popular Front as an agent of Moscow, and threw all its power of persuasion and propaganda into saving Spain from going "Red." Not only did Catholic and conservative elements believe this strongly at the time but they still believe it to be true. Winston Churchill in his book, *Step by Step*, quotes a letter he wrote on August 10, 1936:

... It happened "according to plan." Lenin laid down that Communists should aid all movements towards the Left and help into office weak constitutional, Radical or Socialist governments. These they should undermine, and from their failing hands snatch absolute power, and found the Marxist State. This procedure is well known and well proved. It is part of the Communist doctrine; it is part of the Communist drill book. It has been followed almost literally by the Communists of Spain....[1]

In his World War II memoirs he repeats his early statement almost word for word, and goes further in attributing the murders and violence in the five months before the Civil War to the "Communist pervasion of the decayed Parliamentary Government."[2] Certainly the activities of the

Comintern and the Communist parties in most countries since 1919 seemed to justify such a conclusion as Churchill's. This process of deduction to prove Communist complicity in Spain cannot, however, be used as all-inclusive proof. This can only come with the examination of the particular facts in the specific case. For this, the relations of Russia and the Comintern with Spain before July, 1936, must be examined in detail.

The subject of official relations between the two governments before 1936 can be reduced to one sentence. There was practically no contact between the official representatives of these nations as diplomatic relations were not established until August, 1936.[3]

COMMUNIST STRENGTH BEFORE FEBRUARY, 1936

Soviet relations through the Comintern and its Spanish agent, the Communist Party of Spain, were, on the other hand, extensive. When, in 1921, the Spanish Socialist party refused to accept the Twenty-One Conditions and adhere to the Comintern, a few of the dissident Socialists and also a few Anarcho-Syndicalists formed a Communist party. Two of the best-known leaders of the party were Andrés Nin and Joaquín Maurín. During the 1920's, however, the party amounted to very little and had few followers, all the original Socialists having left the party as well as many of the Anarcho-Syndicalists. The party was so insignificant that Primo de Rivera did not bother to suppress the Communist newspaper. The policy dictated by the Third International was not very popular within the Spanish party so that when Nin and Maurín failed to get the Comintern to adopt a more liberal policy giving increased latitude of action, they quit the party in 1932 and formed a party of Left communism. This problem of deviationists, which was constantly afflicting the young Communist party and which became very serious with the defection of Nin and Maurín, kept the ranks and strength of the party to a minimum. Only the most docile members remained. At the proclamation of the Republic the party numbered no more than 1,000 members.[4] In the June, 1931, elections they put up only eleven candidates for the Cortes, none of whom came close to being elected, and polled only about 60,000 votes in all of Spain.

Taking advantage of the freedom offered by the Republic and also the unsettled conditions of the depression, the Communists were able to build up their ranks. This same phenomenon could be observed in other countries during the depression. In spite of the opportunities of the situation and the growing revolutionary attitude on the part of the lower classes, the Communist party remained small in comparison with the other working-class parties. The Communists were particularly unsuccessful in winning adherents from either the Anarchists or Socialists who remained skeptical and even hostile to the Comintern and foreign control. The Soviet purge trials also turned many away and hurt recruiting. In the 1933 election, however, the party secured one deputy in the Cortes from Málaga, their main stronghold at this time, and polled about 400,-000 votes out of about eight million. By October, 1934, the party claimed 20,000 members, and by February, 1936, 35,000 with 1,500 members in Madrid,[5] compared to the Anarchists with over a million and a half *CNT* trade-union members and the Socialists with over 60,000 members in the party and a million members in its trade-union federation, the *UGT*, which was ninety per cent Socialist with only a handful of Communist unions.[6]

Before the above figures on Communist strength can mean anything, however, they must be carefully scrutinized. In the first place, the 400,000 votes polled by the Communists in 1933 did not all represent Communist sympathizers. Many represented protest votes against the Republican forces and others were the ballots of Anarchists who voted in spite of the no-vote campaign and had no candidates of their own. Second, what are the sources of the figures given above? We have in the main only two basic sources for figures about the Communist party, the party itself and the *Dirección General de Seguridad* (the Security Police) of the Spanish government. The Security Police in November, 1934, put the strength of the Communists at 133,236. Since the figures of the Security Police in Spain have never been considered reliable, and since at the same time they exaggerated the strength of the *UGT* and the *CNT*, it is difficult to accept this figure as correct. Furthermore, the police do not tell how they arrived at this figure. Authorities who were well acquainted with Spain during this period confirm that communism played a very insignificant role. The party, therefore, remains as the only other real source for figures. But are the figures which they released reliable? They could have two reasons in general for concealing the truth, either to hide their weakness or to hide their strength. If they wanted to hide their weakness they could have used much higher figures. Were they then concealing their strength as many assume? This would not have been in keeping with their policy during this period. Throughout the period, both before and during the Civil War, the Communists were proud of their strength, bragging about their growing numbers rather than trying to conceal them. Since the conception of the Republic they even openly claimed to be the leader of the revolutionary proletariat. For example, in the Asturias revolt they pictured themselves as the leaders and as the motivating force behind the formation of the Popular Front in the uprising. They by no means attempted to play down or conceal their revolutionary activities among the proletariat, quite the contrary. The figures they did conceal were the number of Comintern agents in Spain, which would denote foreign interference, but the spontaneous growth of communism in the country itself was not a thing to be concealed. If anything, it must be concluded that the figures above are an exaggeration of Communist power.[7]

In spite of the Communists' inability to gain wide adherence to their method of revolution and to compete with the Anarchists and Socialists, there was a strong sympathy of the Left for Russia as the home of the only successful proletarian revolution. Both the Socialists and the Anarchists, though they resisted the Communist encroachment on the home front, looked toward Russia as a big brother. Symbols, terminology, and methods were copied from the Russian Revolution without regard for the Communist party. It was not unusual for a village without one Communist member to revolt and establish a Soviet on the Russian pattern. They would often raise the hammer and sickle and call themselves "Communist" without any reference to the Communist Party of Spain. Likewise, Russian movies and stories of revolutionary heroism appealed to the masses and, as a result, Russian novels and showings of Russian movies were widespread. It was an expression of the sympathy of one revolution for another but without in any way indicating that the people had become adherents to the policies of the Comintern. The Communists, however, were quick to seize upon this spontaneous feeling for Russia and make use of it for their own benefit. During the Civil War this kindred feeling was very useful to Russia in carrying out her policies in Spain.

In the political events from 1931 to 1934, the Communist party played a very minor role. It took no part in the proclamation of the Republic in 1931 and, in fact, was very negative and skeptical in its attitude toward it, rejecting the Republican government as bourgeois. During the first years of the Republic the Communists ignored the government and concentrated on building a larger following and fighting the Socialists, Anarchists, and particularly the dissident Communists. This followed the international policy of the Comintern, which at this time did not allow for close coöperation with either bourgeois or non-Communist revolutionary groups.

By 1936 the Spanish section of the Comintern was no longer the small, insignificant group of Communist revolutionaries it had been in 1931, and was attracting a sizable political following. Its strength still did not challenge that of the Anarchists or Socialists. Nevertheless the Communists were, by 1936, capable of taking an active part in the politics of the Left. The Soviet Union was developing in the Spanish Communist party a militant and vocal agent in Spain.

THE COMINTERN AND SPAIN

The Communist International had long been interested in Spain as a troubled spot of the world. Articles on Spain appeared frequently in the *Communist International*, the magazine of the Comintern. One article in 1931, for example, declared, "The prospects for the Spanish Revolution are good."[8] From the frequency of the articles and their analysis of the Spanish situation it would seem that the Communists considered the prospects of revolution better in Spain than in most countries of the world, except for China and perhaps India. In the unsettled conditions and extreme poverty and repression of the masses, the Communists saw a revolutionary situation similar to Russia in prerevolutionary days. They were always ready to fish in troubled waters and, through the Communist Party of Spain, tried to gain leadership in the proletarian movement. Because of the small size of the party in Spain, however, the Comintern was able to make very little progress in carrying out its policy there.

The growing threat of fascism with the rise of Nazi Germany in 1933 brought about a change in tactics in the policy of Soviet Russia and her agency, the Communist International. Russia, in her fight against the capitalism and imperialism of the West, decided to declare a truce with the democracies and concentrate her attention on what she considered an even greater danger: the rise of fascism in Germany, Italy, and Japan. Not only did the Soviet Union lessen her attacks on the democracies but she sought their coöperation in containing the Fascist states. In 1934 the Soviet Union entered the League of Nations, followed in 1935 by the signing of a security pact with France. At the same time there occurred a change in the policy of international communism which was first reflected in the pact between the Socialist and Communist parties of France, signed on July 27, 1934.

The actual detailed program of the Communist International following the new tack in Soviet foreign policy was not set down until the Seventh Congress of the Comintern in July and August, 1935, though it had already come into operation before that time.[9] The basic element of the program was the united front of all the proletarian parties against fascism. The idea of the United Front was not new. For example, as early as 1931, the Comintern urged on the Spanish Communist party the formation of a united front:

... The Communist Party must appeal to all workers, to those organized in the reformist trade unions, to those organized in the anarcho-syndicalist National Confederation of Labour, and to the unorganized workers to form a united front in order to carry the democratic revolution to the end and to destroy all the relics of monarchy and feudalism, explaining that Soviets must be organized precisely for this aim, as organs of the struggle against counter-revolution, the monarchists and the feudal lords.[10]

The fulfillment of the United Front in 1931 was on the basis of unity from below, by means of local units and individual workers. The program of the Seventh Congress of the Comintern took this old idea of the United Front and gave it a whole new meaning, which made for a sharp change in Communist tactics.

The new Comintern policy resulted from the Communist analysis as to the causes for the rise of fascism which was appearing as a new "terrible threat to the proletariat." Georgi Dimitrov, in his main report to the Congress on August 2, 1935, gave the Communist rationalization of the rise of fascism:

Fascism was able to come to power *primarily* because the working class, owing to the policy of class collaboration with the bourgeoisie pursued by the Social-Democratic leaders, *proved to be split, politically and organizationally disarmed*, in the face of the onslaught of the bourgeoisie. And the Communist Parties, on the other hand, apart from and in opposition to the Social-Democrats, *were not strong enough* to arouse the masses and to lead them in a decisive struggle against fascism.[11]

Thus the Communist interpretation maintained it was the weak bourgeois policy of the Social Democrats and the ineffectiveness of the Communists which brought about fascism. To reverse this trend toward fascism, they concluded that it was necessary to increase the strength and influence of the Communists through coöperation with other proletarian groups, and prevent further collaboration of the Socialists with the bourgeois Fascists by a United Front program of the working class. This unity of action was to be worked out on all levels, not just on the local level as in the case of the United Front program in 1931. This was a radical change in Communist tactics since it was the first time since the collapse of the German and Hungarian revolutions in 1919 that the Communists permitted coöperation with the leaders and organizations of other parties in Western Europe on a large scale.

Many observers at the time of the Seventh Congress thought the revived United Front program of the Comintern signified that the Communists had given up the idea of world revolution and the dictatorship of the proletariat. This, however, was not the case, as a careful reading of the speeches made by the Communist leaders at the Seventh Congress clearly reveals. It was merely a change of tactics. An awareness that the Communist parties in all countries but the Soviet Union were weak, plus the threat of fascism, seems to have made the Communists realize that the tactic of seeking immediate world revolution and the dictatorship of the proletariat was not feasible. Dimitrov declared, "It cannot be expected that those Social-Democratic workers who are under the influence of the ideology of class collaboration with the bourgeoisie, which has been instilled in them for decades, will break with this ideology of their own accord, by the action of objective causes alone."[12] What was required was time and patience on the part of the Communists to explain the principles and program of communism. Furthermore, the development of fascism among the bourgeoisie was such a danger to the very existence of the proletarian parties and the "proletarian fatherland," the Soviet Union, that its elimination was required before the matter of world revolution could be dealt with.[13] The new rallying words of the International were those of Stalin from his report of the *CPSU* (Communist Party of the Soviet Union):

The victory of revolution never comes by itself. It has to be prepared for and won. And only a strong proletarian revolutionary party can prepare for and win victory.[14]

The idea of revolution was certainly not given up, only delayed. Throughout the speeches given before the Congress the aim of the dictatorship of the proletariat was frequently reiterated. Maurice Thorez, for example, stated very clearly that in the case of France the revolution was merely delayed, and indicated why:

We Communists are fighting for Soviet power, for the dictatorship of the proletariat. We know that this is the only way to put an end to the crisis, to poverty, to fascism, and to war forever. But we also know that *at the present time only a minority* of the working class, and above all, only a minority of the people of France share our convictions *and are fighting with the firm desire to establish Soviet Power*. That is why Soviet power cannot be the immediate goal of our present struggle. But although we are in a minority, we can and we must lead the majority of the country, which today is already determined to avoid the establishment of a fascist dictatorship at all costs. We can and we must convince the masses, in the struggle and on the basis of their own experience, of the necessity of attaining a Soviet Republic.[15]

As mentioned above, the basic element of the new tactic was the United

Front. The major portion of the discussion of the Congress revolved around the content and forms of the United Front. It did not, however, establish an exclusive pattern that the United Front should take.

It was suggested as a basis that agreements be made at all levels in the working-class movements on either a long-term or short-term basis.[16] In the establishment of the United Front the "Communist International put only one condition for unity of action and that was an elementary condition acceptable to all workers, viz., that the unity of action be directed against fascism, against the offensive of capital, against the threat of war, against the class enemy."[17] Though not mentioned by Dimitrov there was also the implied condition that the United Front should aid the Soviet Union in case she were attacked. This is inferred from the resolution put before the Congress which stated:

... in case of a counter-revolutionary war against the Soviet Union, the Communists must call on all the toilers to help by all means and at any cost to bring about the victory of the Red Army against the imperialist armies.[18]

Furthermore, in making a United Front agreement the Communists were to reserve for themselves certain rights. "Communists, of course, cannot and must not for a moment abandon their own *independent work* of Communist education, organization and mobilization of the masses."[19] Finally, "joint action with the Social-Democratic Parties and organizations not only does not preclude, but on the contrary, *renders more necessary* the serious and well-founded criticism of reformism, of Social Democracy as the ideology and practice of class collaboration with the bourgeoisie. ..."[20] As a result attacks against the Socialists continued.[21] There was some effort, however, to distinguish between the right Socialists, collaborators with the bourgeoisie, and the left Socialists. As for example, Ercoli declared:

In the Left wing of the Socialist Party in France there is developing, although with greater vacillations, a tendency towards the position of revolutionary struggle against war, and in particular, to renounce defense of the fatherland under a bourgeois regime. In the Social-Democratic Parties which have been driven into emigration by fascism, there has also been observable tendencies, as yet timid, for linking the struggle against war with the struggle for the overthrow of fascism.[22]

In the struggle against fascism the Communists realized that the proletariat was going to need the help of certain sections of the bourgeoisie. Consequently, starting with the United Front as the basis, they envisaged a Popular or People's Front made up of certain nonproletarian groups to fight against fascism:

In striving to unite, under the leadership of the proletariat, the struggle of the toiling peasants, the urban petty bourgeoisie and the toiling masses of the oppressed nationalities, the Communists must seek to bring about the establishment of a wide *anti-fascist people's front* on the basis of the proletarian united front, supporting all those specific demands of those sections of the toilers which are in line with the fundamental interests of the proletariat.[23]

Dimitrov further explained the role of the People's Front:

For it cannot be seriously supposed that it is possible to establish a genuine anti-fascist People's Front without securing the unity of action of the working class itself, the *guiding force* of this anti-fascist People's Front. At the same time, the further development of the united proletarian front depends, to a considerable degree, upon its transformation into a People's Front against fascism.[24]

This part of the Comintern program at the Seventh Congress was not spelled out in as much detail as the United Front, which was considered of prime importance. Furthermore, it would seem that the People's Front policy was not to affect greatly the Communist attitude toward the bourgeoisie. Except for winning over the peasants and petty bourgeoisie the war against the middle and upper classes was to continue. It was, however, realized that the relations of the Communist parties with the bourgeois republics could not be the same as they had been in the past.[25] Yet nothing was done in the Congress to define this change. In fact, the distinction in the Congress between the democratic bourgeoisie and the Fascist bourgeoisie was only slight. Coöperation with bourgeois governments of any type or composition was still considered taboo. Nor was there any mention of an alliance with any of the democratic bourgeois parties of the West. The Communists maintained their active hostility toward "Parliamentarianism."[26] The Comintern even continued to oppose the Social-Democratic governments of Scandinavia.

As the next move following the formation of the United Front and People's Front, the Communists saw the possibility of a government by a United Front or a People's Front. They saw this development as perhaps a new step in the path toward the dictatorship of the proletariat. Dimitrov declared:

Fifteen years ago Lenin called upon us to focus all our attention on "searching out forms of *transition* or *approach* to the proletarian revolution." It may be that in a number of countries the *united front government* will prove to be one of the most important transitional forms.

Dimitrov later in the same speech emphasized, however, that "it would be wrong to imagine that the united front government is an *indispensable stage* on the road to the establishment of proletarian dictatorship."[27]

The Seventh Congress set up certain conditions for the formation of a United Front government:

(a) When the state apparatus of the bourgeoisie is seriously paralyzed so that the bourgeoisie is not in a condition to prevent the formation of such a government; (b) when the vast masses of the toilers vehemently take action against fascism and reaction, but are not yet ready to rise and fight for Soviet Power; (c) when already a considerable proportion of the organizations of the Social-Democratic and other parties participating in the united front demand ruthless measures against the fascists and other reactionaries, and are ready to fight together with the Communists for the carrying out of these measures.[28]

Finally the Congress considered as the climax in preparation of the proletarian revolution the creation of a unified trade-union organization and a single proletarian party. The resolution on the report of Georgi Dimitrov declared:

The Communists are decidedly for the reestablishment of trade union unity in each country and on an international scale; for united class trade unions as one of the major bulwarks of the working class against the offensive of capital and fascism. . . .[29]

This final stage of the United Front program was also to include the creation of a single mass political party of the working class. This unification was possible only:

First, on condition of *complete independence from the bourgeoisie and complete rupture of the bloc of Social-Democracy with the bourgeoisie;*

Second, on condition that unity of action be first brought about;

Third, on condition that the necessity of the *revolutionary overthrow of the rule of the bourgeoisie* and the establishment of the *dictatorship of the proletariat in the form of Soviets* be recognised;

Fourth, on condition that support of one's own bourgeoisie in an *imperialist war* be rejected;

Fifth, on condition that the party be constructed on the basis of *democratic centralism*, which ensures unity of will and action, and which has been tested by *the experience of the Russian Bolsheviks.*[30]

In summing up the action of the Seventh Congress of the Comintern in 1935, it can be said that in recognition of the strength of fascism and the weakness of the Communist parties the Congress set up a new pattern of action for the sections of the International in preparation for revolution and the dictatorship of the proletariat. The program established certain steps to be followed: first, the United Front; second, the People's Front; third, a United Front or People's Front government; and fourth, trade-union unity and a single party of the proletariat. It was not, however, to be considered a hard and fast plan but merely an outline of the possible path of events.

It was this program of the Comintern which was in effect during the Civil War in Spain.[31] The Communist leaders both in and out of Spain frequently referred to the decisions of this Congress in speaking of activities of the party in Spain. It is one of the purposes of this book in analyzing the role of the Communist party in the Civil War to answer the questions as to how closely it followed the Comintern policy and to what extent it was a test case for this new policy.

THE POPULAR FRONT IN SPAIN

The Communist Party of Spain, soon after the inauguration of the United Front program in France in July, 1934, and before its definition at the Seventh Congress of the Comintern, had its first opportunity to put the new tactic into effect during the Asturias revolt in October, 1934. The Communists controlled about 9,000 workers in the area who, with about 20,000 Anarchists and 30,000 Socialists, allied in their battle against the state. The Communists, of course, claimed that they led this Popular Front movement and that without them the alliance would never have occurred. The fact that this was the first time in Spain that the Communists had coöperated with another party, and this was also the first time there had been any proletarian solidarity in Spain, speaks in their favor. Actually, however, the Communists were in a minority and thus in no condition to lead or force the other two parties to coöperate. The forces of solidarity in Spain were working independently of Russia's foreign policy. The last failure of the Left at the polls in 1933 had shown the need of some kind of working agreement. Coöperation actually had begun to develop early in 1934, but the Communists had only adhered to the alliance in September, 1934. At the same time the Asturias uprising took place, a similar agreement failed to mature in Barcelona, not because there were fewer Communists in Catalonia, but because it meant the Anarchists would have been coöperating with the bourgeoisie, too large a difference for either group to span. Also the Anarchists in Barcelona felt strong enough to seize power on their own when the right time came and did not feel the need to depend on the bourgeoisie. In Asturias, the case was different. Here the Anarchists were in the minority and could never have hoped for success alone. Furthermore, the whole working-class movement in Asturias, both *CNT* and *UGT*, was much more moderate and less doctrinaire in outlook, making an alliance much easier. Finally, it was obvious to everyone, especially to the practical Asturians, that without coöperation there was not the slightest chance of success.

The Communists' claim to be the leaders in this movement can, therefore, be discounted.

The same arguments more or less can be used in respect to the Communists' claim to have inaugurated the Popular Front. There is equally little foundation for this assertion. The electoral law and defeat of the Left in 1933 had made such an alliance very likely. The very fact that the alliance included "Trotskyites" of the *POUM* and was merely for the election and distribution of seats in the Cortes and not for the formation of a government shows that it was not the Communist leadership the Left was following.[32] Nevertheless, whether the Communists were the leaders of the Popular Front or not, they used all their resources to secure the new solidarity of the Left. They very carefully walked a fence between appealing to the revolutionary masses and the moderate Republican elements, sometimes contradicting themselves.

José Díaz, Secretary-General of the Communist party, as early as June, 1935, laid down the program for the party in as mild terms as permissible to appeal to the Republicans as well as the revolutionary elements. The program included four main points:

1. Confiscation of the land from the Grandees, Church, and convents without compensation and the immediate turning over of the land to individual peasants and farm workers.

2. Liberation of the oppressed peoples from Spanish imperialism, giving autonomy to Catalonia, Euzkadi, and Galacia.

3. Improvement in the conditions of life and work of the laborers (increased salaries, respect for workers' contracts, freedom to unionize, freedom of opinion, freedom of assembly and press, etc.)

4. Amnesty for all revolutionary and political prisoners.[33]

The program was very carefully couched in revolutionary terms to appeal to the revolutionaries and in addition called for a United Front of the proletariat, but, on the other hand, it contained none of the usual Communist elements alarming to the Republicans—destruction of the bourgeois state, collectivization, or nationalization. In fact it was a program few Republicans could not support, even the strong Catholic Basque Republicans. It made a direct appeal to the peasants in calling for confiscation of land from the large landowners and for turning it directly over to them. It also made a strong appeal to the Anarchists in demanding amnesty for political prisoners. The inconsistency of the Communist position can be seen in José Díaz' speech at the Colesium Pardiñas in Madrid on November 3, 1935.

We struggle for the Dictatorship of the Proletariat and for the Soviets. We declare this clearly because we, as a Party of the proletariat, do not renounce our objectives. But at the present moment we understand that the struggle taking place is not in the area of the Dictatorship of the Proletariat but in the struggle of democracy against fascism as its immediate objective.[34]

The Communist policy of unity, although it was not the main factor in the creation of the Popular Front, did help to increase the prestige of the Communists among the Left. In bargaining for seats in the Cortes the Communists were able to secure sixteen out of 267 seats. This figure indicates an increase in the force at the Communists' command but on the other hand, it also shows its over-all weakness in being able to command only six per cent of the deputies of the Popular Front and only three per cent of the total number of deputies in the Cortes.

GROWTH OF COMMUNISM AFTER FEBRUARY, 1936

Following the victory of the Popular Front in February, 1936, the Communists put on pressure for new recruits. They continued to play an opportunistic game, setting up their program deliberately to catch in their net as much of the Left as possible. The Communist postelection program was very similar to the one successfully developed before the election but with more of a revolutionary fervor. This program called for the immediate seizure of large estates without compensation, complete separation of Church and state, the end of Church subsidies, and the formation of a people's army under the direction of the people.[35] It did not press for the formation of a Popular Front government to replace the weak Left Republican government formed after the election. The Communists did demand, however, that the Popular Front should continue in existence and that the government follow the Popular Front campaign program, in exchange for which they promised full support to the government.

The Communists' tactics proved effective in bringing in recruits. The polarization of opinion and the stirring of the lower classes with the victory of the Left led to a general arousing of political activity and an increase in the number of supporters for all parties of the Left. The Communists claimed 117,000 members by the outbreak of the war. Other authorities put the strength of the party much lower—citing generally figures around 50,000—a gain of about 15,000 members since February. It seems very likely that the Communist figures for July were an exaggeration. Moreover, in viewing this increase, the important fact must be borne in mind that this additional strength was not the usual well-disciplined group generally associated with the Communist party. Time was required before these new members could develop "revolutionary efficiency." Few of the Communist recruits had come from other parties; most of them had not previously belonged to any party. A large portion of the new candidates were youths attracted by the Communists' here-and-now policy backed by the concrete example of Russia in contrast to the Socialists' and Anarchists' programs of mere hopes. In spite of their support of local autonomy, the Communist strength continued to center around Madrid and had little appeal in Catalonia or the Basque country, except in the mines.

The Communists' growing influence did not merely depend on the increase in their number, which was still small, even if the figure 117,000 is accepted. The most important conquest was rather in their influence over the Socialist party. Since the establishment of the Third Communist International, the Communists and Socialists throughout the world had been the bitterest of enemies. The Communists had always reserved their first line of fire for the Socialists, whom they considered renegades from the cause of the revolution. In 1934, with the *rapprochement* of France and Russia, there was a change of attitude on the part of the Communists. They sought close association and coöperation with the Socialists. The Socialists in France, although glad to have an ally against the growing Fascist tendencies of the Right, were wary of this new alliance. Content to call a truce in their war against the Communists, they were skeptical of any close association and resisted all Communist advances for closer unity. In Spain, on the other hand, the Communists had never seriously threatened the Socialists' influence over the workers, unlike the Anarchists, who had always been powerful and equal competitors for the proletarian vote and allegiance. In their rivalry with the Anarchists, the Socialists were not above accepting the Communists as allies, especially as Communist party membership increased. Two other factors also aided in bringing about a closer association between the two parties. The Socialists, as mentioned previously, under pressure from the masses and because of the failure of the parliamentary system in Spain, had become more and more revolutionary in outlook and, therefore, were growing closer to the Communists in ideology. The deep-rooted sympathy of the Spanish people for the Russians also pushed the Socialists into seeking the Communists as allies.

The Communists were fortunate that the leader of the largest segment of the Socialists was Largo Caballero, who was susceptible to influence and flattery.[36] They were perhaps even more fortunate in having Álvarez del Vayo as one of Largo Caballero's right-hand men. Some authorities, such as Indàlecio Prieto and Colonel Segismundo Casado, have sought to argue that Álvarez del Vayo was actually a Communist or a Communist agent. Actually, the dispute over this question is unimportant since the fact remains that Álvarez del Vayo apparently supported the Communist program and was strongly favored by the Communists. On his advice, it would seem, Largo Caballero moved into closer and closer coöperation with the Communists. The Communists also played on the vanity of Largo Caballero by calling him the "Spanish Lenin."

The most important immediate consequence of this friendship between Caballero and the Communists was unification of the Communist and Socialist youth in March, 1936. The Socialist youth consisted of about 200,000[37] and the Communist of no more than 50,000, if that many.[38] Before February the Communists had claimed only 14,000 youths. In the new *Juventudes Socialistas Unificadas (JSU)*, the Communists gained control from the beginning. As a result, not all the Socialist youth joined, particularly in northern Spain, and many soon dropped out until the ranks of the *JSU* were depleted to about 150,000 members.

The Communists' influence over Caballero and the Socialists, however, was by no means complete. Although the Socialists were willing to come into closer coöperation with the Communists, they refused to form a United Front with them, insisting that the Popular Front of all the Left was sufficient. Furthermore, the Communists were often embarrassed by the rash and utopian statements made by Caballero. They tried unsuccessfully to urge moderation in his speeches and advised him to prepare for a possible counterrevolution by the Right instead of weaving dreams of the future.

The growth of Communist membership and influence before the beginning of the Civil War, especially in the last months, seems to be clear evidence as to the success of the Communists in the first steps in adapting the United Front program to Spain. The idea of a close alliance of workers, peasants, and petty bourgeoisie into a Popular Front corresponded to the trend which the parties of the Left in Spain were already following, and allowed the Communists to fit their United Front tactics closely into the political realities of Spain. Furthermore, their stressing of the immediate aim to fight fascism, and the playing down of their ultimate end —the dictatorship of the proletariat and Communism—was applicable to the Spanish scene. All the parties of the Left were fearful of domination by the Right, which was not truly Fascist but fitted into the Communists' broad definition of fascism. The soft pedaling of the Communists' revolutionary aims appealed to the lower-middle class and small landowners who feared the Right but did not want revolution. The successful integrating of the Comintern program into the Spanish situation, which showed in the rapid increase of the Communist party's strength, augured well for the final success of the United Front program in Spain.

Although the Communists by July, 1936, had increased their membership many fold over what it had been before 1934, they still remained a small group compared to the Anarchists and Socialists. Had the Communist party, however, become strong enough, as the Spanish Nationalists claimed, to be plotting a coup against the government, so that it was necessary for the army to "save" the country? And was immediate seizure of the state part of the Communist plan?

CHAPTER IV

RESPONSIBILITY FOR THE INSURRECTION

THE NATIONALISTS ACCUSE

THE MILITARY *putsch* of July 19 was hardly a day old when the Right attempted to declare the Left government illegal and without the support of the majority of the people, and to throw all blame on the Communists. They, the Rightists, were saving Spain from communism and had revolted in order to forestall a planned Red insurrection. How successful were Franco and the Right in proving these accusations? Their success in making the people of Spain and other countries believe their statements is a problem which will be dealt with later. This chapter will deal only with an analysis of the proofs of a Red provocation and the legitimacy of the Left government.

One of the first claims of the Nationalists after their revolt was that the Right and not the Popular Front had really won the February election. The Right, in totaling up the election returns for February 16, 1936, claimed that the popular vote gave them about 200,000 votes more than the Left. If we accept the Right's figure of approximately 4,300,000 for the Popular Front,[1] and add together the Center and Right, this gives to the opponents of the Left between 4,500,000 and 4,900,000 votes, depending on the source of figures. This would give to the Right a popular majority, and there is little to prove that these figures are very far wrong. Even Republican figures are quite close to the accounting given above. It would, however, be wrong to conclude from this, as did the Nationalists, that since 4,500,000 or more voted against the Popular Front these same voters supported Franco, and therefore his government was "the legitimate government" chosen by the people. Large sections of the Center and the Basque Nationalists (130,000 voters) went over to the Republic after the insurrection, and it would be difficult to prove absolutely the majority on one side or the other once the war started.

No one can deny that the division of seats in the Cortes did not strictly follow the popular vote in giving the Popular Front about 256 and the Right and Center only 198 seats. The argument that it was undemocratic can certainly not be refuted easily. But such a division is by no means unusual in a parliamentary system, and without proportional representation there is no way to prevent such an occurrence.[2] In most democracies it is but a temporary phenomenon which is changed by the next election. It must also be noted that the Right in Spain had benefited in 1933 by the very election laws they complained of in 1936, because in the 1933 elections they received more seats in the Cortes than the popular vote would have allowed.

The other challenge brought up concerning the election was that it had been fraudulent. Alcalá Zamora, the first President of the Second Republic, writing in the *Journal de Genève* on January 17, 1937, accused the Popular Front of fraud:

At first the Popular Front was believed to have been beaten. But, five hours after the arrival of the first results, it was found that the Anarchist masses, which are so numerous and hitherto had abstained from the polls, had voted in a solid block. They were anxious to show their power and to claim the price for their aid—the peace, alas, the very existence of the country.

In spite of the Syndicalist reinforcements, the Popular Front obtained only a few, a very few, more than 200 seats out of a total of 473. Thus it became the largest minority group, but did not secure a majority in Parliament. It managed, however, to obtain this majority by hurrying through two stages of procedure in defiance of all legality and with utter disregard for scruple.

As to the first stage, as early as 17 February, and even from the late afternoon of the 16th, the Popular Front, without awaiting the final scrutiny or the proclamation of the results of the voting, which were to be given out on 20 February by the provincial commissions appointed for the purpose, launched its attack by starting disorder in the streets and using violence in demand for power. A Government crisis ensued, and the Civil Governors of several of the provinces resigned. At the instigation of irresponsible agitators, the mob seized the balloting papers, with the result that false returns were sent in from many places.

As to the second stage: the majority thus secured was easily rendered crushing. Reinforced by strange allies, such as the Basque reactionaries, the Popular Front elected the Committee entrusted with the task of verifying the elections in each constituency, a task the Committee carried out in an arbitrary manner. In certain provinces where the opposition had been victorious, all the mandates were annulled and candidates who were friendly to the Popular Front, although they had been beaten, were proclaimed Deputies. Several members of minority groups were expelled from the Cortes. Nor was this done in blind party passion, but in execution of a deliberate plan conceived on a large scale. The end aimed at was twofold—to convert the Chamber into a packed Parliament by crushing all opposition, and to ensure the obedience of the more moderate groups of the Popular Front. . . .

Before making conclusions about the validity of this accusation several factors should be noted. In the first place, election fraud in Spain had always been common. The Conservatives and Liberals had kept their power throughout the nineteenth and early part of the twentieth centuries by a system of political bosses and election fraud. It was, therefore, a usual practice, particularly on the part of the Right, though there is no reason to believe that the Left, given a chance, would refrain from using this technique of getting elected. Out of this results the counter-accusation that the Right had employed fraud to get its votes in the February election. In February the Right was in control of the governmental apparatus and, in a country where it was rare for the government in power to be voted out of office involuntarily, it would not be too much to assume that the Right used its power for its own benefit. In fact there is good evidence that in the more backward districts caciques and fraud were successful in securing the vote for the Right, and that where the landowners were still strong, coercion was frequently used to gain the vote of the people.

Another factor which must be borne in mind is that Alcalá Zamora was a Conservative writing in 1937, when Spain was locked in the death struggle of the Civil War. Furthermore, it must be remembered that Alcalá Zamora was voted out of his presidency by the Popular Front before the end of his term, which made him especially bitter toward the Left.

Alcalá Zamora's indictment of fraud stands almost alone. In the five months before the outbreak of open hostilities there was little mention of fraud by the Right.[3] It was hardly out of fear of the government since the Right accused the Left of every other form of chicanery. It was perhaps to avoid an embarrassing counterinvestigation of fraud which prevented them from accusing the Left of illegal acts during the elections. The Left, on the other hand, probably did not investigate the use of fraud on the part of the Right because it was the accepted thing. If the Right had refrained from using all its influence, legal and illegal, to win the election, it would have been considered by the Left only as a sign of weakness.

It is quite true that there were cases in which the mob seized the ballot boxes after the elections, but an investigation of the reports of the time shows these instances were very few and hardly enough to substantially alter the voting returns. Moreover, if the Left had deliberately planned to change the results as Alcalá Zamora claims, they would have come out with figures more beneficial and flattering to themselves than those described above.

There is little doubt that in the supplementary elections held on March 1, the results were prejudiced in favor of the Popular Front since they controlled the election machinery at this time. Whether their methods were any worse or more fraudulent than those used by the Right would be difficult to answer. It can be said in conclusion that the charge of fraud in the election, to cast the slur of illegitimacy on the Popular Front government, was not proved by the Nationalists.

Another alleged illegitimate act of the Popular Front was voting Alcalá Zamora out of office. The Popular Front, on their own admission, feared the Conservative President might use his powers for the benefit of the Right and made use of trumped-up charges to dispossess him of his office after they had failed by threats to make him resign. The discussion here is concerned, however, only with whether his deposition was legal according to the Constitution. Article 81 of the Constitution, in discussing the President's power of dissolving the Cortes, says, "If there should be a second dissolution, the first act of the new Cortes will be to examine the necessity for the Decree of Dissolution of the last Cortes. An unfavorable vote by an absolute majority of the Cortes shall mean the President's end of office." Using this as the pretext, the Cortes voted that the dissolution of January, 1936, had been unwarranted—a ridiculous resolution for the Popular Front to favor since the dissolution had brought them into power. In spite of the trumped-up excuses, however, the forms of legality were followed in voting Alcalá Zamora out of office. Diego Martínez Barrio, President of the Cortes, said legal form had been observed by the participation of many of the Right in the election of Manuel Azaña as President when they abstained by handing in blank ballots.[4]

THE "RED MENACE"

The problem of the "Red Menace" is more complex than the problem of legitimacy and also more important, since it was the main source of the Nationalists' propaganda fire. It is useful to point out in the beginning that the "Red Herring" was a technique which had already been used over and over again with much success. Mussolini had used it very successfully in rationalizing his march on Rome in the early 'twenties, and Hitler had used it to even more advantage in assuming extraordinary powers in Germany. The word "Red" had become the "open sesame" of dictators. The use of the Red scare by the generals in 1936 was not the first time the technique had been used in Spain. The fear of "Moscow agents" had helped Primo de Rivera into power in 1923, and the Red threat was called into use by the reactionaries throughout the turbulent events of the Second Republic. Such allegations before 1936, as discussed previously, were groundless as shown by the size of the Communist organization in Spain. Rarely was there any attempt at proof; it was purely for emotional effect. By a process of association it would seem that the generals' use of the "Red Herring" in July, 1936, was equally groundless and a pure hoax. But since it was considered invalid to accuse the Left of being Communist-dominated on the basis of association, it is equally unreasonable to condemn the Right as prevaricators by the same method of deduction. The specific facts in the case must be investigated.

The proofs which the Right used to establish the allegation that Russia was behind the Popular Front and was moving to set up a Soviet state in Spain were in general of four main types: statements by Communists, newspaper accounts of Red domination, claims of the presence of Comintern agents in Spain, and documents found proving the existence of an organized Communist plot to seize power. Not all supporters of the Nationalist cause carried their indictment of Communist complicity to the same extent. Some stated the Communist plotting began at a very early date in 1931, but others say it was later. Most authorities on the "Red Menace," however, made little distinction between the various parties of the Left but declared when pushed to it, "As for the alleged distinctions between centre and left Socialists and Communists, they seem to me unimportant."[5] A few did draw a distinction between the various groups of the Left but put the motivating force of the revolution entirely in the hands of the Communists.

As mentioned previously a great deal of proof relied on condemning the Communists' actions by association, and by statements as to the Comintern's aims in Spain. Gertrude M. Godden wrote two books on Communist activities in Spain basing a large part of her evidence on just such statements in Communist publications.[6] First she tries to implicate the Communists on the basis of their general revolutionary aims, quoting from Lenin and Stalin. On the basis of activities the Communists had conducted in other countries, such as expenditures of large sums of money in England, she implicates the Red International in Spain.[7] Finally she makes use of the frequent statements in Communist literature of the "ripeness" for the revolution in Spain, and Communist sympathy for the Spanish people. From the *Communist International* of November, 1934, comes the statement, "The workers of Asturias fought for Soviet Power under the leadership of the Communists," and from the following month the prediction, "The events that took place represent, not the end of the developed struggle for power, for Soviets, but only its beginning. . . ."

One reference which was frequently used by both Franco and conservative writers was a trip made to the Revolutionary Museum in Moscow in 1936 by M. Delbos, the ex-Foreign Minister of France, where he found a whole section of the museum devoted to the "future Communist Revolution in Spain."

As far as it goes, this method of proving the involvement of the Comintern in Spain is very good. But as was mentioned before, association alone cannot be allowed as conclusive proof. Nor can statements by Communists regarding Spain be considered definitive. As mentioned before, the Communists have never attempted to conceal their aim in Spain; that is, the creation of the dictatorship of the proletariat.[8] They looked upon every rumbling as a step toward this goal, and they were forever declaring themselves the leader in this movement. But these were merely expressions of a wish and cannot be taken as expression of true facts. On the contrary, the fact is that all the evidence available points to the insignificance of the Communist movement and its inability to play any role of leader or instigator among the Spanish proletariat before the Civil War. Consequently, such a method of trying to involve the Communists as the plotters of the Civil War collapses and serves only as propaganda.

The claim that Comintern agents were employed in Spain is not so easily dismissed, if it can be completely dismissed at all. Rumors of Comintern agents (Béla Kun usually headed the list) going to Spain in April, 1936, were prevalent. It is impossible to trace these rumors to their source. It would not have been unreasonable for the Right to have deliberately started such rumors as they had done previously. On the other hand, it is not unlikely that in the unstable conditions of Spain agents were sent if not to plot at least to spy for Moscow and send back reports on what was going on. Walter Krivitsky, a Comintern agent who headed the activities in Spain after the Civil War started, does not mention the presence of any agents before the outbreak. Yet it could be true that they were sent unknown to him. Joaquín Maurín, a former Spanish Communist, mentioned the presence of General Mikhail Borodin and Béla Kun but failed to mention exactly when they came or how he learned or knew of their presence in Spain.[9] In all the references by Nationalists, however, to Comintern agents, none attempted to offer any really concrete proof of their presence in Spain during this period.[10] Consequently, in the absence of any real evidence, it is necessary to throw out this imputation as mere rumor.

To the realm of rumor must also be relegated the various references to Soviet arms and money sent to Spain, as well as the various dates given for a Communist-planned uprising, since no evidence or proof of any kind was given for the validity of these statements.[11]

Another source often used by Nationalist sympathizers in support of a Communist plot was the reports of newspaper correspondents in Spain. One frequently used was H. E. Knoblaugh's interview with Largo Caballero in which the leader of the left Socialists supposedly proclaimed, "Lenin declared Spain would be the second Soviet Republic in Europe.

Lenin's prophecy will come true. I shall be the second Lenin who shall make it come true.'"[12] In the first place it is doubtful that Lenin could ever have made such a statement, since it was in Germany that Lenin expected and hoped for the next step in the world revolution. Furthermore, the words of correspondents on the Spanish situation must be used carefully because for every statement which supported the Nationalists there was at least one statement, if not more, by pro-Republican correspondents refuting the pro-Nationalist opinion.

In the field of international relations, the Nationalist recriminations of Red provocations were supported by the Fascist states. It was Portugal which actually laid the bill of indictment before the Non-Intervention Committee in London, accusing the Soviet Union of helping the Loyalist forces and plotting a Communist uprising, but Germany and Italy supported these claims in the committee and in their propaganda.[13] In a long detailed document to the Non-Intervention Committee on October 24, 1936, the Portuguese government presented an indictment purportedly proving a Red plot in Spain.[14] The indictment, however, contained no proof beyond newspaper statements alleging Communist plots in Spain.

There remain to be discussed three documents found by the Nationalists which they claimed were plans concerned with the preparation of a Communist uprising. The first document, found supposedly in three separate towns, was a typewritten general plan for the uprising giving the composition of the new Soviet government, organization of the militia, passwords, and the plan to be followed in Madrid. Cecil Gerahty, in his book *The Road to Madrid*, alleged it to be an Anarcho-Syndicalist plan, although most other pro-Nationalist authorities attribute it to the Communists. There is little probability that it could have been an Anarchist plan. In the first place Anarchists do not believe in leadership from above and feel all revolutionary plans must originate spontaneously from below. That such a comprehensive plan for all of Spain would have been worked out by them is not probable. Even more unusual would be an Anarchist plan which set up a new government, since it is a basic tenet of anarchism to be rid of the state for good and always with the coming of the revolution. Furthermore, it does not seem reasonable that the Anarchists, having overthrown the government, would turn power over to the other parties, keeping for themselves only a couple of minor posts in the new government.

That the document was of Communist origin is equally improbable. The document names 150,000 shock troops as the basis of the revolt, yet the Communist party did not total anywhere near that number at this time. Furthermore, if such a plot was planned it would have depended on the previous arming of the working class, yet when the military uprising occurred there was a great scarcity of arms among the workers. It was only the distribution of arms by the government on July 19 that allowed the workers to form into militias.

Some other general facts might be mentioned about this document. It is significant that, though the document was said to have been found early in the war, it was not published until the summer of 1937. It is also perhaps significant that the contents of the document were made known to the British government, which did not consider them important enough even to communicate to the Spanish government. The document likewise called for an uprising between May 1 and June 27, yet no such uprising occurred. Several authors claim it was postponed but base their supposition only on hearsay evidence. The one possibility is that this was a plan on the part of the whole revolutionary Left to revolt and establish a Popular Front government. But why was a revolt necessary when the Popular Front, through its majority in the Cortes, already controlled the government? The revolutionaries certainly could have gained the support of the Left Republicans under Azaña who all along had been in favor of the formation of a Popular Front government. No force, therefore, was necessary to carry out the aims of this alleged plan. Finally, the only deduction which can be made concerning this document is that it was prefabricated by the Nationalists for propaganda purposes.

The other two documents found were general instructions to Red agents in Spain; one, supposedly issued at the end of April, 1936, concerned the Red militia, and the other concerned a meeting and the resulting decisions of Comintern agents on May 16, 1936, in Valencia. The contents of these documents are filled, in contrast to the first document, with such unimportant details or such very general facts that an analysis of the contents alone reveals nothing. The authorities using these documents do not indicate how they were discovered or how their validity can be checked. It seems that one first appeared in the Paris newspaper, *Echo de Paris;* the source of the other has never been mentioned. Since no proof whatsoever has been brought forth to support the origins of the documents, they must be disregarded as evidence in the case.

Up to this point, the specific evidence investigated would not lead to a conclusion that there had been a Communist plot to seize power. A consideration of the general Russian policy at this time equally reveals the impossibility of such a plot. In 1934 Russia had adopted the system of collective security to fight the threat of fascism which had long aimed its most virulent ire against the USSR. In adopting this policy Russia sought close coöperation of all anti-Fascist parties within the various states. Russia found that this wooing of the democratic states of the West was not an easy task. Her past reputation for subversive activities was not easy to conceal and the din of anti-Communist propaganda from the Fascist states had a very telling effect on many groups in the Western world who turned a cold shoulder to Russia's advances. At the same time that the Communists were trying to develop a security system with the democracies they tried to maintain their influence among the proletariat and revolutionaries. This delicate balance, which we have already witnessed in Spain, was very precarious and constantly threatened. Such a threat existed in a revolution in Spain. For Russia's prestige among the proletariat of the world she dared not ignore a Spanish revolution because she felt that the Communists must take the leadership in any proletarian revolt. Yet to lead a revolution in Spain would endanger her new foreign policy of collective security by alienating the Western democracies. The charge of subversion and violence could not, in such a case, be overlooked. It was, therefore, absolutely necessary for the Soviet Union's foreign policy to keep the Spanish situation as stable as possible, to forestall a revolution by the masses or the military, and to try to find some compromise through a bourgeois government. A plot to seize power was unthinkable under these circumstances.

On the other hand it was as important for Franco, as it had been for Mussolini and Hitler, to justify himself by means of a Red plot. Hitler created the Reichstag fire plot, and Franco tried to make the world believe the threat of a Communist uprising, but with less success, for it was by no means universally accepted by the Spanish or the world. The known facts of the insurrection in July pointed to a clear-cut military uprising to establish a military dictatorship. With the blame falling at the very beginning on the army, it was especially necessary for the generals to make an attempt to throw the blame onto the most likely group of the Left—the Communists.

A Fascist Plot

If the Civil War was not provoked by the Communists, was it plotted by Germany and Italy? The evidence in this case is more readily available since the German and Italian archives have been opened. The implications of Germany and Italy, however, will be discussed only briefly since their interventions remain a side issue to the general discussion of communism in Spain. Mussolini was interested in activities in Spain since it bordered and dominated one of the entrances of the Mediterranean, which he wanted to make an Italian lake, and because Spain controlled the strategic Balearic Islands. Mussolini was always ready to fish in troubled waters and was displeased with the growing strength of the Left in Spain. As early as 1934, he promised aid to the Monarchists in any attempt to restore the monarchy.[15] He was, however, by no means willing at this time to plot a semi-invasion for the restoration of the monarchy, but if a Monarchist revolt broke out, he would have been willing to lend a hand. The German government, up to the insurrection, had made no commitments to the generals, but this does not indicate that they did not know an insurrection was being planned. Although the German government had no direct relations with the military plotters, it knew what was going on through the Nazi party, which was in close contact with the revolt. In the sizable German colony of 12,000 to 15,000 in Spain the Nazi party had a very strong following and an extensive organization throughout the country, especially in Spanish Morocco.[16] Hitler was, therefore, in a very good position to keep track of events and lend aid if necessary. There is no evidence that the Nazis had a significant role in planning the revolt, though relations were already closely established between the Nazis and Franco before the insurrection. This was clear when on July 22, 1936, Franco sent Johannes Bernhardt, a German businessman from Morocco, and Adolf Langenheim, the local Nazi leader, to Germany by air to ask aid of Hitler, who received them immediately.[17]

From the documents it appears that both Germany and Italy were interested in Spain economically, strategically, and ideologically, but not to the extent that they actually plotted the military revolt.[18] They were, however, ready to take advantage of the situation once the generals had made the first move, and by their benevolent attitude had encouraged the generals to go ahead with their plans for a coup.

A Domestic Problem

The result of investigating the various alleged plots leads to the conclusion that the Civil War in Spain began essentially as an internal matter and only later took on the international scope usually associated with the war. The internal conflict between the extremes of Right and Left had worked itself to the point of spontaneous combustion and needed no ignition from the outside. With the victory of the Popular Front in February, the Right realized that the balance of power was now with the Left and if the reforms of the Popular Front went through, that is, turning over the land to those who worked it and the democratization of the army, they would lose most of their power and the revolution would have been won by the Left. They further realized that the moderate Republican parties were losing out and that power was passing into the hands of the extreme Left who would not wait for reforms or gradual changes. In the case of a government of moderate Republicans, the Right saw a chance to sabotage the reforms and allow only a few scraps to be thrown to the revolutionaries until they could once again return to power as they had done in 1933. But such a repetition of events now seemed impossible. The Socialists and Anarchists were moving into closer coöperation and, with their combined following, were demanding changes immediately, and in some cases were already resorting to illegal action. On the Right the situation had also deteriorated. The Fascist Falangist movement, which had had only a small following before the elections, doubled and tripled in size after February and began carrying out a campaign of terror in order to force the Right into taking an uncompromising, irrevocable stand against the Left. The army, too, refused any longer to follow a road of moderation and the lead of the Conservatives. They saw a repetition of the early 'twenties, with an opportunity to "save" the country and seize power for themselves. As events moved more and more rapidly after February, the Conservatives and the moderate Republicans found themselves helpless before the extremes. The result was the inevitable disintegration into the Civil War, first in the streets and then in the battlefields.

CHAPTER V

THE GENERALS REVOLT

The Attempted Army Coup

THERE WAS A general awareness from May, 1936, not only in Spain but elsewhere, that a military revolt would take place. Nevertheless, the government took an optimistic and unconcerned attitude toward the future. The Prime Minister, Casares Quiroga, even mentioned the plot in the Cortes but did not consider it of very much importance.[1] He took only a few precautions to prepare the government's defense against the coup. Beyond moving some of the more reactionary army leaders such as Franco from Madrid, practically nothing was done to prepare for the protection of the capital or the country from an uprising. The Socialists and Anarchists seemed similarly unperturbed; they were riding on a wave of optimism and refused to heed the signs. Their leaders seem to have considered their strength so great and so awe-inspiring that no group would dare attack a government as long as they supported it, and that should a coup be attempted, the all-powerful masses would bring it to heel quickly. Consequently, only the most superficial preparations were made by the parties of the Left. Largo Caballero asked for arms for the workers and got the expected refusal from the government. This seems more or less to have ended his attempts at preparedness. Even the well-disciplined Communist party was carried along by the optimism of the times. Unlike the Socialists, however, they did not remain blind to the threat. Eugene Varga, discussing the Spanish situation in the *International Press Correspondence* (*Inprecorr*) on June 4, 1936, summarized this feeling of complacency, yet combined it with a certain amount of caution:

Although great dangers still threaten the Spanish revolution, there are undoubtedly many new factors present in Spain which are favourable to the revolution, and with a correct and courageous application of the united front strategy the final victory of the revolution should be secured.[2]

As the plotting of the Right became more and more obvious the Communists took steps to warn the government and to force it to take action.[3] During the first part of June the Communist newspaper, *Mundo Obrero*, ran a series of articles demanding these measures against the threat of the Right: purging of the army, the outlawing of the Fascist organizations, steps against Fascist terrorism, and the closing of the Fascist press.[4] The warnings were to no avail because the Communists were too weak to have much influence.

On July 17, the army in the Spanish zone of Morocco rose and occupied Ceuta and Melilla. The government still did nothing and issued a proclamation that everything was perfectly normal. Within a few hours after the proclamation there were military uprisings throughout Spain. In desperation, the government of Quiroga resigned and on the second attempt a new government under José Giral, a colleague of Azaña, was formed.[5] Soon the government saw itself powerless before the scope of the revolt and turned to the only ally left to it, the working masses. Immediately, on the night of July 18, orders were given to arm the workers. Though it was too late to stop the coup, it was not too late to stop the Civil War. Jean Raynaud in his book, *En Espagne "rouge,"* describes how the workers were called upon to help in Catalonia. His picture may not be historically accurate but it shows the trepidation and apprehension of the Left Republicans in calling for help from the revolutionaries, knowing it meant civil war and a reign of excesses verging on anarchy:

It is reported that on July 18, 1936, when it was suspected that there was a military rebellion in progress, M. Companys, President of the Council of the Generalitat of Catalonia, called before him Durruti, one of the Anarchist chiefs whom he had previously thrown into prison, to beg for the aid of his troops in order to put down the revolt which was beginning to take form. Durruti, jeering (and there was good reason for it) accepted on the condition that the arms depots be opened to the Anarchists. Companys had no choice. . . . The agreement was sealed over a cigar for which, it is said, Companys offered with a trembling hand a light to Durruti.[6]

Immediately and spontaneously there developed workers' militias organized primarily around the trade-unions. Within a few days the separate militias in each area founded coördinating committees, as for example, on July 21, a Central Committee of delegates from all parties and all syndicates was set up in Barcelona, and issued a decree establishing the Militias for the Defense of the Republic. This first decree in Barcelona called for 2,000 men from the *UGT*, 3,000 from the *POUM*, 13,000 from the Anarcho-Syndicalists, and 2,000 from the Generalitat. Similar militias were organized throughout Spain. In fact, the real power of government almost immediately passed to these committees as it had passed to the Soviets during the Russian Revolution. The government could carry out its administration only with the sanction of these committees.

Within a few days the people of Spain had aligned themselves on one side or another, only a few changing sides at a later period. Militarily, the strength fell primarily to the Nationalists.[7] All the army, except for a few officers and a few conscripts, went over to the side of the generals.

The navy split about half and half, while the air force mostly went over to the side of the Republic.[8] The insurgents also had the aid of several other important military forces: the Moroccan troops of about 11,000 men, the Foreign Legion with 5,000 troops, the *Guardia Civil* with over 30,000 men and officers, the Falangist army, and the Carlist *Requetés*, dating from the Carlist Wars and reported to have 14,000 men. The Republicans, on the other hand, had only a few army officers, the air corps, part of the navy, 6,500 *Guardias de Asalto* founded by the Republicans in 1931, and the militias.[9]

As to which side had the majority of the population supporting it, there can be no positive answer, because no free elections were ever taken after February, 1936. Both sides claimed majority support but the various observable factors favor the Republican side. In the first place the generals had on their side, as mentioned above, the overwhelming military and financial strength, and yet were not able to gain control immediately. Only after three years of hard fighting were they able to put down the last resistance. Secondly, as will be discussed in later chapters, Franco was successful only because he received large quantities of arms and troops from Italy and Germany. This help surpassed that given to the Republicans, in every respect.[10] Moreover, there was scarcely an instance reported, except in Navarre, where the civilian population arose and took over power in the name of the Nationalists. For example, in the book *Communist Atrocities*, published by the Burgos or Nationalist government, there are described the "crimes committed by the Reds in southern Spain." The book is a detailed account of the atrocities committed by the "Reds" in all the various important towns of southern Spain. In every town described, except those with sizable army garrisons, the Loyalists at the beginning seized power and were overthrown only by Franco's troops which had been transported from Morocco. In no town was there reported an uprising by the people for the Right. Finally, German intelligence reports from the German Ambassador in Nationalist Spain in October, 1937, and again in May, 1938, stated that forty per cent of the population in the "liberated" areas were considered politically unreliable. "This fact is emphasized," the Ambassador said, "by the number of assassinations, on some of which I have made separate brief reports; attempts to destroy bridges; accidents in powder magazines; acts of incendiarism; and the guerrilla fighting still in evidence in southern Spain (Cáceres) but especially in Asturias. Severe reprisals—which naturally produce counter-action, however—have prevented these events from assuming dimensions which could be dangerous to the security of the regime. . . ."[11]

The generals, by taking advantage of the weakness of the government, were able to seize about half the territory of Spain before the militia troops could slow down their advance. The Loyalists continued to hold Madrid, the whole of the eastern coast, the Mancha, New Castile, and an important strip of Estremadura which cut the rebel territory in two. The Loyalists in turn were cut off from the northern territories under their control, Guipúzcoa, Biscay, Santander, and Asturias. The rest of the country was held by the rebels. The isolation of the important industrial section of the north from the rest of Loyalist Spain had very serious consequences, making it difficult to coördinate the economies and defenses of the two sections.

Thus the generals, by controlling the majority of the armed forces, were able to take advantage of the unpreparedness of the government and the working class. Although the mass of the population did not appear to support the insurrection, the rebels' military strength alone was able to secure them half the country.

THE COMMUNISTS AND THE ARMY COUP

The Communist reaction to the insurrection was that it was a Fascist plot. They did not, however, really make full use of this idea or expand it until the Italian and German press talked of a Red plot and of aid to the government by the Soviet Union. From that point on, in all the Communist press and literature, the rebels were referred to as Fascists aided by Hitler and Mussolini. Before this the supporters of the Right were more generally referred to as reactionaries and counterrevolutionaries. To accuse the generals of being Fascists contained no more truth than calling the government forces Reds. Actually, the only really Fascist Spanish organization was the *Falange Española*, which had been founded by the son of Primo de Rivera, José Antonio, in 1932. It remained, as in the case of the Communist party, very small until February, 1936, and then taking advantage of the fears and uneasiness of the middle classes, began recruiting vast numbers. The exact number of members at the time of the insurrection is not known, but from the records available it appears that they had little to do with the actual plot of the insurrection, which was purely an army affair.[12]

From the beginning the Communists played up the fact that it was the workers who had saved the Republic. It was only by arming the workers, which they had urged, that the garrisons in the important proletarian centers such as Madrid and Barcelona were prevented from falling to the rebels. Even before the revolt the Communists had urged the proletariat to be the vanguard of the Republic and organize against any attempt of a counterrevolution by the Right. To the Communists, of course, it was the vigilance of their party and their program of the United Front and the People's Front that made the difference.

Immediately after the coup the Communists almost entirely stopped their criticism and attacks on the Anarchists and Socialists.[13] Though they had formed the Popular Front with the Socialists and allied with the Anarchists, they had never quite ceased to pin-prick them with attacks. Now, in the first few weeks after the insurrection, coöperation between the various workers' parties was the order of the day.

The Communists, contrary to the general opinion of the Left during the first days, were not so confident of victory, particularly since behind the rebels they saw Hitler and Mussolini as the "chief councillors." For the failure to stop or prevent the revolt the Communists threw the blame immediately on the weak Republican government. "It allowed their [the enemy's] economic positions of vantage to remain practically untouched, and particularly because it held in check the agrarian revolution. It also left undisturbed the political key positions of the enemy, both in the machinery of state and in the army. This leniency is now taking its bitter revenge."[14]

COMMUNIST ANALYSIS OF THE CAUSES

Before going into the detailed program developed by the Communist party during the Civil War and the success they had in forcing this policy on the government, it is necessary to summarize the Communists' view of the historical background of the conflict because it affects the course of their later policy.[15]

The Communist analysis of modern Spanish history stressed, above all, the poverty and backwardness of the country. To them, it had remained in the era of "feudalism," and the "bourgeois-democratic revolution" was still to occur. The landowners dominated the entire agricultural scene and the little industry which existed. Thus, by controlling the means of production they dominated the government. Through this alliance with the Church, which was the "largest landowner" and capitalist in the country, they made use of the army to maintain control or to seize power when the Right had been forced out by the masses. The landowners kept their position and were able to compete on the world market by keeping the workers and peasants in a state of semi-starvation. Real wages were only about forty per cent of those in England and unemployment was generally around a quarter of a million and closer to a million during the depression following 1930.

The role of the bourgeoisie gave Spain a special character according to the Communists. The bourgeois revolution had not come about in Spain up to 1936, and by that time the bourgeoisie were reactionaries in the age of imperialism. Already, the threatening proletarian revolution made them fearful of any change. The Communists concluded that Spain was in the same state as Russia in 1917, and the words of Lenin in 1908 about Russia applied to Spain in 1936:

> The victory of the bourgeois revolution in Russia as the victory of the bourgeoisie is impossible. This appears to be paradoxical, but it is nevertheless true. The preponderance of peasant population, its terrible oppression at the hands of the (semi) feudal large landowners, and the strength and determination of the proletariat, which is already organised in a Socialist party—all these circumstances lend a special character to our bourgeois revolution.[16]

The Communists, therefore, concluded that the bourgeoisie were generally a very vacillating class who usually sided with the reactionaries, especially since many had become members of the landowner class.[17] The petty bourgeoisie and the intellectuals were divided between those who supported the Church and the anticlericals. The anticlericals could be relied upon as allies in a Popular Front. The peasants, whom the Communists generally think to be of bourgeois mentality, were in Spain, as they had been in Russia, in such desperate need of the bourgeois revolution that they could be relied upon as allies for many years.[18]

In spite of the fact that the "Spanish proletariat is one of the most revolutionary detachments of the international working class,"[19] the failure of the revolution in Spain, according to the Communists, was due to the division of the proletarian class.[20] In most countries the workers had become divided into two groups, but in Spain the disorganization was even greater, with the splintering into three groups on geographic lines, as well as ideological divisions. It was only by the unity of the proletariat through the United Front, the Communists predicted, that victory could be achieved. This was the task of the Communist party.

A further complicating factor in Spain, as it had been in Russia, was the national question. Eugene Varga declared, "Another important hindrance to the co-ordination of the struggles of the workers and peasants throughout Spain, is the *unsolved national question.*" It was in the form of the Popular Front that the Communists hoped to coördinate the aspirations of the workers, peasants, and oppressed nationalities.[21]

Ventura, the Spanish delegate to the Seventh Congress of the Comintern in 1935, summarized the Communist analysis of the situation in Spain at the time:

> The alignment of forces in Spain may be characterized as follows. On one side we see the ruling classes with their internal struggle for economic group interests, as well as with serious differences of opinion on the question of tactics to be pursued in order to throttle the revolution and establish a fascist dictatorship. The monarchists and the vowed fascists stress the necessity of a coup d'état, whereas the supporters of the tendency represented by Gil Robles fear the resistance of the masses and recommend that the German method be followed. These differences of opinion, as well as the mass struggle, have so far hindered them in building up a totalitarian party for the establishment of a fascist dictatorship. It would, however, be a serious mistake to overlook the efforts that are being made by the reactionary sections to rally and speedily organise their forces. On the other side, we see the proletariat, steeled in the crucible of five years of revolution, rich in revolutionary experience and trained in the various forms of the class struggle—from parliamentary struggle to the general strike, from partial struggle to armed uprising—but still split and disunited.
>
> This is the most vulnerable spot of the Spanish Revolution, and the source from which fascism is drawing its energy. Thus in Spain it is now a question of tempo—a question of who will first succeed in uniting their forces: the bourgeoisie and the landlords, or the workers and peasants. This is what will decide the issue; this is what will decide the fate of the working people for the entire ensuing period.[22]

Actually the Communists' analysis of Spain did not differ greatly from that of many impartial observers from the Western democracies, except for the roles assigned to the bourgeoisie and the Communist party.

CHAPTER VI

THE COMMUNIST PROGRAM

Spain and the United Front

In the policy of the United Front laid down by the Seventh Congress of the Comintern in 1935, the Communists sought coöperation with the Socialists against fascism.[1] This was further to be expanded to include the peasants, petty bourgeoisie, and the unorganized masses in a Popular Front. In proposing this alliance, however, the Communists did not intend to stop attacking either the Socialists or the bourgeoisie, or to give up their activities of seeking control over the proletariat. In other words, though the USSR wanted and needed the coöperation of the Socialists and democratic bourgeoisie against the threat of fascism, she was not willing to give up her revolutionary aims or her striving for control over the world proletariat through the Comintern. For example, at the same time the Communists in Spain were seeking an agreement with the Socialists, Georgi Dimitrov was attacking the Spanish Socialists in the Congress of the Comintern:

Was it inevitable that the bourgeoisie and the aristocracy should have triumphed in Spain, a country where the forces of proletarian revolt are so advantageously combined with a peasant war?

The Spanish Socialists were in the government from the first days of the revolution. Did they establish fighting contact between the working class organizations of every political opinion, including the Communists and the Anarchists, and did they weld the working class into a united trade union organization? Did they demand the confiscation of all lands of the landlords, the church and the monasteries in favor of the peasants in order to win over the latter to the side of the revolution? Did they attempt to fight for national self-determination for the Catalonians and the Basques, and for the liberation of Morocco? Did they purge the army of monarchist and fascist elements and prepare it for passing over to the side of the workers and peasants? Did they dissolve the Civil Guard, so detested by the people, the executioner of every movement of the people? Did they strike at the fascist party of Gil Robles and at the might of the Catholic church? No, they did none of these things. They rejected the frequent proposals of the Communists for united action against the offensive of the bourgeois landlord reaction and fascism; they passed election laws which penalized popular movements, laws under which the heroic miners of Asturias are now being tried. They had peasants who were fighting for land shot by the Civil Guard, and so on.[2]

By August, 1936, however, the Comintern found that a policy of receiving all and giving nothing was not going to work, particularly in Spain. The Socialists, even in Spain where there was closer affinity between the two parties than in most other countries, had not responded to the offer of the Communists for a United Front pact on this unequal basis. The Socialists in Spain, by their experience, had been won over to the idea of a solid alliance of the Left, but would enter a compact on a *quid pro quo* basis only. The Communists also found that the Socialists were even less willing to respond to their invitation in view of the Communists' numerical weakness. They were in fact without even the power to have their prosposals accepted as a basis for negotiating. The Socialists in Spain did not desire a pact with the Communists, but were interested in an alliance of all the Left, of which the Communists were only a very small minority. (On the basis of the number of seats they received in the Cortes they constituted only about six per cent of the Left's strength.) Consequently, if the Communists wanted to be a part of the Popular Front they had to accept the terms of the other parties, and not dictate terms. The Communists were thus faced with a dilemma. Was it better to stick strictly to the program of the Seventh Congress of the Comintern which insisted that the core of the Popular Front be the United Front of the proletariat, or should they modify their program to coördinate their policies with those of the other parties of the Left in Spain? An uncompromising attitude on their part would have meant an alliance of the Left without them. Two reasons probably influenced them to choose the latter path: the increasing threat of fascism in Western Europe and Spain, and the fear of losing all influence among the elements of the Left if they abstained. The result was that the Communists shifted the emphasis of their program in Spain and stressed the idea of an alliance against the Fascists in the form of the People's Front rather than a United Front of Communists and Socialists.[3] Furthermore, the Communists stressed it was a pact not only of the proletarian parties, peasants, the petty bourgeoisie, and the unorganized masses, but of all democratic elements who opposed the "black hordes" of fascism, including the very conservative and Catholic Basque Nationalists and the Catalan Esquerra. Jesús Hernández, as managing director of the Communist party newspaper *Mundo Obrero*, published the following statement on August 9:

> It is absolutely false that the present workers' movement has for its object the establishment of a proletarian dictatorship after the revolution has terminated. It cannot be said we have a social motive for our participation in the war. We, Communists, are the first to repudiate this supposition. We are motivated exclusively by the desire to defend the democratic republic established on April 14, 1931, and revived last February 18.

The idea of the United Front, however, was by no means forgotten and was pushed forward whenever possible, as for example, the unification of the Socialist and Communist youth in April, 1936. Likewise, articles and speeches by the Communists continued to demand the unity of the working class through a United Front pact and stressed even more the idea of the creation of a single working-class party and trade-union federation.[4] Finally, even though the Communists failed to achieve a formal United Front pact with the Socialists, in practice there was close cooperation between the two parties.[5]

The Communists' coöperation with the Popular Front included the entrance of two Communists into Largo Caballero's Popular Front government on September 4, 1936, although a United Front pact still did not exist with the Socialists, and the Communists remained in the minority in influence and strength in the Popular Front. In France, the Communists had previously refused to enter the government, hoping in this way to lose nothing should the Popular Front fail and to use the mistakes of the Blum government to build their own prestige among the proletariat. In Spain, however, where the situation had deteriorated into civil war, the Communists could not afford to weaken the solidarity of the Left by remaining out of the government. Antonio Mije, member of the Politbureau of the Spanish Communist party, stated the reasons the Communists had entered the government:

Already at the commencement of my speech I showed how our party has always consistently fought for the furtherance of all slogans of the democratic revolution.

Today the conditions exist for the realisation of these slogans. First, there exists the situation of a civil war, brought about by the enemies of the people, and the necessity for us to unite closely together for the fight against reaction and against fascism in the framework of the democratic republic. Second, the proletariat, as the most important and active force, is fighting in the front ranks with weapon in hand. Third, a profound change is taking place in the economic sphere, especially in the country districts. Fourth, in immediate connection with the war, the main tasks of the democratic bourgeois revolution are being fulfilled.

In these circumstances a government was needed which can count on the confidence of all the various social strata of the population, in order to put an end to the military-fascist insurrection as quickly as possible. Such a government has now been formed. Having regard for this situation the Central Committee of our Party decided to take part in the Government.[6]

It should be noted that the conditions under which the Communists entered the government corresponded very closely to the prerequisites set down by the Seventh Congress of the Comintern in 1935 for the formation of a Popular Front government: (1) the breakdown of the old bourgeois state, (2) the masses in revolt against fascism, and (3) the

Socialists and other workers' groups actively fighting the Fascists and reactionaries.[7] As a result, even though the Communists gave up their demand for a formal United Front pact with the Socialists as a prerequisite, they still closely adhered to the United Front program.

A DEMOCRATIC REVOLUTION

The most startling development in respect to the Communists' program in Spain was the length to which they went in denying the nearness of the proletarian revolution and Socialism, the basic concepts of Communism. In earlier chapters the gradual change in the idea of the proletarian revolution was traced through increasingly more opportunistic policies. It was not, however, until the Communists entered the government that this idea was fully defined and they absolutely rejected the proletarian dictatorship as an immediate aim. It was rationalized that Spain, slow in developing, had not yet had a democratic revolution and must go through that first. Unlike its Russian counterpart, where the democratic revolution and proletarian revolution came within a few months of each other, according to the Communists, the democratic revolution in Spain was not to be accomplished so quickly. In fact, with the entrance of the Communists into the government, comparison with the Russian Revolution was made less and less frequently by Communist authors; they stressed only the differences and, therefore, the impossibility of transposing the solution of 1917 to 1936.[8] The support of the democratic republic and revolution was emphasized time and time again, as, for example, in the statement by José Díaz, Secretary-General of the Spanish Communist party, on October 1, 1936:

> We, of the Communist Party, consider that we, together with the honest ranks of the working class, will have to go a long road with the Spanish democrats. Some try to portray this government as a Communist government or Socialist or generally give it a name of some peculiar Socialist viewpoint. In answer we say with complete decisiveness that this government is a continuation of the previous government.[9]

Furthermore, the emphasis changed from a world revolution to one of "national character":

> *The revolution in Spain bears a national character,* not only because it is directed against the attempts of German and Italian imperialism to enslave the country but because it seeks the freedom of all oppressed peoples.[10]

The opportunism of the Communist policy was, however, obvious on closer examination of their statements. The Communists, in supporting a democratic Popular Front government as their aim in Spain, still held to the idea of proletarian leadership under the Communists though its program was to remain within the confines of the bourgeois revolution. For example:

It is the great merit of the Communist Party of Spain that, while tirelessly and consistently struggling to overcome the split in the working class, it fought and is still fighting to create the maximum prerequisites for ensuring the hegemony of the proletariat, the prime condition for the victory of the bourgeois-democratic revolution. The formation of a united front between the Socialist and Communist Parties, the establishment of a single organisation of young workers, the creation of a single party of the proletariat in Catalonia, and, last but most important, the transformation of the Communist Party itself into a huge mass party enjoying tremendous and ever-growing influence and authority are all a sure guarantee that the working class will be able still more effectively to exercise its hegemony by assuring leadership over the whole revolutionary movement and carrying it to victory.[11]

The program of the Communists on entering the government in September, 1936, clearly indicates this rejection of the dictatorship of the proletariat as an immediate aim:

We intend in the first place to master completely the military-fascist insurrection; secondly, to reorganise the people's army, after it has been purged of all monarchist generals and of all fascists who occupied commanding positions; thirdly, to solve the question of land and credit for the peasants and for the landworkers; the land belonging to the landowners who financed the military-fascist movement will pass into the hands of the millions of peasants and landworkers, who were terribly exploited, thereby putting an end to starvation and misery on the land; fourthly, to destroy the economic and political power of the clergy, whereby real freedom of culture will be established. We shall respect the religious convictions of everybody, but at the same time we shall not allow the churches ever again to be centres of conspiracy nor places from which the people can be shot down; fifthly, generally improve the standard of living of the workers, secure minimum wages, fix the working time so that the workers shall not be exhausted, introduce social insurance (unemployment, sick and old age insurance); sixthly, introduction of a democratic regime in Morocco; seventhly, to fight in the government for the peace of the whole world.

The slogan at the moment must be, to win everything through the Government and everything for the Government, to strengthen its authority and power.[12]

Although the above program might have been considered quite radical in Spain a year before, in September, 1936, the country was in the throes of civil war and revolution. The Anarchists and peasants were carrying out their revolution of *comunismo libertario*. In most places where the Anarchists had any strength they had formed local committees and had taken over from the governmental authorities, if not in name, at least in fact. They were rapidly socializing and collectivizing the land and industries wherever possible. Along with this they were carrying on a reign of terror, seeking out former landowners and priests, and burning churches. The Communists, on the other hand, directly contrary to Lenin's April thesis of "all power to the Soviets" (workers' and peasants' councils) in a revolution, supported the bourgeois government and authority. The Communists were not against change but wanted all reforms to be within the scope of the bourgeois revolution[13]—that is, they supported the claims of the lower-middle class, small entrepreneurs and small landowners, against not only the exploitation by the "feudal" elements of the Right but against nationalization and collectivization being forced on them by the parties of the extreme Left. M. Ercoli (Togliatti) stated the maximum demands of the Communists in Spain:

... in the interest of the economic and political development of the country, the agrarian question must be settled by abolishing the feudal relations which dominate the countryside. It means that the peasants, the workers, and the working population as a whole must be relieved of the intolerable burden of an outworn economic and administrative system. It means further that the privileges of the aristocracy, the Church and the religious orders must be done away with and the uncontrolled sway of the reactionary castes must be broken.[14]

The Comintern was particularly anxious that their policy be well propagandized among the Western democracies. Consequently, all Communist front organizations in the various countries and sympathetic observers of the Communist policies, such as Louis Fischer in the United States, stressed the bourgeois aspects of the new policy. Louis Fischer, in his pamphlet *War in Spain*, declared:

... Some have regarded the Communists' advocacy of democracy in Spain as a tactical maneuver to mislead foreign democracies and bourgeois liberals into supporting the Loyalists. This interpretation is wrong; such a trick would soon become too transparent for use. The democratic slogan means that the Communists have no desire to establish in Spain a dictatorship guided by one party as in Russia. Spanish conditions are different. . . .[15]

The Communists, in supporting the bourgeois-democratic revolution in Spain against both the Right and extreme Left, did not give up the dictatorship of the proletariat and the establishment of socialism as their final goal. They never denied that this was the ultimate aim they were seeking, but their propaganda referred to it less and less. In the thousands of Communist speeches given during the war it was rarely even mentioned. José Díaz, the Secretary-General of the Communist party, explained one reason for its omission:

... it is necessary to mobilize everyone and unite everyone in order to win the war. . . . Libertarian Communism, dictatorship of the proletariat, socialism of the State, a federal Republic: we will speak of all these later. For the time being, let us win the war![16]

Thus, to the Communists, the immediate task of winning the war was the most important aim. They did not want to allow the war to be lost because of the various revolutionary programs competing for recognition behind the Loyalist lines. Such a confusion, and the possibility of a civil war within a civil war, would have allowed the rebels an easier victory. It may also be argued that the Communists felt that their numerical and political weakness at the beginning of the war would have put their revolutionary program at a disadvantage. It was, therefore, necessary to hold off the final revolutionary struggle until they could increase their forces. In the meantime they felt it best to ally with the middle-class parties in support of the *status quo*.

Furthermore, the omission of the Communist revolutionary propaganda for the dictatorship of the proletariat and the establishment of socialism was in keeping with the general Comintern strategy at this time. The immediate concern of the Third International was not so much how to spread revolution but how to stop the "counterrevolution" in the form of Nazism and fascism. The interest of the Comintern in Spain, therefore, was primarily not as a new outpost for a Communist revolution or a Soviet Republic, which strategically could be of little help to Russia, but how to keep Spain out of the hands of the dictators, who could use it to encircle Russia's ally, France.

Another integral part of the Soviet Union's foreign policy and a part aimed at German aggression was coöperation with the democracies. This was a further reason why the Communists decided to omit in their propaganda in Spain the demand for the immediate establishment of the dictatorship of the proletariat and of socialism. The Communists probably hoped that such an omission would lull the fears of the democracies concerning Comintern activities and help strengthen Russia's alliance with the West.

Consequently, the Communists in Spain developed a program which was almost identical to that of the middle-class parties on the Loyalist side. And although that program was actually revolutionary, when compared with the programs of the other workers' and peasants' parties of the Left, the Communist program can be described as extremely mild.

THE AGRARIAN POLICY OF THE COMMUNISTS

Even before the actual beginning of the Civil War in July, the Communists, following Lenin's thesis that in relatively backward countries final victory of the revolution was possible only in alliance with the peasants, advocated supporting the peasants and acceding for the time being to all their demands.[17] Thus, while collectivization was still being pushed by means of coercion in the USSR, the Communist party condemned forced collectivization in Spain.[18]

The Anarchists and some Socialists had gone into many sections of the countryside in the first months of the war and had organized the farmers into collectives, and wherever the Anarchist militia penetrated they left collectives under control of Anarchist committees in their wake. The Anarchist utopia of *comunismo libertario* called for the organization of local collectives as the basis of the new society. With the destruction of all governmental authority the Anarchists believed society would remain organized on the local level both economically and socially through collectives presided over by locally selected committees. Although in the new Libertarian society everything was to be voluntary, the Anarchists could not conceive of any deviation from the collective principle and, consequently, all peasants were expected to join. Actually, the collective in many parts of Spain would very likely have been a sound basis for organizing agriculture, especially in the arid sections of large estates and areas where the use of agricultural workers had long been the custom. It was in these regions of southern Spain that the Anarchists had had their largest following among the peasants, but these areas had almost immediately come under rebel domination. In Aragon and Catalonia, where the Anarchists were trying to carry out collectivization, they had only a scattered following. Moreover, most of the peasants in these regions had long been small, individual farmers and strongly resisted the forced collectivization.

The Communists made good use of this peasant antagonism toward collectivization in order to push their more moderate policy to the fullest extent in the country. They attacked forced collectivization as merely a continuation of the cacique system by the "Committees."[19] Their program was based rather on the expropriation of all the estates held by supporters of Franco, which included most of the large estates. These estates were then to be divided among the individual farmers who worked them. As José Díaz explained, "Then, when the peasant finally holds in his hands the land which has been given him by the Republic, he is determined that it is in his interest to defend it on the front and in the rear."[20]

Although forced collectivization was condemned by the Communists, they strongly encouraged volunteer coöperatives. Vicente Uribe, Communist Minister of Agriculture, stated the Communist attitude:

You know, and we Communists have repeated this forty thousand times, that we cannot tolerate the creation of collectives by violence. On the other hand we have also continuously reiterated that all the collectives formed voluntarily have from us the support and affection which they need to become ideal labor organizations in the Spanish countryside. We have called attention continuously to the significance of the present rush to form collectives.[21]

The Communists also supported other types of volunteer farm coöperatives besides production coöperatives, particularly consumer coöperatives and government-sponsored credit organizations, giving the peasant a source of easy credit instead of forcing him to resort to the high fees of the moneylender. Through their instigation the Institute of Agrarian Reform was revitalized and a Department of Coöperatives was set up. In conclusion, it can be said that the Communists from the beginning paid special attention to the peasants and stressed their importance to the defense of the Republic:

Truly, the part of the peasants in the armed struggle against the rebels is still in every way scanty. This shows that in large measure all the parties of the People's Front in the past have underestimated the role of the peasants in the struggle for the Republic; while some have even neglected the demands of the many millions of the peasants. Not enough work was done by the Communists in the villages. . . .[22]

The agricultural program of the Communists was not unique. The Socialists who had previously backed collectivization were willing to forgo their aim in exchange for support of the peasants and bourgeoisie. Even the Republicans backed the Communist volunteer collective program against the Anarchist coercive methods. The Caballero government, however, was not immediately successful in breaking up the collectives created by the Anarchists. Only gradually was it able to reassert its power over the areas which had fallen under Anarchist domination. The process had to be slow so as not to antagonize the Anarchists unduly.[23]

The Anarchists did what they could to stop the encroachment of the government into the countryside and openly attacked the Communists as counterrevolutionaries. The Anarchists established a peasant newspaper, *Campo Libre*, which opposed all the Communist and government policies.[24] In spite of their efforts the Anarchists were not able to stop the anticollectivization movement supported by the government.

INDUSTRY

Immediately after the beginning of the war the Communist policy on industry followed closely that which it adopted on agriculture. The Communists opposed the wholesale collectivization of factories, which was being carried out by the Anarchists wherever the *CNT* was in control.

They condemned the Decree of Collectivization issued by the Generalitat of Catalonia on October 24, 1936, and backed the government in sabotaging it. This law, forced through by the Anarchists, provided for the collectivization of all industries employing more than one hundred workers. In Barcelona, where the Anarchists were the real power, almost all the industries had already been collectivized and control had passed into the hands of workers' committees. In opposition the Communists set up a much milder plan for industry. Those factories which had been owned by rebels were to be expropriated and nationalized, but not collectivized —that is, owned and managed by the workers. The Communists, however, did include in the program "workers' control," but they meant something very different from the Anarchists by "workers' control." To the Anarchists it was complete control of the factory in every aspect by the workers, but to the Communists it meant workers' control subject to the orders of the manager and owner and to the over-all direction of the state. Under the Communist plan, rebel-owned industries were to be nationalized by the state; all other industries were to continue under private ownership and management, except that a workers' committee was to be formed to help management run the plant. The Communists were particularly insistent that foreign capital should be respected: Failure to protect foreign capital "would be an error in international relations, because then England would decisively intervene in Spain not on our side but with Franco because England has economic interests in our country to defend."[25]

The Communists also were opposed to the equalitarian policy of the Anarchists in industry. The tendency to equalize pay "promotes irresponsibility and indolence which impedes the attainment of the maximum efficiency of the worker."[26]

In attacking the Anarchist program the Communists found their best support in the reports of the Ministry of Industry whose head was an Anarchist. The Ministry reported 11,000 instances in which it was asked to intervene to give economic aid to various factories because of unwise management.[27] The Anarchist attempt to develop workers' control had not proved successful. Confusion and lowering of output were the general results of the program.

In the beginning the Communists were not as successful in altering the industrial program adopted in Anarchist areas as they had been in agriculture. The Anarchists were very strong in the industrial area of Catalonia and the Ministry of Industry was in their hands. In the non-Anarchist areas, however, their program was put into effect, not because the Communists dominated or controlled these areas, but because the Socialists had a program for industry similar to that of the Communists.

THE CHURCH

One of the most potent elements of the Nationalists' propaganda about "Red" Spain was the alleged Communist burning of churches. As has already been pointed out, the burning of churches by the masses was an old tradition in Spain and, therefore, did not originate with the Communists. Churches had been burnt in 1823, 1835, 1868, 1873, and 1909. It was generally a spontaneous act by the people, rarely having organization or leadership. The burnings were the most widespread in Anarchist areas because the Anarchists generally encouraged these acts and had less control over their followers. The other parties and groups in Spain tried, whenever possible, to discourage such excesses. The Communists were very outspoken in their condemnation of these acts. In April, 1936, José Díaz expressed the Communist attitude toward the Church saying, "We do not want to attack the religious feelings. Though we are not supporters, we respect in others the feeling of religious faith. [On the other hand] we do not want these sentiments to be abused as arms of oppression . . . we will not consent that the churches be enormous concentrations of riches, while the poor people [*parado*] die of hunger."[28] The Communist attitude was one of refraining from open persecution of the churches as a dangerous policy but at the same time taking from the Church its riches and political power. There is no evidence to show that they supported the burning of churches in any way. They countered such propaganda by saying, "That the fascists have been responsible for the burning of many churches in Spain is certain. Their aim is to whip up a general panic among the population under cover of which to seize control. Also, and this is not the least important of their objects, to create public antagonism towards the left organisations."[29]

That this policy of the Communists toward the Church was not purely a hoax is proved by their attitude later in the war when their influence was great and they actually attempted to restore religious life in the country. The strongly Catholic President of the Basques in 1938 stated:

The efforts of our Manuel de Irujo in favor of normalization of the religious life in the territory of the Republic have received from President [*sic*] Negrín the most comprehensive consideration. In this country where, at the beginning of the struggle, criminal excesses were committed against the persons and edifices of the Church, today there reigns tolerance and respect for the beliefs, supported by the authorities and profoundly professed by the people.[30]

AUTONOMY

The Communists opposed the Anarchists on still another question—that of regionalism. The theory of anarchism does not consider the problem of regionalism. It is a theory of extreme localism without consideration of different nationalities or the historical backgrounds of different areas. All men are alike in *comunismo libertario*—the masses know no distinction of nationalities. Consequently, the Anarchists, though strong in Catalonia, completely ignored the ardent regionalism in that area, and considered it purely a bourgeois phenomenon. The pragmatic Communists saw that regionalism was strong and used this as bait to gain support. "It was for this reason that the Communist Party of Spain places in the forefront of its attention the question of the relations between the Spanish and Catalonian peoples. 'There can be no national unity which is not based on fraternal relations between Catalonia and Spain, the Catalonian people and the other peoples of the Iberian peninsula.' "[31] The Communists continuously made a strong appeal to Catalonian pride, even to printing a large amount of its propaganda in the area in Catalan, a practice adopted by neither the Socialists nor Anarchists.[32] The actual plan for fitting Catalonia eventually into their scheme of the Republic was never worked out by the Communists. In fact, as will be seen later, the Communists, when in a position of power, tended to overlook Catalonian and other regionalism and to reduce effectively the autonomy of these areas.[33]

The program of the Communists during the first months of the war was, therefore, mostly against the Libertarian revolution being "perpetrated" by the Anarchists and in support of the Republican parties. It was mainly a defensive policy dictated by the comparative weakness of the Communist party which was not yet strong enough to launch an aggressive program of its own.

CHAPTER VII

FORMATION OF THE POPULAR FRONT GOVERNMENT

SEÑOR GIRAL'S CABINET composed of only the three moderate bourgeois parties—the Republican Left, the Republican Union, and the Radical-Socialist—came into power on July 19, but served as only a temporary solution to the problem of government pending further developments and the balancing of forces in Republican Spain. If the generals' insurrection had been limited to only a small area and had not posed such a serious threat, perhaps a moderate Republican government could have continued in power. Likewise, if the Western democracies had supported the Republican government instead of sponsoring the Non-Intervention Pact, the moderate Republicans might have remained in control. As it was, the defense of the government fell more and more onto the workers' militias, and workers' committees took over the powers of the government either separately from the municipal authorities or merged with them. For example, in Valencia the area was controlled by a People's Executive Committee completely independent of the central authorities. Manuel Azaña, whose name had once carried so much prestige and weight, was completely overshadowed by the more revolutionary Left and particularly by the name of Largo Caballero. More and more frequently demands were heard to put the "Spanish Lenin" at the head of the government. Azaña, who virtually controlled the Giral cabinet, could have followed the path of trying at all costs to save the moderate government but most likely would have been overthrown by the force of the people's committees, as Kerensky was in the Russian Revolution. But even before the Civil War, Azaña had wanted the formation of a Popular Front government under the domination of the Left Republicans. By the end of August, however, their leadership over a Popular Front government was impossible because the Republicans could never command the necessary respect. Consequently, bowing to the popular demand, Azaña and the Republicans turned over power to Largo Caballero and used all their influence to moderate his cabinet as much as possible. In this task they had the alliance of the right faction of the Socialist party under Indalecio Prieto and also of the Communists, but at this time the latter were not an important political factor.

On September 4, the new government was formed with Largo Caballero as Prime Minister and Minister of War. Indalecio Prieto became Minister

of Air and Navy;[1] Juan Negrín, Minister of Finance; and Álvarez del
Vayo took the post of Minister of Foreign Affairs. In all, there were six
Socialists, two Communists, two representatives of the Republican Left,
and one member each from the Catalan Esquerra, the Basque Nationalists, and the Republican Union. The Communists held the portfolios of
Agriculture and Public Instruction. Though considered minor posts the
Communists made the most of them. The outstanding feature of the
cabinet was not so much its tendency to the Left as the strength which
the moderate elements were able to hold for themselves in the growing
revolutionary condition of the country. The new government provided a
means of closing the gap between the revolutionary committees and central control by including the revolutionary elements in the government,
so that they would not attack it. The Communists had advocated this
solution all along, though it was by no means their suggestion which
brought it about. The Communists had from the beginning attacked the
Giral cabinet as unreliable, saying that, "Had the course of events been
different, some of these people [of Giral's government] would possibly
have sought for a compromise with the reactionaries."[2]

The *FAI* and the *CNT* at first refused to be represented in the government, although they had been asked. They still held as unsavory anything connected with government. As the situation became more desperate
with the possible fall of Madrid, the Anarchists were persuaded to take
the plunge and accepted four posts in the government.[3] Not only did the
Anarchists share the fear of general collapse, but they had also come to
acknowledge the need of some type of centralized command and organization. Furthermore, in accepting the positions they hoped to get more
war material from the government.[4]

This beginning of coöperation between the *CNT—FAI* and the Socialist trade-unions and party, which resulted in the Anarchists' entrance
into Caballero's government, was a significant step forward in building
a unified defense. Luis Araquistain explains it as follows:

...The *U.G.T.* has already become more radical, both in political and trade union
questions. The majority of the unions have adopted revolutionary socialism and have
accepted the revolutionary mission which, according to Marx and Lenin, should be
that of the trade unions in the period of transition from capitalism to socialism.

The *C.N.T.* has become socialistic in the sense of recognizing the necessity of the
state as an instrument of struggle and as a means of consolidating the revolutionary
conquests in the internal and external affairs of the country. What a pleasure for a
socialist to read the program of nationalization, collectivization and municipalization
contained in the proposals of the *C.N.T.!* These measures seem to have been taken
from our own Socialist program and, above all, from the program of the Socialist

Group of Madrid, which I have already mentioned. Bakunin and Marx would embrace over this document of the *C.N.T.*[5]

Although all parties had verbally agreed on the need for centralizing defense, it was quite another thing to get the groups to give up their hold in various areas to the central authorities. Localism and the persistence of the groups in holding onto their gains were so strong that Largo Caballero found himself pushed into a position where he had to use force against the revolutionary groups he had wanted first to support, and to carry on a campaign against these "uncontrollable elements." He had come to power a revolutionary but found this position difficult to maintain. For instance, the Anarcho-Syndicalist Iron Column, on its return to Valencia from the Teruel front, preferred to fight the central government rather than accept "militarization." It was defeated with many casualties. The army also had to be called against the town of Cullera, near Valencia, which refused to submit to the central authorities. At the end of December, 1936, it was decreed by the central government that the town and village committees should be replaced by regular municipal councils bringing an end to the revolutionary committees. Likewise, Caballero had to give way against the resistance of the peasants. He had to suspend the decree on forced collectivization and allow expansion of individual farming.[6] In respect to industry Caballero had to bow before the necessity of foreign relations and not nationalize foreign firms.[7] The nationalization of other industries was also slowed down, and those that were nationalized were brought under central control whenever possible. Consequently, the Caballero government found itself everywhere putting the brakes on the revolution, and soon revolutionary elements began to call it "counterrevolutionary." This antirevolutionary drive, however, was due not only to pressure from the moderate elements, including the Communists, but dictated by the needs of war. Caballero himself said soon after taking power, "Our first task is to establish unity of command and power. The leadership of the fighting forces of the whole Republic, including Catalonia, is now concentrated in the hands of the War Minister, whilst all threads of operations are in the hands of the General Staff."[8] Thus the disrupting element of revolution which tended to further divide the country and to slow down production, at least temporarily while changing over to a collectivized system, had to be brought to a halt in order to organize for the immediate necessity of defending Madrid and the country.

The course of events in the Catalan Generalitat followed that of the central government. On September 27, the *CNT*, the *POUM*, and the *PSUC* (United Socialist Party of Catalonia) entered the Generalitat Council, which, as in the case of the central government, was not the signal for a further turn to the Left, but, on the contrary, meant the beginning of a "counterrevolution." Soon the Militia Committee and Economic Council were merged into the Generalitat, and the Committee for Internal Security, which formerly had been a branch of the Militia Committee, was now made responsible to the Councilor for the Interior. The militias were gradually welded into the regular army of Catalonia. Collectivization of farms was gradually ended, but collectivized industry still remained paramount in Catalonia.

Thus, the pressing demands of preparing for and carrying on a prolonged fight against the rebels, after the first flush of popular enthusiasm, had kept the army from seizing the government and brought the policies of the Caballero government more and more into line with the program adopted by the Communists in the early days of the war.[9] In the first months of intensive revolutionary activity the strength and prestige of the Communist party had been insignificant. It could do little to stop the left Socialist workers from carrying out an immediate Socialist revolution and nothing to stop the Libertarian revolution of the Anarchists in Catalonia. Even when further revolutionary acts had come to a halt in the face of military defeats, the Communists were still weak. Although the program they advocated became the order of the day, they were not its leaders. Rather Largo Caballero, Indalecio Prieto, and the Republicans were the instigators. The Communists remained a political force of little consequence. But at the end of 1936 there occurred an event which altered completely the balance of forces on the Loyalist side in favor of the Communists—the arrival of military aid from the Soviet Union.

CHAPTER VIII

SOVIET AID

SUPPLIES FROM RUSSIA

BY THE TIME the monarchy collapsed in 1931, the accusation of "Moscow agent" was already an old term in respect to the Left in Spain, as was the claim that Moscow was sending aid in the form of money and guns to Spanish revolutionaries. During the Asturian revolt of 1934 the cry reached a virtual din. The allegation was accepted by the Right as good propaganda and no one bothered to investigate the truth of the matter. Money was supposedly smuggled in on Russian ships, which were also reported to have landed arms on the Asturian coast. It is true that the Socialists, Anarchists, and Communists were all building up caches of arms and made little attempt to deny it, though it is doubtful that they obtained them from the Soviet Union. Gerald Brenan, in his book *The Spanish Labyrinth*, says that the arms used in the October uprising originally came from the Spanish government's arsenals. "The principal supply had been ordered by Echevarrieta, the well-known Basque financier and a friend of Prieto, from the Consorcio de Fábricas Militares in 1932."[1] The only known aid the Soviet Union did give to the Asturian workers was in funds raised in Russian factories to feed and clothe the survivors and the dependents of the revolt, but these funds did not reach Spain until after the revolt was over.[2]

After the victory of the Popular Front in February, 1936, to no one's surprise the stories of Russian aid again began to circulate even before the July 19 uprising. After the beginning of the insurrection the propaganda machines of the Right issued reams of "evidence" of Soviet aid to the Republicans. It is difficult to check the so-called facts, but where it was possible to find the source it was usually a newspaper report or a rumor. Actually, there was little attempt by the Right to prove the existence of Soviet assistance. No attempt, for example, was made to send a group of unbiased investigators to check the rumors as was done by the Left. The reports seem to have been only propaganda to cover up the rebels' own outside source of supplies and to justify their use of foreign material when it was impossible to conceal it. It was, and still is, the favorite game of dictators to multiply the charges to such an extent that it is impossible to investigate them thoroughly and to blame the other side for what they are doing. In conclusion, it can be said that after carefully investigating the multitude of reports on Soviet material landed in

Spain up to October, 1936, there are no grounds for believing the existence of this kind of aid. The very fact that there is plenty of proof of the presence of Russian aid after October, 1936, even though the Soviet Union was trying to conceal it, leads to the conclusion that if Russia had given arms before this date more substantial evidence would be available.

Nationalist and Fascist reports on Soviet help after October, 1936, when there were good indications of Soviet war material from the Republican camp itself, were a peculiar combination of fact and fiction. Even where there seemed to have been some basis in fact, there were only meager attempts to cite evidence or indicate sources. An outstanding example of this is a speech by a master in the art of propaganda, Dr. Joseph Goebbels, in support of Franco. In the first part of the quotation below he uses figures which independent checking of other sources reveals were within reason (only altered in respect to time) and were probably based on good intelligence reports. Then, in the last sentence, he uses figures which appear completely out of line with the first figures he cited. The later figures were by his own evidence, therefore, exaggerated and made up for propaganda purposes:[3]

... Within the short period of time from March 6 to May 14, 1937—that is to say after the control plan had come into force—through the Dardanelles there passed 190 munition ships belonging to Soviet Russia and 88 ships flying the flag of the Red Party in Spain, on their way to Spanish harbours within the Red domination. These ships brought 162 tanks, 130 cannons, 86 aeroplanes, 395 motor transport cars, 12 anti-aircraft guns, 31,420 tons of other war material and munitions. During February and March 101 Russian Soviet aeroplanes were shipped from Reval to Spain. And on March 1st, 50 heavy guns from Soviet Russia were brought overland to Almansa. Recently one single large consignment of war material from Soviet Russia to the Reds in Spain included 100 heavy tanks, 500 medium-size tanks, 2,000 light tanks, 4,000 heavy machine guns, 6,000 light machine guns and 300 aeroplanes, with their pilots.[4]

Soviet material assistance took two forms, relief and war material. Relief, consisting of food and clothing for women and children, started at the very beginning of the Civil War. In every city and town in the Soviet Union meetings were held during the first weeks of the rebellion to demonstrate solidarity with the Spanish people. The pages of *Pravda* and *Izvestiia* were filled with speeches and pledges of help from the Russian people. On August 6, 1936, Secretary Shvernik of the All-Union Central Soviet of Trade Unions announced the sending of 12,145,000 rubles (over two million dollars) to the Spanish people collected from Russian workers.[5] It was expected that in the month of August contributions would reach over four million dollars. The reasons for this immediate support for the Republican side are several. First, the Soviet Union had been watching all along the growth of the revolutionary situation in Spain, and as the alleged leader of world revolution she had to champion it for her own prestige. Since at first Russia was unwilling to commit herself in respect to armed aid, she had to make the most of the propaganda value of verbal solidarity and of supplies of food and clothing. On the other hand there appeared to be a genuine feeling of fellowship on the part of the Russian people with the Spanish masses which grew up spontaneously and was merely put to use by the Soviet government for its own purpose. Finally, Russia urged support of Spain because she wanted to arouse the democracies to aid the Spanish people. Russia feared a totalitarian regime in Spain which would tend to isolate France, the new keystone of Russia's security system.[6] As a result the Soviet government itself actively encouraged and sponsored the collection of funds for Spain.

With the adherence of the Soviet Union to the Non-Intervention Pact at the end of August, the collection of relief funds for Spain was allowed to lag, in order not to give grounds to the claim of the Fascist powers that the Soviet Union was violating the pact. Some authorities have alleged it was due to French pressure that the collections stopped. When it became obvious, however, by the middle of September, 1936, that Germany and Italy had not stopped supplying the rebels, the Soviet government launched a new campaign for funds for Spain. The newspapers again were filled with reports of meetings, letters, and contributions. By October, the collection had reached a total of 47,600,000 rubles. And by the end of October, five ships laden with food had been sent to Spain from the port of Odessa.

Not only were the Communists active in collecting in the Soviet Union but through Communist-sponsored organizations throughout the world large sums were collected for Spain. Besides the already established societies the Communists created a new network of organizations solely for the support of Spain, so that those people who would not work through a Communist organization could still aid Spain. A typical organization was the *Comité International d'Aide au Peuple Espagnol* in Paris, which between August, 1936, and June, 1938, had collected over half a million dollars. It would be difficult to estimate how much money was given through the Communist parties and organizations, as there is no complete accounting and much of it was sent in the form of food. It would not, however, be an exaggeration to say that the total aid was in the neighborhood of fifty million dollars.[7]

This source of food and clothing was extremely important to the welfare of the Spanish Republic. The most important wheat and dairy area

had fallen to the rebels and the Republican regions were generally deficient in food, having a surplus of oranges and wine only. Furthermore,
the collectivization program and alteration of the usual channels of trade
in the early months of the war had greatly reduced agricultural production and exchange. Consequently, Spain found herself approaching the
winter of 1936 with a shortage of food, even after the channels of trade
and transport had been restored. This made outside contributions very
helpful, especially since Spain did not have the opportunity to earn
foreign exchange because most of her production was being used for war.
The importance of this nonmilitary aid from the Soviet Union can be
seen in the USSR's trade with Spain as published by the Soviet government: In the course of the first six months of 1937, Russia exported to
Spain 322,000 tons (51,442,000 rubles) compared with 47,000 tons (2,-
582,000 rubles) for the same period in 1936, thus making Spain Russia's
second best customer (Great Britain being first with over 100,000,000
rubles). Imports from Spain went from 900,000 rubles to 16,934,000
rubles. From January to October, 1937, the Russians exported to Spain
105,283 tons of coal, 163,841 tons of oil products, 85,739 tons of grain,
7,864 tons of trucks, 30,802 tons of fertilizer, and 16,687 tons of cotton.
Soviet imports from Spain were only 17,303 tons of lead and 26,621 tons
of oranges and lemons.[8]

Although the Soviet Union well publicized the fact that relief aid was
being given by her people to Spain, the sending of military aid was never
acknowledged.[9] The Soviet government came as close as it ever did in
admitting it was proposing to send military help when the Russian representative to the Non-Intervention Committee sent a note to the
secretary of the committee saying, "The Soviet Government is therefore
compelled to declare that if violations of the Agreement for Non-Intervention are not immediately stopped the Soviet Government will consider itself free from the obligations arising out of that agreement."[10]
Beyond this, no official Communist publication ever mentioned the sending of military equipment. Frequently, however, the Communist Party
of Spain mentioned Soviet succor but did not designate exactly to what
they were referring. By the importance they ascribed to it in the saving
of Spain, military aid must have been included. For example, José Díaz'
speech on November 13, 1937:

> The decisive importance of the aid from the Soviet Union is recognized by all our
> people. As expressed very well by Señor Martínez Barrio, President of the Cortes and
> and of the Union Republican Party, without the aid of the Soviet Union our Republic
> would not still exist today. This is certain. The aid came at just that moment which

permitted us to overcome the critical hour of our struggle and resolve the great problems of the war with vigor. Only the Soviet Union understood, at that tragic moment that the cause of peace of the entire world was at stake. . . .[11]

At first the Soviet Union tried to keep the sending of military supplies a complete secret, but the numerous reporters throughout Loyalist Spain had few restrictions placed upon them which, combined with the inability of the Spanish government employees to maintain the secret, made all efforts at concealment futile. As a result, the Soviet Union continued to maintain official ignorance, but in unofficial declarations made full use of the propaganda value of being the only great power to help democratic Spain. Communist apologists followed this line and published quite freely the fact that the Soviet Union was sending military aid.[12]

The first time Soviet equipment was used in the fight against the Nationalists was about November 7, 1936, in the siege of Madrid when the enemy was already in the suburbs.[13] José Martin Blazquez reports that the first Russian supplies arrived at the beginning of October, at Alicante. This fits in very closely with November 7 as the first day of the appearance of Russian equipment in the form of planes seen in the fighting.[14] Walter Krivitsky, in his book *In Stalin's Secret Service*, mentioned that the Politbureau of the Communist party of the USSR made the decision to intervene with arms in the Spanish conflict at the end of August or the first part of September,[15] which is also in keeping with the arrival of material during the first part of October and its use at the beginning of November.[16] Krivitsky stated that the sending of material was divided into three sections. The first part was headed by the Soviet army which sent technicians and pilots to supervise the use of the matériel. In the absence of skilled Spanish personnel, Soviet drivers were used in the tanks and Soviet pilots in the planes. Otherwise, no Soviet personnel were to enter combat but were merely to serve as technical advisers. Krivitsky reports that Stalin had warned all his men: "Stay out of range of the artillery fire!" This order follows the reports of other observers in Spain. Stalin had no desire to expend the skill of his army in Spain when at home there was a great shortage of technicians and trained soldiers. He also did not want to give any grounds to the accusations that a Soviet army was invading Spain since Italian troops were being accused of this by the Republicans. Stalin, under no circumstances, wanted to be charged with being an aggressor. He kept within the provision of international law which allowed for the supplying of arms to the legitimate government in a civil war, though in doing so he violated the Non-Intervention Pact.[17] It is also probable that he feared defeat of Russian soldiers would lower his prestige and might even force Russia into war with Germany. Furthermore, to put his troops into action in Spain would only have begun an undeclared war between Russian, German, and Italian troops.

The second section of Russian succor for Spain was under the *GPU* (secret police) in Russia and headed by Captain Oulansky. This provided for the clandestine supplying of material from Russia through the port of Odessa to Spain. The main problem was to prevent knowledge of the traffic going to foreign capitals and in this respect the Russians were only partially successful. The German Consulate at Odessa reported the loading of ships bound presumably for Spain during October and November, 1936.[18] At first it was planned to use only Spanish ships, but because of the small number available, Soviet ships had to be used.

The third branch of Communist arms trade with Spain was through a system of Communist International agents and companies under Krivitsky himself. It was their purpose to act as agents for the Spanish government, using their connections and world organization to buy war materials from wherever possible in the world. Krivitsky stated, "We made large purchases from the Skoda works in Czechoslovakia, from several firms in France, from others in Poland and Holland. Such is the nature of the munitions trade that we even bought arms in Nazi Germany. I sent an agent representing a Dutch firm of ours to Hamburg, where we had ascertained that quantities of somewhat obsolete rifles and machine guns were for sale. The director of the German firm was interested in nothing but the price, the bank references and legal papers of consignment."[19]

To answer the question of how much material Russia sent to the Loyalists is by no means easy. With the delivery of the arms to Spain, Russian control did not end, and the tendency was to move all the material into fields and camps set aside for the Russians. These depots were under exclusive Russian or Communist control and even high Spanish government officials did not appear to know what they contained. In these depots supplies remained, to be doled out and used as the Russian advisers thought fit. Colonel Casado, in his book *The Last Days of Madrid*, relates:

... I can state clearly that during the whole war neither the Air Force nor the Tank Corps was controlled by the Minister of National Defense, nor in consequence by the Central General Staff. The Minister and his Staff were not even aware of the quantity and types of their machines and only knew the situation of those which were used in actual operations. In the same way the Minister and his Staff were not aware of the situation, and even of the existence, of a great number of unknown "flying fields" (aerodromes) maintained in secret by the "friendly [Russian] advisers" and certain of the Aviation Chiefs who were entirely in their confidence.[20]

José Martin Blazquez, on the other hand, gives the impression, "In the Air Force we exercise full control. The Russians are very tactful, and realize that we wouldn't take orders from them."[21] The evidence available does not support Martin Blazquez, however. A study of the statements made by the top leaders in the Loyalist government and discussion with several of them reveals the fact that, although all were aware of Soviet arms, none knew how much was sent or where the material was. Indalecio Prieto, Minister of Marine and Air or Minister of Defense for most of the war, declared, "In regard to keeping accounts on Russian aid, never was it carried out with intransigence because on numerous occasions it was permitted the Sub-Secretaries of Armament and Aviation [usually Communists] sign invoices on matériel which had not even arrived and furthermore I, myself, have signed invoices under such conditions."[22] Consequently, it is almost impossible to make an intelligent estimate of the quantity of material. The only way to arrive at any evaluation is to rely on reports of observers in Spain, on Nationalist reports, and on intelligence reports of the Fascist powers.

From the reporting of foreign observers one gets the impression that aid from the Soviet Union never reached the magnitude of Italian and German supplies to Franco.[23] Nor was Spain ever used extensively by Russia as a training ground for troops, or as a laboratory to test new equipment and techniques, as she was by Italy and Germany. This empirical judgment agrees with the conclusion arrived at by inductive reasoning. In contrast to Germany and especially Italy, the Russian supply lines to Spain were long and circuitous. Furthermore, shipments from Russia to Spain were easily observable in the various narrows through which the ships had to pass. Nationalist and Italian submarines and planes plotted the course of Russian ships through the Mediterranean, and at Loyalist ports rebel observers watched the unloading of the ships. As a result it was difficult for Russia to hide her shipments.[24]

To Germany and Italy the Non-Intervention Pact was merely a scrap of paper. They tried to stall their fulfillment of the agreement as long as possible and at the same time keep the democratic powers from going to the aid of the Loyalists. This they could easily do by merely throwing out a few false promises in the Non-Intervention Committee. To Russia, on the other hand, it was important and essential that in breaking the agreement she should not in any way alienate her potential partners, the Western democracies, and that the West should not lose faith in Russia as an ally because she failed to abide by the pact. Consequently, it was particularly important to Russia that she hide her activities in Spain.

Russia was perhaps also fearful of consigning too much to Spain if perchance a world war suddenly broke out, in which case all her commitments to Spain would have been immediately isolated and lost. In the event of a world war, the long lines of communication between Russia and Spain would have been impossible to maintain in terms of the military advantage obtained. Italy, however, would have been in an excellent position to continue her aid and thus menace France on her Spanish frontier and disrupt her African communications.

In the grand strategy of Italy and Germany for the conquest of Europe, Spain played an important role as a training ground, as a base, and as a pincer against France. The outcome of the Spanish conflict, therefore, was of particular importance to them. The Soviet Union entered the Spanish war as a side issue in her security system. In a war with the Fascist powers, Spain could serve no immediate role in the defense of Russia. In addition, Soviet supplies were kept to a minimum by the activities of the Nationalist and Italian submarines which carried on an extensive war against all Republican trade.[25] Consequently, it is not surprising that the observations by correspondents should conclude that Russia's aid to the Republicans never reached the proportions of Fascist aid to Franco.

From Italian and German intelligence reports, from information reported by the Secretary of the Sea Observation Plan of the Non-Intervention Committee, and from newspaper reports some estimate can be made of the amount of shipping from Russia to Spain. From the middle of October, 1936, to the inauguration of the Non-Intervention Control Scheme on April 20, 1937, there left Russia for Spain between thirty and forty ships per month of varying tonnages. Over half the ships were Russian-owned and the rest were Spanish, plus a few Greek and Scandinavian. None of the ships carried war material exclusively, because legitimate cargo was needed to disguise the arms and because Spain had good use for legitimate cargo as well as for war material. Half or more of each shipload was food, clothing, medicines, fuel oil, or transport trucks; all legal cargo under the Non-Intervention Pact. The rest consisted of arms, ammunition, tanks, and planes.

By the time the Non-Intervention Control Scheme went into effect in April, 1937, there was a considerable drop in the shipments to Spain. Piracy had begun in the Mediterranean at the end of 1936 and became more and more serious during 1937. At the time it was difficult to place the blame because the sinkings were made by submarine or by unmarked airplanes, but it is now known that the attacks were carried out primarily by the Nationalists and Italians to cut down shipments to Republican Spain and to stop Russia from sending aid.[26] The piracy had the desired effect.[27] The foreign trade of Loyalist Spain was reduced considerably, and Russia became more and more fearful of losing her none too plentiful merchant marine and of becoming too deeply involved in a crisis over the sinkings of Soviet ships. After the sinking of the *Komsomol* in December, 1936, Russian ships were used less and less to supply Spain. By the time of the inauguration of the control scheme, use of Soviet ships for Spanish ports had stopped completely. Russia did not want to participate in the control scheme in any way. Consequently, no Russian ships were ever reported by the intelligence system of the Non-Intervention Committee as going legally or illegally to Spain.[28] Since the Spanish government's shipping facilities were limited, and since only a few foreign companies were willing to ship illegally at very high costs, the elimination of Soviet ships brought a considerable decrease in the supplies going to Spain. Another factor to be considered is that in 1936 and the early part of 1937, when Spain was in a state of turmoil, when the Nationalists were winning all the victories and Madrid was seriously threatened, there was an immediate need of large quantities of arms to save the Loyalists. With the stabilizing of the fronts, the development of armament industries, and the general improvement of conditions in Republican Spain during 1937, the Loyalists were in a position to supply their own forces with at least part of their equipment, and the urgency of Soviet aid consequently decreased.

From Nationalist sources some idea can be gathered as to the proportion of Russian material in relation to that from other sources. The Nationalists claimed that between August, 1936 and April, 1937, 759 planes were delivered intact to the Loyalists. Of these 46 per cent came from the Soviet Union, 28 per cent from France, and the remaining 26 per cent from various other countries.[29] Reports reaching the Department of State in Washington in March of 1937, on the other hand, indicated that Russian planes accounted for 92 per cent of the Loyalist Air Force.[30] These two sources are not necessarily incompatible, however, because one set of figures is for the strength of the air force in March, and the other set is for deliveries up to August, 1937. The differences can also be explained by the fact that after February, 1937, the Soviet Union decreased her own shipments to the Loyalists, making it necessary for them to find aircraft elsewhere. For this, however, they had the help of Communist agents throughout the world, as discussed above. In any case it is clear that by far the largest supplier of aircraft to the Republicans was Russia.

By August, 1937, the Nationalists listed the following equipment as part of the foreign arms still usable which had been captured in the campaigns:[31]

    318 French machine guns
    565 Foreign machine guns of varying types
    948 Russian machine guns
    954 Spare gun barrels (various)
  1,358 French machine rifles
2,600,000 Cartridges for 8-mm Lebels (French)
 120,000 Loaders for French machine rifles
  2,800 French rifles
 12,575 Russian rifles (two types)
   886 Czech rifles
  3,852 Mexican rifles
4,875,000 Cartridges for Russian rifles
    24 French mortars (stock type)
    53 37-mm French guns
    32 75-mm French guns
    16 155-mm French guns
    18 124-mm Russian guns
 52,000 Shells (French and Russian)
   110 Russian tanks

Thus, using Hericourt's figures above as a basis, it can be estimated that of the foreign arms furnished, the Russians supplied about 100 per cent of the tanks, 50 per cent of the machine guns, 60 per cent of the rifles, and only about 15 per cent of the larger guns. France supplied about 20 per cent of the machine guns, 20 per cent of the rifles, and 85 per cent of the larger guns.

In analyzing the figures above, certain factors must be kept in mind. First, the figures do not include the Spanish-made material which admittedly at this time was not too great. A large quantity of the French-made material can be explained by prewar supply commitments, as before the war France had an agreement with Spain to supply her with the major portion of her war material. Furthermore the material sent by the Communists does not include only that made in the Soviet Union but also other material sent through Comintern agents. In addition, the Spanish, under Soviet direction, had begun manufacturing Soviet-type material. As a result Russian *Chatos* airplanes[32] and rifles were coming off the assembly lines in Spain, though by August of 1937 it is doubtful if large quantities had yet been produced in Spain. Finally, it is impossible to check the Nationalist figures for accuracy though they seem to agree with other evidence available.

From the figures above, the broad conclusion can be drawn that during the first days of the war about half the equipment and all the tanks used by the Spanish Loyalists came from Communist sources. This material in the beginning saved Republican Spain, since without it there is little doubt that Franco, with German and Italian help, would have been successful, perhaps as early as the end of 1936.[33]

Authorities disagree as to when the Soviet Union ceased to send material to Spain. Again there is no absolute evidence because of the shroud of secrecy which accompanied all Soviet assistance. Some have put the end as early as the beginning of 1937. It is certainly true that less and less is heard of Soviet aid after this time. But from events in Spain and the growing power of the Communists, it would seem that supplies did not end abruptly. The maximum Loyalist military strength was reached only in December, 1937, when they launched their major offensive against the rebels in the direction of Teruel. The scarce but continued evidence from the Axis' intelligence reports and newspaper accounts leads to the conclusion that Russian aid continued after the beginning of 1937.[34] Moreover, in the numerous accounts by government leaders and other participants on the Loyalist side in the war there is no mention of Soviet aid ending at this time. Certainly if the substantial flow of Soviet aid had come to a halt, its absence would have been noticed by at least some of the participants. Likewise, by 1937 the Soviet Union still appeared not to have lost hope of the democracies coming to the aid of the Loyalists. It was only after the continued procrastination of the West in the Non-Intervention Committee during 1937, that Russia was convinced the Western democracies would not be aroused by their own interest in Spain to protect the Republican government.[35] It would seem that aid probably did not cease until the middle of 1938. The German Foreign Office documents mention Russian aid during April, 1938, and the promise of continued support.[36] By the summer of 1938, however, the military situation was such that the victory of Franco seemed assured. His offensive along the Ebro in the spring had been successful in cutting the Loyalist territory in two and showed that the Republican troops, in spite of strides toward a modern and efficient army, were not a match for the Nationalist army.[37] Further, the Munich crisis was turning Russia's attention elsewhere. One indirect indication of the end of Russian aid was the withdrawal of the International Brigade from Spain in the summer and autumn of 1938.

THE SUPPORT OF NON-COMMUNIST GROUPS

Although Russia was the largest supplier of Loyalist Spain, she was not the only one. Many countries, particularly England, continued to trade with Spain in nonmilitary materials. Furthermore, there were other organizations besides Communist-sponsored ones which collected relief for Spain. The British Labour party was very active in collecting money and agitating for Loyalist Spain, and the *Action de Secours pour l'Espagne*, a Socialist organization in France, collected several million dollars for relief. In fact liberal and left-wing organizations all over the world, including Gandhi and his following in India, supported and collected for Spain.[38] It would give an entirely wrong impression to say that aid for Spain was a Communist monopoly. In numbers of supporters other organizations were vastly stronger. It was the Communists' well-developed international organization and discipline which made their aid more effective and influential.

Likewise, arms were not supplied to Spain by Russia alone. Mexico never adhered to the Non-Intervention Pact and openly backed, and sent arms to, the government forces. France also, in the very early days of the war, sent arms. At the time of the insurrection a government of the Popular Front under Léon Blum was in power in France. The sympathies of the Blum government definitely lay with the Spanish government against the revolting generals. Within a few days after the outbreak, arms began to cross the border of France into Spain.[39] Léon Blum feared, however, that, with Germany and Italy supplying the generals, the Spanish Civil War would soon turn into an armaments race and very likely a war between France and Germany. By proposing the Non-Intervention Pact he hoped to bring a halt to this race before it really got under way. With the signing of the pact, France ceased to send arms, though there were constant reports of smuggling across the border. The validity of these rumors is doubtful. Some arms no doubt were smuggled out but the quantities could not have been very great, or more substantial evidence, as in the case of Russia, would be available.[40]

SPANISH GOLD

Even though the Communist war material sent to Loyalist Spain was in support of Soviet foreign policy, it was by no means given gratis. The Communists collected in terms of influence, as will be discussed in the next chapter, and also in gold. At the beginning of the war Spain had a very large gold reserve deposited in the Bank of Spain.[41] With Madrid being besieged, Negrín, then Minister of Finance, and Largo Caballero decided that it should be moved to safer keeping. It was sent temporarily to the naval base at Cartagena, but having no permanent and safe depository for the gold in Spain they decided to send a large part of it (7,800 cases) to Russia and this was carried out in December, 1936. When the information leaked out, there was a cry in Spain and over the world that the Russians had stolen the Spanish gold. The Nationalists were particularly bitter because it meant that even with victory the gold could never be theirs. If it had been deposited in some other country their chance of recovery would have been very good. There was strong criticism, however, even on the Republican side. Indalecio Prieto, who was Minister of Air and Navy at the time, did not exactly say it was stolen, but deplored the fact that the gold from Spain was used to increase the Russian gold reserve.[42] Julian Zugazagoitia, former Republican Minister of Interior, felt that it was not an unjustifiable move and believed Spain received a good exchange in goods. He did criticize, however, the manner in which the gold was shipped. In this he was supported by Prieto. The decision to send the gold to Russia was never put before the rest of the ministers of the government and was not even communicated to them, thus leaving the decision open to criticism of subterfuge and dishonesty.[43] Prieto, who as Minister of Air and Navy was responsible for shipping the gold safely, claims that even he did not know the destination of the gold.[44]

It is not known exactly to what extent the Russians were responsible for the removal of the gold, though there is little reason to believe that it was the result of coercion on their part. The suggestion, as Alvarez del Vayo points out, no doubt came originally from the Russians who did not want to see the gold fall into Nationalist or Fascist hands. The final decision, however, seems to have been voluntary, and an analysis of the reasons leads to the conclusion it was by no means unwarranted. Russia was at this time almost Spain's only ally, and as the largest supplier of materials would eventually receive a considerable portion of the gold anyway. London, New York, or Paris were out of the question as depositories because of the fluctuating feelings in these countries.[45] In all three countries there were forces strongly opposed to Republican Spain and these might have been able to block the use of the gold reserves by the government. This fear was by no means unjustified because Franco supporters had been able to block certain Spanish funds in France. The one dark note in this transaction as mentioned by Prieto seems to be the fact that the Spaniards who accompanied the shipment were never allowed to return to Spain. Julian Zugazagoitia says the accusation made by some Spanish *émigrés*, that the depositing of the gold held up the purchase of equipment which might have saved the Republic, is without any foundation.[46] Louis Fischer even asserts that, "When the war came to a close in 1939, the Loyalists owed the Soviet Government $120,-000,000, which was never paid. Of this debt, $20,000,000, approximately, represented Loyalist imports of food and raw materials from Russia, and $100,000,000 imports of arms."[47] Actually a fair and equitable accounting is impossible, since most of the material did not have a set market price. The balance depended entirely on what price the Russians chose to charge for the planes, guns, tanks, and other equipment.

THE INTERNATIONAL BRIGADE

As the war began to reduce itself to a stalemate, Italian troops found their way to Spain to help Franco to a quick victory. By April, 1937, Mussolini had four divisions and two brigades, about 70,000 men, fighting for Franco in Spain.[48] Hitler's contribution included the Condor Legion, pilots, and tank drivers, as well as a couple of thousand instructors for Spanish troops. The Nationalists rationalized their use of foreign troops by saying that there were Russian divisions on the side of the Loyalist government. In fact, however, there is no evidence of Russian ground troops having been in Spain. The Russians limited their personnel to a few pilots, tank drivers, technicians, instructors, and top military advisers. It is doubtful whether the entire Russian military forces in Spain ever reached more than four to five thousand.[49]

The Soviet Union realized, however, the importance of building up manpower on the Loyalist side. Well-trained foreign troops were considered necessary because Italian troops were being used more and more by Franco and because the Communists considered that the Spaniards, in general, made very poor soldiers, tending to resist discipline and to retreat before any open attack. Nevertheless, Russia refused to send her own troops, probably for fear of becoming too deeply involved and for fear of having her troops become contaminated by contact with the outside world. Consequently, only a few picked men could be spared, primarily instructors and advisers. To make up the deficiency the Comintern began the organization of the International Brigade. By utilizing the local Communist parties and organizations a world-wide recruiting network was set up. The Comintern, in selecting candidates, sought primarily not Communists but men of democratic sympathies. They opposed recruiting too many Communists because this would have depleted the ranks of communism in the various countries.[50] All recruits, however, were carefully screened as to their reliability. Revolutionary elements were eliminated and only men of democratic, liberal views were accepted. In Spain itself the International Brigade was kept completely separate from the Russians, though they held control through reserving for Communists the command posts and particularly the positions of political commissar. Many of the recruits on entering were not even aware of the Communist control. The only contribution which the Soviet Union made to the International Brigade was the sending of about five to six hundred foreign Communists who had been exiled from their own countries and were living in the USSR, but no Russian was allowed to volunteer.[51]

It is difficult to estimate the approximate size of the brigade. Its strength has been estimated as low as 15,000 and as high as 200,000, depending on where the sympathy of the appraiser lies. The figure of 200,-000 is excessive and was manufactured only for propaganda purposes. In June, 1937, Franco declared to the German Ambassador that the strength of all foreign volunteers, most of whom were in the brigade, was between 40,000 and 50,000.[52] From the reports of various observers it is probable that this figure would still indicate a number in excess of the maximum strength the brigade reached.[53] There is no question that for most of its existence the brigade was in the center of the fighting, that its casualties were, as a result, very heavy, and that many of the men were war weary and left even before the end of their terms of enlistment.[54] This kept its fighting strength down. Another factor limiting the size of the brigade was the various restrictions on recruiting put into effect in many countries of the West and the difficulty of transporting men to Spain across the closed borders and through the Naval Control Scheme. Probably the total number of volunteers in the International Brigade throughout the war was about 60,000 with the maximum fighting strength at any one time no higher than 30,000.[55]

CHAPTER IX

THE COMMUNIST LEADERSHIP—
DISCIPLINE AND UNITY

THE EFFECT OF SOVIET AID IN SPAIN

IN A PREVIOUS chapter the policies of the Spanish Communist party immediately after the beginning of the war and before the intervention of Russia on the side of the Republic were discussed. The Communist program at that time can be most generally characterized as mild for the times, and especially moderate for a so-called revolutionary party. The motivation of this program, as was seen, had its basis in the strategy of the United Front and the People's Front and in the foreign policy of the Soviet Union. It was an effort to rally all anti-Fascist groups in the struggle against the spread of fascism. Before October, 1936, the influence of the Communists in Spain was negligible. They were able to do little but complain about the revolutionary actions of the Anarchists and left Socialists, which were tending to disrupt the Popular Front. The Communists claimed that these actions were alienating the bourgeoisie and peasants through forced collectivization of agriculture and industry and were disrupting the defenses of the Republic by putting the revolution before victory over Franco.

When aid arrived from the Soviet Union in October, 1936, the Communists found their bargaining power greatly strengthened. With the tacit threat of withdrawing Soviet aid if the Communist demands were not heeded, the Communists began to speak with the voice of authority. The entrance of the Communists into the government of Caballero in September, 1936, followed by the arrival of Soviet aid, marked a change in the Communists' tactics in Spain from that of passive criticism of the parties and the government to active participation in, and support of, the government. Their program, likewise, took on a dynamic quality and was modified to correspond to their new leadership role and to the immediate problems of defending the Republic. From this time on their primary task in Spain was to bring all the groups and parties into absolute support of and subordination to the rule of the Caballero government, and to help the Republic win a victory over Franco. In this connection they carried out a vigorous campaign of discipline in the army, in industry, and on the home front.

In a radio broadcast on January 3, 1937, Dolores Ibarruri of the Spanish

Communist Party Politbureau set down the "Eight Conditions of Victory":

1. The entire power must be placed in the hands of the government....
2. The introduction of compulsory military service—the only way of rapidly creating a great, organised, disciplined and powerful people's army.
3. Iron discipline must be established in the rear....
4. The principal branches of industry, and primarily the munitions industry must be nationalised and reorganised to meet the needs of the front and the rear.[1]
5. A Council of Industrial and Economic Co-ordination must be set up consisting of representatives of the People's Front from all branches of industry...this government body should administer and regulate production. The decisions of the council must be obeyed unreservedly.
6. Workers' control must be set up over industry, which must work in accordance with a plan laid down by the Council of Co-ordination.
7. Agriculture must produce everything required by the front and the rear in accordance with a plan....
8. Agricultural production and industrial production must be co-ordinated....[2]

A REGULAR ARMY

Even before the intervention of Russia, the Communists had supported the efforts of the government to develop an army of defense. José Martin Blazquez, one of the few regular army officers who remained with the government in the Civil War, describes how the Communists helped in the first days:

The streets of Madrid swarmed with militiamen promenading with rifles, but when we needed them very few presented themselves.... I must, however, give the Communists their due. If they had no armed men, they improvised them, heaven knows how, and always gave us effective aid.[3]

And further on he describes:

The Communist Party must be granted the credit of having set the example of accepting discipline. By so doing it enormously increased not only its prestige, but its numbers. Innumerable men who wished to enlist and fight for their country joined the Communist Party.[4]

Martin Blazquez was not writing as a supporter or an apologist of the Communists and in most respects was very critical of them.

It is difficult to comprehend the stand of the Communists at this time without knowing the status of the armed forces in Spain. The truth is that no one knew exactly the composition of the defense forces. At the outset every trade-union, every party, and every Republican organization recruited for its own separate militia in each town, making for many separate forces. Besides this there were still organs of the old army and police which had remained loyal. Gradually, some of these forces consolidated within provinces and within parties, especially those under Communist and Socialist influence, but there still remained several separate forces. Each group had its own idea of defense and fighting, and each sought arms and material from the government. Coördination was almost nonexistent, either between the forces or along the front. This popular enthusiasm had saved the government in the first days, but for prolonged resistance it was ineffective against the centralized and trained army of rebels. Few of the militia, however, were willing to give up their autonomy. Most of the forces did not even see themselves primarily as an army to protect the state, but rather considered themselves revolutionary forces now able to put forth their own pet schemes of revolution and a new society. Against these revolutionary armies the government had to move slowly and cautiously. The first step was the formation of a Popular Front government on September 4, which was later expanded to include the Anarchists. This was an attempt to include all groups so that each would feel a stake in the government and thus be more willing to turn over their militias to a regular army.

The Communist party was one of the first groups to offer to disband its militia into a regular army under the government. As early as August 20, the Communists issued the following memorandum:

... It is necessary that this heroic army of the people should receive the discipline it requires. Every operation, every armament, must be in accordance with an organised plan of a war necessity. When we speak of discipline we mean conscious discipline, respectful, democratic discipline for the highest positions as for the lowest, as much for the units as for the Commands.

The hinterland must be organised—We must realise that we have to carry on a long war. Our comrades at the front can only put up resistance to the extent that matters are being organised in the hinterland, including the organisation of supplies for the civil population as well as for the fighters at the front.[5]

In August the plea of the Communist party was only a weak voice in the wilderness, even though Azaña and the right Socialists were in agreement.

By October, the situation had changed. Even the most revolutionary groups, including the Anarchists, realized that something had to be done to organize and coördinate defense. Furthermore, the Communist party no longer spoke with an insignificant voice but had behind it all the force of anticipated Soviet help. There is no doubt that if the Western democracies had, likewise, offered their aid to the Loyalists, the power of Soviet material would have lost most of its punch, and the prestige of the Republican parties would have been raised. But since the Soviet Union, along with Mexico, was the only important source of arms outside of Spain, the voice of its agent, the Communist Party of Spain, became nearly all-powerful.

The words of the Communist party no longer pleaded but demanded. José Díaz declared: "Consolidate the army of the people. These problems must be resolved by all the organizations making up the Popular Front and a unified command."[6] All the pressure at the Communists' disposal was used to push the formation of a regular and strong army:

> It is a problem of discipline and organization concerning which our party has constantly insisted in the press, in meetings, and within the Government. A mass of armed people which does not have severe discipline, which has not been instructed or prepared militarily, which is not acquainted with the fundamentals of an attack against the enemy, in time decomposes, becomes demoralized, loses its combativeness and continues to represent a danger to the rearguard. . . .[7]

Within the newly organized army itself the Communist party urged the creation of a system of political commissars to reinforce the new "People's Army." A corps of commissars was established in October, 1936, and, according to André Marty, a foreign Communist serving in Spain, "the political commissars transformed the 'columns' and militia battalions which met defeat during the whole of the summer of 1936 into brigades, divisions and army corps of a victorious army, the army of Madrid, of Guadalajara and the Southern front."[8] The Communists dominated the corps of commissars from the beginning.[9]

Franz Borkenau describes the work of the Communists in the army:

> With the siege of Madrid, military leadership, from November 1936 onwards, fell into the hands of the Communists, who launched a totalitarian scheme instead of a revolutionary one. The basic ideas of Communist military policy were: No revolution during the war; strict discipline, including terrorism within the ranks; strict political control of the army, by a system of political "commissars," with the aim of creating an ideology adapted to this policy, an ideology, that is, mainly based on nationalism.[10]

The Communists continued throughout the war to press their slogan of "absolute unity in our army," but the individualistic Spaniards never completely submitted to Communist discipline. The Anarchist militias continued in existence and not until the end of 1937 were they brought under central authority; even then they did not submit completely to rule from above.[11] Nevertheless, all observers agree that out of general chaos the government, driven by the Communists, created a modern army capable of withstanding for three years the combined forces of Franco, the Moroccan legions, the Spanish Foreign Legion, several Italian divisions, and sections of the German Army. It would be quite true to say that without the Communists as the unifying and driving factor, the Loyalist forces would have been defeated long before 1939.[12]

DISCIPLINE IN INDUSTRY

The Communist attitude toward industry changed from one of reluctantly "following the trend" to demanding discipline, a central plan, and absolute control by the central government. The primary object of the Communist program was to model the industrial plan after that of the Soviet Union with some modification to take care of private industry. Although never openly attacking workers' control of industry, the Communists tried to sabotage it from every side. They never called for the abolition of the workers' committees but they pushed for "all technical direction under one person, with full powers to carry out completely his orders on production and with full responsibility."[13] The over-all production program was to be set by the state through a Council of Industry. Private enterprise was still to remain with the joint control of workers and management under the state, but the important armament and transport industries were to be nationalized, at least during the war, and brought under the immediate supervision of the state. Raw materials were to be allocated by the state, and war needs were to have absolute priority. The syndicates were, likewise, to develop a new outlook in respect to their industrial and production relations. The two main tasks of the trade-unions were:

> First, to improve the situation of the working class, to aid the worker in organizing an improvement in his living conditions, to help improve the conditions of work, to obtain for the workers' benefit all the comforts compatible with the supreme interests of war, to struggle against speculation, against monopolizing the articles of prime necessity and to raise the cultural level of the workers.
>
> Second, to collaborate with the Government to better organize production, in reorganizing the system of salaries and the system of direction in the plants, to rationalize production, to create a new discipline of work and a discipline of war in the plants and factories in general, to struggle against subterfuge and sabotage by the fascists and counter-revolutionary elements in the factories and especially in the industries of war.[14]

The trade-unions were, consequently, to become the instrument of the state, as they had become in the Soviet Union, and they were to subordinate all their demands to the interest of the war.

The Communists, in advocating the mobilization of industry for war, had altered their attitude toward private ownership and control. Previously they had supported continued private ownership with some workers' control except for "Fascist-owned industries." The new Communist program demanded nationalization, at least temporarily, of all industry essential to the war irrespective of ownership, and its complete subordination to a central plan. Private ownership was to remain only in nonessential industries. In this way, the Communists continued to support the small capitalists and businessmen whom they considered important Loyalist supporters.

Although the Communists never completely achieved the desired centralized efficiency in industry against the resistance of Spanish indolence, they had made great strides in this direction by the end of the war. The criticism of attempted dictatorship can certainly be made with justification against the Communist program in Spain. On the other hand, it was such a program of centralized planning which was necessary for fighting a war against Franco and his Fascist allies. The Non-Intervention Pact and Franco's naval blockade made it impossible for the Republican government to receive all the supplies it needed. Furthermore, the economy had been disrupted internally because the normal sources of raw material had been cut off and many of the factory owners and managers had deserted to Franco. The industrial economy of Spain had not been extensive, and thus every bit of output was needed for the war. The Communist pressure, particularly that from the "friendly advisers," as the Russian technicians were called, was just the impetus needed to put industry on a war footing. It is difficult to measure in figures exactly the increased industrial war production,[15] but from an economy which in 1936 produced a negligible amount of arms there developed a steady flow of munitions. President Companys of Catalonia, who is no doubt a prejudiced observer, gives some idea of the magnitude of the tasks accomplished in Catalonia, the largest industrial section remaining to the Loyalists, in his letter to Prieto on December 13, 1937. For example, in September, 1936, only 4,000 artillery projectiles were produced and in less than a year in April, 1937, 90,000 a month were being produced. By September 30, 1937, a total of 718,830 projectiles had been produced.[16]

An important element which accompanied the Communists' new program was the demand to purge the army and the rear of the "Fifth Column." The parties, the government, and the syndicates were asked to root out all counterrevolutionaries.[17] In a civil war the problem of spies and "copperheads" is always greater than in a national war. It was known that in every city there existed a large underground movement in favor of the rebels and in the later days of the war these groups operated in the open to sabotage the Loyalists. There is no doubt that vigilance against sabotage by these groups was necessary. The Communists, as later chapters will show, put a much broader interpretation on the terms counterrevolutionary and Fascist agent, using them to rout out all those who tended violently to disagree with them.

A New Type of Democracy

With the support of most of the members of the Popular Front government, except the Anarchists, the Communists put less and less stress on the proletarian revolution. In spite of their declaration that by supporting governmental authority and unity "we have strengthened the popular revolution,"[18] and that "the Communists do not lose sight of the historic need for the revolutionary overthrow of capitalism, which has outlived its day, and for the achievement of Socialism, which brings emancipation to the working class and the whole of mankind,"[19] the fact remains that in the Spanish situation the Communist revolution had been completely ignored for the moment. Dolores Ibarruri, *La Pasionaria* (the Passion Flower), was much closer to the truth when she said, "Today the most revolutionary thing is to win the war, which means winning the first battle against fascism on an international scale."[20] The Communist argument that victory was necessary before there could be any thought of revolution may have been sound reasoning, but does not alter the fact that the Communists had become a "counter-revolutionary force in the proletarian revolution" being carried out by the Anarchists, *POUM*ists, and left Socialists.

The Communists, in following the program of the Seventh Congress of the Comintern and also in trying to get the support of both the proletarian elements and bourgeois elements, developed a new stage, "a new type of democracy" which was to be the prototype of the present "People's Democracy." The idea, of course, was based on the resolution of the Congress of the Comintern in 1935, when it was stated that a United Front government could serve as a possible transition stage in the development of Soviet power.[21] It would appear, however, that it was first defined in detail during the Spanish Civil War. The "new type of democracy" in Spain was primarily an attempt to gain the support of all democrats, whether proletarian or bourgeois in outlook, and to establish unity between them in the fight against fascism. This sentiment certainly was an excellent one for the Loyalist cause, in the light of history, though the Communist application of the idea was not always honest.

The idea of this "new type of democracy" developed very early in the Civil War, though it was not specified as such:

But the democracy which the Communists are collaborating to defend or gain is not that faint-hearted democracy which left open the path to fascism in Italy and Germany, nor the democracy which capitulates before the threats and blackmail of Hitler and Mussolini! It is, on the contrary, that democracy which fights energetically against fascism with the aid of the People's Front, which is increasing its forces at home and its international authority by a progressive social policy in the capitalist countries, as in France, for instance; it is that democracy which accomplished agrarian reform in Spain, and is defending itself victoriously in that country against the fascist generals who have betrayed the country.[22]

As the Communist policy on other matters solidified, so also did its ideas on the "new type of democracy." M. Ercoli (Togliatti), in his book on the Spanish problem which was released in December, 1936, describes the characteristics of this new democracy:

It is a distinctive feature of this new type of democratic republic that fascism . . . is being suppressed by the armed force of the people, and that in this republic there will be no place for this chief and bloodthirsty enemy of the people. Should the people be victorious, fascism will never be able to enjoy there such freedom as, for instance, in France, the U.S.A. or England, where it makes use of bourgeois democracy and the rights granted under it to destroy democracy and establish completely arbitrary rule. Secondly, the material basis of fascism will be destroyed in this republic. All land, all enterprises belonging to participants in the fascist revolt have already been confiscated and handed over to the Spanish people.[23]

José Díaz later rationalized this new stage by saying that "to have attempted to establish the dictatorship of the proletariat would have meant skipping a necessary stage of development; it would have narrowed the social basis of the struggle of the Spanish people and would have made it easier for the international reaction to destroy the revolutionary movement in Spain."[24] Such reasoning is not without basis, because the division between the Anarchists and Azaña's Republicans in respect to aims was actually much greater than the differences between Azaña and the Conservatives on the side of Franco. It was only the threat of military dictatorship and a civil war that brought the various groups of the Left together. The ideas and outlook of the various groups—Republicans, Socialists, and Anarchists—were so fundamentally different and so strongly held it is doubtful that, if the Loyalists had been victorious, they could have gotten together to establish a stable or lasting government. Only a common enemy made it possible for them to associate, and even then during a good part of the war they traversed diverse paths. The Communist program of "the new type of democracy" was actually a very realistic program for a country made up of Republicans and revolutionaries who had at all costs to defeat a military dictatorship. And such a program would have been the only possible and enduring basis for a settlement after the war in Spain. It is doubtful, however, that the Communists would have supported this solution once peace had been attained, because they considered it as only a transitional stage to the dictatorship of the proletariat.

The idea of a new transitional stage between bourgeois democracy and socialism continued to develop. José Díaz, in his report to the Central Committee of the Communist Party of Spain, on March 5, 1937, expanded in detail the workings of the "new type of democratic parliamentary republic":

In our struggle, we are striving to bring about the *destruction of the material basis of semi-feudal Spain,* in order to root out fascism once and for all. . . .

We must liquidate the class of big landowners, who have participated to a man in the military-fascist rebellion; we must nationalize their estates, and turn them over to the agricultural laborers and peasants, for cultivation either individually or collectively.

It is also necessary *to destroy the economic and political power of the Church,* which was the center of the conspiracy against the interests of the masses, and one of the strongest mainstays of semi-feudal Spain. To this end the property of the Church must be confiscated and nationalized. The *struggle against* the semi-feudal economic and political rule of *the Church* does not by any means signify *a fight against religion.* On the contrary, only a republican and democratic Spain, a free and progressive Spain, will ensure freedom of religion in our country.

We must also set about *putting an end to militarism,* to the remnants of the caste spirit of the old army, which served semi-feudal Spain and was used to suppress progressive tendencies. . . .

We must *put an end to the financial oligarchy,* to the bankers and manufacturers who were closely connected with the landowners and the Church and hindered the normal development of the national economy. We must proceed to the nationalization of the Bank of Spain and the chief industries of the country. This is the only means of satisfying the needs of the front and the rear.

In addition to these main points, the solution of which will lead to the disappearance of the semi-feudal castes which were dominant in Spain, and will lead to the reorganization of the material and social basis of our new, democratic, parliamentary republic, we must introduce genuinely universal suffrage and secure the direct participation of the entire people in the political and economic life of the country.[25]

The concessions to the regionalism of the various minorities and to the type of collectivization envisaged by the Anarchists are conspicuous by their absence. In previous Communist programs discussed, such factors were taken into account through workers' control and regional autonomy. Their absence here is primarily because in the thick of the war, when this report was given, all emphasis was on unity and centralism, and because the Communists at this time were struggling with the Catalonian Generalitat and the Anarchists for their submission to the control of the central government. Nevertheless, the plan was an attempt to balance collectivism and destruction of the old ruling class with bourgeois democracy—"a transition stage."

This attempt at compromise was only partially successful. The Socialists and some of the Republicans endorsed it, but most of the other factions, and especially the Anarchists, stubbornly clung to their own utopias and were suspicious of any solution proposed by the Communists whom they considered foreign agents. The Communists and the government, as will be discussed in later chapters, frequently resorted to force and underhand methods to carry out their project, which only made the factions more adamant against compromise. If the government and the Communists could not rally the people together in war, how could they have done any better in peace? It would seem that a victory over the Nationalists would only have been the beginning of a new civil war between the factions of the Left. Perhaps if some other group besides the Communists had been the focal point of compromise the results would have been different, but what group could it be? What party was strong enough alone to win over the other groups? What party was capable of sacrificing its own prejudices for the benefit of pushing a scheme of compromise?

THE COMMUNIST PARTY ORGANIZATION

Neither the Communist nor the Socialist party at the beginning of the war had had a large following in Catalonia, the stronghold of the Anarchists. The Communist party was almost nonexistent and the Socialists had only a few thousand members. The Communists of Catalonia, under Nin and Maurín, had split off from the Comintern as early as 1931, and the Third International was never again able to build up a following in the Barcelona area against the competition of the Left Communists. The Left Communists had further subdivided into various factions and parties and only in February, 1936, did they come together into the *POUM*. The number of adherents to this party was never very large at any one time, as it was recruiting among the same class as the powerful Anarchists. The *POUM*ists themselves claimed 40,000 members, whereas other authorities estimated the membership at 5,000 to 6,000.

A couple of weeks after the beginning of the war, in an attempt to create some following in Catalonia and under pressure from the Communists, who had been urging a single proletarian party throughout Spain, the Socialist League, the Catalonian Proletarian party, the Com-

munist party, and the Catalonian Federation of the Socialist Party of
Catalonia formed into the United Socialist Party of Catalonia, number-
ing about 5,000 to 6,000.[26] From the beginning the Communists assumed
leadership and the new party affiliated with the Third International.
This party also assumed control over the Socialist trade-union in Catalonia, the *UGT*, with about 40,000 members.[27] The new United Socialist
party (*PSUC*) soon after its formation claimed a membership of 42,000.
Although the actual number of members was not a significant increase
in the total Communist membership in Spain, it was an important addition because they were essentially the first adherents from this area and
provided a core for Communist activities in this vital industrial region.
The *PSUC* was able to attract very few industrial workers, who remained
strongly pro-Anarchist and the party admitted that its rolls were increased primarily from "office workers, civil servants, peasants."[28]

In respect to the Communist membership in the rest of Spain, there
continued to be a rapid increase. From about 117,000 at the outbreak of
the war the party claimed 249,000 in March, 1937, and by June of the
same year, 301,000. These do not include 22,000 in Biscay and the *PSUC*,
which by this time had claimed a growth to 64,000.[29]

What is even more revealing are the figures on the social composition
of the party as officially given out:

> 87,660 Industrial workers
> 62,250 Agricultural workers
> 76,700 Peasants
> 15,485 From the middle class
> 7,045 Representatives of the intellectuals
> and the liberal professions[30]

The Communists do not reveal how the groupings were defined, but from
looking at the figures themselves it would seem that the category of
peasant would include all those farmers who owned land. It also would
appear from the figures that the party was no longer an exclusively proletarian party, but that the recruitment from the middle classes had
been heavy and, what is more significant, the majority of the party was
composed of peasants and agricultural workers. Of the members in the
rural areas the majority appear to have been landowners at least to some
degree. It was apparently the Communists' resistance to forced collectivization that won them the adherence of so many landowning peasants.
The number of industrial workers still remained high, though other figures which the Communists published indicate that this grouping of in-

dustrial workers is quite broad, including even artisans and perhaps small shopkeepers. For example, in Madrid, with a comparatively high percentage of the industrial workers organized into unions—usually the very core of the Communist strength—the party had only 10,160 trade-union members in 1937, and this increased only to 18,160 trade-union members by 1938, when the membership of the Madrid section of the party totaled 63,426. Thus, in a city where most of the factory workers were unionized, it would appear that Communist strength was primarily not among the industrial proletariat, which composed less than a third of the membership, but among the bourgeoisie and artisans.

The Communist party had tripled itself in one year. The causes for this phenomenal rise are multiple. Perhaps half this increase can be explained by the general trend upward of the membership of all trade-union and political groups. For example, the Socialist trade-union, the *UGT*, nearly doubled its strength in the same period of time to almost two million. Only the Anarchists showed a decline in strength because nearly half their prewar membership had fallen under the domination of Franco; even so their strength was about 1,200,000. This trend was a movement on the part of the large mass of unaffiliated people in Spain, who had been awakened politically by the war, to take part in events. Moreover, membership in a trade-union or political group brought protection and even rations in the uncertain conditions of the war and revolution. In Catalonia, furthermore, at the end of August, 1936, a law was passed in the Generalitat that all workers, even private shopkeepers, must be affiliated with some syndicate. Although the factors above probably explain half the Communist rise in this period, the other half must be explained by other causes. No doubt the prestige given the Communist party through the aid rendered by the Soviet Union to the government was tremendous, and attracted a number of people. It also attracted a number of careerists who hoped to use the rising Communist party as a means to power. A large number, however, joined because they believed in the program of the party. José Martin Blazquez describes this movement from his own experience:

> It often happened that, when I came across a man who was just leaving for the front, I asked him:
> "But why did you join the Communist Party? You were never a Communist, were you? You were always a Republican."
> "I joined the Communists because they are disciplined and do their job better than anybody else," was the answer.[31]

Numbers of the middle class joined the party because they saw it as the most stable and conservative element of the Left. This was particularly true in Catalonia where the fear of the *CNT* and the compulsory unionization forced them into the *UGT* and the Communist party. As a result the *PSUC* and the Catalonian *UGT* were almost exclusively a petty bourgeois party and union. The conservative policy of the Communists also explains the large influx of the middle class and peasants into the party, from all over Spain as described above.

Direction of Communist activities in Spain during the Civil War did not come under the control of the Spanish leadership of the party. The split of the party in the early 1930's seemed to have eliminated most of the potential leaders. None of the new leaders of the party had had any previous record of leadership and were not destined to become well known even during the Civil War. Only Dolores Ibarruri, *La Pasionaria*, had any color. She, by her emotional, maternal character, had a tremendous appeal to the masses, and her speeches always commanded a large audience. From the various articles on Spain in the *Communist International* from 1931 to 1936, it would appear that the Comintern was displeased with the leadership of the Communist Party of Spain. For example, an article in the December 1, 1933, issue discussing the trend toward revolution in Spain declared, "The failure of the Communist Party to keep pace with this exceptionally sharp and prolonged revolutionary struggle of the masses of workers and peasants forms a serious danger to the further development and the complete victory of the revolution."[32] Other articles on Spain in the *Communist International* during this period contained similar admonishments. Even in the Seventh Congress of the Comintern in 1935 the Spanish section was subjected to severe criticism:

The fight in Spain is not over. The Party must now develop still greater initiative in organising the masses and must make still greater efforts to establish a united front with the Socialist and Anarchist workers in order to prepare itself for the impending political struggles. Yet, the Communist Party of Spain is still suffering from grave weaknesses. After the armed fighting in October 1934, our comrades in Spain, unlike the Communist Party of Austria, were not able to enlighten the masses as to the mistakes of the Social-Democratic leaders of the fight, nor to induce large numbers of Social-Democrats to turn towards Communism.[33]

The very small size of the Communist party in the revolutionary situation of Spain before the Civil War was another indication of the weakness of the leadership of the Communists.

After the outbreak of revolution and Civil War in Spain, the Comintern and the Soviet Union took control of Communist activities in Spain. Exactly when they actually assumed direct leadership is difficult to determine. It may be that agents of the Comintern came to Spain in the spring of 1936 for this purpose as the Nationalists claimed. Such a supposition is not unreasonable since with the victory of the Popular Front in February, 1936, the situation in Spain had become highly critical. But after the intervention of Soviet Russia on the side of the Loyalists there is no question that the leadership of Communist activities in Spain passed into the hands of Soviet and Comintern representatives. The detailed activities of these foreign Communists in Spain will be discussed in the next chapter. It need only be said here by way of conclusion that, except for public announcements and agitation, all the important functions of the Communists in Spain were carried out by the foreign Communists. This is borne out by the testimony of various participants, who, in discussing dealings with the Communists, rarely mention the activities of the Spanish leaders of the Communist party.[34]

CHAPTER X

INFILTRATION

THE STRUGGLE FOR POWER

BY THE END of 1936, the Communists were ready to assume a larger role in the Loyalist government. Membership in the party was increasing rapidly and the party had gained a favorable reputation, especially among the peasants and petty bourgeoisie. Through unification, the party had gained control over the Socialist youth and over the Socialist parties in Catalonia. The Communists had developed a program which could serve as a rallying point for the rival factions and their cadres were being trained and prepared to carry it out. Finally, as a lever to increase their power, the Communists had the backing of Soviet aid and the International Brigade.

To what extent the Communists were limited by moral factors in their efforts to extend their power in Spain is a matter of doubt. In the Spanish political scene all parties were accustomed to seeking power by every means available with little regard for ethics. Some parties, as for example the Anarchists, would stop at absolutely nothing to gain power, resorting to terror and even glorifying the annihilation of the opposition. This attitude on the part of the Anarchists was held not only in relation to the Right, but even toward other Left parties. They tended, however, to restrain their use of terroristic methods against other workers' parties for practical motives. The insurrection itself is proof that the parties of the Right were willing to employ force. Thus, in the years before the war, no holds were barred in the struggle for power, both between Right and Left and within Right and Left coalitions.

The formation of the Popular Front was the first effort of the various factions of the Left at coöperation which was strictly limited to a joint effort to gain advantage from the electoral law of the Republic. Although there were local instances of closer coöperation, such as when the revolutionary parties allied in the Asturian revolt of 1934, up to the Civil War a close alliance of the Left on a national scale did not exist. The insurrection by the Right marked a change, and a truce was established among the factions of the Left which gradually developed into a governing alliance. Though this new coöperation limited the methods which could be considered legitimate in seeking power under the Popular Front, there was by no means a complete cessation of the parties' vying for an improved position. All the parties realized that the Popular Front, in the long run, would be merely a truce until victory could be secured over the Right, at which time open and savage competition would begin again. Realizing this, all the parties during the truce of the Popular Front government prepared for the eventual struggle, and if intrigues could improve a party's position they were used without the slightest compunction. As a result, evidence of intrigue can be traced to all parties. The Anarchists were constantly attempting to sabotage the position of the middle class, their most powerful opposition in Catalonia. On the other hand, the Republican parties used every method possible to protect their property and position, even to the extent of trying to use the Communists as their foil and protector, hoping later to be able to otherthrow them. There was even subterfuge among the various factions within a political party and among individuals. As will be discussed later, the right wing and the left wing of the Socialists tried by every means to undermine each other, using principally the Communists as the instrument.

The Communists likewise participated in this subversive rivalry. It might be argued that the Machiavellianism of the Communists was a little more ruthless and a little less considerate of the bond which was supposedly holding the parties together. On the basis of conduct, however, it is doubtful whether the other parties would have acted differently, given the advantages of the Communists. The one distinguishing feature about the Communist party in its rivalry for dominance was that it, unlike the other factions, was an agent of an alien power.

It is necessary to preface any discussion of Soviet techniques of infiltration with a discussion of sources of information. When the Loyalists were defeated by Franco in 1939, there was an attempt by all groups participating in the Republican cause to throw the blame for defeat on someone else. The Communist party was unanimously chosen as the scapegoat by all non-Communist elements among the Spanish *émigrés*. In their rush to throw the stigma on communism, attempts at careful analysis and truth were often forgotten. Old hates which had been laid aside during the war were focused on the Communists. In their turn the Communists threw the guilt on everyone but themselves. This fanatic recrimination makes most of the Spanish reports written after the war almost worthless to the conscientious investigator. A further difficulty is that these denunciations began even before the war was over. As each leader and group fell into disfavor, no matter what the cause, the defeat was rationalized to throw the blame on the Communists; consequently it becomes a very difficult problem to measure the soundness of the various indictments against them.

The Siege of Madrid

As mentioned previously, Soviet material aid first began to arrive in Spain at the time of the siege of Madrid, and was initially used on the front protecting Madrid. Even before the arrival of help, however, the Communists had assumed, as their main task in Spain, the defense of Madrid. From the first they realized the importance of Madrid as the capital and the threat to Loyalist morale if it should fall. They also were fully aware of the prestige it could bring the Communists if they should lead its defense and it was successful. Consequently, even before the fall of Toledo on September 28, 1936, the Communists were clamoring for the building of Madrid's defenses. The entire propaganda machine and all cadres of the Communist party were organized to mobilize the city. The party's slogan was, "Madrid must become the grave of fascism!" The Fifth Regiment, which was the Communist militia of about 70,000, placed itself at the disposal of the government for the defense of the city, and the party's cadres exhorted and cajoled the city's population to dig defenses. To the Communists' support during the first part of November came the newly formed International Brigade, which immediately went into action around Madrid. With the addition of newly arrived Soviet tanks and airplanes, the Communists were able to create and concentrate a considerable force around the city and thus influence the course of events in that area. Felix Morrow (Joaquín Maurín), a member of the dissident Communist party, the *POUM*, describes the importance of Madrid to the Communists:

... If Madrid fell, the jig was up for the Stalinists. In Spain, their prestige was bound up with the Fifth Regiment of Madrid—in reality an army of over a hundred thousand—and the Defense Junta which from October 11 was responsible for Madrid's defense and which was Stalinist controlled. Internationally, the prestige of the Comintern and the Soviet Union would have collapsed irrevocably with the fall of Madrid. The retreat to Valencia and Catalonia would have found a new relationship of forces, with the Stalinists taking a back seat. . . .[1]

On the night of November 6, it was decided that the government should be evacuated to Valencia immediately. All the members of the cabinet favored the change except the four Anarchists, who at first refused their sanction but later acquiesced. The Communists had mixed feelings on the move. Although they realized the military necessity, they disliked the government leaving the vicinity of Madrid where the Communist party had its greatest influence. They did, nevertheless, support the evacuation of the cabinet, though later they condemned Largo Caballero for sneaking away.[2]

Even after eight months of assaults by Italian and Nationalist troops, Madrid continued to hold out. The Communists, without any show of modesty, assumed full credit. Francisco Anton, member of the Politbureau of the Communist Party of Spain, asserted:

But why is our Madrid being defended? Why has our Madrid been defended from the beginning? Apart from the bitterness of the struggle, which has developed the vigor of our soldiers in the course of the eight months that we have been in bitter combat in the defense of Madrid; apart from the spirit of combativeness of our soldiers; apart from the clear comprehension that in Madrid we are fighting for world freedom and democracy—one of the factors most appropriately underscored here—is the role of our Communist Party and the role played by the United Socialist Youth [controlled by the Communists].[3]

The defense of Madrid remained a special interest of the Communists throughout the war and they fought to hold it to the end, even when it was isolated from most of the rest of Spain.

COMMUNIST INFLUENCE OVER THE GOVERNMENT

From the core of Madrid the Communists gradually tried to extend their control over the rest of Loyalist Spain and over the government at Valencia. One of the first steps in this direction was the spreading of propaganda and control of censorship. The natural affinity of the Spanish revolutionaries to the hero stories of the Russian Revolution was exploited to the utmost. Soviet works were pushed to such an extent that complaints began to be heard that Spanish tradition was being completely forgotten. Colonel Casado, without doubt a prejudiced observer, blames the general lack of patriotism, the failure to use patriotic propaganda among the Nationalists, and the ineffectiveness of propaganda abroad to the overdose of the Soviet line.[4] Such a sweeping conclusion is largely without basis. An examination of propaganda works in Spain at this time, although showing a vast amount of Soviet material, indicates it was by no means written exclusively by Russians or by the Communists. Furthermore it must be borne in mind that the feeling for Russia in Spain at this time was very strong and spontaneous.

On the other hand, that most of the propaganda abroad was communistic is quite true.[5] The government forces had no ready-built international method of propagation at their disposal. Unlike the wealthier elements among the Nationalists who had relations and resources abroad, the parties of the Left, except the Communist party, had few international connections. Anarchism as an international force had almost ceased to exist and the Socialists, although adhering to the Second International, had never been close to the other Socialist parties of the world because of their difference in outlook and background. The general isolation of the Iberian peninsula from Europe made it difficult for the Loyalists to bridge the gap in order to explain their problems to the world. It is not surprising then that the Comintern was the main source of Republican propaganda abroad, and logically, it tended to stress the role of the Communists and their supporters in Spain.

The matter of Communist control of censorship was much more serious. Luis Araquistain, another prejudiced observer but in a position to know since he was a Socialist leader and the Ambassador to France during the war, says that the department which was in charge of censorship came under the Ministry of Foreign Affairs of which Álvarez del Vayo, strongly supported by the Communists, was Minister. In this department "more than ninety per cent of the officials, beginning with the Under-Secretary himself, were Communists, out of a total of five hundred, most of whom were shirkers who had sought refuge there so as to escape serving at the front."[6] From a strongly pro-Communist source comes a partial confirmation of this accusation of Communist control over censorship. Constancia de la Mora describes in her autobiography her work for the foreign censorship bureau during the war. Although she disclaims Communist domination of the bureau, the reader is left with the impression that the work was done harmoniously under the guidance of the Communists.[7] Araquistain further points out:

> The chief official in charge of the code was a Communist, with the result that the Republic's secret communications with its agents abroad were known to the Russian Embassy before the Spanish Government itself learnt of them.[8]

The result of Communist control of censorship was that it was considered treasonable and an aid to Franco if anything were said against the Communists or Russia in the press. The Communists, on the other hand, could insult the various groups and persons they wished, as they freely did the *POUM*, the Anarchists, and the various ministers who lost favor in their eyes.[9]

THE SOVIET ADVISERS

The corps of Russian advisers also played an important role in the increased influence of the Communists over the government. Theoretically the Soviet personnel was to act only in the military field and in an advisory capacity. But as the Soviet Union held the whip hand, being the only large source of supply, their advice actually became orders. The

Russian "advisers" fell into the three groups discussed in the following paragraphs.

There was one political group connected directly with the Spanish government. Most authorities put Marcel Rosenberg, the Soviet Ambassador to Spain, at the head of this group. Antonov Ovseenko, the Russian Consul in Barcelona, was the government adviser in Catalonia. However, Krivitsky says that it was Rosenberg "who was making speeches and keeping in the public eye, but the Kremlin never considered him important. Silently and effectively, Stashevsky [a Secretary in the Soviet Embassy] did the work of Stalin."[10] Arthur Stashevsky was especially busy in gaining control of the finances of the country and, according to Krivitsky, suggested to Largo Caballero that he send the gold to Russia. Stashevsky took under his wing Negrín, the Finance Minister. Negrín had been unknown in politics before the war, holding the Chair of Physiology in the Faculty of Medicine at Madrid. He was a member of the Socialist party but had not been one of its outstanding leaders. Many of his critics have called him "gullible and naïve." Irrespective of how his personality is judged he was a nonrevolutionary Socialist and saw, in closer coöperation with the Communists, a chance for victory and the best chance for a peaceful democratic Republic in Spain. In spite of all the rumors to the contrary, those who knew him say that he was sincere in his beliefs and not a Communist.[11] Stashevsky saw in Negrín, however, a docile ally for the Communists when Caballero could no longer serve a purpose.

While one group of Russians was busy in the politics of the government, another was busy in the military. General Berzin had collected around him a group of Russian staff officers, first, to influence the course of events around Madrid, then on all the fronts and in the Defense Ministry. As their choice of commander-in-chief, according to Walter Krivitsky, they selected José Miaja, who was a good soldier without political ambitions. He first became head of the military junta of Madrid in October, 1936, and later became commander of all the armies. Miaja did not, however, turn out to be the docile follower they expected.[12]

The Russians seem at times to have assumed direct control over military operations. Indalecio Prieto, in his speech to the National Committee of the Socialist Party of Spain on August 9, 1938, mentioned several instances in which his orders were countermanded by the Russians. Prieto, as Minister of the Navy, had ordered the dispatch of the destroyer *Ciscar* across the Straits of Gibraltar from where it was anchored at Gijón. The chief of the Soviet advisers asked that Prieto revoke his

order, which he refused to do. In spite of Prieto's refusal, Communist
agents on the spot kept the ship from sailing and, as a result, the ship
was sunk. Another incident occurred when the Russians demanded that
Antonio Ruiz be relieved of his command of the Naval Base at Cartagena, which Prieto flatly declined to do. In respect to aviation, he related
other instances of Soviet interference. After the northern provinces had
been lost, Prieto wanted to bomb the cities behind the eastern front. In
this project he was opposed by the Communists. Prieto, nevertheless,
made his opinion prevail and orders were issued to bomb to the east.
The raids, however, were never carried out and the Communists' only
excuse was that "there had been difficulties." Another instance was the
case of the erroneous bombing of Valladolid, which Prieto had crossed
off the list of objectives as strategically unimportant. When asked how
it happened, the acting commander of the air force, Lt. Col. Martín
Luna, said, "I have no alternative but to tell the truth, Señor Minister.
I had been told to say that the planes were headed in the direction of
Salamanca, but that they had to go off course, but the truth is that the
Russians had ordered the bombing of Valladolid." In conclusion, Prieto
mentioned instances of German planes which went down behind the
lines. The Russians, in these cases, refused to allow French technicians
even to take photographs. These are some of the instances related by
Prieto in his address before the Socialist party.[13] It is essential to consider that the speech was in explanation for his dismissal as Minister of
War after being under pressure and attack by the Communists.[14] It is
impossible to check the evidence on the incidents, or assuming their validity, to know whether the Communists countermanded orders more
often than the other parties and forces on the side of the independent-
minded Spanish Loyalists, such as the Anarchist militias. Nevertheless,
it can be said there is a strong indication that the Communists and the
Russians were doing the very thing they were so bitterly condemning
the Anarchists and other forces for doing—undermining the discipline of
the government.

Colonel Casado corroborates Prieto's evidence:

As time went on, Russian influence was increased at the War Ministry. They looked
over the plans of the General Staff and through the Minister they rejected many technical proposals and imposed others. Generally speaking, all the proposals of the
"friendly advisers" were opposed by the Ministry's General Staff, but very often their
advice prevailed. Their suggestions nearly always had a political objective....[15]

He specifically goes on to support Prieto's contention that the Russians frequently interfered in the operations of the air force and even goes a step further in his condemnation:

I can affirm that in all the operations in which I took part as an Army Commander, in order to find out anything about what aeroplanes and tanks were at my disposition, or how they could be tactically used, I always had to enter into direct relations with the "friendly advisers" and only sometimes with the Spanish Chiefs of Aviation and Tanks. Frequently during the carrying on of the war operations, in order to have the support of aircraft, we had to change our time-table for one which they imposed, often with lamentable results.[16]

It was Colonel Casado's final conclusion that the Russian advisers prevented the development of a coherent plan of campaign during the entire war, and that the general behavior of the Russian technicians and the Communists was a major cause of the defeat of the Republican forces. He declared that plans to strengthen army organization, such as turning the two hundred mixed brigades into divisions of a regimental kind, had been vetoed by the Russians to the detriment of victory.[17] In analyzing these conclusions a factor of primary importance is that Colonel Casado, just as Indalecio Prieto, was defending himself against Communist attack. He was accused of betraying the Republic by seizing power and negotiating peace with Franco during the last days of the Civil War. He was, therefore, particularly anxious to free himself of blame and throw it onto the Communists. It would be impossible to conclude whether the advice given out by the Russian staff, oftentimes in the form of orders, was to the impairment of the Republic. In the first place, it would be difficult to trace the various plans and orders back to the Russian staff as the originators. Secondly, any judgment on the quality of the plans and the judiciousness of the orders must be subjective in view of the complexity of the whole situation. Only one thing should be mentioned before leaving this subject: before the arrival of the Russian staff there was no army, only armed masses without organization, coördination, or plans. Shortly after the Russians arrived there was a radical change in the whole defensive structure. Within six months an army had been created which could defeat the up-to-date Italian Army at Guadalajara, and slow down the advance of the armies of Franco which had been trained by the Germans and Italians and aided by the divisions of Mussolini for almost three years. How much of it was attributable to the Russian and Communist leaders and how much of it was hindered by them can never be finally ascertained, but the extent of their authority in the army would lead to the conclusion that they were an important and an essential factor in the long resistance of the Loyalist troops.

The third group of Russians in Spain was the *GPU*, the Russian government's security agency, under the chief agent, Orlov. It was the purpose of this group to support the other two in their activities to organize the Republicans along the lines the Soviet Union desired. They also had the job of ridding the Republican side of Fascist agents and "uncontrollables." The activities of this group will be discussed later.

To complete the picture of Soviet forces in Spain something must be said about the International Brigade. Though not composed of Communist elements only, it was a very carefully picked brigade in respect to "reliability." In Spain itself the units were kept separated, as far as possible, from the Spanish troops and the men in general were not allowed to mix with the Spaniards. All contacts of the brigade with the outside were through reliable Communists and all important posts from General Kleber, the Commander, down to the post of political commissar were held by Communists. As a result the International Brigade was essentially a Soviet force in Spain and there were always rumors and fears on the part of the Spanish that the International Brigade would march on Valencia and seize power for the Communists, which they doubtless could have done.

The Power of Soviet Aid

There was always the threat to withdraw all aid behind the advice of the Soviet advisers and behind the demands of the Communist party. The threat was tacit and merely remained a possibility, but within the various groups in Spain the power over distribution of supplies was used extensively by the Communists for political purposes. It is not surprising that at the beginning it was the Communist troops which first got the supplies, not merely because they were Communists but because they were one of the first groups to submit to regular army organization, which the Russians felt to be an essential element in defense.

One incident, which has been attributed by some to Communist refusal to send supplies and air and sea support, was the fall of Málaga in the spring of 1937. The central government, it is said, persistently refused to send help and hoarded supplies for the defense of Madrid.[18] This policy, the claimants declare, was the result of Communist influence on the government. But before accepting the condemnation of the Communists immediately, it is necessary to analyze the evidence a little closer. The material available does point to a lack of supplies in Málaga; though to attribute its fall entirely to the shortage of material would be a hasty judgment. The panic which ensued among the militia defending Málaga even at the rumor of an attack would indicate that another cause of the defeat was the lack of seasoned and disciplined troops. Supposing, nevertheless, the lack of ammunition and arms as an important contributory cause, it does not follow that the reason for this deficiency was avoidable. In the first place, there was not a great abundance of supplies anywhere in Republican Spain at this time and it was, therefore, necessary to use them where they would do the greatest good. Madrid, then under a similar siege, had strategic as well as morale importance, whereas the holding of Málaga could not claim either. It was essentially cut off from the rest of Republican Spain and without strong sea support it could never have been used even as a jumping-off place for the invasion of Andalusia, assuming a strong Republican army which did not exist. Nevertheless, postulating that there was the extra equipment to send to Málaga, the difficulty of transportation still made it almost impossible. There was great danger in sending it by sea because of frequent sinkings by the rebels, and furthermore, after December the harbor at Málaga was unusable. Motor transportation was over a precarious, narrow, mountain road, which was easily patrolled by the Italian Air Force. Then to make a still further assumption that equipment could have been readily sent to Málaga, it is difficult to prove whose decision it was not to try to send aid. The Communists claimed that Largo Caballero, in his attempt to assume complete control over military strategy, forgot about Málaga and regarded it as unimportant.[19] From the evidence available it is impossible to say whether the Communists or the government made the decision.

The accusation of Communist intrigue in the fall of Málaga has been analyzed in detail to show how an alleged case of Communist domination and treachery, which seems logical and foolproof at first glance, has little foundation. Such accusations were invented out of rumor and a desire to find a scapegoat.

In respect to Russian aid to Catalonia and the Aragon front there is more evidence of political control. Catalonia was dominated largely by the Anarchists and, unlike Largo Caballero and the Socialists, the Anarchists were not willing to follow the Communist lead and forget the revolution until the war had been won, even though they had agreed to participate in the government and to organize a centralized command. They resisted particularly efforts to turn their private army into a regular army. Consequently, the Communists decided to use the force of their equipment to bring them around. Walter Krivitsky reports that at the very beginning:

...I received strict instructions from Moscow not to permit the boat to deliver its cargo in Barcelona. Under no circumstances were those planes to pass through Catalonia, which had its own government, very much like that of a sovereign state. This Catalonian government was dominated by revolutionists of anti-Stalinist persuasion. They were not trusted by Moscow, although they were then desperately holding one of the most vital sectors of the Loyalist front against fierce attacks from Franco's army.

I was ordered to send the planes to Alicante. But that port was blockaded by Franco's vessels. The master of the ship made for Alicante, but had to turn back to save his ship and cargo. He attempted to head for Barcelona, but was prevented by my agent on board. My ship load of aircraft plied back and forth in the Mediterranean. Franco kept it from Alicante. Stalin kept it from Barcelona. In the meantime Loyalist Spain was fighting desperately and was woefully short of planes. At last my agent on board directed the ship to proceed to Marseilles.

This fantastic development was part of Stalin's fierce but silent battle to gain complete control of the Loyalist Government, a battle which went on behind the open theater of war....[20]

Krivitsky is quick to draw the conclusion from this event that the Soviet government sought domination over Catalonia. There is perhaps another explanation for this refusal of aid to Catalonia. As discussed above, the Communists saw in the Madrid sector of the front an element of particular importance. They hoped that in rallying to the defense of Madrid, the whole country would follow in a general rally to save Spain. The militias, as was typical of all revolutionary forces, had started out with a burst of enthusiasm but as the war settled down to a long struggle and extreme hardships, their spirits began to wane. It was these groups the Communists hoped again to arouse, directing their enthusiasm this time toward a well-organized defense system. Events proved their plan feasible. Consequently, they wanted to be sure that the new Soviet equipment would first get to the Madrid front and save the situation there. If it had landed in Barcelona, it would have been virtually impossible for the central government to get the equipment since Catalonia had in fact an independent government. Furthermore, the Anarchists, after seizing the equipment, would have no idea how to fly the planes or run the tanks, so that they would have been useless to the defense of Spain. Still another factor in the Communists' favor was that the front held by the Catalonian militia at this time was largely inactive, irrespective of Krivitsky's reference to "fierce attacks from Franco's army."

Nor was Stalin without supporters in Spain for this policy of keeping the equipment out of Catalonia. There had long existed competition between Catalonia and the government of Madrid. The revolutionary groups in both governments had fallen heir to this tradition. During the Civil War Catalonia had secured virtual independence from the central government. Although the Socialists and Republicans did not believe in absolute dictation from the center, they believed that the general policy for the whole country should be decided by the central government and felt that the Civil War made it all the more necessary that Catalonia remain an integral part of the rest of the country. The Republican forces were in desperate need of the industrial production and troops of wealthy Catalonia because the only other large industrial section left to the Republicans was the Basque provinces, which had been completely cut off by Nationalist troops from the main part of Loyalist Spain. Up to the time of the intervention of Russia, Catalonia resisted all efforts to submit even to the slightest show of authority by the central government and sent only a few troops to the Madrid front. Furthermore, the Anarchists in their efforts and rush to collectivize and carry out the revolution had failed to develop any munition or war industries in Catalonia. Consequently, it is not surprising that the majority in the central government, at least tacitly, supported the moves of the Soviet Union to bring Catalonia under control.

Soviet aid was used to discriminate against the revolutionaries in Catalonia in several ways. There is good circumstantial evidence that the Soviet Union set these conditions for aiding Catalonia: that the dissident Communist *POUM* should not be allowed to participate any longer in the Catalonia Generalitat, and that the Catalonian government must submit to the over-all program set down by the central government.[21] Aid to Catalonia began in December, and immediately the *POUM* representatives were dropped from the Council, the Catalonian militias submitted to the long process of being organized into a regular army, and the central government began gradually to assume authority over industry in Catalonia.

An accusation has also been brought against the Communists that they deliberately withheld grain supplies from Catalonia to discredit the Anarchist control and particularly Domenech, the *CNT* representative, who was in charge of the Council of Food Supplies of Catalonia, in order to replace him with a *PSUC* man.[22] This is difficult to prove. It may be quite true that the shortage of grain and the resulting food lines and riots were due to the failure of the Soviet Union to send grain, but it may also be true that the shortage was due to inefficiency and maladministration by the *CNT* and to the resistance of the peasants to *CNT* control, so that a change was needed to restore the normal channels of trade. It may also be argued that the central government paid for the grain from Russia from its own gold reserves and, therefore, was entitled to the grain.

Evidence in respect to the Communist refusal of material for the Aragon front is much more clear. When the Madrid front had been secured by Soviet material aid against the first assaults, nothing was done to help the important Aragon front which was manned primarily by the militias of the *POUM* and the *CNT*. Failure to support this front is impossible to explain. It clearly shows the political motive for the distribution of supplies. Katia Landau states the case:

> No sacrifice, they say, must be held back for the saving of Madrid. It is not only in Madrid, but also in the Aragon front that arms are needed. At the Aragon front there are the militias of the *C.N.T.—F.A.I.* and the *P.O.U.M.* who wait. With the modern Russian arms, they would go on in the conquest of Saragossa, which would thus contribute in the most effective and definite way to forestall the encirclement of Madrid [and hinder Franco's offensive against Bilbao.] And the arms, at this time, are not a far-off dream; they are there in the port of Cartagena.
>
> But at the Aragon front the Anarchist militia and that of the *P.O.U.M.* wait in vain; and slowly they recognize the cruel truth; the Russian arms are political arms, directed against the revolutionary elements of the *C.N.T.*, of the *F.A.I.* and the *P.O.U.M.* . . .[23]

There is no doubt from the evidence that strategically this refusal of aid for an Aragon offensive was a mistake of serious consequences. To what extent the Socialists and Republicans are free from implication in this decision is not clear. At least they gave it tacit support as the blockade gave rise to no serious objections from these quarters. The prohibition of arms to the Anarchist and *POUM* militias was protested frequently by the Anarchists. They sent several deputations to the government, including the famous leader of one of the *CNT* columns, Durruti, but to no avail.[24] Finally matters became so serious that at the *FAI* conferences held February 21–23, 1937, it was resolved that:

> The conference agrees that, taking into account that it has been fully proved that there exists a boycotting and a sabotaging on the part of the Government of the Aragon Front and other fronts where there are volunteer and Anarchist forces, to set a term of eight regular days in which to send war material of all classes in a spirit of equality.
>
> If this is not carried out by the Government, then our ministers will be withdrawn from it, and the national and international public will be informed how the sabotage was carried out and who were its victims.[25]

Because of the pressure by the *CNT*, the Communists and the government finally relaxed their boycott in part until they felt strong enough to bring the Catalonian government completely under their authority. In conclusion, it can be stated from the evidence reviewed above that the Communists made extensive political use of their aid in order to undermine their political opponents, the *POUM* and the Anarchists. To what extent they used it against other parties and groups is, however, not clear.

COMMUNIST INFLUENCE IN THE CABINET

In seeking governmental authority the Communists were very careful to maintain on the surface a truly Popular Front government. Throughout the entire war the Communists never had more than two members of the party in the cabinet, and these two members always held the comparatively insignificant posts of Minister of Public Instruction and Minister of Agriculture. At the time of the original formation of the Popular Front government in September, 1936, this was a true reflection of Communist strength. After Communist authority had increased as a result of the inauguration of Russian intervention, the party still chose to keep before the country and the world the idea that the Communists remained only a minor element. Their sway over the government took other forms —primarily putting their followers in other parties into positions of authority and infiltrating the lower echelons of the governmental hierarchy. Finally they made use of factional disputes and personal jealousies, to gain their ends.

Up to this point several instances have been discussed where Communists had obtained supporters in other parties. For example, there was Álvarez del Vayo, whom the Communists continually supported as Foreign Minister and as General Commissar of the army. They also supported Largo Caballero as long as he could be flattered and cajoled into following the policies of unity and centralization of governmental and army authority. When he was no longer docile, the Communists trained Juan Negrín, Finance Minister, to take his place.[26] They further made use of the personal jealousies between Prieto and Caballero for control of the Socialist party and of the animosity of the Socialists and Republicans toward the Anarchists to get rid of Caballero and reduce the influence of anarchism. These maneuvers will be discussed in detail in the following chapters.

COMMUNIST INFILTRATION OF THE ARMY

Although manipulation of ministers required the most daring and finesse, the real core of Communist domination was their hold over the lower echelons in the government. They showed special preference for those branches of the government which had most to do with carrying on the war. They were very strong in the Foreign Office and especially the department of propaganda and censorship. It was, however, in the Ministry of Defense that they concentrated the greatest effort.[27] We have the testimony of four former officials in the government as to the predominance of Communist strength in the departments of defense; Largo Caballero, Luis Araquistain, Colonel Casado, and Indalecio Prieto. All four men were prejudiced against the Communists, but they also were in a position to know. Colonel Casado claims:

... more than sixty per cent of the commands of the first units of the People's Army were given to the Communist Party. This was following the political tactic of the party, and complying with the demands of the U.S.S.R., whether with the consent of the War Minister, or without his realising the manoeuvre.

This percentage of commands in the People's Army was held by the Communist Party throughout the whole campaign and even rose higher during the last months, when it reached the exorbitant figure of seventy per cent. There were many protests and complaints from other political parties and syndicates, but without any result, since later on the Communist Party had in its service both the Minister of National Defense and the Sub-Secretary of the Army.[28]

In support of his claim, Colonel Casado reviews the various command positions and their party affiliations. In a report to Prime Minister Negrín dated February 28, 1939, Colonel Casado repeated his contention that at that time seventy per cent of the commands were Communist and that "some of them, the minority, have joined the Party in good faith, others through fear, or through ambition."[29]

Indalecio Prieto in describing the predominance of the Communists discusses their representation in the Superior Council of War:

... The figures reveal that the Communist officials represented a percentage infinitely greater in proportion to the number of members belonging to that party; moreover there were many other officials of the United Socialist Youth governed by Communists and the United Socialist Party of Catalonia, also under control of the Soviets, and many others, who disguised their affiliation behind the simple initials of the *U.G.T.*[30]

Prieto defends his own failure to take action against the Communists by saying that in spite of his protest Negrín refused to alter the system of representation. Prieto then goes on to mention all the various significant positions held by the Communists in the government, including the important posts of Undersecretaries of Army, Air, and Navy, Director General of Security, and Director General of Supply and Transport. Prieto further agrees with Colonel Casado that the Communists "gained absolute predominance in the sectors most decisive in commanding all the armed forces," which included the chief of the naval base at Cartagena; the military governors of Albacete, Alicante, and Murcia; command of the army of the east; and command of the army of the Ebro. Prieto again excuses himself as Minister of Defense against the encroachment of the Communists by throwing the blame on Negrín and Largo Caballero, who refused to reduce the number of Communist appointees in the ministries and in the army commands in spite of Prieto's requests.

The testimony of Colonel Casado and Indalecio Prieto is corroborated by other authorities. Luis Araquistain, González Inestal, Under-Commissar General of War, and several others confirm the growing power of the Communists in the armed forces.[31] Even the Communists seem to have admitted their accession to a position of power in the army. Jesús Hernández, in speaking in Valencia on May 28, 1937, alludes to the Communist prevalence already assured on the central front around Madrid: "It is not chance that the slogan of 'united army and united command' was accepted fully and carried out precisely in the Central Sector where the influence of our party is decisive."[32] The Communists persistently praised the work being done by their party to create a disciplined army and attributed to their own efforts the success which was being achieved in spite of resistance on the part of some groups.[33]

Although the Communists were interested in controlling the command positions, it was the corps of political commissars on which they depended to keep the rank and file of the soldiers in line. Realizing that without the support and submission of the regular soldier their over-all control would mean little, the Communists put special emphasis on the job of political commissar. On their insistence a Commissariat of Army, Navy, and Air was created in October, 1936. Its aim was to direct the political activity of the soldier and keep him aware of the ends for which he was fighting. A special newspaper *El Commissar* was published to help the commissar in this work. Certainly the principle of this new organization was creditable in a revolutionary and mass situation where enthusiasm was very likely to wane. All the parties except the Communist, however, seemed to have overlooked the importance of this new group until it was too late. From the beginning the Communists sought to take over, and were successful in having appointed as the General Commissar, Álvarez del Vayo. Largo Caballero describes how Álvarez del Vayo appointed thousands of commissars on his own, which Caballero considered illegal since the Commissar General could not alone designate commissars. When Caballero asked Álvarez del Vayo why "the vast majority of the commissars of war which he had appointed were Communists," the answer was that it had been an accident.[34] But the surprising thing is that Largo Caballero, even though he knew of Communist predominance among the commissars of war, did nothing about it.

The prestige of the political commissars was enhanced whenever possible by the Communists. "The commissar is the nerve and the soul of our People's Army" was the Communist slogan. On him was placed the responsibility of "political unity" in the army and of carrying out the program of the government.[35] "The effectiveness of the functions of the Commissar General, of the under-commissars and the commissar delegates will in large part be measured on how much they contribute to establishing the necessary coördination between the commanders and the troops."[36] Thus the Communists conceived of the commissars as the links between the government and the military command on the one hand and the common soldier on the other. The Communists persistently urged that their powers should be extended to include actual participation in the formulation of operations. "We have insisted, as the actual facts have already demonstrated, that it is very convenient to have the direct participation of the commissars in the political preparation of the military operations and prior knowledge of the plans of the command."[37] It was not uncommon for the political commissars to actually share command with the military leaders. Their influence over the troops made them a force which no commander dared ignore for fear of having his men turn against him.

The propaganda of the commissars followed closely the line of the Communists and the Republicans—supporting military discipline, complete mobilization, love for the fatherland, independence for Spain, and democracy. Revolution, socialization, collectivization, and dictatorship of the proletariat were never mentioned.

The proportion of the Communists among the political commissars cannot be determined exactly, but the Communists' own figures give some indication. Dolores Ibarruri in discussing the importance and bravery of commissars, especially the Communists, listed the casualties among them in an article in *Mundo Obrero*, March 19, 1937:

Killed: Communists—21; Socialists—1; members of the United Youth League—7; members of the League of Left Republican Youth—1; members of the Republican League—1; others—1.

Wounded: Communists—31; members of the United Youth League—1; Socialists —3.[38]

From these figures it would appear that the proportion of Communists approached ninety per cent. Even if it is assumed, as Dolores Ibarruri contends, that more Communists were in the front lines than members of the other parties, and if it is assumed further that the figures may exaggerate the Communist strength on purpose, it would still seem that the Communists had a preponderance. The complete absence of Anarchists and *POUM*ists from the figures indicates that the Communists made sure few members of the "uncontrollables" were allowed to hold these important positions.

In defense of the Communist efforts to influence and control military matters, it must be said that at the same time the Communists sought special control over the defenses of the country the Socialists were also active in their special interests, using their efforts to influence and control industrial policies, the distribution of raw materials, local government, and the police.[39] This, however, does not detract from the conclusion in respect to the evidence above, that the Communists were well on their way toward absolute domination of the defenses of the country by the end of the war.

Communist Front Organizations

In attempting to spread their influence over the population the Communists in Spain made use of the familiar Communist technique of front organizations. The party realized that there were many people who could not bring themselves to join but who were still in sympathy with the aims of the party's war policy. Many people were not willing to submit to the discipline of the party and others had a strong prejudice against anything communistic. It was partly to catch these groups, but also partly to permeate all aspects of society with their program that they set up front organizations. The Civil War had started a wave of patriotic and aid societies for support of the Republican cause. A strong feeling of community had replaced momentarily the strong individualistic outlook of the Spaniard, and the Communists were quick to take advantage of this new emotion. The societies of the Communists were quite extensive in number. To name a few: *Socorro Rojo Internacional, la Unión de Muchachas, las Mujeres Antifascistas, las Milicias de la Cultura, los Amigos de la Unión Soviética, la Alianza de Intelectuales Antifascistas*, and *la Unión de Madres Jóvenes*. Several of the groups had large memberships and were widespread. For example, the *Socorro Rojo Internacional* had 992 local committees and 353,000 members by February, 1937. This organization was of particular importance because it was responsible for the distribution of relief and aid to the population, which meant that it was able to wield tremendous power in a community and could do a great deal to raise the prestige of the Communists and the Soviet Union.

THE ACTIVITIES OF THE *GPU* IN SPAIN

The rebel general, Mola, during the siege of Madrid had boasted that he had five columns attacking the city; four armed columns from without, and a "fifth column" from within. The alleged "fifth column" of spies and sympathizers was no idle boast. The Civil War had cut the country both along geographic lines and along class lines, and as a result many Nationalist adherents found themselves behind the Republican lines. Furthermore, like all civil wars the break between those on one side and those on the other was by no means clear-cut and it was easy for spies, sympathizers, and espionage agents to slip from one side to the other. Consequently, the "fifth column" always stood as a threat to the Republican government, ready to take over a city as soon as the Loyalists relaxed their vigil and in the meantime making use of every tactic to obstruct the Republican defense.

Against this inside enemy the government developed a secret police to purge the rear. The newly organized force was composed of all the parties of the Popular Front including the Anarchists. The Communist representatives were agents of the *GPU*. As mentioned previously, one of the groups sent by Russia to supervise the use of Soviet equipment was a *GPU* organization under one of the Russian Embassy secretaries, Orlov. This *GPU* group or *Cheka*, as it was often called in Spain, took its place as a section of the Loyalist secret police and as a department of the Ministry of Interior. It had the very innocuous name of Special Information Section of the State. From the evidence available it would seem that a large portion of at least the top men of the agency were foreign Communists, though not Russian. The number of Spanish Communists who could be trusted, it appears, was not very great. From the very beginning the *Cheka* section of the secret police worked independently of the rest of the organization and before long they were in fact a separate entity, with their own prisons, their own investigations, their own trials, and their own executions. Why were they able to gain such autonomy from the regular channels of justice? In answer the Minister of Interior, Julian Zugazagoitia, is reported to have said, "Well, we have received aid from Russia and have to permit certain actions which we do not like."[40]

As the activities of the *Cheka* spread over Spain complaints were heard more and more, particularly from the revolutionary parties. Condemnations such as those below became quite common.

Solidaridad Obrero, Barcelona *CNT* organ, declared on April 20, 1937:

> We have no adequate word for the attempted tyranny of the Madrid Communists who seek to run the capital. There have been arbitrary arrests, unpunished murders, secret jails, persecution of the press ... shameless protection of Falangists and reactionaries. ...

Again on April 25, 1937:

> It is becoming clear that the *Chekist* organizations recently discovered in Madrid, for which the Commissioner of Public Order, Cazorla, was chiefly responsible, are directly linked with similar centers operating under a unified leadership and on a preconceived plan of national scope. The situation has grown worse and worse. Our Madrid daily, *C.N.T.*, was suppressed and suspended for commenting on the monstrous role played by Cazorla. ... Not only the Madrid *C.N.T.* but all our press outside Catalonia has been suppressed and suspended. ...

The activities of the *Cheka* rapidly developed, as the evidence clearly shows, into a reign of terror, especially during 1937.

Though all the various indictments against the Communists in Spain differ as to what were their aims and methods, all authorities from the Nationalists to the Anarchists agree on the widespread activities of the *Cheka* in Spain. The dissident Communists and Nationalists have both produced abundant testimonies of those who at one time had been confined in one of the private prisons of the *Cheka*.[41] With corroborating evidence from all quarters it is impossible not to accept as fact a large portion of the testimony.

The widespread terrorist acts of the *Cheka* show that though the Communists were allied with democratic elements in Spain in respect to their war aims, they had not by any means adopted their methods. The Communists were trying to gain democratic ends by the methods of an oriental despot. It must not be assumed, however, that such methods were uncommon. On the Nationalist side Franco admitted quite openly to the German Ambassador to Salamanca that "he was determined, since he was fighting a war, to nip in the bud any action directed against him and his Government by shooting the guilty parties."[42] The Anarchists in their turn had made use of such methods at the beginning of the war, though as the situation of the Republic became worse and worse they tended to refrain from the use of terror against their opponents within the Popular Front. Nor can the Socialist and Republican parties be freed completely from guilt. Even though they knew about the extensive activities of the *Cheka* against the Anarchists and the dissident Communists, they made but few protests and even collaborated with the Communists in their purges.[43] They seemed almost secretly to rejoice in the elimination of their strongest opponents on the Left.

It is questionable whether the cost in bitterness and enmity, created by the *Cheka* in Spain, was worth what it accomplished in the way of securing Communist control. It tended to alienate the Spanish people and liberal supporters everywhere from the Loyalist cause. That the Communists employed terrorism, however, is not surprising. The use of forceful inducement and elimination follows the line of action frequently used by the Russian Communists, who have never been content to depend on mere persuasion to gain their support among the masses. It would appear also that the *GPU*'s activity in Spain was partly a spill-over from the widespread purges which were being carried out in the Soviet Union. Trotskyism was anathema to the Communists in the 'thirties, and even though the *POUM* was not a Trotskyite party the Communists considered it as such and seized upon it for their revenge in Spain. It became the scapegoat for all the ills and sadistic desires of the *GPU* agents.

In the main, however, the *Cheka* or *GPU* was set up to accomplish three ends. The revolution of the extreme Left in Republican Spain in 1936 was almost the only active revolutionary movement in a world which appeared to be moving to the Right and toward fascism and, therefore, it immediately became the focal point and refuge of all types of revolutionaries. Russia was particularly alarmed about this migration because the only revolutionaries she wanted in Spain were her own, which she could control. She feared other elements would bring about an uncontrollable revolution in Spain whose excesses would only alienate the democracies from the Left and from the idea of a Popular Front. It was, consequently, one of the main jobs of the *Cheka* to keep the number of foreign non-Communist revolutionaries at a minimum by carefully overseeing the recruitment of the International Brigade, and by eliminating the foreign revolutionaries who became too outspoken against Soviet interference.[44]

The *Cheka*'s second task was to eliminate all opposition to the Communists' program. The brunt of the *GPU* attack was leveled at the Anarchists and *POUM*ists, who wanted immediate revolution and were the strongest opponents of what they called the "totalitarian" program of the Communists. The Socialists and Republicans who were in agreement with the Communist war policies, on the other hand, were generally immune to the *Cheka* terror. It was, therefore, the job of the *Cheka* to split up the revolutionary parties and eliminate the most outspoken opposition to the Communist policy.

The final task was to maintain the unchallenged supremacy of the Communist program once it was in force. The Communists were fully aware that the authoritarianism of the Communist program had never and would never appeal to the Spanish people. It was this that had kept the Communist party very small in Spain. In addition, they realized that as the vicissitudes of the war became more burdensome, the Spanish populace would be more and more willing and anxious to compromise and even surrender to the Nationalists. This the Communists wanted to prevent at all costs. It was the job, therefore, of the Communist secret police to keep the people in hand and docile to the aims of Soviet foreign policy.

CHAPTER XI

A PLEA FOR A SINGLE PARTY
OF THE PROLETARIAT

THE COMMUNISTS AND LARGO CABALLERO'S LEADERSHIP

AT THE SAME time that the Communists were strengthening their position in the government administration through infiltration they sought to ingratiate themselves with the Socialists and Anarchists and increase their influence in the trade-unions. Through close coöperation among the workers' groups the Communists hoped to create a united party of the proletariat which they considered absolutely essential to the success of their war program and to the final victory of the bourgeois-democratic revolution over Franco. From the experience of the United Socialist Youth (*JSU*) and the United Socialist Party of Catalonia (*PSUC*), it was implied that in establishing a united party the program of the Communist party would serve as the basic policy and that the Communists would dominate.

The Communists had supported the government of Largo Caballero from its inception. Their propaganda and press were full of praises for it and they unceasingly used their influence to bring about Caballero's control over the military and economic life of the country. Although there is evidence that as early as January, 1937, they lacked confidence in Largo Caballero, at least in the open they continued to give him unswerving support.[1] In return, Caballero coöperated to the fullest extent with the Communists, allowing them to extend their control more and more over the Socialist youth, and to gain important and dominant positions in the Ministry of Defense and in the Army. It may be quite true to say: "Caballero did not understand. He believed in the sincerity of the Russian intervention and in the sincerity of the feeling of unity of the Spanish Communists."[2] Largo Caballero did not wake up to the ultimate aims of the Communist policy until it was too late. He seemed quite naïve in overlooking the fact that the Communists were using the split between himself and Prieto and all the concessions he had granted to them to secure their own position in the government. It is surprising that he should have been so gullible in regard to the Communists' activities on the one hand, while on the other hand he was perfectly aware of the intrigues of the Anarchists, Republicans, and particularly Prieto, against him. Perhaps he was not simple at all; perhaps he feared that Soviet aid would end if he failed to coöperate with the Communists. It is possible that he saw in the Communists the best ally to secure his position in the Socialist party and in the country. The Communists were, after all, primarily dependent for their prestige in Spain on Soviet aid. Their membership was composed mostly of fair-weather friends who would leave the party as soon as a democratic government was victorious and go back either to being nonpolitical, or to one of the various democratic, bourgeois parties, because in time of peace the Spanish had never taken to communism with its authoritarianism and foreign control. In that event Caballero could easily have ended his alliance with the Communists and been the sole leader in the country. Perhaps he felt assured that his own prestige would remain strong while the Communist influence would be depleted.

Both interpretations of Largo Caballero's attitude can be reconciled by available evidence. That he was not completely duped by the Communists can be seen in that he refused to accept the unification of the Socialist and Communist parties. On the other hand his naïveté or duplicity is shown by the manner in which he kept Communist sympathizers as his chief advisers. Neither interpretation can be proven absolutely. But the fact still remains that no matter on what basis his policy was founded, it was unsuccessful. The Communists made very good use of him to gain their own ends and then discarded him when he would no longer serve their interests.

A Single Proletarian Party

The Communist hope for the unification of the proletariat into one massive proletarian party had always remained paramount—the next step to be achieved after the formation of the Popular Front government. The Communists had never ceased in their propaganda to urge upon the Socialists the need for going ahead with unity immediately. Though the policy of a United Front pact had been shelved, unity of the proletariat had not been forgotten. The Seventh Congress of the Comintern had designated it as the ultimate and final stage of the United Front program preparatory to the dictatorship of the proletariat. The idea of the unity of the proletariat, of course, was as old as both communism and socialism. From its inception the Comintern had been seeking this unification with, of course, the unified parties consolidated under its control.

In Spain, the steppingstones toward a united party had been carefully laid by the Communists—unification of the Socialist and Communist youth, the creation of the United Socialist Party of Catalonia, and the development of closer coöperation between the Socialists and Communists. By December, 1936, the Communists felt that the foundation had been completed and, in contrast to 1935 when the unity idea was first broached, they were now a party of some size with tremendous prestige throughout the country as a result of Soviet succor. Consequently, the Communists were ready to launch a new campaign for unity with the Socialists: "The eight months of war with all its lessons, the necessity to create conditions indispensable for the winning of the war within the present national and international situation, as well as the great tasks of building the economy and developing the expanded country after the victory demands above all the realization of this unity...."[3]

The example of the United Socialist Youth (*JSU*) was used to urge the Socialists to take action on the Communist request. Every effort was made to cover up Communist domination of the *JSU*. Santiago Carrillo, Secretary to the *JSU* and a Communist, declared:

The Socialist Youth and the Communist youth were unified creating a new organism which was no longer composed of the two youth movements but was a new Federation. And in this new Federation which was begun, neither the Communists, the Socialists, nor any elements of any political or union tendency can claim the right to direct or the right to govern the life of this organization of youth. Our federation is a new Federation ... we declare in the name of the Executive Committee that we consider to be absolutely consummated the process of unifying the Socialist Youth and the Communist Youth. By the dialectic of our unity we have created an organization of youth absolutely new, absolutely distinct from its predecessors.[4]

But neither the use of the dialectic explanation nor constant reiteration could convince the Socialists that the *JSU* was not a Communist organ. The only thing Socialist about it was its name. The example of the *JSU* more than anything else made Largo Caballero and the Socialists wary of unity with the Communists. In spite of the constant rumors by the Communists to the contrary,[5] there is no evidence that the Socialists even allowed the policy of unity to get into the negotiating stages.

Along with the policy of unity the Communists carried on an undercover program for more influence in the *UGT*. It was, after all, in the trade-unions that the Socialists had their real strength. Caballero's prestige and leadership among the Socialists were not based on his position in the party but on his position as Secretary-General of the *UGT*. Before the Civil War the Communists were able to control very few unions. Except for a small number in Madrid, Communist unions were almost nonexistent. In the early years of the Republic the Communists had formed a Communist Federation of Trade Unions (*CUGT*), but it did not prove very successful since it was so small as to be without much significance. At the end of 1935 the Socialist *UGT* allowed the few existing Communist trade-unions to adhere to its federation. Although the Communists hailed this as the beginning of the United Front, it had no effect on the *UGT* since there were so few Communist unions and since the Communists were not given a representative on the Executive Committee. It did, however, allow the Communists to use their association with the Socialist trade-unions to infiltrate the Socialist unions. By 1937, the Communists had made some gains by this process. The unionization of the various petty bourgeois proprietors, craftsmen, and professional men at the beginning of the Civil War also added greatly to the strength of the Communists in the *UGT* because their influence among the non-industrial workers was generally greater than that of the Socialists. By these methods, very early in the war they gained control of the *UGT* in Catalonia. In respect to the rest of Spain it is impossible to calculate exactly how many of the unions the Communists actually controlled by 1937. Many of the unions had Communist leadership and a Socialist membership and vice versa. Furthermore many of the leaders, although supporting the Communist line, were not considered members of the Communist party. It would seem from the evidence that as far as total union membership went the Communists were still a small minority, but in respect to the number of unions affiliated the proportion was much greater, though still far from a majority. The reason for the discrepancy in total individual membership versus the number of separate affiliated unions is that the strength of the Communists was in the small professional unions, as for example the dental union of about five hundred, compared with the large mass unions of industrial workers of several thousands supporting Caballero, as for example the Federation of Land Workers with about 750,000 members.

On the basis of their increased strength the Communists began pressing for new elections of the Executive Committee, on which there was not a single Communist. It had been agreed previously that elections for a new committee would not be held during the war. Nevertheless, the Communists, beginning as early as January, 1937, pressed for new elections on the basis that the old Executive Committee no longer represented the true reflection of *UGT* opinion. Antonio Mije, in the Central Committee of the Communist party, declared:

We, Communists, hold that we now have an indisputable right to participate in the direction of the *U.G.T.* It is not to be treated as a whim but a right which is the reflection of the enormous amount of influence which our party holds in the affiliates to the *U.G.T.* and within the middle ranks of the central [*U.G.T.*].[5]

The Communists hoped they not only would get some representation on the Executive Committee, but that in alliance with the right Socialists, they would have a majority. They claimed that three-quarters of the unions would support this alliance.[7] This claim is not without basis and was verified in part at least by the defeat of Caballero for Secretary-General of the *UGT* later in the year.[8] Largo Caballero, however, resisted all the Communists' efforts to bring about new elections.

The Communists' Changing Attitude toward the Anarchists

As has been seen in previous chapters the Communists and the Anarchists were poles apart in their aims and program. The enmity of Marx and Bakunin was as strong in 1936 as it had been at the time of the First International. The difference, however, was that the Communists were not intellectual revolutionaries as Marx had been. The Communists were operating in the sphere of power politics and hard political realities. Their ideology was not the absolute end and means it had been with Marx, but served the Communists as a guide to be overlooked when the realities of the situation made it inconvenient. Such was the case of the Communists' relations with the Anarchists in Spain. Although the Communists were bitterly antagonistic to *comunismo libertario*, they realized that an openly intransigent policy toward the Anarchists would prevent the defense of Loyalist Spain. The Communists, being a minority, dared not arouse the antagonism of any large groups. Consequently, the Communist policy was very ambivalent—on the one hand opposing the policies of revolution carried out by the Anarchists and on the other hand striving for closer coöperation with them. In order to attack the Anarchists and at the same time gain their coöperation, the Communists chose to distinguish between the various leaders of the Anarchists:

Some leaders of the Anarchists try, as they can, to carry out a better and more organized participation of the Anarchist workers, to lead them into a role in the People's Front and direct them into the real struggle against fascism. To this point they have accomplished little. On the other side others of the Anarchist leaders struggle to suppress those who side with other parties, especially fighting against the Communists.[9]

In attacking the Anarchists the Communists not only opposed them in their policies of collectivization of industry and agriculture but criticized them for their support of the "Trotskyite" *POUM* and for allowing Fascist agents to infiltrate the ranks of the *CNT*.[10]

It was during the first few months of the Civil War that Communist recriminations against the Anarchists were the most severe. The Anarchists at this time were straining every effort to put into effect their Libertarian program. It was partly out of fear of a rebel victory and the need to concentrate all effort on defense that the Communists, along with the other parties of the government, assailed the Anarchists' action:

... The transfer of the factories to separate groups of workers and scattered trade union federations would be a blow to the defense of the Republic. The task of serving the needs of the front cannot be solved along the lines of decentralizing the leadership of the economic life of the country. In addition, the seizure of the factories of the small and middle bourgeoisie would strike at circles which are today supporting the democratic republic and the People's Front. Such a measure could only drive these strata into the camp of reaction.... [11]

The entrance of the Anarchists into the government marked a sharp change in Anarchist policy. Probably the rapid initial victories of the rebels more than anything else made them realize that without victory of the government forces there was not a chance of success for their Libertarian revolution. Added to this were the difficulties with the peasants and bourgeoisie and their resistance to the Anarchist program, which had turned what the Anarchists had thought would be a glorious transformation into an economic chaos and a breakdown in the productive apparatus. Some of the collectivized factories worked very well, but the lack of raw materials and the absence of coördination over the whole economic system forced even the successful collectives to seek remedies through government plans and aid. To what extent the propaganda of the Communists and the pressure of other parties were responsible for the change in attitude is difficult to surmise. Certainly the antagonism of even the revolutionary parties, except the *POUM*, to their actions made the Anarchists realize that the fulfillment of the revolution would be all but impossible against the rising hostility.

Although the majority of the Anarchist leaders were in favor of slowing down the revolution, entering the government for defense against the rebels, and establishing a regular, centralized army, the minority and large segments of the rank and file still held to the old idea. The complete absence of discipline among the Anarchists made it virtually impossible to coerce these groups into coöperating with the government. In spite of efforts by the government and Anarchist leaders, there always remained a group among the Anarchists who refused to go along with the policies of the government and the majority, and who tenaciously held to their revolutionary policies and aims.

The results of the Anarchist change in policy were the signing of an agreement between the *UGT* and the *CNT*, the inclusion of Anarchists in the Generalitat, and the entrance of four Anarchists into the central government as already mentioned. The *UGT-CNT* agreement was signed on October 22, 1936. It was considered by the Communists, who controlled the Catalan *UGT*, an important step in the creation of a United Front in Catalonia. The pact contained the following main conditions:

1. We agree to carry out the resolutions and decisions of the Generalitat and use all the influence of our organizations to execute them.

2. We aspire to the collectivization of production, that is the expropriation without compensation of the capitalists and the transfer of private property to the Community. ... We do not wish the collectivization of the small proprietors, except those small proprietors who are found to be fascists, and except those needed in war production. In this case, the small proprietors must be compensated in such a manner that their living will be assured by their participation, according to their professions, in the collectivized works. All foreign owned industries will be taken with compensation.

* * *

4. We aspire for the ultimate concentration of all the forces for the final victory. We consider as a means of arriving at a single command, which will coordinate the activities of all the unified combatants, the creation of obligatory military service which will mark the beginning of a grand people's army, and the strengthening of discipline. All this will be completed by the creation of a grand industry of war. The organization of this industry will be directed in common by the *C.N.T.*, the *U.G.T.* and Ministries of Finance, of the Economy and of War.[12]

Other clauses included the nationalization of banks, the control of export, and freedom of action for the work of trade-unions. Absent from the agreement was consideration of the difficult problems of collectivization of agriculture, a matter on which the two groups could not agree. Although the alliance was not based on the nonrevolutionary war program of the Communists, who controlled the *UGT* in Catalonia, it was a significant shift in the antigovernmental and antibourgeois policies of the *CNT* to the protection of small proprietors and centralized control over the army and industry.

This reversal in the Anarchists' viewpoint brought an end to the acrimonious attacks on them by the Communists. The emphasis was now shifted to the fraternity between the two proletarian parties. The Russian Consul at Barcelona, Mr. Antonov Ovseenko, in an interview granted to the correspondent of the *Manchester Guardian* published on December 22, 1936, "expressed the greatest admiration for the Catalan workers, especially for the Anarcho-Syndicalists." He went on to speak in glowing terms of the work they were doing. When Buenaventura Durruti, a famous and colorful leader of the Anarchist militia, was killed in defending Madrid on November 20, 1936, José Díaz on behalf of the Central Committee of the Communist party sent a telegram of condolence:

We have learned with profound sorrow of the glorious death of our comrade Durruti, son of the working class, courageous defender of proletarian unity....[13]

The *UGT-CNT* agreement in Catalonia of October had been considered a step forward by the Communists, but before long they wanted the Anarchists to absorb even more of their program. The expansion of Communist power at the end of 1936 led to another drive to bring the Anarchists into line with the Communist policies. The first move was to get Anarchist approval for the removal of the *POUM* from the Catalan government. This was accomplished on December 16, 1936. The existence of the *POUM* had been energetically protected by the Anarchists, not because the programs of the two groups were similar but because the *POUM* supported immediate revolution and was the underdog suffering continuous attacks by the Communists.

The next step was to reopen discussions between the Communists and the Anarchists during December, 1936, and January, 1937, in an effort to gain better understanding. Even though the Communists declared these discussions a success, little in the way of concrete results ever developed from them.[14] The joint declarations published amounted to little more than pious declarations of friendship between the two working groups.[15]

TRADE-UNION UNITY

At the same time that the Communists were attempting to establish a united party with the Socialists and closer relations between themselves and the Anarchists, they were promoting closer coöperation between the Anarchists and Socialists through the unification of the *CNT* and *UGT*. The Communists realized that their foreign connections had made the Anarchists and Socialists shy away from close association with them. Such a suspicion was not involved, however, in bringing about the unity of the *UGT* and *CNT*. The Communists put into action all their propaganda devices to persuade the Anarchists and Socialists to create a single trade-union. At the time of Durruti's death in November, 1936, the Communists even attempted to enlist his popularity into their cause by declaring, "Durruti was an energetic supporter of the ultimate unification of the two industrial confederations."[16] In March, 1937, at the meeting of the Central Committee of the party, the Communists resolved that trade-union unity was one of their main tasks and required the immediate attention of all party cadres: "The syndical unity of the proletariat, once realized will be an event of maximum importance and will play a decisive and a very great role in the acceleration of a victorious end of the war as well as in the solution of the great problems of organizing the life of new Spain after the victory."[17] Unification of the trade-union movement, voluntarily brought about, had a lot of arguments in its favor both for winning the war and solving the deep division in the Republican camp. The Communists probably had two aims in striving for the single trade-union movement in Spain at this time. Their short-range aim was to influence the *CNT* to modify its revolutionary demands and accept the Communist nonrevolutionary war program supported by the Republicans and Socialists. The long-range aim was domination through infiltration, though the act of unity itself would have put them at least temporarily farther from this goal. They were still a minority in the *UGT* and in any combined union they would have been even more insignificant.

The idea of unity between the *UGT* and *CNT* was not new. As early as February, 1936, José Díaz had suggested, "Why not introduce into our conferences and congresses the problem of fusion of the *U.G.T.* and *C.N.T.*?"[18] At the time the idea was not within the realm of probability. Only when the policies of the unions had moved closer together in supporting the government and winning the war was such action feasible. But even then, at the beginning of 1937, it met with hostile reception from both federations. Pascual Tomás, Vice-Secretary of the *UGT*, summed up the feeling of the *UGT*:

... some five months of destructive war have modified the passions which both federations had during the days before the struggle and destroyed many of the prejudices ... [but] the fruit is not yet ripe enough to carry out complete fusion.[19]

The Anarchists, on their part, had moved as far right as they would go. The leaders, except a few, felt that another concession was impossible when they could not even bring all their supporters to sanction the step of entering the government. They declared, "unity of the *U.G.T.* and the *C.N.T.* cannot exist except as an idea between us. ..."[20] At the *FAI* congress during February, 1937, without exception all the representatives agreed that the time was inopportune and that neither the *CNT* workers nor the Socialist workers were in favor of the union. They nevertheless agreed that the watchword of the *CNT* would remain "revolutionary unity between the *U.G.T.* and the *C.N.T.*"[21]

The Communists were thus rebuffed again in their efforts to unify the working class by means of friendly persuasion. The Socialists and Anarchists remained suspicious both of the Communists and of each other. Coöperation in the government was as far as they were willing to go. The Communists, however, were not discouraged. They still had other means to gain their ends. Because of Soviet aid the prestige of the Communists was still high among the people and there was always the *GPU*.

CHAPTER XII

THE KLEBER INCIDENT

THE COMMUNISTS' first real play for more direct control over military operations and for a larger role in the government after the inauguration of Soviet aid apparently took place in January, 1937. By means of Soviet aid, the Communists' Fifth Regiment, and the International Brigade, the immediate danger to Madrid had been reduced and the war around Madrid had settled down to a long siege. The Communists were riding on a wave of popular enthusiasm emanating from gratitude for the saving of Madrid which resulted in a general renewal of Loyalist enthusiasm for the saving of the Republic. The Communists considered themselves the leader of this rally since they credited themselves with the sole responsibility for having saved Madrid. Thus, thinking themselves at the head of a popular movement they decided the time was opportune to make a bid for more power. The attempt revolved around General Emil Kleber, who was at the head of the International Brigade. By January, he had become the legendary hero of the siege of Madrid. The Communists had been letting the world know that it was the arrival of the International Brigade which saved Madrid in the nick of time.[1] Zugazagoitia describes how fame came to Kleber, "who arrived in Madrid surrounded by mystery and who left Madrid under the same mysterious conditions":

... A council of war was held on the very field of operations, not far from the enemy, in which Kleber won the adherence of the chiefs of the forces to his military plan. One of these chiefs, who knew his craft, was heard to say that the position of Kleber was, militarily, uniquely wise and feasible.[2]

Following the saving of Madrid, Kleber suggested to the command that the successful defense be turned into an offensive against Franco. General Miaja, who was head of the military Junta of Madrid, and the government had become jealous of Kleber's fame and refused to consider an attack at that time, claiming that the troops were not yet prepared to take the offensive. Simultaneously there were constant rumors that the Communists were going to attempt a *coup d'état* against the Caballero government using their newly won prestige and the International Brigade. It was also at this time that the Communists were pushing for unity with the Socialist party and for unity of the *CNT* and the *UGT*. All indications seemed to reveal that the Communists were riding the crest of popularity and were hoping to bring about a government crisis in order to put themselves and their allies into power.

If the Communists thought this an opportune moment they had calculated incorrectly. The Spanish, in their isolation from the rest of the world, had developed a strong feeling of antipathy toward foreigners. They did not like the idea being spread about, that Madrid had been saved by the foreigners in the International Brigade and under the leadership of a foreigner, General Kleber.[3] As a result General Miaja in his personal jealousy for Kleber found an ally in the sentiments of the Spanish people. Added to this antiforeign feeling among the Spaniards was the fear that the Communists might be attempting a coup. Consequently, the Spanish leaders were anxious to cut down to size the Communists' prestige and fame before it was too late. These motives combined to drive the Anarchists, who in all their relations with the government and army had remained aloof and suspicious in spite of their participation in Caballero's cabinet, to give their wholehearted support to Miaja against Kleber. Furthermore, both the right and left Socialists and the Republican parties rallied around Miaja against the foreigner. The Communists thus found themselves helpless and isolated. They knew that to attempt to control or enforce their demands without the alliance of at least the Republican parties would be to invite disaster and the victory of Franco.

The Communists gave in and Kleber was removed from his post, and surrendered to the mercy of his Spanish enemies, from whom he barely escaped. The Communist Fifth Regiment was merged into the regular army and an entirely Spanish Junta was appointed for the defense of Madrid. Another indication of Communist retreat was the recall, in February, of Marcel Rosenberg as Ambassador to the Loyalist government, and his replacement by the Counsellor of the Embassy, M. Gaikis.

The Kleber incident marked a sharp change in the policy of the Communists in Spain. Before this they had relied primarily on the popularity of Soviet aid and the appeal of their moderate program to maintain their strength. Likewise, they had considered the right Socialist and Republican parties strong allies who would help them carry out their program. They were disappointed in the Kleber crisis on both counts. From this date the tactics of the party changed and to accomplish their goals they no longer used primarily the forces of prestige and alliances but used terror to gain their ends when it was necessary.

CHAPTER XIII

A CHANGE IN COMMUNIST METHODS

THE END OF THE COMMUNIST-CABALLERO ALLIANCE

DURING THE first months of 1937, after the Kleber incident, the Communists withdrew their support from Largo Caballero not only because he backed General Miaja against Kleber but because of his persistence in resisting all Communist overtures to closer unity, and, even more, his refusal to put an absolute end to the revolution in Spain. Although he agreed to the necessity of unity and centralized control to win the war, he refused to reverse entirely the revolutionary program inaugurated by the parties of the extreme Left at the beginning of the war. Likewise, he refused to carry the attacks on the Anarchists and the *POUM*ists to the extent desired by the Communists. Although he was glad to undermine the control of the Anarchists in Catalonia, he was not willing to resort to terror against them and to the annihilation of the *POUM* altogether. In ending their support of Caballero the Communists sought an alliance with the right Socialists. Making use of Prieto's rivalry with Largo Caballero over the leadership and the program of the Socialists, the Communists hoped to unseat Largo Caballero from his dominant position in the *UGT* and in the government. The Communists, however, had to move cautiously. They did not dare attack Largo Caballero openly and were forced to wait until some unfavorable event occurred which could be turned against him. The prestige of Caballero was still very high following the successful defense of Madrid and the defeat of the Italians at Guadalajara in March, 1937.

TERROR AGAINST THE ANARCHISTS

The Communists, having failed to make an impression on the Anarchists with their program of unity, resorted to coercion and terror after the Kleber incident.[1] The main object of this method was to get rid of those elements in the *CNT* who sought to undo unity and to carry out the Libertarian revolution immediately, and also those who preached against the counterrevolutionary activities of the Communists. It was under the pretext of eliminating the "uncontrollables" that the campaign was carried out.[2] Doubtless there were "uncontrollables" and even rebel sympathizers among the Anarchists as the Communists claimed. The Anarchist method of recruitment was not the well-developed screening system used by the Communists and to a lesser extent by the Socialists.

Records and administrative procedure meant little to the proletarian followers of the Anarchists. To them men were proved by deeds; consequently they opened their doors to almost anyone who wanted to come in. The result was that many rebels sought to lose themselves in the mass unions of the *CNT*, waiting for the day of liberation and in the meantime stirring up trouble where they could among the Republicans. There is no doubt that some action was needed to screen the Anarchists. The government had begun the project but the Communists superimposed the *GPU* to make a thorough job of it. The Communists searched out not only uncontrollables, however; they also sought any anti-Communist elements and those who still resisted the nonrevolutionary program of winning the war first.

From February, 1937, on, the *Cheka* moved against the anti-Communist elements in the *CNT* and reports of this terror became more and more frequent. The Anarchists claimed that in the central region alone between February and May, 1937, eighty of their comrades were assassinated.[3] There were also frequent reports of Anarchists being imprisoned by the *GPU*, some of them prominent leaders such as Maroto, chief of the Anarchist militia in Almería and Alfredo Martínez, a leader of the Anarchist youth movement. The terroristic activities began to grow in intensity and hardly a day passed in Barcelona when several *CNT* members were not either assassinated or apprehended by the secret police. In these months there were more than one hundred and fifty unpunished murders in that city alone. As pointed out above, the attack was not a frontal assault on all Anarchists but was concentrated on those who resisted centralized control and those who had openly criticized the Communists. The Communists tried to allay the fears and ire of the rank and file Anarchists by saying the purge was not against the body of Anarchists but only against certain minorities. José Díaz declared:

We want closely to cooperate with the Anarchists not only during the war but after the victory. We must fight side by side with the Anarchist comrades against the lawless buccaneering of numerous "uncontrolled groups." Many such groups use the name of the Anarchists. But it would not be right to attribute to the C.N.T. as an organization the lawless acts committed by the "uncontrolled" elements. . . .[4]

Special attention was always given by the *Cheka* to the foreign Anarchists, whom the Communists considered the most dangerous. The outstanding example of such an attack was the murder of Professor Camillo Berneri, who was an Italian Anarchist. Berneri had been greatly honored as an Anarchist philosopher by the Anarchists in Spain and they considered his opinion of great value. Berneri, from the beginning, had been openly hostile to the Communists and to the Russians. Throughout the war he wrote a number of articles condemning any coöperation with the Communists and attributing to the Russians aggressive motives. He was particularly opposed to the Stalinist regime in Russia. "Stalinism is," he wrote, "nothing more than remnants of the Leninist approach to the political problems of the social revolution. To attack the effects without getting at the causes, at the basic faults of Bolshevism (bureaucratic dictatorship merged with a dictatorship of the party) is to simplify arbitrarily the chain of causes which stretches from the dictatorship of Lenin to that of Stalin having no profound solutions linked by continuity."[5] In respect to the situation in Spain he wrote:

Already today, Spain is between two fires: Burgos and Moscow.... The policies of Madrid are on the point of success. She had refused arms and money to Catalonian revolutionaries in order to put herself into the hands of the U.S.S.R. who has furnished arms and staffs destined to control the antifascist struggle and stop the development of the social revolution in its struggle against fascism.

The dilemma: "Madrid or Franco" has paralyzed Spanish Anarchism. Today, Barcelona is situated between Burgos, Rome, Berlin, Madrid and Moscow. Besieged.[6]

The Communists would not allow such polemics against themselves and when the terror was at its height against the Anarchists, on May 5, 1937, Berneri was arrested and shot by the city police of Barcelona in conjunction with the members of the *GPU*.

Coercion against the Anarchists was not only in the form of terror, but pressure was applied to get the Anarchists out of high positions in the government and generally reduce the effectiveness of their control. On March 1, 1937, the Generalitat reorganized the Department of Public Order abolishing the Workers' Patrols and putting all armed power in the hands of the regular police. On March 12, the Valencia government ordered all parties and trade-unions to collect arms from their members and surrender them within forty-eight hours. This decree was aimed mostly at the Anarchists who were alleged to have large caches of arms around Barcelona. Furthermore, pretexts were found to close several of the Anarchist newspapers during this period: the *Nosotros*, an *FAI* publication in Valencia, was suspended on February 27; *C.N.T. del Norte* at Bilbao was seized by the Basque government on March 26; and the *C.N.T.* of Madrid and *Castille Libre* were temporarily suspended on April 11.

After the Loyalists were defeated in 1939, the émigrés generally attributed this attack in 1937 to the Communists exclusively, but from the evidence it would appear they had accomplices. It may be true that the

Communists instigated the terror and took an active lead in it, but in their activities they received the coöperation and assistance of the Socialist and Republican groups. The Socialists and Republicans both feared and hated the Anarchists. They were extremely anxious during the Civil War to reduce their strength for fear of a violent Anarchist revolution following a successful conclusion of the war. As Franz Borkenau reported in January, 1937, in his book, *The Spanish Cockpit,* "both sides notoriously kept large numbers of armed men back in Valencia—not on account of the local situation, but because it was supposed that here the issue would be fought out for the republican camp as a whole."[7]

A further indication of the strong antipathy between the Anarchists and the Republicans was the open declaration by Azaña and other Republicans during January, 1937,[8] that they were against any further revolution and supported parliamentary democracy as the ultimate end of the Civil War. This was practically an affirmation of war on the Anarchists and to a limited degree on Caballero's government, since Caballero was in favor of further revolution when the war was won against Franco.

The Socialists even supported the terrorist action against the Anarchists. The Communist propaganda against "uncontrollables" among the *CNT* was echoed day after day in the Socialist press.[9] Furthermore, Largo Caballero took no concrete steps to stop the reign of assassinations and kidnappings, and his government actually participated in several of the arrests of "uncontrollables." Likewise, it was his government that passed the various decrees designed to disarm the Anarchists and bring their police and militia under the regular control of the government forces.

It is also significant that the Anarchists, at the time, in condemning and accusing those who perpetrated this war on them, indicated not only the Communists as ringleaders, but in Catalonia put the blame equally on the Esquerra, and in the rest of Spain on the Republicans and "the Socialist Party without distinction of factions, from Indalecio Prieto to Largo Caballero."[10]

"THE TROTSKYITE TRAITORS"

The bitterest spleen of the Communists was always saved for the *POUM.* This small party of Left Communists with only a few thousand members was the demonophobia of the Communists.[11] More pique of the Communist propaganda was aimed at the *POUM* regardless of its small size than against all the other parties put together.[12] The *POUM* had a following mainly in Catalonia and a few scattered cells in the rest of Spain. Yet it was a constant source of irritation to the Communists for several reasons. It opposed the Communist policies and aims from the beginning and attempted to expose them to the world as the opportunistic means to Communist domination of Spain. The *POUM*ists fought for revolution immediately and condemned the Communists and bourgeoisie as counterrevolutionaries. But most important, the Communists considered them renegades and traitors to the Communist cause, and for the same reasons that anti-Stalinists in Russia were feeling the torturers' wrath, they too felt it in Spain. Zugazagoitia described it as "transplanting to Spain, the violent quarrel of legal Communism, Leninist-Stalinist, against the opposition, Trotskyism, which had such regrettable repercussions."[13]

The activities against the *POUM* did not end with its elimination in December, 1936, from the Generalitat in Catalonia, the *POUM*ists' only position of power. During January and February the various newspapers and radio stations of the *POUM* outside Catalonia were seized. In Barcelona, where the *POUM* was under the protecting wing of the *CNT*, the Communists still dared not bring about the suppression of the *POUM*'s newspaper, *Batalla*, and its radio station.

By March, 1937, the Communists had actually declared open war against the *POUM*ists. "The enemies of the people are the fascists, the Trotskyites and the 'uncontrollables'." The *POUM*ists were declared to be traitors and the agents of fascism:

Our principal enemy is fascism. We are concentrating all the vigor and hatred of the people against it. We are setting against it all forces ready to destroy it, but our hatred with the same degree of concentrated force, is likewise being leveled against the agents of fascism, who are the *POUM*ists, disguised Trotskyites, who hide themselves behind the pretended slogans of revolutionaries in order to carry out their major mission of agents of our enemies lurking in our own territory.[14]

In their attack on the *POUM* the Communists made some attempt to separate the rank and file members from the leaders by saying that the members actually did not support the anticommunist line of Nin, who was merely following the orders of Trotsky,[15] but such tactics proved ineffectual because there was no indication that the membership ever disagreed with the leadership in the *POUM*.

The intransigent and bloodthirsty attitude of the Communists toward the *POUM* gave rise to a great deal of criticism by the parties of the Left both in Spain and outside. The Socialists and the Anarchists both criticized this war on the *POUM*. They declared it to be destroying the unity of the Popular Front. The Communists, however, whenever called upon to defend their terroristic methods, always met these criticisms with further acts of persecution against the *POUM*. Georgi Dimitrov answered the criticism of the Second International against the purges in Russia which were overflowing into Spain:

... They [Citrine and the Second International] try to create the impression that the trial of the counter-revolutionary terrorists in the Soviet Union endangers the fulfillment of this proletarian solidarity with the Spanish people. But this is an obvious lie.

The trial of the terrorists, agents of fascism, is an integral part of the anti-fascist struggle of the international working class. True solidarity with the Spanish people is not compatible with the protection of agents of fascism in other countries. One cannot sincerely support the Spanish people, which is fighting against fascism, and at the same time play the part of protector of the terrorist rabble in the Soviet Union which is helping fascism....[16]

Against the Anarchist criticism along the same line *Pravda* retorted:

The central organ of the Anarchists in Barcelona, *Solidaridad Obrero*, carried in its March 6 issue, an insulting attack on the Soviet press. It is significant that the writer directs his attack more particularly at those reports in the Soviet press which related to the counter-revolutionary activities of the Trotskyist *P.O.U.M.*, and made the assertion that 'these injurious tactics are meant merely to arouse dissension in the ranks of the anti-Fascist front in Spain.'

This obscene defense of the Trotskyist traitors proceeds from those shady elements which have sneaked into the ranks of the Anarcho-Syndicalist organization....[17]

In their oppression of the *POUM*, the Communists made full use of the facilities of the *GPU*, as they had with the Anarchists. All members of the *POUM* were subject to arrest, secret trials, and even execution with no chance to defend themselves.

The Communists and the Bourgeoisie

Although the relations between the Communists and the revolutionary parties of the Left were strained during most of the war, their contact with the Republican parties of the bourgeoisie was always very amicable and rarely was there any disagreement between the two groups. The Communists made every effort to keep on good terms with these parties and win their support against the "uncontrollable" revolutionaries. José Díaz, in his speech to the Central Committee of the Communist Party on March 5, 1937, in which he attacks Caballero's government and certain elements of the Anarchists, has the following to say about the Republicans:

We maintain good relations with the Republicans. The Republicans have consciously participated in the great anti-fascist movement hand in hand with the proletariat. They knew in advance that they were fighting not for an abstract republic but for a new type of republic. The Republicans, the petty bourgeoisie, have suffered as much as the proletariat from the semi-feudal oppression of the ruling section — landowners, bankers and the military clique. They fight nobly and bravely at the front, and are capably carrying out leading work in the economic and political life of our country.... This position [of Azaña and Martínez Barrío, whose speeches are quoted] reflects the comprehension by the republicans, and the republican parties of the necessity of cooperation with all the forces of the Popular Front and with all the working forces who are represented on the Popular Front. This position proves that the alliance between the forces of the proletariat and those of the petty bourgeoisie has a firm political basis. It is the duty on our part to see that this basis is never undermined. (Great Applause).[18]

The Communists and bourgeoisie also were in complete agreement as to the policies the government was to follow. Azaña declared in January, 1937:

... we need a war policy, both on the battle front and behind the lines. A war policy which has only one expression, discipline and obedience to the responsible Government of the Republic. (Hear, hear.) ... For I am never tired of saying that there is only one manner of waging this war, the one which leads to victory, and that is the one which we must pursue. There are no two ways of organizing an army, and a war is won with a well-organized army....[19]

The Republicans, although fully supporting the Communist war program, were critical of the extreme terrorism being carried out by the Communists. Furthermore, the predominance of Communists in some of the more important positions of the government alarmed them but it never resulted in a rift during this period up to May, 1937. The bourgeoisie were glad to have a strong ally against the revolutionary Left which they feared almost more than Franco. They realized that the Communists were becoming a very powerful influence in the government, but many felt that the Communists had truly adopted democratic methods and would not use their newly gained position to the detriment of the bourgeoisie. Others felt that the Communists' authority was only temporary, lasting merely as long as the Soviet Union was the sole great power ally of the Republic, and in support of this prediction they pointed to the weakness of the Communists before the Civil War.

Reasons for the *Cheka* Terror

The Communist campaign of discrediting and terrorizing the Anarchists and *POUM* was not based so much on sadism or a religious zeal to convert the revolutionaries to communism as it was motivated toward a political maneuver to bring Catalonia under Communist and the central government's control. By breaking the strongest single political force in Catalonia, the Anarchists, they hoped to subjugate this important industrial province. Although the Communists had been very successful in carrying out their policies in the central government, Catalonia still had not been mobilized to the Communists' satisfaction in the fight against Franco. Juan Comorera, leader of the *PSUC*, describes the Communist feeling about Catalonia:

... Catalonia has not understood and has not been able to do its duty in the war. It has not been able to organize a regular army. It has not been able to apply itself to the needs of the moment, which is to give aid to the men who fight in the Basque country, Madrid, and Andalusia; nor to co-operate as it is necessary to do for the victory of the people. It has not been able to organize its economic life in accordance with the needs of war and its own revolution. It has not even been able to make the struggle against the invader the fundamental question which it ought to be. Catalonia has stood apart; it has been a disturbing element in the Republic; it has been a burden to the Republic.[20]

By the integration of Catalonia with the rest of Spain the Communists hoped to build a defense industry to supply the Loyalist forces and to obtain reserve manpower to build up the armed forces to defeat Franco. Up to this point Catalonia had acted as almost an independent government and had refused to carry her share in the defense of the Republic, even failing to mobilize an army. The Communists complained:

... Catalonia ... could have done much more for the defense of Madrid which at that moment was the central task. At the time when Franco was drawing off from all fronts reserve troops for action in the direction of Madrid, Catalonia did not show the proper initiative. Only under the influence of the blow received by the Republic caused by the fall of Málaga and the direct danger for Catalonia (the bombing of Barcelona) did the Catalonian Government decide to put into action the decree for mobilization....[21]

Since the Franco troops nowhere directly threatened their borders, the Catalonians of all classes had not felt the pressing need of fighting the Nationalists and building an armament industry. The Anarchists in Catalonia were more interested in revolution than in defense, whereas the Esquerra was more concerned with preserving its property against expropriation and in protecting the newly won Catalan autonomy from encroachment by the central government. The Catalan government ignored the orders and pleas of the central government. There were even frequent rumors that Catalonia would seek complete independence from Valencia and make a separate peace with Franco or seek to be recognized as independent by the French government, hoping that France would protect her territorial integrity from the rebels. The German Ambassador to France reported to the German Foreign Ministry in October, 1936, that the French were considering very seriously recognizing the independence of Catalonia.[22] Any attempt they may have made, however, to come to an agreement with Franco on the basis of preserving Catalan autonomy would only have met with frustration since Franco was a strong believer in central control and was in no mood to compromise with any of the Republican groups as long as he had German and Italian aid to help him defeat the Loyalists.[23] It was against this threat of separation and failure to coöperate with the Valencia government that the Communists aimed their attack against Catalonia by undermining the strength of the Anarchists.

By purging the Anarchists the Communists hoped to establish the hegemony of the *PSUC* (United Socialist Party of Catalonia) over Catalonia in alliance with the Esquerra. In doing this the Communists, however, wanted to be sure that the real power was in the hands of their party, the *PSUC*, and not the Esquerra. The Esquerra, although it was a middle-class and peasant party, was too much in favor of complete Catalonian autonomy which the Communists opposed in fact, if not in their propaganda.

The Communists also had other reasons for their purge of the extreme Left. They were interested in bringing the only remaining land contact with France, along the Catalan-French border, under the central government's control. Since the beginning of the war it had been under the control of the Anarchists who sequestered most of the goods which came across the border, stopped many of the nonrevolutionaries and Communist supporters, and allowed in many foreign revolutionaries who were anti-Stalinists and hoped to find in Spain their revolutionary utopia.

For their own personal satisfaction the Communists also wanted to see the complete annihilation of the *POUM*. This small dissident Communist movement never posed a really serious revolutionary threat to the war program of the government and the Communists, but the political enmity of the Communists demanded its complete liquidation.

In their attacks the Communists also hoped to divide and discredit the revolutionary Left all over Spain so that it could no longer threaten the Communist program. Once this had been done, the final features of the Anarchist and left Socialist revolution could be destroyed and the program of the Communists and their allies would have complete sway.

Most likely the Communists also hoped that in any government crisis which might ensue as a result of their activities, Caballero would be so discredited that it would be possible to eliminate him as head of the government. They would then replace him with someone more conservative who did not insist upon continuing the gains accomplished by the revolutionaries early in the Civil War, and was not in favor of protecting the left-revolutionary elements.

CHAPTER XIV

THE MAY CRISIS

"The Barcelona Revolt"

THE CULMINATION of the Communist purge of the revolutionary Left came in May, 1937. A crisis had slowly developed throughout March and April of 1937. The *Cheka* terror had aroused the anger of all the Anarchists and the *POUM*, and the growing severity of the attacks had alarmed many of them for the safety of the whole revolutionary Left. The factions most outspoken in the need for action to protect the revolution from encroachment and annihilation by the Communists and the government were the Libertarian Youth, a youth group of the *FAI*, and the Friends of Durruti, along with the members of the *POUM*. These groups began to retaliate with assassinations of Communists.

The conflict first appeared openly in governmental circles in the Generalitat on March 27, when the representatives of the *UGT* resigned in protest at the refusal of the Anarcho-Syndicalist Minister of Defense to apply the mobilization decree issued by Valencia in Catalonia. Negotiations for a new Council for Catalonia went on for three weeks, the Communists insisting that all the decrees of the preceding ministries should be carried out including mobilization, disarmament of the workers, and unification of the police. The Anarchists persistently refused, fearing a further retreat of the revolution. The new Council, which was finally formed, was similar to the previous one, each party holding the same proportion of seats. The new Council, however, had not come to an agreement on the basic issues and compromise was even farther away than before. Feelings between the *PSUC* and the Anarchists began to run dangerously high. On April 25, Roldán Cortada, secretary to one of the *UGT* Councilors, was killed. A few days later this was followed by the murder of Antonio Marti, who was a leading Anarchist and the mayor in the large village of Puigcerdá on the French border. It is significant that Marti's band had been in control of the customs and had only recently been replaced by customs guards of the Valencia government. Feelings throughout Spain had become so strained that all May Day demonstrations were banned for fear of riots.

Another move of the Valencia government and its vanguard, the *PSUC*, was to bring the People's Courts in Catalonia under the regular system of justice used in the rest of Spain, thus further limiting the control of the revolutionary leaders. The next step taken by the central government and the Communists, leading to the complete incorporation of Catalonia into the program of all Spain, proved to be too much for the *POUM* and the more virulent elements among the Anarchists to accept. Since the previous October they had watched their revolutionary accomplishments and control gradually give way before the pressure of the Republican bourgeoisie, represented in Catalonia by the Esquerra, the *PSUC*, and the forces of the central government. The capitulation had reached its peak in April and May, 1937, and these groups felt that to give way another step would sacrifice the revolution for good. Even after a victory over Franco, they would have been too weak to reassert their control. Consequently, when the police arrested several *CNT* members for the murder of Roldán Cortada and then on May 3, moved to take over the Telephone Exchange Building in Barcelona, the more radical groups of the Left rose.

The *CNT* had been in control of the Telephone Exchange Building in the center of Barcelona since the first days of the revolt and all efforts by the Generalitat to dislodge it had been futile. As a result, the *CNT* had complete control over almost all telephone communications in Catalonia. On the afternoon of May 3, the Director of Public Security, Rodrígues Salas of the *PSUC*, sent a police patrol to relieve the *CNT* of control of the building which it refused to do voluntarily. This was the spark igniting an outbreak of hostilities all over Barcelona, a city long used to rioting and open warfare. Each group brought out its hidden stores of arms, including machine guns and tanks, and set up barricades and gun emplacements to protect its particular section of the city. Uprisings also broke out in Tarragona and Gerona.

The resistance of the revolutionaries was doomed to failure from the beginning when the vast majority of the leaders of the *CNT* decided not to support an armed uprising as long as the Civil War was in progress. This left primarily the *POUM*, the Libertarian Youth, and the Friends of Durruti as the core to fight against the police, the *PSUC*, and 5,000 assault guards from Valencia, who arrived toward the end of the uprising. In spite of the opposition of the leaders to the uprising, many of the rank and file Anarchists also participated with the revolutionaries against the government.

The police on the afternoon of May 3, had not been successful in taking the Telephone Building, except the ground floor. By that night most sections of the city, especially the suburbs, were in the hands of the workers barricaded for protection. The government was in control only in the area around the government offices.

One of the participants described the opening of the first real day of the struggle on May 4:

... The housewives went out in order to get in their provisions, then returned rapidly to their homes while the merchants who had opened their doors hastily closed them again. The streets, one moment alive, again became empty and those people who had been bold enough to show themselves at the windows were begged, politely but in a tone which would not permit a refusal, to immediately close them again and to retire into the interior of the apartment. This was done without wasting time. And the battle began....[1]

The fighting was conducted mostly in house-to-house combat and from behind barricades. By the evening of the first day the representatives of the *UGT* and the *CNT* called on both sides to cease fire until a compromise could be reached. From Valencia the Anarchist Ministers, Garcia Oliver and Federica Montseny, rushed to the scene to try to persuade the participants to listen to reason. Garcia Oliver, in his plea, declared: "A wave of folly has passed over the city. It is necessary to put an end immediately to this fratricidal struggle. Let each remain in his position without trying to use the truce in order to conquer the others. The Government is going to be reunited and will take the necessary measures. ..."[2]

From Aragon came a section of the Durruti column and five hundred soldiers from the *POUM* militias. They assembled near Lérida and prepared to march in help of their comrades in Barcelona, but they were persuaded to stop when it was found that the Anarchist leaders were not in support of the rising and when the government threatened to move troops against them and also against Barcelona if they did not return to the front.

In the meantime, the regional leadership of the *CNT-FAI* had met and decided to use all its efforts to bring about a truce as rapidly as possible. The *POUM*, on the other hand, continued to call for resistance to the government and was supported by the Friends of Durruti. During the nights of May 4 and 5 negotiations were carried on between the Valencia government, the *UGT*, and the *CNT* which resulted in an armistice and a joint appeal by all groups for an immediate cease fire.[3] The Friends of Durruti countered with a leaflet calling upon the workers not to leave the streets and for death to all those responsible. The *CNT* leadership completely disavowed the leaflet[4] and as a result the workers gradually left the barricades during May 5 and 6. On May 6 even the *POUM* issued the call, "back to work, but be on your guard." By May 9 the uprising had completely subsided. The casualties had been high, running into several hundreds—the deaths alone were estimated at anywhere from two hundred to eight hundred and fifty. The conclusion was a truce in name only; it was really a defeat of the revolutionary elements which the main body of the Anarchists had failed to support. The results of their failure had very profound consequences in Catalonia, as will be seen. In spite of the defeat, however, the ferocity of the struggle shows that had the *CNT* been united behind it, the uprising would have developed into very serious proportions which could have led to a civil war within a civil war. The Anarchist leadership showed both patriotism to the Republic and restraint by coöperating with the government in bringing about an immediate cease-fire.

THE ANARCHISTS ACCUSE

After the fighting subsided the battle of bullets was replaced by the battle of words—each side accusing the other of a plot. Several groups among the Anarchists began publishing evidence of a government-Communist plot, including speeches by government officials alluding to the subjugation of the *CNT-FAI*, documents purporting to be plans for plots by the *PSUC* against the Anarchists, and reported meetings of Comorera with Fascist agents.[5] None of the evidence was well enough substantiated to be considered too seriously. A further unconfirmed story, which was widely spread about, was that on March 5, the *PSUC*, by means of forged documents, secured ten armored cars from the Barcelona arsenal in preparation for the revolt.[6]

One accusation of the Anarchists, however, which was difficult for the Communists to refute, was the claim: "The action of Rodríquez Salas and Ayguadé of sending the guards [in an attempt to seize the Telephone Exchange Building], was not legal. The proof is that when the Council of the Generalitat reassembled, it recognized that the Chief of Police and Councilor of Internal Security had overstepped their powers."[7] This indictment could easily have been refuted if it had been false, but neither the government nor the Communists challenged this statement.

The idea that the May 3 plot was preconceived on the part of the central government and the *PSUC* is really only a half truth. They certainly consciously worked toward the integration of Catalonia into the general Republican defense system and wanted to eliminate the independent actions of the Anarchists in particular. This they had freely admitted in their announced program which called for just such a coordination. Likewise, all the actions and decrees of the Valencia government and the Communists during the spring of 1937 had been in this direction.[8] In pushing their aims they must have realized too that there was a good chance the Anarchists would not accept an unlimited amount of coercion and would attempt to fight it. As a result this made it necessary to be prepared for the worst by having troops and arms ready, which available evidence indicates was the case. That the action of May 3 was an attempted coup, on the other hand, does not seem probable, because neither the police nor the *PSUC* were alerted for the uprising. It would seem rather that the attempt to take over the Telephone Exchange Building was just one more act in the gradual disarmament and subjugation of the Anarchists by the nonrevolutionary elements of the Republic.

The bitter recriminations by some groups of the Anarchists against the Communists and government were not supported by all sections of the *CNT*, particularly those which had favored participation in the government in the first place. They tended to shift the blame on some unidentified "foreign element."

We recall also that during the events of May 1937 the executive of the *U.G.T.* found itself immediately in agreement with the Central Committee of the *C.N.T.* because it well understood that the provocation of Barcelona had not been the work of the *C.N.T.* or the *U.G.T.* nor that of the workers, but was clearly that of ambitious politicians and politicasters from well identified sectors who were attempting to introduce foreign methods in Spain.[9]

This moderate group among the Anarchists, however, did deplore the recriminations being made by the Communists who were accusing sections of the Anarchists and the *POUM* of being Fascist agents. The editorial in the Anarchist newspaper *Solidaridad Obrero* on May 13, 1937, admonished the Communist paper *Mundo Obrero* for its attitude:

We are engaged in a task of pacification. If we want to restore the lost tranquillity to the region of Catalonia, we must do so without the tone of Jupiter adopted by the organ of the Communist Party of Spain.

In Madrid, perhaps, the origin of the affair is not known very well. But in Barcelona we all know the original causes. And the best that we can do is for each of us to assume part of the responsibility, without trying to put it all on our neighbor. We know all the truth in Catalonia. And out of this knowledge should come the formula to re-establish calm and facilitate the immediate repair of the splits that arose in our anti-fascist bloc.

The Communists, it is true, carried their recriminations to the extreme and in their accusations of treason were not too careful this time to distinguish between the main body of the *CNT* and the extreme elements which had supported the uprising. Juan Comorera, for example, asserted concerning the events of May, "The correct political line put forward by us, and the concepts and actions which have been rejected, are those put forward by the *F.A.I.*"[10] He overlooked the fact that the Regional Committee of the *FAI* had supported the government. This was, however, part of the Communists' strategy—to use the Barcelona uprising to discredit the whole Anarchist movement.

AN ANTI-COMMUNIST PLOT?

The Communists declared, "it was a premeditated act, an act from which concrete results were desired—in the first place these irresponsibles sought to recover from their political defeats; to subject the *U.G.T.* to violence; to eliminate the *P.S.U.[C.]* from the political life of the country, and lastly to bring pressure from Catalonia on the Government of the Republic to do the same."[11] The accusation that the revolters wanted to be rid of the Communist domination was certainly true, but it is doubtful whether it was a preconceived plot. The Communists went so far as to allege that the Barcelona uprising was a Fascist plot carried out basically by their chief "agent provocateur" on the Republican side, the *POUM*. Their line of argument was: "What order could Franco, or more exactly Hitler, have given his agents in Republican Spain with a view to paralyzing the Republican troops, the war industry and the whole life of the country? It could have been no other than this: 'Do everything possible to introduce schisms, to reduce confidence in the government, to effect acts of sabotage, to engage in assassination, and if possible in *putsches*, try all possible means to weaken the armed forces of the republic and the war industry.' "[12] Although such accusations against the extreme Left seem fantastic and on the same pattern as those used in Russia where Trotsky, Zinoviev, Bukharin, and others were declared to be agents of Nazism, there is an interesting item of evidence which might support the Communist imputation. The German Ambassador to Franco's government reported to his superior as follows:

As for the disorders in Barcelona, Franco informed me that the street fighting had been started by his agents. As Nicolás Franco further told me, they had in all some 13 agents in Barcelona. One of these had given the information a considerable time ago that the tension between the Anarchists and Communists was so great in Barcelona that he would guarantee to cause fighting to break out there. The Generalissimo told me that he had not at first placed confidence in the statements of this agent but had then had them checked by others, who had confirmed them. He had intended at first not to make use of this possibility until a military operation against Catalonia was begun. Since the Reds, however, had recently attacked at Teruel in order to relieve the Euzkadi Government, he had judged the present moment to be right for the outbreak of disorders in Barcelona. Actually the agent had succeeded, within a few days of receiving such instruction, in having street shooting started by three or four persons, and this had then produced the desired success.[13]

This evidence can be considered only circumstantial. The agents were not by any means necessarily members of the *POUM* and the very fact that Franco claimed only thirteen agents in Barcelona proves that the mass of the *POUM* membership could not have been implicated as Fascist agents. It would be equally possible to claim that the agents were in the *PSUC*. It is even plausible that the agents were not members of any party or trade-union whatsoever. This bit of evidence does serve to show, however, that the charge of Fascist treason by both sides cannot be dismissed lightly, though as the rebels themselves admitted the basic cause was still the difference between the Anarchists and the antirevolutionary parties of the government.

THE ALLIES OF THE COMMUNISTS

To impute to the Communists the role of being the only "agents provocateurs" in the government against the Anarchists and the *POUM* is a distortion of the truth. Caballero, leader of the left Socialists, sanctioned, if by nothing other than his silence, the actions carried out by his government against the Anarchists and urged by the Communist party. He did, however, refuse until May 7, to sanction the sending of shock troops against the Anarchist dissidents in Barcelona.[14] Indalecio Prieto, leader of the right Socialists, was openly active in his support. In a letter to Fernando de los Ríos on May 25, he is quoted as saying:

... Finally there is the resolved part which is the most important, the cleaning up of our rearguard. In Barcelona as in all the surrounding provinces, the machinery of the *F.A.I.* and the *C.N.T.* has today been disarticulated; their most dangerous elements are dead or prisoner. What is still more important is that those who return to reason are today satisfied or at least appeased. The cleaning, however, is not yet complete. But with the strongest resistance broken it will be very easy to carry out a repression without violence and without effort but so effectively that in a short time the work will be achieved. We still fear, however, that the brigades of these elements who are still actually on the front will abandon it in order to rush to the aid of their organizations. But I believe that they will not dare. Besides it will be very difficult for them to organize such a movement. We have further decided to proceed on various fronts with a series of offensives in which we will employ first the elements of the *F.A.I.* and the *C.N.T.* as troops of the first wave. We have decided also to transfer these elements into the most dangerous sectors. In this way the factions themselves will aid in carrying out the complete cleansing for which we must be grateful to them.[15]

Although the validity of this letter cannot be vouched for, the actions of Prieto would confirm it. He fully coöperated with the suppression of the uprising by sending troops and ships to Barcelona and favored the subjugation of the Anarchists to the unity and discipline of the army.

THE CONSEQUENCES OF THE BARCELONA REVOLT

Prieto's letter above gives an indication of the activities on the part of the central government which followed the suppression of the Barcelona uprising. Even before the uprising was over the central government had sent 5,000 assault troops, in spite of vague promises to the Anarchist militias that if they remained on the front the government would not send troops. These assault guards arrived after most of the fighting had ceased, but they immediately took over control of the city. Meanwhile, as early as May 6, under the terms of the Autonomy Statute, the Valencia or central government had taken over control from the Generalitat, appointing its own ministers. In spite of the questionable activities of Ayguadé and Rodríguez Salas in ordering the seizure of the Telephone Exchange Building and the enmity they aroused among the workers, the central government allowed them to keep their positions and lead the cleaning up and the persecution of those who had "perpetrated" the rising. Under their direction a wave of arrests began throughout Catalonia. Although Valencia's control over Catalonia was to be only temporary, the government leaders saw to it that the independence of Catalonia was never reasserted. The Ministry of Defense of the Generalitat, even in theory, was never allowed to function again and it was absorbed directly into the Defense Ministry of the central government. To be sure of continued control the central government was moved from Valencia to Barcelona in November, 1937.

At the same time the government moved in and took over the Aragon front. The defense of Aragon at the beginning of the war had been taken over by the Catalonians and especially the Anarchists. They also had taken upon themselves the task of government in that portion of Aragon still remaining to the Republic, and this had become their own special domain. All subsequent efforts on the part of the central government to bring the front and the province under its control had failed. But when Catalonia was temporarily weakened by the suppression following the Barcelona revolt, the central government moved into Aragon, dissolved its Council, and brought it under central command. The various collectives, particularly the farm collectives, were disbanded and declared illegal. Communist and other government troops were moved in to be dispersed among the Catalan troops to insure their loyalty to the new command.

In order to secure their newly won positions, the government and the Communists extended their attacks on the Anarchists to new extremes. On May 14, the government issued a proclamation ordering the surrender of all arms, other than those held by the Popular Front army, within seventy-two hours. Although the government had issued such decrees before, this time the law was vigorously carried out. Furthermore, the police, contrary to the spirit of the armistice, began rounding up any persons who had had any connection with the rising and put them into prison. The Communist *Cheka* also was very active in this business, and in apprehending collaborators in the uprising—its definition of an accomplice being very broad and its justice swift and arbitrary.

Another action against the Anarchists was the closing of their presses, newspapers, and radio. These were allowed to reopen only if they adhered to strict censorship which allowed for no criticism against the government. As a result, all Anarchist publications of any importance or interest had to be mimeographed and distributed surreptitiously. In the same repressive spirit large mass meetings were prohibited.

The Reaction of the Anarchists

The remarkable aspect of the May days and their aftermath was the attitude taken by the majority of the Anarchists. From the beginning they preached moderation and coöperation with the government. It is true that they shifted the blame of the uprising onto certain elements of the government, in particular the Minister of Interior of the Generalitat, Ayguadé, who "did everything in his power in order to disarm the members of the *C.N.T.* and the *F.A.I.* with the aid of adherents of certain parties, in order to break the revolutionary power of the unions of the *C.N.T.* and the *F.A.I.* which constitute the best guarantee of the working people...."[16] Comparatively speaking, however, this accusation was very mild. This attitude of temperance by the Anarchists was continued in respect to the subsequent repression of their followers.

Forbearance. There was no other alternative. We were suffering the consequences of our own inexperience and the excess of sanguineness of our movement. It was inevitable that the new Government would apply the decree concerning the disarmament of the rearguard, approved two months previously and directed now especially against us, the force which rose up in arms against the Governments of the Generalitat and Valencia in which we formed a part.[17]

What was even more surprising was that there was no resistance to the invasion of Aragon by the government in spite of the fact that the Anarchists' and *POUM* troops were still very strong in this sector.

. . . We had the power easily to crush Lister [Commander of the Communist troops] and his men if, at a given moment, our Divisions which amount to many thousands of men, had abandoned the front and fallen upon those who were destroying the collectives and were persecuting the comrades of the rearguard. We told them: Be still. . . .[18]

This docile attitude on the part of the Anarchists is difficult to understand. It certainly shows a restraint on their part which is unusual. Never before had the Anarchists shown such discipline to the decisions of their leaders. This obedience on the part of the great mass of Anarchists to their leadership can be explained by several factors. In the first place the press and radio of the *CNT* and *FAI*, in coöperation with the government, had been preaching the necessity of unity of command and discipline for the winning of the victory over Franco. By this time the propaganda had begun to pay off. Secondly, the great bulk of the rank and file of the Anarchists were confused and felt the need of leadership. It was no longer the simple problem of destroying all forms of exploitation and the annihilation of all rulers. The Civil War had made the Anarchists realize that there were governments and governments, some to be immediately destroyed and others to be coöperated with even to the extent of participating in their activities. Thus the Anarchists' clear-cut philosophy of destruction had been replaced by an intricate dogma which required a leadership to interpret it, and which made the masses more dependent on this leadership to guide their actions. Further, the bulk of the Anarchists were reluctant to fight against a government which was composed in part of their compatriots. Finally, in the cruelty of the Civil War, the Anarchist masses were having their fill of bloodshed and had no desire to add to it by another civil war against the other parties of the Left.

The motivation of the Anarchist leaders in their decision to refrain from an open break with the government forces was even more complex. No doubt the main consideration was the realization that a serious split in the ranks of the Popular Front could only mean the victory of the rebels. But that they should have allowed their party to be shorn of power with only verbal protest is astonishing. Perhaps they felt the strength of anarchism was so vital it could not be destroyed by the Republican government, just as the governments of the Right had failed to root it out in all their long years of rule. Such an assumption did not prove to be too far wrong, because, as will be seen later, in spite of the oppression the Anarchists still remained an important political force. Perhaps, too, the Anarchist leaders felt that they had already sacrificed so much they could not stop but had to go on to derive any benefit from the policy. Another possibility is that they considered the counterrevolution had progressed so far that it was impossible to stop it when behind it were the Soviet Union, the tacit sanction of the Western democracies, and the threat of fascism as the alternate solution. Against such odds the failing strength of the revolution had to accept democracy as second best. Finally the influence of Soviet aid may have affected their decision —the fear that it would end if the mass of Anarchists dared oppose the counterrevolution. Anarchist literature at this time frequently mentioned Soviet aid and the conditions of antirevolution which went with it.

This acquiescence of the Anarchists stood the strain of the May days, but as the oppression of the government and particularly the Communists became more and more ruthless the tractability of the Anarchists reached its limit, as will be discussed below.

COMMUNIST PROPAGANDA IN CATALONIA

Against the resistance on the part of Catalonians toward their integration into greater Spain the Communists carried on a propaganda campaign calling for unity of all Spaniards:

All Catalonia knows that the part of the People's Army that is now on Catalan soil has nothing in common with the old caste army of the semi-feudal monarchy, that it is the army of the people which has come at the order of the Government of the Republic to check the advance of the enemy on Barcelona, to defend at the same time the liberty of Catalonia and the independence of Spain.

It is one of the slogans of Italian fascism to separate Catalonia from the rest of Spain; it is one of Mussolini's aims, which he wants to achieve both with his own forces of intervention and with the aid of his Spanish agents—the provocateurs and Trotskyites.[19]

The Communists persistently tried to persuade the workers to support control of their industries by the Valencia government and attempted to make the bitter pill a little sweeter:

The direction of the industries of war has to depend on the Government of the Republic which holds the maximum command and the maximum authority and the maximum responsibility and to which all of us must contribute, if we want to attain loyally, the maximum facilities. It is clear that in the administrative organization of the war industries of Catalonia, although it may be an official organization dependent directly on the Government of the Republic, the Generalitat cannot be eliminated because it . . . cannot be disinterested in one of the activities most fundamental to our country. . . .[20]

While on the one hand trying to soften the blows, the Communists on the other hand called for the deepening of the purges. Their charge that:

"The recent *putsch* in Barcelona gave a particularly clear demonstration of how the Fascists make use of Trotskyist organizations to stab the People's Front in the back," became the cry for the absolute annihilation of the *POUM*.[21] The Communists not only made free use of the *Cheka* against them but demanded that the government outlaw the party and imprison all the leaders.

CHAPTER XV

THE RESIGNATION OF LARGO CABALLERO

The Communists *vs.* Largo Caballero

PRIOR TO THE May uprising, Largo Caballero had more or less tolerated the activities of the Communists and their allies, the Republicans and right Socialists. But when the Communists demanded that his government outlaw a workers' party, the *POUM*, it was a step Caballero refused to sanction. The differences between Caballero and the Communists by this time had become considerable, and the patience of both had worn thin. The warning note against Caballero and his government had been struck by the Communists at the March meeting of the Central Committee of the party. José Díaz declared:

The fact that these fundamental points [of the Communist program] are recognized by all the parties and trade unions participating in the People's Front and represented in the Government is a big step forward. But the fundamental problem of the present day is not only the recognition of the correctness of these points; the decisive point is the *speed at which they are put into operation.* It required eight months of war for the sum total of the problems raised by the Communist Party from the very first day of the war to be understood. If the Government does not take steps immediately to fulfill the economic, military and political tasks necessary to win the war; or, in spite of the support of the entire people, the Government proves incapable of carrying into life the things which the situation urgently demands, the Government will be doomed. Either the Government carries out the measures necessary to win the war or the Government will cease to be the Government.[1]

It was over the matter of the role and leadership of the armed services that the disagreement between Caballero and the Communists was most serious. The Communists had wanted a purge of the officer staff of the army to get rid of the dead weight.[2] They had wanted to start with the punishment of all those responsible for the fall of Málaga but Caballero refused to do this.[3] The Communists were able to obtain only one resignation, that of General Asensio, Under-Secretary of the Army. Zugazagoitia describes the dismissal of General Asensio:

... The myth of Largo Caballero had been broken [after the fall of Málaga]. The Communists got ready to pulverize him. They began without too much discretion the discrediting of the Chief of the Government and attacking him, head on, with one of his weaknesses: General Asensio, whom they accused as responsible for the fall of Málaga for which they demanded his dismissal. The responsibility, if there was any, did not fall on the under-secretary but his minister. They felt, however, that this was too much to demand. They attacked by degrees. For the moment they resigned themselves to the under-secretary and held against him old grudges. The pressure of the

Communists swept away Asensio. Largo Caballero, with his habitual tenacity, defended him to the maximum limit. When he was convinced of the uselessness of his defense, he cried tears of rage. He knew that this was a battle which he had personally lost....[4]

Zugazagoitia concludes his discussion by saying, "after the defeat of Asensio, the campaign of the Communists heightened against Largo Caballero."

The Communists, after this episode, began to treat Caballero more and more coldly and even occasionally attacked him in public. Santiago Carrillo, Secretary-General of the United Socialist Youth, went so far as to declare, "He has been a mistake. He is not the man who can win the war." The right Socialists and the Republicans also joined in condemning Caballero. "They all maintained that, as Minister of War and Commander-in-Chief of all the armies in the field at the time of our defeats, the responsibility ought to be attributed to him and not to General Asensio who, though a traitor, had only been Under-Secretary."[5]

Caballero in his turn tried to reduce the growing influence of the Communists in the defense of the Republic.[6] He sought first to cut their hold over the corps of political commissars. He ordered restriction of the powers of the commissars and assumed greater control over their nomination. Previously they had been appointed almost exclusively by Álvarez del Vayo and the result had been an overwhelmingly Communist domination.[7] Now, in order to counteract Álvarez del Vayo's influence, Caballero put into effect exact rules for appointment of the commissars with the final decision up to the Minister of War—himself.

Another deep-seated disagreement between Caballero and the Communists was over military strategy. The Communists objected to the continued personal command of Caballero in military operations and felt that in holding the job of both Prime Minister and Minister of War he could not give sufficient time to strategy. The antipathy came to a head over Caballero's planned offensive to the west to cut the rebel army in two. Caballero spoke sarcastically about this disagreement, referring to himself in the third person:

The then Minister of War [Caballero] had the absurd idea of starting a campaign which he had already prepared—a campaign to cut the enemy's communication between Córdoba and Seville, capturing Penarroya and Merida. That was a delusion of grandeur, vanity, madness, a desire to be a "little Napoleon." Why such sacrifices? Something had to be done to prevent the execution of this campaign, which would benefit only the enemy if it were successful. The campaign was made impossible by the crisis. In the last analysis, the facts have shown that this operation was unnecessary, inconvenient and dangerous—as long as the command was not turned over completely to the Communists![8]

In connection with this operation both Colonel Casado and Luis Araquistain said that it "undoubtedly would have been a triumph for the Republican Army." The assumption that it "could have changed completely the course of the campaign; the north could have been saved, all Andalusia could have been recovered,"[9] is merely the personal opinion of these two observers. Actually, the complexity and uncertainty of many factors made any operation in the Spanish Civil War unpredictable as to its outcome. It is very possible that the Communists, supported by the moderate Republicans and the right Socialists, had very good reasons for opposing the offensive. The general lack of success in the Republic's offensives during the summer and autumn of the same year indicates perhaps that an attack against Merida and Badajos, in the west of Spain, might have created an extended salient into Nationalist territory which could have been easily decimated by an assault on the two flanks. In support of Casado and Araquistain there is, on the other hand, the fact that the Communists and their allies had political reasons for not wanting an offensive. The Communists at this time were maneuvering to remove Largo Caballero from the War Office at least, if not out of the premiership. They wanted to take no chances in allowing an offensive, which, if victorious, would restore Caballero's prestige or which might come at the moment of crisis, when it would be unwise to change leadership for fear of confusion and for fear of destroying the confidence of the army during the assault.[10]

A CABINET CRISIS

In order to stop Caballero's planned offensive, Araquistain says that General Miaja, who was at that time under the sway of the Communists, refused at first to transfer from Madrid the necessary troops, but relinquished under direct order from Caballero. After failing by this method to stop Caballero, the Communists created a cabinet crisis by walking out of the meeting.[11]

Disagreement over military matters, however, was not the only element in the cabinet crisis of May, 1937. From the evidence it would appear that the actual effectuation of the crisis and the crowning dissent was over the punishment of the so-called perpetrators of the Barcelona uprising. The Communists demanded that the government purge the revolutionary Left which they had already begun to do on their own. In this connection the Communists demanded rigorous castigation of the dissident elements and the dismissal of Caballero's "Minister of Interior [Galarza] who failed or did not want to perceive the open preparations for a counter-revolutionary *putsch.*"[12] Caballero refused to take any such action and the conflict soon came out in the open. On May 11, Caballero's newspaper, *Adelante*, editorialized:

> If the Caballero government were to apply the measures of suppression to which the Spanish Section of the Communist International is trying to incite it, then it would come close to a government of Gil Robles or Lerroux; it would destroy the unity of the working class and expose us to the danger of losing the war and shipwrecking the revolution. . . . A government composed in its majority of people from the labor movements cannot make use of methods that are reserved for reactionary and fascist-like governments.

Within the cabinet it is reported that the Communists not only demanded retribution for the revolutionaries, but outlawing of the *POUM* and reduction of Anarchist representation in the cabinet from four to two posts. The break came in the cabinet meeting of May 15, when Largo Caballero declared, in respect to the proposed persecution of the *POUM*, that he was above all a worker and would not consent to preside over the dissolution of a brother organization of workers.[13] In this he was supported by the Anarchists, who further claimed that the Barcelona events had been provoked intentionally by the nonrevolutionary parties of the Republic. At this juncture the Communists, followed later by the Republicans and right Socialists, left the cabinet meeting, bringing about the collapse of the government. Caballero handed in his resignation to the President on May 16.[14]

As to the next step in the crisis Araquistain had this to say:

> President Azaña begged Señor Largo Caballero to continue at the head of the government until the [planned military] operation was carried out, saying that if the Communists insisted on resigning the Cabinet would be reorganized without the help of that party. Señor Largo Caballero accepted and returned to his office, resolved, like President Azaña, to eliminate the Communists from the government. If this plan had been successful, the fate of the war would have been changed entirely.

> Having heard—perhaps through President Azaña himself, who used to be in constant communication with Indalecio Prieto, Socialist Minister of Navy and the Air—about President Azaña's conference with Señor Largo Caballero, a few hours later two Socialist Ministers presented themselves at the latter's office. Dr. Negrín was one of them. They told him that, in view of the attitude of the Communist Ministers and bearing in mind that under the circumstances the government could not do without the Communist Party, the two of them, and Señor Prieto also, were resigning.[15]

The unknown second party with Negrín was probably Álvarez del Vayo whose name was not mentioned out of delicacy since he and Araquistain had once been close associates. It is not surprising, however, that the right Socialists refused Caballero's solution since they did not have a strong feeling of fellowship with him and because they considered Russian aid absolutely essential to win the war. Furthermore, it is very likely that if the Republican parties had been approached, they too would have refused to enter a government without Communists.

It was also reported that Largo Caballero made a pact with the *CNT* to form an entirely Syndicalist cabinet. The strong resistance of the moderate groups, however, made this solution impractical and almost impossible without a revolution.

The attempt to form a completely non-Communist cabinet having been nipped in the bud, the next step was taken by the Communists who were supported by the moderate Republicans and Socialists. They sent a note to Caballero giving him the following conditions for their adherence to a cabinet headed by him:

1. Democratic direction of all political, economic and military life of the country by means of discussion and collective resolution of all the problems by the Council of Ministers.

2. The normal functions of the Superior Council of War which will deal, conjointly with the Minister of War, with all problems of the Department, the status of the troops, the nomination of the high military commands, the armament of the army, the general progress of operations and measures to direct and assure its execution, etc., etc.

3. The immediate reorganization of the Staff and the nomination of a Chief of Staff, responsible to the Minister of War and the Council of War, but with full authority to direct and plan all the operations which are to be carried out in the country.

4. The reorganization of the Commissariat of War and the creation of a collective directorship, composed of the representatives of all the organizations which form the government. This Commissariat will be responsible to the Minister of War and the Council of War, but will have possession of autonomy in everything relating to the nomination and political direction of the Commissars.

5. The President of the Council will deal exclusively with the matters of the Presidency. The portfolio of War will be filled by a minister from that Department.

6. The elimination of Galarza from the new cabinet for his notorious incapacity and his leniency in the problems of public order.

7. The Minister of War as well as the Ministers of Government must be persons who have the support of all the parties and organizations which enter and form part of the government; therefore, their names must be known before proceeding with their definite nomination.

8. The creation of a program of government which must be made known to the public on the same day that the new cabinet is constituted.[16]

The Communists thus put forth very stiff conditions for their continued adherence to a government led by Caballero. Essentially, they were asking for the end of Caballero's interference and his direction of military matters of the government.

Caballero completely rejected such a solution. This action he rationalized later: "I could not leave the post of Minister of War for various reasons; first, because there was no cause to expel me from the Ministry of War and secondly, I believe that as a Spaniard I had the obligation to defend the Spanish army and to direct it in a manner that will bring us victory...."[17] By refusing to compromise he ultimately lost all say over the conduct of the war and the government.

As was to be expected the Executive Committee of the *UGT*, controlled by Largo Caballero, refused to support any government of which he was not the head. The downfall of Caballero also aroused the Anarchists, who began to retaliate. They stopped being the docile revolutionaries of the Left who had been pushed around by the bourgeoisie. The counter-revolution had gone too far. The editorial in the Anarchist newspaper, *Solidaridad Obrero*, on May 16, declared:

> The *C.N.T.* knows perfectly well the objective pursued by the servants of the democratic powers, enemies of our revolution, in trying to overturn Largo Caballero, and declares with all confidence its indestructible agreement with the *U.G.T.* not to accept any solution that does not have as its fundamental condition the return of the said comrade to the presidency of the cabinet and to the Ministry of War. His presence in these posts is the most solid guarantee that the proletariat has that the war against international reaction will not be called off for anything or anybody.
>
> The solution of the conflict provoked by the arrogance and the stupidity of the Communist leaders, can only be the formation of a new government similar to the last; that is a government that has as its base the proletarian organizations to which the other anti-fascist sectors give all their cooperation. The proletariat conquered with weapons in hand the right to govern the destinies of the country, and no one can negate our right to be the determining force in the Government of the Republic.

Even the most moderate elements among the Anarchists condemned the crisis brought on by the Communists and bourgeoisie. Such moderate leaders as Garcia Oliver, who had helped the government end the Barcelona insurrection, supported Caballero unreservedly.[18] The *FAI*, in a manifesto distributed secretly, came out unconditionally "for solidarity with Largo Caballero and the *U.G.T.*"[19]

The Government of Negrín

In an effort to get a compromise Azaña called upon Dr. Juan Negrín to form a government. He did not call Prieto, the next logical choice, because the personal feelings between Caballero and Prieto were too strong and Azaña felt any government that was to be formed needed at least the tacit support of Caballero and the *UGT*. Furthermore, Prieto was considered to be too anti-Communist to satisfy the Communists.[20]

Although Prieto was not called upon to play the role of Prime Minister he was given the most important post in the cabinet, that of Minister of Defense. The new cabinet formed on May 17, was as follows:

Juan Negrín—Premier and Finance Minister .   Moderate Socialist
Indalecio Prieto—Minister of Defense .   .   .   Moderate Socialist
Julian Zugazagoitia—Minister of Interior .   .   Moderate Socialist
Jesús Hernández—Minister of Education .   .   Communist
Vicente Uribe—Minister of Agriculture   .   .   Communist
José Giral—Minister of Foreign Affairs   .   .   Republican
Giner de los Rios—Minister of Public Aid and
    Communications .   .   .   .   Republican
Manuel Irujo—Minister of Justice .   .   .   .   Basque Nationalist
Jaime Ayguadé—Minister of Labor.   .   .   .   Catalonian Esquerra

Absent from the cabinet were representatives from the Anarchists, *POUM*, and the left Socialists. Also absent from the cabinet was the name of Álvarez del Vayo. His name had been so closely associated with Caballero that he could not be given a post, though he did take on the job of representing the Republic in the League of Nations and kept his job as head of the political commissars.[21]

From the evidence it seems clear that the Communists had been in the lead in instigating the crisis, being in basic disagreement with Largo Caballero and being the first to resign from the cabinet. But without the support and active coöperation of the Republican parties and the right Socialists, the Communists would have found it difficult to carry out their attack on Caballero. The excuse that it was only the factor of Soviet aid which made these elements ally with the Communists does not follow either the theories or the practices of these groups. The bourgeoisie wanted at all cost to avoid a violent social revolution. They feared the great popularity of Largo Caballero and thus sought in every way to sabotage his prestige and power. They seized upon the opportunity which the Communists offered to rid them of Largo Caballero, and without any qualms accepted posts in the new government.

Although the moderate groups were in complete agreement with the war program of the Communists and willing to ally with them in intrigues for power, once in possession of the government they were unwilling to share this power with anyone, particularly the Communists whom they considered to be at the bid of a foreign government. The alliance was good only to obtain the reins of the government, not to hold them. Even Negrín, who was purported to have been trained for a powerful position by the Communists, proved to be a Socialist above all else.[22] Consequently, the Communists after the crisis found themselves still in the position of a minority in the cabinet and the government. Particularly distressing for the Communists was the new Defense Minister, Indalecio Prieto, who was well known for being anti-Communist. Even if the vote of Negrín is counted as being Communist, against three Communist-held votes, Prieto had six votes plus the support of President Azaña, a strong anti-Communist. As a result it would seem that the Communists had gained nothing by the change except the doubtful value of splitting the Anarchists and left Socialists from the Republicans and right Socialists, which was really only bringing into the open something which had long been present under the surface.

Communist Aims

The conclusion of the cabinet crisis in May, 1937, leaves the analyst with a very confusing collection of evidence concerning the aims of the Communist Party of Spain. The actions of the party from February to May, 1937, had all the marks of a political group seeking to increase its political control by every means: coercion, terror, splitting and discrediting of the opposition. Yet, with the successful conclusion of the campaign which had resulted in a cabinet crisis in its favor, the party refrained from seizing what they had won. Why had the Communists not made political gains in the crisis?

Did the Republicans and right Socialists stop their attempts? The evidence does not show this to be true. The Communists did not make even the slightest verbal objection to being relegated to a minority position in the government nor had their demands for a solution of the cabinet crisis included an increase of power for themselves. If the Communists were not interested in more political control immediately, then why had they provoked the crisis? Perhaps they had not been shrewd enough to realize that their alliance with the bourgeoisie would end as soon as Caballero had been removed, and that the chicanery which had once been used against the extreme Left in the government would now be aimed at them. The Kleber incident, however, should have shown them the infidelity of the moderates.[23] It is also possible they thought that getting rid of Largo Caballero was a necessary step on the road to power. Dissident revolutionaries had always been considered by the Communists as the most dangerous obstacle in their search for domination. This attitude, however, is not in line with the pragmatic policies of the Communists in Spain, nor the Comintern policies of coöperating with the

Social Democrats of all countries at this time. Although Caballero had refused to unite the Socialist and Communist parties, he had gone a long way in coöperating with the Communists. On the other hand, from Indalecio Prieto, leader of the right Socialists and a professed anti-Communist, the Communists could expect little help in carrying out their United Front program. A further explanation for the Communist attitude is that by splitting their opposition irrevocably they thought their enemies would never be able to combine in order to oppose them in the final coup. But, if such were the case, why had the Communists worked so hard previously to try to get the revolutionaries and nonrevolutionaries to work together?

The Communists were well aware that they could never have assumed control alone at this time, but this does not explain why they did not seek to gain more influence, particularly in the field of the armed forces in which they had special interest. Is it possible, perhaps, that the Communists had not incited the crisis as a bid for power after all? From the evidence available it is plausible to conclude that the Communists were not interested in dominating the government. Their policy had a single purpose—to sacrifice everything to carry on the war against Franco. They felt that their program of unity and discipline, to which the Republicans and right Socialists also adhered, was the only logical way to oppose effectively Franco's forces, which were supported by Hitler and Mussolini. "All must be subordinate to winning the war" was their slogan, and they felt that Caballero's policies had not been strong enough in this direction. Even though he had accepted the logic of this slogan early in the war,[24] he refused to take the necessary drastic actions to put the Communist war program into operation, as for example, the complete absorption of Catalonia into the defense of the Republic.

Even the Communist move to put the *PSUC* in control of the Catalonian Generalitat can be explained by the fact that it was the only reliable element in that province which could be counted on to carry out the central government's program, the bourgeoisie in Catalonia being very autonomous-minded. In greater Spain the Communists had, on the other hand, made no attempt to undermine the Republicans who were in favor of the Communist program in almost every respect.

The thesis that the Communists were not interested in working toward a seizure of power so much as they were intent on resisting fascism in Spain follows the Soviet foreign policy at this time. A Soviet satellite in Spain would advance the revolutionary prestige of the Communists, but in all other respects would have damaged the policies being pursued by the Soviet Union. In the first place, a satellite in Spain would have no strategic value to the Soviet Union which feared above all a threat of Nazi and Japanese aggression. A satellite would instead have been a serious liability. If Spain became a Communist state the Soviet Union would be forced by self-interest to protect it. If she did not, she would have alienated Communists and sympathizers everywhere, because through the Comintern she had always demanded first that they sacrifice all for the protection of the great Socialist Fatherland, Russia. It would have been a serious blow to her prestige if she allowed a Spanish Soviet Republic to go down in defeat before Franco and the Italian troops. Thus the Soviet Union wanted to avoid the dilemma of having to choose between sacrificing the support of her sympathizers or maintaining a Soviet state under serious handicaps.

Secondly, it is very probable the Soviet leaders had included in their speculations that once Germany, and especially Italy, had committed their forces to Spain, they would not leave Spain without a Nationalist victory short of a world war. To do so would have been a serious blow to the prestige of Mussolini and Hitler both at home and throughout the world and might have threatened the aura of invincibility which Hitler was trying to develop around the German Army. Considering this, it is doubtful whether the Soviet leaders ever thought a Loyalist victory possible without the democratic states coming to the aid of the Spanish government. The Soviet Union had already indicated her unwillingness to commit herself to a Loyalist victory by strictly limiting the personnel and supplies which she sent to Spain. In any event the Soviet leaders did not see the possibility of a Soviet Republic in Spain at this time. If the democratic states came to the Loyalists' aid, it would have undermined Soviet influence and the democracies would have inevitably demanded a freely constituted government for Spain. This analysis of the situation, of course, was never made known to the Communists in Spain who continued to act as if they would some day come to power. To have told the Communists in Spain that the Soviet leaders would never let them assume control would have shattered their morale and support.

A further deterrent to the increase of Communist control was that it would have alienated the Western democracies with whom the Soviet Union was seeking friendship. A Communist-ruled Spanish Republic would have alarmed the West and given substance to the Fascist propaganda about Soviet aggression and the danger of the "Red Menace."

In conclusion, the Soviet foreign policy would have been embarrassed in every way by the emergence of a Communist government in Spain which she would be called upon to protect for the sake of continued support of the Communist cause abroad. The Soviet government was satisfied when the Communist Party of Spain was strong enough to prevent an uncontrolled revolution on the Loyalist side and to prevent an early Franco victory. Otherwise, the Communists were anxious that the party stay out of the limelight and let the other parties suffer the consequences and disgrace of defeat. The Communist policy in Spain was, therefore, as they stated it: sacrifice everything (including the creation of a Soviet Republic) to make war on the Fascists.

This appeared to be the Communist policy from the events of the May crisis. The remaining question is whether subsequent happenings in Spain supported such a thesis.

CHAPTER XVI

THE AFTERMATH OF THE CABINET CRISIS

THE ANARCHISTS STRIKE BACK

THE ANGER OF the Anarchists had been aroused by the overthrow of Largo Caballero. As long as the *CNT* was represented in the government the majority of Anarchists had refrained from seriously attacking its policies. The cabinet crisis had now freed them from this restraint and had incited them against the antirevolutionary role of the government. Though Negrín made repeated attempts to gain their reëntrance into the cabinet, or at least their agreement to support the program of the new government, he was unsuccessful.[1] The Communists also tried to gain the adherence of the Anarchists.[2] The party sent a note to the *CNT* deploring their reaction to the crisis and concluded by saying:

> Do you really want the loyal union of all the anti-fascist forces on the basis of a practical program to win the war and enjoy together the victory? We are ready. Do you want to discuss fraternally with us in order to arrive at an agreement concerning these problems and immediately proceed in common to a solution? If this is what you want and we have no doubt that it is, we await you.[3]

The Anarchists, however, avidly maintained their support of Largo Caballero and only reluctantly agreed to do nothing to obstruct the work of the government. Groups which had remained silent immediately after the Barcelona outbreak began to speak their minds. A manifesto of the *FAI* distributed clandestinely declared:

> We have in our possession documents, trustworthy proof of persons who took part in the organization of the May uprising. They are of the secret meetings held in Paris by men of the Catalan State, of the Socialist Unity Party of Catalonia with other elements of the Esquerra in which they prepared the provocations, by which they hoped to produce an insurrectional uprising in May by means of using the natural reaction of our people.[4]

The National Committee of the *CNT* issued a similar manifesto in June, 1937, condemning the parties of the bourgeoisie for their provocative role in the May events,[5] and indicted them for their subversive role previous to the May crisis. The manifesto further castigated them for the events after "peace" had been established: "A wave of blood and terror has assaulted the people of Catalonia. Unpunished assassinations have become the order of the day." As to the blame, "the Catalan State, the Communists and the Esquerra pursue different objectives in the interests of their parties. But all agree, though from different points of view, in the object of exterminating the *C.N.T.*"[6]

THE COMMUNISTS ATTEMPT TO REASSERT THE POPULAR FRONT

The Communists became alarmed at the turn of events after the cabinet crisis. They had intended to reduce the strength of the Anarchists and left Socialists, but they had not meant to alienate them. It was merely to obtain a wider acceptance of the Communist and Republican programs that they had carried on their terror against the "uncontrollables." They had hoped to continue to hold the support of the majority of the trade-unionists. The evidence also indicates that they were even hopeful of keeping Caballero in the cabinet as a figurehead prime minister, but they reckoned without taking into account the sensitive Spanish character which is extremely proud and will not accept second position once first place has been held. Consequently, the Communists were distraught when they saw all the work of building a Popular Front of revolutionaries and nonrevolutionaries disintegrate within a few days. They had miscalculated; in despotically forcing their program on the government they had disregarded the desires of the participants. They had coerced the Anarchists and left Socialists one step too far and had won for their efforts the alienation of the working classes from the government and its program. Consequently, after having created the government they desired, the Communists had to retrace their steps and try to restore harmony among all the parties of the Left under this new regime.

The first move of the Communists was to win back the mass of the *CNT*. This they did by the usual technique of distinguishing between the loyal majority of the Anarchists and the "uncontrollable" minority, and in this way wooing and attacking the Anarchists simultaneously. The unreliable element of the Anarchists they considered to be the *FAI*, which was at this time leading the attack against the government. In a speech in June, Jesús Hernández, Communist Minister of Education and chief theorist of the party, speaking of past associations with the Anarchists, indicated the line the Communists were to follow:

... we felt great respect for the Syndicalist organization, the *C.N.T.*, and we appreciated its contribution to the struggle against Fascism, but we demanded that its Ministers and responsible leaders should disassociate themselves from certain uncontrollable elements who call themselves the *F.A.I.* (which is a political party although they say the contrary), and who, by their conduct, have brought dishonor on their comrades who were fighting on the Madrid and Aragon fronts.[7]

The main tactic of the Communists in their attempt to win back the proletariat was to discredit Largo Caballero. Caballero's prestige among the masses had been overwhelming when he first took office in September, 1936. The long hard months of war had, it is true, reduced it somewhat; yet among the proletariat his influence was still strong. The masses, who had realized the necessity of giving up their revolutionary utopia for the moment, felt that their future was still protected as long as Caballero remained head of the government.

Since Caballero had refused to coöperate any longer with the Communist policies by remaining in the government, he became to the Communists a dangerous and formidable opponent who had to be destroyed. Caballero actually helped the Communists destroy his own popularity by his vindictive character. His monomania against the Communists soon made him sacrifice everything to it, including all coöperation with the government, even in the cause of winning the war. Although the proletariat shared his dislike of the Communists and middle classes, they realized more than Largo Caballero that a victory over the Communists and Republicans would be empty without a victory over Franco at the same time. This was exactly what Largo Caballero himself had taught them while he was in power, but what he forgot as soon as he had been thrown aside.

All sorts of abuses were heaped on Largo Caballero; events for which the Communists had once praised Caballero were condemned as his mistakes. For example Caballero's role in the siege of Madrid and the government's evacuation to Valencia was reinterpreted as follows:

> And the Government? What was it doing? Concerning this all asked, but no one knew. Caballero, as before, avoided everything and was indecisive. He would not consent to publish an appeal to the people. He made no decision as to the evacuation of Madrid. And he, on the word of many who surrounded him, was inclined to the theories of [General] Asensio, that is to forgetting about Madrid, that Madrid was not worth defending, that the army should be evacuated and the battlefields around Madrid be given up.[3]

On May 28, Jesús Hernández, Communist Minister of Education, made an extensive analysis of the Communists' revised attitude toward Largo Caballero and set down the line of attack to be followed against Caballero. Following is a summary of his expressed views:

> 1. "Caballero had a very personal conception of politics, a 'boss' conception.... Instead of collecting and weighing up the opinions of the Ministers, Caballero saw himself as the one and only person responsible for all the governmental policy, and alas for the Minister who demanded a discussion of the problems of the war, or who took an interest in problems which were not the specific care of his department!...
> 2. "The Caballero government, owing to the personal attitude of its President could

not create a policy arising out of the needs of the war; and as a consequence did not direct it. It had no clear view of the solution of the problems of the war, but it carried on anyhow, under the pressure of the situation but without clear vision of the whole group of problems presented by the war, and without the exact notion of the efforts that had to be made to reach victory. . . .

3. "His activity as Minister of War has shown his lack of foresight and understanding of the most elementary problems of military and political tactics and strategy. Ill-advised by his collaborators, he could never understand the changes of situation produced on the fronts or at home, or as a result adopt the means of struggle to new necessities of the war. And when our Party stated those problems, Caballero got irritated, he protested; he did not solve them. And what is more serious, giving signs of criminal pride, he tried to deceive everyone else, thereby deceiving himself, by saying that he had foreseen and solved all the problems which were brought up."

4. He did nothing to prepare "the necessary fortifications for the defense of the capital."

5. In evacuating the Government from Madrid he sneaked away secretly without calming the population or explaining the causes for which the capital was being abandoned.

6. "Caballero refused to purge the traitors and saboteurs from the command of the army, and these organized defeats. . . .

7. "The fall of Málaga was the result of incompetence and treachery . . . of the incompetence of the Minister of War [Caballero]."

8. He maliciously attacked and tried to undermine the influence of the Communist Party.

9. "The people demanded 'the establishment of a unified command for the army.' Caballero understood the unified command of the army as the personal command of the Minister of War. Is this the unified command? No. The unified command means the creation of a single administration for the fronts of Spain, Catalonia and the Basque provinces; the single direction of all war activities by this administration. What has the government of Caballero done in this sense? Nothing, or almost nothing."

10. He was jealous of the popularity and glory of General Miaja and refused to raise him to the position of Chief of Staff he deserved.

11. The difficult plight of the northern provinces, which were under an assault by the Nationalists and which were gradually being conquered, was traceable also to the incompetence of Caballero as Minister of War.

12. Caballero since the cabinet crisis continuously in his speeches has been giving away military secrets to the enemy.

13. "Largo Caballero had never realized a policy which depends on reserves. On the contrary he has always obstructed it. . . .

14. "Largo Caballero's Ministry was incapable of establishing order in the rear-guard. . . .

15. "Largo Caballero did not fight to avoid economic and financial collapse."

16. He did nothing to develop a war industry.[9]

Communist speeches and propaganda continued to be full of recrimination against Caballero. No opportunity was allowed to slip by without trying to discredit him in some way. This not only indicates how completely they had rejected him but how dangerous they considered him to the safety of the Negrín government and how important to the Communists was the overriding necessity of gaining the support of the workers, essential to carrying out their industrial and war program.

CHAPTER XVII

ELIMINATION OF THE OPPOSITION

THE ACTIVITIES AND CHARACTER OF THE NEW CABINET

THE NEW GOVERNMENT under Negrín meant a victory not only for the war program of the Communists and nonrevolutionaries, but raised the Republic's prestige in the eyes of the Western democracies. The conservative elements in these countries were particularly pleased at the turn of events. It meant not only the possibility of saving their Spanish investments, which they feared under a revolutionary regime would have been eventually expropriated, but it was a check on revolution and radicalism in the West.

The role of Dr. Negrín in this new government has come under bitter attack. As discussed previously he was considered by many to be a fellow traveler; however, the people who were most intimate with him declared him to be sincere, though perhaps naïve as to the purposes of the Communists in Spain.[1] Indalecio Prieto indicates Negrín's motivation for supporting the Communists by quoting a statement Negrín made to the Executive Committee of the Socialist party in March, 1938:

> I cannot ignore the Communists because they represent a factor of very considerable importance in international politics and because their removal from power would be internally a serious inconvenience; I cannot ignore them, because their compatriots abroad are the only ones who effectively aid us and because we would put in danger the aid of the U.S.S.R., the only effective aid we have in regard to material of war. . . .[2]

The evidence of Negrín's activity indicates that he supported the Communist program for winning the war and resisting Franco to the end, but he was by no means in favor of all the Communist tactics. For example, he resisted the unification of the Socialist and Communist parties and supported Prieto in ridding the army of the Communist-dominated political commissars.

Without the restraining influence of Caballero and the Anarchists in the cabinet, the suppression of Catalonia and the revolutionaries reached new intensities. An uprising of Anarchists in Almería was put down in the usual fashion with little show of mercy. Under Prieto's direction the Catalan army was integrated into the regular army of the central government and the militias were completely obliterated. The control of industry gradually passed into the hands of Negrín's cabinet, though it was necessary here to proceed with some caution since strikes and crippling delays had to be avoided.[3] The *CNT* still controlled a large percentage of industry in Catalonia. The *UGT* was strong only in transport, government employees', farm, and shopkeepers' organizations but was very weak in industry itself which remained under the sway of the Anarchists. The transformation of control, therefore, had to be subtle and slow so as not to arouse the Anarchists unnecessarily.

The Communists, as their contribution to the undermining of the Anarchists, continued to attack the *FAI* with terror and propaganda in an attempt to weaken and separate the leadership from the main body of Anarchists:

> In the bosom of the *F.A.I.*, the political party of the *C.N.T.*, there are hidden many enemies of unity of the working class because they know that the attainment of this unity would represent for them the loss of hegemony over one sector of the proletariat and the possibility of using the syndicalists' attempts at "collectives," which have done so much damage to the economy of the country, as much as their attempts at *"putsches"* and uprisings. Thus we have political terrorism in a myriad of syndicates of the *C.N.T.*, where any idea of unity of the workers is opposed by these people, who impose conditions and who sabotage unity. In order to unmask these enemies of unity it is necessary that the unions of the *C.N.T.* come out for unity and prepare themselves to carry out unification on the basic concrete platform of the struggle.[4]

The Anarchists on their part struck back with pin-prick attacks of propaganda, but were able to do little to stop the growing control of the central government and the Communists. There was some passive resistance in the factories, but the threat of Franco kept this sort of movement from becoming widespread.

THE OPPOSITION

The Anarchist strength, however, in spite of government inroads, still remained a large potential force, which, if aroused, could have easily upset the government. Making use of this latent power Largo Caballero, defeated and resentful of the manner in which he had been overthrown when he was still the popular leader of the masses, began to rally around him the left Socialists and Anarchists. Throughout the summer of 1937 there were continuous rumors of Caballero leading Anarchist revolts in various sections of Spain. At the same time negotiations were started between the Executive Committee of the *UGT*, under Caballero's domination, and the *CNT*, looking toward some kind of alliance and even unity in their opposition to Negrín's government. Such a rallying of the opposition around Caballero could have been a serious threat to the government and steps had to be taken immediately to break up any attempts at alliance. Terrorism against the more obstinate leaders and members of the Anarchists was intensified and the absorption of Catalonia was pushed ahead rapidly. The government isolated Largo Caballero from the people and the *CNT* as much as possible. The government crushed his newspaper support either by seizing the plants for some misdemeanor, as in the case of the two largest Caballero newspapers, *Claridad* in Madrid and *Adelante* in Valencia, or by putting them under strict censorship. He was forbidden to make public speeches and eventually was even put under house arrest so that he could not participate personally in any rally of the revolutionary working class.[5] It appears nevertheless that in spite of the government's efforts negotiations for some type of fusion between the *UGT* and the *CNT* went on through the summer, though without avail. The Anarchists were especially anxious at this time for unity. They had declared at the end of May, "The Union of the *U.G.T.* and the *C.N.T.* is as necessary to our organization as water and salt."[6] They hoped through unity to strike back against the "perpetrators of the May crisis." The basic differences between the two groups, however, were too great for them to unite even as outcasts in a struggle to gain back supremacy. Largo Caballero admitted this later:

...Consequently it seems to me that if we cannot fuse with the *C.N.T.*, we can at least have some bounds of unity, of understanding, or relationship, so that we shall not attack each other, so that we may respect our own organizations, and so that we may become more convinced that at some future time we must unite as one. I feel this can be done.[7]

Except for reasserting their friendship, the *UGT* and *CNT* remained separated and isolated in their struggle against the encroachment of the government. Consequently, the rally of the opposition never occurred because of their own differences and because of the resistance and purging by the government. The Communists, for their part, helped the government in this task by trying to win back the Anarchists and slandering Caballero before the people.

The lack of organization and resistance to discipline by the membership was rapidly becoming the Anarchists' undoing. Their strong individuality and localism made it impossible for the members of the *CNT-FAI* to present a united front of opposition with the *UGT* or even a solid front of their own federations. A united Anarchist policy would have saved them from terror and protected their interests in the government and in the economy. As it was, the government was able to force them to retreat more and more from their own interests and force them into support of the war program of the Communists and Republicans.

THE END OF THE *POUM*

The defeat of Caballero achieved by the Communists had particularly severe consequences for the *POUM*, the pet mania of the Communists. The Communists had precipitated the crisis by their demand for the outlawing of the *POUM* and upon achieving success they extracted their price and moved rapidly toward the complete annihilation of the *POUM*. On the urging of the Communists, Julian Zugazagoitia, Minister of the Interior, gave the order on June 16, 1937, for the arrest of the Central Committee of the *POUM*. The members were immediately arrested and a short time later the popular leader of the party, Andrés Nin, disappeared from prison. The evidence seems to point to the fact that he was picked up by the *Cheka* and was either murdered or sent to Russia. After the incarceration of the Central Committee all members of the *POUM* became subject to arrest and were terrorized by the Communists. A total of over a thousand *POUM* members were reported to have been seized. Prieto denied that the government ever gave approval to these arrests. This may be true,[8] but it is equally true that the government took no real steps to stop the terror.

The wave of arrests and attacks on the *POUM* created a very bad impression among the liberal elements abroad. All the non-Communist labor and leftist parties of the world condemned the Communists for their actions. Two separate international delegations of leftists went to Spain to verify the activities and to see if the *POUM* was guilty of treason. Both investigations concluded that the *POUM* and its leaders were innocent and falsely arrested by the police without the sanction of the government.[9]

In the face of unfavorable opinion both abroad and in Spain the Communists allowed the trial of the leaders of the *POUM* to be delayed until October, when the antagonism had died down. Since the leaders were in prison and harmless, there was no immediate hurry to conduct the trial. In the meantime the Communists built up their case against the *POUM* by an elaborate propaganda campaign resembling the one they had been using to uphold similar purges in Russia.

The main object of the Communists in Spain was to parallel the line followed in Russia. As one Soviet writer stated, "Just as here [in Russia] the Trotskyites are on the side of the reactionaries against the power of peace, so too in Spain the Trotskyites carry out the role of assistants and agents of fascism. . . . Trotskyites work hand in hand with the agents of the 'Fifth Column' who disorganize the work of the army and in the rear, help in the foul plans of General Franco."[10] To support their contention the Communists developed an elaborate case with documents purporting to show the treason of the *POUM*. In their propaganda the Communists played up the following points as activities which they claimed the *POUM*ists carried on in their underground work:

1. Attacked the parliaments of the Republic and Catalonia
2. Campaigned against the Popular Front
3. Attacked and undermined the Republican and Communist parties
4. Tried to sow dissension between the *UGT* and *CNT*
5. Resisted Soviet aid and administration of supplies and supported the Fascist propaganda that the Soviet Union was trying to set up a Red Republic
6. Opposed establishment of the Regular army and united command
7. Instigated the revolt in Barcelona in May, 1937
8. Spread Fascist propaganda in the Republic[11]

Most of these points, except the last, it should be noted, can without question be verified as methods used by the *POUM*. Being a self-professed revolutionary party their activities corresponded quite closely to the Communist propaganda above.

But the Communists' real case depended on proving the *POUM*ists were Fascist agents. The Communists unearthed a large quantity of police records, subversive plans, letters from the *POUM* to Franco and vice versa, including a letter to Andrés Nin from a Gestapo agent.[12] The validity of these documents is doubtful, and it is beyond the confines of this book to discuss them in any detail. The proof or disproof of these documents is closely associated with the validity of the whole series of documents which came up during the purge trials in Russia at this period concerning the dissident Communists' association with the Fascist powers. It need only be said here that the Spanish courts found them to be invalid and it is doubtful that a revolutionary party of the laboring classes would have had extensive dealings with the leaders of a professional army coup and Fascists.

When the leaders of the *POUM* were tried in October, 1937, the cases against them were dismissed for lack of evidence. Five, however, were convicted and imprisoned for taking part in the Barcelona uprising in May, 1937. In spite of the final vindication of the *POUM* the Communists had achieved their desired end, the complete elimination of the *POUM* from the political scene in Spain.

A Schism in the *UGT*

The elimination of the *POUM* had been comparatively easy because of its very small size and influence. Likewise, the organizational weakness of the *CNT* had made it easy to nullify and pacify the aroused feelings of the Anarchists. The question of how to cancel out the effect of Caballero and his hold on the *UGT*, however, was a much more difficult problem. First of all his popularity made it necessary to proceed with caution. He could be temporarily put under house arrest, but this arrangement could not remain permanent and might incite his supporters if it lasted too long. Secondly, Largo Caballero's power over the *UGT*, as Secretary-General of the Federation, and the fact that his supporters controlled the Executive Committee made his position very formidable, especially since the *UGT* was the most powerful trade-union federation in Spain, centrally organized and with about a million and a half members. (The *CNT* had more members perhaps but it was decentralized.) Thus in order to end Caballero's supremacy over the *UGT* it was necessary to eliminate him as Secretary-General and cut his majority on the Executive Committee—not a simple process.

At the beginning of the Civil War in July, 1936, the Communists and the right Socialists had been in a distinctly minor position in the *UGT*. The right Socialists controlled those unions primarily from the northern provinces, and the Communists were in the lead in only a handful of union locals. But, as discussed previously, by 1937 the situation had greatly changed and the right Socialists and Communists together felt strong enough to challenge Caballero's supremacy.[13] Caballero had persistently refused to call elections for a new Executive Committee, since it had been agreed to forgo these until the end of the war. Before May, 1937, the Communists merely objected verbally. Caballero's resignation from the government, however, spurred the Communists and right Socialists into direct action, especially since Caballero adamantly denied the *UGT*'s support to Negrín's government. Using their predominating position in some of the affiliated unions, they were able to obtain, in spite of Caballero, adherence of many of the *UGT* units in Madrid, Catalonia, Biscay, and Asturias to the new government. The next step was to call the National Committee to censure the actions of Caballero's Executive Committee. The meeting was held on May 28, 1937, and it decided by a vote of twenty-four to fourteen to reprimand the Executive Committee for taking a negative attitude toward the new Prime Minister. This adverse vote against the Executive Committee represented not only the votes of the Communists and the right Socialist federations but those federations which were reluctant to oppose the government in time of war. It was, therefore, not a clear-cut denial of Caballero as leader of the *UGT*; it merely censured him on this one issue. His continued persistence in actively opposing the government of Negrín, however, made him later lose many of his supporters. Furthermore it should be noted that this was a vote by federations affiliated with the *UGT* and does not represent a vote by individual workers. The fourteen federations which supported Caballero were generally the mass unions with many thousands of members, whereas the opposition was composed mostly of the federations of professional and skilled unions with only a few thousand members. The mass federations which supported Largo Caballero were of particular importance because they included a large portion of the workers in war industries, such as the Federation of Metal Workers' Unions. Thus the National Committee vote did two things. In the first place, it was a propaganda victory for the Communists and their allies. Secondly, it showed that Caballero was still very strong among the mass of workers and that his opposition was a threat to the stability of the Negrín government.

As a result further steps had to be taken. The Communists and right Socialists began pressing for another meeting of the National Committee to remove Caballero from power and elect a new Executive Committee. In calling for a meeting the Communists also asked for complete reform of the structure of the *UGT*. Manuel Delicado, member of the Politbureau of the Communist party, stated the Communist proposition:

... The direction of the *U.G.T.* cannot and must not be the patrimony of one single ideology or of one group, rather the responsibility of the direction should be shared in a proportional manner between Communists, Socialists, and non-party members. I repeat for this purpose the words of our Secretary General, Comrade José Díaz. . . .

"In order to consolidate more completely the forces of the *U.G.T.* to which belong the immense majority of Communists, it is necessary to cordially ask if it is not possible to hold a Congress at which can be elected democratically a new executive, which will produce in the Executive a Communist representative and will strengthen the work of direction."

Secondly, on the basis of past experience with methods of direction, contrary to syndical democracy, the directors in most basic organizations of the *U.G.T.* were imposed from above. It is necessary that there be a change and to set in practice syndicalist democracy which would permit the workers to discuss and resolve problems in assemblies convened regularly and in which the opinion of the majority would prevail.

Third, since the organic structure of the *U.G.T.* does not answer the necessities of its own revolutionary aims, a revision of this structure should proceed on the basis of a truly national federation of industry and national unions of industry and not as it is now, called federations of industrial workers when they are federations in name only.

Finally, it is necessary that the Executive and National Committees of the *U.G.T.* introduce into their regulations the recognition of local and provincial organs on the basis of local federations and provincial councils which can direct the activities of the unions in each locality and in each province. . . .[14]

Caballero refused to consider any such changes or even to reconvene the National Committee. The results would only have been detrimental to his control of the *UGT*. About his position on the matter Caballero had this to say:

> When they come to demand the convening, we observe that among those who make the request there are many who claim to represent Federations which do not pay dues, others which have not yet joined the Union like the tobacco workers and the urban letter carriers, and others like the sugar workers, the location of whose headquarters is not even known to us. They come to demand a convening of the National Committee to pass judgment on the Executive Committee, and we observe that the intention is to attack the Union and to take over the offices of the leadership of the Union. In fulfillment of our elementary duty, since this is the principal responsibility we have, we say that we shall not hand over the Union.[15]

Caballero countered the Communist attack on the *UGT* with the expulsion of several of the federations "for failure to pay dues." In order to insure his position he was soon forced to expel over half the federations which had been affiliated with the *UGT*, although the basic strength of the *UGT* still remained intact. In another move Caballero said that he would call a National Committee meeting once he had received the proper documents from enough of the federations. He claims, however, never to have received these documents.[16]

Since the Communists and right Socialists failed after several months to get Caballero's sanction to a meeting of the National Committee and since well over half of the federations had been expelled, they convoked their own meeting of about thirty of the dissident federations. This meeting took place on October 1, 1937, and created another Executive Committee in opposition to Caballero's. At the head of the committee was placed Gonzales Peña. It should be noted that Peña was a right Socialist and a close associate of Prieto—the new committee was not in any way Communist-dominated though they had representatives on it. After this date there existed two executive committees. It would be impossible to estimate the number of followers of each group since membership counts were flexible and many of the men were at the front. Likewise, the adherence of the leadership of a union did not mean the unqualified adherence of all the members.

When a rally of the revolutionary Left around Caballero had ceased to be a serious threat, and when the moderate Socialists and Communists had persuaded the dissident unions to follow a new Executive Committee, the government decided to let Largo Caballero give a series of speeches in the hope that he would talk himself out of popularity. He began the series in Madrid on October 17, and in his first speech bitterly attacked the Negrín government and the Communists.[17] The response to the speech was such that the government decided he should not be allowed to proceed. The discouragement over the course of the war in which the Loyalists were slowly being pushed back by the rebels and Fascist troops, resistance to the regimentation of the economy and the army, fear of Communist domination, and regret over the reversal of the Libertarian and Socialist revolutions found a sympathetic chord in Caballero's words. He thus remained an important factor, representing the discontent of a large segment of the working people.

The Communists continued to carry out a very active defamation campaign against Caballero even though they declared he was no longer of importance as a leader of the proletariat. In their propaganda he was made responsible for the treason of the Trotskyites because he "permitted all types of provocateurs, spies and agents of the Gestapo, masquerading in the *P.O.U.M.* to carry out tranquilly their work of demoralization and provocation. . . ."[18] And as the military situation of the Republic was growing worse, Caballero was blamed for the military mistakes and defeats during his administration and after. The Communists insinuated that because of his mistakes, the Republic had been put into a gradually worsening position after his fall.[19]

The condition of having two leaderships for the *UGT* was very unsatisfactory and attempts were made by the Communists and right Socialists to restore unity, but Caballero held fast to his position. Finally Leon Jouhaux, leader of the French trade-unions, was called upon to find some compromise solution. He met with the leaders of both sides and a conference of delegates from the various unions and provinces was held on January 3, 1938. At this meeting a compromise was drawn up. Caballero resigned his position as Secretary-General and gave way to Gonzales Peña. Further, Caballero's supporters agreed to disband their executive and in exchange were given four seats on an Executive Committee expanded from eleven to fifteen. This was not strictly following the *UGT* statutes but served as the only basis on which a compromise could be reached. Finally it was agreed to give unconditional support to the Negrín government. The Communists were quite pleased with the outcome, declaring:

. . . It is not an ideal solution, but is *a good solution*. The schism has been liquidated. Consequently, the *U.G.T.* will arise more powerful and is secured from this possible danger. The re-establishment of the unity of the *U.G.T.* will increase our international prestige and eases the work of our compatriots who work abroad in order to increase

the amount of aid to our cause. . . . The fact of having re-established this unity makes
it more possible, easier to carry out the basic aims of the Popular Front and the unification of labor. . . .[20]

The outcome of the negotiations was a serious defeat for Caballero,
and resentful, he refused to coöperate with the new Executive Committee and maintained a personal opposition to the government of Negrín.
Even in August of 1938, when he was asked to participate in the fiftieth
anniversary celebration of the Spanish Socialist party he refused.[21]

Most of Caballero's supporters did not go along with him in opposing
the compromise arrived at by the factions of the *UGT*. Most of those
unions which had supported Caballero realized that his cause was a lost
one. Over the previous six to eight months Caballero's prestige had declined under the defamation campaign of the government and Communists, helped by the fact that Caballero was held incommunicado. Furthermore, the necessity of carrying on the war and the horrors of war
made most of the unions less interested in bearing grudges against certain
factions of the Loyalists. When the dissident federations returned to the
UGT, Largo Caballero was left with but a few supporters and his cause
was forgotten in the hardships of the last battles of the Civil War.

The Communists felt the small group that remained loyal to Caballero
had been sufficiently discredited and weakened to attach to it the stigma
of being enemy agents:

. . . The Caballero group carries on criminal, disrupting activities directed against the
unity of the People's Front, against the government of Negrín and especially against
the Communist Party in Spain. "This small group which is attacking the unity of the
universal workers' union, spreading absurd rumors, carrying on defeatist propaganda
and taking an equivocal position in their attitude towards the People's Front have
turned into agents of the enemy [José Díaz]."[22]

Though less extensively, the Communists continued even after January,
1938, to attack Caballero but more as a scapegoat for the war hardships
than because of his strength, though many of the discontented among
the workers still supported him.

CHAPTER XVIII

THE COMMUNISTS AND THE RIGHT SOCIALISTS

NEGOTIATIONS FOR A UNITED PARTY

THE COMMUNISTS, having achieved in the May crisis the creation of a cabinet which accepted the policy of discipline, centralization, and the subordination of all social and economic ends to the winning of the war, felt it was an opportune time to reopen the question of unity with the Socialist party. Although winning the war or postponing Franco's victory was the prime necessity of the moment, the Communists never ceased to be interested in fulfilling the program of the United Front in Spain. The two aims, however, were not mutually exclusive. The Communists considered that an important factor in strengthening the defenses of the Republic was the unity of the proletariat. They felt that by the removal of Caballero as the influential leader of the Socialist party a great obstacle had been overcome in their unification plans.

The decision to intensify the unity campaign and to reopen negotiations directly with the Socialists was made at the meeting of the Central Committee of the Communist Party on June 18, 1937. All organs of the Communists were mobilized for the campaign. The Communists, making use of the newspaper *Claridad*, which had been seized by the government and turned over to Communist sympathizers within the Socialist party, began to carry out a campaign from within the Socialist party for unity of the two groups. One of the chief Socialist supporters of unity was Álvarez del Vayo. Dolores Ibarruri described Álvarez del Vayo's activities in this respect:

... Among these champions of unity a most prominent place is held by Álvarez del Vayo. (All rise and cheer Comrade Álvarez del Vayo.) Comrade Álvarez del Vayo has been indefatigably striving for an alliance of the Socialist and Communist Parties....[1]

On the decision of the Central Committee of the Communist Party a letter was sent to the Executive of the Socialist party proposing the opening of negotiations for unity.[2] The letter itself did not contain the conditions upon which unification was to be brought about—it merely mentioned that the first task of the new party would be the creation of a war program similar to that supported by both parties already. In the discussion of the resolution in the Central Committee, however, the Communists made clear the type of party they expected from unification. Dolores Ibarruri, in her report to the Committee, described the new party:

Our claim that it is necessary for the United Party to be constructed on the principles of democratic centralism is based on the experience of the glorious Bolshevik Party and on the teachings of Lenin, Stalin and the Communist International, which is the true heir of the revolutionary traditions of the international workers movement.

* * *

It is perfectly obvious that if iron discipline is to be established, the party must be ideologically united. Without such ideological unity, which leads to conscious discipline and the growth of the party, there will always be the danger that various political lines, various tactics, may appear within the party, which is exactly what has happened to the Socialist Party, where each group interprets the tactics and policy of the party in its own way. And sometimes we meet with the strange phenomenon that the Socialist paper published in Valencia has a different line from the organ of the Socialist Party published in Madrid, and then whereas one paper declares for unity, the other tries to split the working-class movement.

* * *

The United Party of the proletariat must defend the Soviet Union and fight its enemies.

* * *

And we are Stalinists, because the great theory of Marx-Engels-Lenin has been enriched by Stalin, who teaches us Communists to be staunch even in the most difficult situations, to observe unflinching, Stalin-like firmness in our struggle and work, to be irreconcilable towards the class enemies and renegades of the revolution....[3]

Dolores Ibarruri in this same speech was also extremely frank in admitting the opportunism of the Communist policies:

We are Marxist-Leninists-Stalinists and, consequently, we adjust our theories to the revolutionary possibilities of each moment without renouncing our final aspirations.

The surprising thing was perhaps that in spite of the example of the United Socialist Party of Catalonia and in spite of these freely admitted aims of the Communists in respect to unification, the Socialists, now mainly under the control of Prieto and Negrín, allowed discussions with the Communists to begin soon after the crisis. The discussions continued on through the summer beneath a barrage of Communist propaganda for the complete merging of the two parties. The motivation of the Socialists in carrying out these negotiations, however, was not love for the Communists although they were in complete favor of their war program. They realized that the Communists had become an important political factor in Spain and that they, the moderate Socialists and Republicans, could not stand alone against the personal popularity of Largo Caballero backed by the working masses of Socialists and Anarchists. It was during this same summer of 1937 that Caballero was attempting to rally around himself the opposition to Negrín's government in order to return to power, and throughout the summer there were frequent rumors of uprisings being led by Caballero. The success of the government of the moderate Socialists and Republicans depended, therefore, upon the establishment of a working agreement with the Communists. Negrín was particularly in favor of an agreement with the Communists since he felt it to be necessary to secure victory over Franco; difficulty with the Communists might lead to withdrawal of the essential supply of arms from the Soviet Union. Unlike Prieto, he did not fear Communist domination in the long run, and, therefore, from a temporary standpoint, he was not greatly concerned about it.

The idea of a united party of the proletariat was by no means repugnant to the Socialists. It had been the dream of the Socialists in every country to develop a party of all the working classes. After the formation of the Popular Front in Spain the idea was of particular interest to the Socialists. Largo Caballero had been anxious to absorb the Anarchists into the Socialist party, which would have given him a predominance of revolutionaries and assured the supremacy of his program. The right Socialists, on the other hand, were more interested in the absorption of the Communists who represented a more moderate element of the working and professional classes and whose program corresponded to their own.

Just as the Communists wanted the merger based on Stalinism, the right Socialists wanted it based on principles of Socialist democracy. On entering into discussions with the Communists, the Socialists had no intention of giving up their basic aims and principles and certainly would never have agreed to the abdication of their leadership. On the contrary, they hoped, just as the Communists, to assume control over the whole hierarchy of the new party. But after the example of the United Socialist Party of Catalonia, which had fallen immediately under Communist leadership, the Socialists were wary of entering into any new negotiations with the Communists and wanted to make very sure that the case of the *PSUC* was not repeated in any future arrangements. They, therefore, entered the new negotiations very cautiously.

Since neither side had any intention of compromising its leadership or principles, the discussions were of necessity long and arduous. Not until August 17 was a working pact agreed upon. In their adherence to this agreement the Socialists made sure that it was to be considered as only an accord in respect to ways the parties would work together and not as a pact of unity, though they agreed to continue the discussion toward a merger. The reservation signed by Gonzales Peña was as follows:

. . . It is fitting to state clearly that this is a program for unity of action, which for the large part is already in effect, and that it is not to be confused as the basis for organic fusion, which we have begun to outline in order to undertake seriously and officially the transition work of endowing the Spanish proletariat with what it so much desires; one single party.[4]

The Communists for their part made no reservations, being optimistic that they could not lose. They declared it an important step toward the final goal of unity. It could, in fact, be considered a belated United Front pact which the Socialists in 1935 and 1936 refused to consider. The first eleven clauses were a repetition of the war program on which both the Communists and the right Socialists were already in complete agreement, such as a powerful war industry, strict public order, good relations with the bourgeoisie, a planned economy, and autonomy for the various peoples of Spain. The only new element of significance was the agreement as to the need of purging the revolutionary Left of all elements who were in violent disagreement with the government and its moderate policy, such as the *POUM*. The remaining five articles dealt with elements which looked toward the following: closer unity of the Left; strengthening of the Popular Front; recognition of the necessity for the unity of the trade-unions, the *UGT*, and the *CNT*; the support of both parties for the United Youth (*JSU*); the encouragement of closer coöperation between the Second and Third Internationals; and the defense of the Soviet Union. These clauses, however, were not of too much importance since they merely expressed the desire for these ends without requiring definite action. They were in such a nebulous form that they did not represent a yielding by either side. It might be said that agreement to defend the Soviet Union was a concession, but since the Soviet Union was supplying large quantities of war material it was not much of a sacrifice on the part of the Socialists, especially since it entailed no concrete obligations.

The last paragraphs of the agreement are of much more interest since they looked to the development of coördination among the rank and file organizations. Two exceptions that hindered complete freedom of co-operation at the local level, however, were introduced presumably by the Socialists—the necessity "to conserve the party principle for the two organizations," (that is, both local units of the Communist and Socialist parties were to act separately and there were to be no premature mergers on the local level) and the requirement that local programs of joint action must be presented "for confirmation to the National Coordination Committee."[5]

The agreement was mainly an indication that both parties desired the elimination of revolutionary dissidents, favored some kind of unification, and would allow the local units of both parties the freedom to work closely with each other if they so desired; but the actual amalgamation of the parties was a long way off, and it could not be said that the differences of the two organizations had been lessened significantly by this pact.

It would seem that, except in isolated localities where the Socialist party was very weak or where it had previously been infiltrated with Communist sympathizers, the local coördination committees were established on a strictly two-party basis with both hierarchies jealously holding their own prerogatives.[6] Likewise, on the national level the negotiations, which were continuing to try to develop terms of a merger, began to bog down with neither side willing to make concessions. The threat of Caballero's getting back into power had lessened, and the hostility of the Anarchists toward Negrín's government was no longer so pronounced. There was even talk of the Anarchists sending representatives to the Cortes which reconvened on October 1, 1937. Consequently, the Socialists no longer felt the pressing need of a close alliance with the Communists and were not so willing to go on with the risky business of negotiating unity with them.

The Socialists did, however, allow the Communists to participate as a minority in the new Executive Committee of the *UGT*, set up as a rival to the original Executive Committee dominated by Caballero. Communist help was still needed to eliminate Largo Caballero's control over the fourteen federations of the *UGT* which remained outside the control of the new Executive Committee. It was, after all, primarily due to the efforts and pressure of the Communists that Caballero had been removed from his pinnacle of power and was losing his popularity.

It is possible that the Communists could have achieved the unification of the proletariat into a single party under their leadership if they had used different tactics. They were on their way to success, having accomplished the unification of the Communist and Socialist Youth movements and the creation of the United Socialist Party of Catalonia. Perhaps if they had not been so impatient in seizing control over the United Youth and the United Socialist Party of Catalonia at the very beginning they would have been successful in the unification of the Socialists and Communists all over Spain. More than any other single factor it was the example of Communist domination of the *JSU* and *PSUC* which made the Socialists shy away from unification with the Communists.

THE DISSIDENT SOCIALIST YOUTH

When the United Socialist Youth was established in March, 1936, many of the original Socialist Youth refused to enroll after it became known that the Communists would dominate. Many of these groups created un-official "Socialist Youth" organs closely associated with the Socialist party in their locality, as for example in Jaén, Albacete, and Almería. These groups persistently refused to enter the *JSU* and the Communists carried on a continuous campaign to bring these dissidents into the fold. When direct attack did not work they tried to apply pressure through the Socialist party and one of the articles in the Communist-Socialist Pact of August 17, 1937, stated:

14. United Youth: Given the enormous importance of the *J.S.U.* which has in its fold hundreds of thousands of combatants on the fronts and in industry, who are col-laborating unselfishly with the Government and join with the rest of the organiza-tions in solving the problems of war, the Socialist and Communist Parties must sup-port with all their forces the United Socialist Youth and their political, economic and cultural recovery which will assure a worthy and happy life for the youth and must struggle against the enemies of unity of the youth, who are those who struggle against the unity of the two parties, against the Government and the Popular Front.[7]

In spite of these pious phrases and promised support by the Socialist party, the *JSU* made few converts from the dissident youth. The Com-munists continued to regret the presence of these "Socialist Youth" groups and declared:

We hope that the Socialist Party will correct these violations. The National Execu-tive has in its hands the power to prevent any provincial organ of the Party from in-vading the area of youth and from provoking a division which the youth do not want....[8]

As the Socialist party, however, was resisting more and more the merger plan of the Communists the chance of recovery of the dissident youth to the *JSU* became less and less. Thus the Communists received still another setback to their United Front goals.

ANTI-COMMUNIST ACTIVITIES

The Socialists had secured their position in the government during the summer and fall of 1937 and, therefore, felt strong enough to move against the Communists' overwhelming predominance in the Defense Ministry. The activities of the corps of political commissars (about ninety per cent of whom were Communists) were increasingly restricted and on November 18, 1937, Álvarez del Vayo resigned from his post as Chief Political Commissar. Following his resignation steps were taken gradually to disband the corps. On the other hand, the government did not feel able or desirous of acting against the Communist generals since some of the best generals on the Loyalist side were Communists or Communist sympathizers such as Lister, Modesto, El Campesino, and Miaja.

Another setback for the Communists was the trial of the Central Committee of the *POUM*. Manuel Irujo, the Minister of Justice, made sure that the judges were reliable and that the charges of treason were quashed because the weak evidence of the Communists seemed too obviously trumped up.

On October 1, 1937, the Cortes was reconvened by Negrín with about half its members. Among them were deputies of Lerroux's Radical party and of the Centre party, including Portela Valladares, who had been Premier in February, 1936. The Communists, with only sixteen deputies out of about two hundred, were in the small minority. "Indeed, at least one Communist deputy rose up in protest against the presence of so many reactionaries."[9] The Communists found themselves overshadowed in the Cortes by the Socialists and Republicans, which came as somewhat of a blow to their prestige since the overwhelming majority favored a moderate non-Communist government. The Communists, fearing that their opponents would take advantage of this supremacy in the Cortes, started a campaign for new parliamentary elections. Their demand was not without justification. Certainly the tide of opinion had greatly changed since February, 1936. The Communists, in particular, would have shown a much greater following, which explains their enthusiasm for the idea. The Communists also brought forth other arguments in favor of an election:

... it is evident that the uprising of the Spanish fascists supported by the troops of Italian and German occupation troops has aroused against it all the Spanish people who are struggling for national independence. But the fascist propaganda, the reactionary press, including some of the conservative English politicians and French reactionaries, say that our people are subject to a Communist dictatorship and that the devil of red dictators will not allow them to manifest their opinions freely. Under these conditions, a democratic consulting of the people organized under the banner of the Popular Front will have the significance of a true national plebiscite and will demonstrate to the entire world the truth; it will demonstrate that while in the bourgeois democracies they permit the aggression of German and Italian fascism against the Spanish people, the immense majority are behind the government of the Popular Front, support democracy and are against fascism.

A democratic consulting of the people will mobilize more completely the masses in the struggle against fascism, increase their enthusiasm, increase and consolidate the authority of the Government of the Popular Front, and will create the conditions for ending the war victoriously before very long.[10]

The Negrín government, however, refused to consider the Communist request for calling an election at this time. The main argument against it was the enormous problem of carrying out an election during a war, especially a civil war. The task of registering the voters and then balloting them among the army and a population which had large sections of refugees shifting from place to place was impossible. Consequently, the Communists again had to give way to the moderate Socialists and Republicans.[11]

After the Prieto Socialists had achieved a curtailment of Communist power in the army and a setback in Communist prestige by quashing the *POUM* trial and convening the Cortes, Negrín took the final step. In a speech at the end of October, he brought an end to the discussions of unity between the Communist and Socialist parties, saying that such a rigid framework was more suitable to Franco than to the Republic. As a result of these countermoves on the part of the Socialists, the Communists' efforts to establish a single proletarian party were frustrated, at least for the moment. Thus, by the fall of 1937, the battle lines over the remaining spoils of power were clearly drawn between the Communists and the moderate Socialists under Prieto, who were also supported by the Republicans. The Communists, not wanting to upset unduly the conduct of the war and recognizing that they could not win an open struggle with the moderate Socialists because most of the Spanish Loyalists would have rallied around Prieto against the "foreigner," refrained from any overt act against the Socialists. This restraint on the part of the Communists is further support of the thesis that the Communists were not seeking domination but only active resistance to Franco. The Socialists, for their part, also took no drastic measures against the Communists because of the strong and influential positions of the latter and because their own position in power was not secure enough to launch such an attack. The two factions remained in awe of each other and continued to rule the country in an uneasy alliance. As to the program to be followed by the government there was little disagreement, so the government's operations during this period ran smoothly for the most part.

In spite of rebuffs, the Communists continued to declare that their most essential project was to bring about the unity of the two parties, but they were able to make very little progress in this direction beyond the continued functioning of the coördination committees.[12]

CHAPTER XIX

THE RENEWAL OF THE POPULAR FRONT

THE POLICY OF the united proletarian party having again failed, the Communists turned their attention to the restoration of the Popular Front for the final struggle against Franco. Its revival depended on bringing the Anarchists back into close coöperation with the government. The Communists, from the time of the May crisis, had urged the Anarchists to come back into the government and restore good relations with the Communist party. The Communists were continually sending them fraternal greetings:

> Comrade Anarchists . . . we extend our hands to you in a sincere spirit of fraternity. We want to form a solid and strong union against which every attack of our enemies will be shattered. Can it be that our proffered hand will be ignored?[1]

The terror against the Anarchists during the summer and fall of 1937, however, made it impossible for them to coöperate with the Communists, though surprisingly enough they did refrain from open opposition to the government.

The first move toward the reëstablishment of friendly relations between the parties of the Left was among the youth. The Communists had long been pushing an Alliance of Anti-Fascist Youth (*AJA*).[2] In November, 1937, the Communists, through the *JSU*, were finally successful in establishing the desired alliance. The main contingents of this new union were the Libertarian Youth and the United Socialist Youth. The Communists estimated that seventy per cent of all Spanish youth adhered to the *AJA*. The program of the new league of youth (*AJA*) was similar to that backed by the Communists and Republicans though in milder form in order to appeal to the Anarchist youth. Its policy aimed solely at winning the war: support of the government, greater production of war material, discipline in the army, and defense of the independence of Spain from fascism.[3] The *AJA* was strictly an alliance between the leadership of the youth groups on both national and local levels; at the same time each youth movement maintained its separate entity. The Communists hoped that it might develop into a unified youth movement of all Spanish youth, but the components jealously held to their own hierarchy.

With the successful restoration of the Popular Front among the youth, the Communists had laid the foundation for the return of good relations with the Anarchists. The terror against the Anarchists for the most part had come to an end by November, 1937, and the breach between the *CNT* on the one hand and the Communists and government on the other had begun to heal. By the beginning of January, 1938, reëstablishment of the Popular Front with the Anarchists became possible. The Communist Politbureau as early as October had set the winning over of the Anarchists as one of its main tasks. "... The Politbureau of the Communist Party is not only ready to resume conversations with the leading committees of the *C.N.T.*, but points out the necessity of fraternal collaboration with the *C.N.T.* to all the organizations of the Party in order to solve the concrete problems raised by the war and revolution."[4] The Communists not only hoped for the Anarchists' support of the government of Negrín but their actual participation in it. Dolores Ibarruri, in an address to the Cortes on October 2, stated:

> I know that it is not the fault of the Government that the workers belonging to the *C.N.T.* are not represented in it. I know that it is not the Government that is to blame for this, but we cannot ignore the importance of the *C.N.T.* in our country. In revolutionary policy none of us should be guided by personal likes or dislikes, and therefore we must find ways and means of getting the really revolutionary workers in the ranks of the *C.N.T.* to take a share in the Government.[5]

The moderate Socialists and Republicans, however, having successfully held power without the Anarchists for six months, saw no reason to take in these revolutionaries and persistently refused to do so.

The Communists had to be content with alliances outside the government. They showed particular interest in close coöperation between the *CNT* and the newly reconstituted *UGT*. They urged the revitalization of the coördination committees between the two trade-union movements and, of course, in line with their United Front policy urged that the committees go the limit and establish one great trade-union.[6]

Although neither the *UGT* nor the *CNT* was willing to consider unification, they were both anxious to come to a working agreement in regard to the pursuit of the war. Negotiations between the two central unions began in January, 1938. The Communists for their part, though they only represented a minority in the *UGT*, pressed with all their vigor in the discussions and outside for the successful conclusion of the negotiations on the basis of their own war program.

The discussions finally bore fruit on March 18, when a joint program was signed by both central unions. The pact marked a further retreat by the Anarchists from their ideal of Libertarianism. Its terms included the primary objective of the Communists and government—the subjugation of industry to centralized control and to an over-all economic plan. As compensation the Anarchists obtained some support by the *UGT* for collectivization of agriculture, but only on a volunteer basis. The *UGT* agreed also to urge the government to cease its dissolution of collective farms in Catalonia and Aragon and to pass a law legalizing the remaining collectives. As another concession to the *CNT*, the *UGT* assented to legalization of workers' control of industry for the protection of the workingman's rights.

The Communists reported that in their original proposals the Anarchists had asked for a great deal more: the control of all military units by means of councils with proportional representation of all anti-Fascist groups, liberal credit for collectivized enterprises, forced collectivization of agriculture except where a peasant farmed the land alone, and the municipalization of all houses.[7] These proposals were, however, either stubbornly refused by the *UGT* or only allowed after they had been greatly watered down. Thus, in arriving at an agreement the Anarchists were forced to retreat again and again. The *UGT*, on the other hand, was highly successful in getting the Anarchists to acquiesce to its main demands which dealt mostly with the control of industry. The Anarchists yielded to government control over the armament industries, transport, and the main raw materials. They further agreed that it was the job of the unions above all else to promote greater production in the factories. They consented to nationalization of mines, railroads, heavy industry, air transport, and banks, rather than their preferred aim of collectivization. Finally they assented to an over-all national economic plan for industry to be supervised by the state.[8]

The seriousness of the war situation (Teruel had fallen and the Republic was being cut in two) and the fear of the rebels' "white" terror made the sacrifices by the Anarchists possible. They did not feel that the momentary shifting of aims was as dangerous as the threat of Franco. At this time the feeling of community and coöperation was at its highest among the working classes who had come to realize that only through unity was there a chance of success. For this they sacrificed their most cherished utopias.

The Communists, by means of the coöperation of the working classes, had succeeded in restoring the Popular Front. The Communists, of course, only saw it as a step toward complete unity: "This pact opens up new prospects for us which lead us to hope that very soon it will be possible to raise the question of forming one single united trade union organisation in our country."[9] They continued to press for the next step.

Under continuous Communist pressure the bourgeoisie were gradually urged to accept the collaboration of the Anarchists. The Republican and right Socialist groups in Spain had only narrowly won a battle over the Libertarian revolution the previous year and were not easily persuaded to give up any of the fruits of their victory. But the difficulties of war and the fact that the Anarchists had renounced more of their revolutionary aims convinced the government leaders that the Anarchists should be again allowed to share in the rule of the Popular Front. Consequently, during the serious defeats of the Loyalist troops in the spring of 1938, two members of the *CNT* were given posts in the cabinet. This was only half their previous representation, but for the sake of the defense of the Republic and compromise, the Anarchists accepted this reduction.

CHAPTER XX

THE REMOVAL OF PRIETO

PRIETO AND THE COMMUNISTS

THE COMMUNISTS had a strong opponent in the Minister of Defense, Indalecio Prieto, who tried to reduce their influence in the armed forces. Prieto was actively backed in his attempts by the Ministers of Interior and Justice, Julian Zugazagoitia and Manuel Irujo, who tried in their departments to cut down the activities of the Communist *Cheka*. As previously discussed, Prieto started his attack with the gradual elimination of the system of political commissars. From this he carried his attack to the Communist position in the *SIM* (*Servicio de Investigación Militar* created in August, 1937) whose job it was to hunt out spies and traitors. He dismissed Durán, the Communist chief of the *SIM*, and sought to replace some of the Communists in the bureau with reliable Socialists. Furthermore, whenever possible he protected non-Communist commanders from persecution and favored them over Communist commanders. But the Communists were too deeply entrenched in the army for these reforms to unseat them, though in time they might have had that effect.

The reaction of the Communists to these reforms was a surprise. Instead of fighting them and campaigning against Prieto as a Fascist, which was their usual tactic, they took no overt actions against him or against any of the moderate Socialists and Republicans who were opposing the Communist party sway in the government. By January, 1938, it looked as if the Communists were slowly being forced to retreat into the background before the general hostility of Negrín's moderate government. Perhaps the explanation for this Communist docility can be found in the fact that although there was jealousy between the two groups over personal prerogatives, there existed no variance in respect to general war policies.

Up to the fall of 1937, the Republic had not done very well militarily. October, 1937, had marked the final conquest of the northern provinces and on almost all fronts the Loyalists had been forced to lose ground. In the meantime, however, Prieto, with the help of the Communists, had been slowly creating an effective, well-disciplined army. Because of Prieto's efforts and success in the reorganization of the army and because of the still delicate military situation, the Communists were reluctant to create any internal dissension with anti-Communists in the government.

By December, 1937, the new army had been completed and sought redress for the Republic's previous losses by attempting an assault against Teruel, a Nationalist stronghold standing at the head of a salient into Loyalist territory and in a position to cut the Republic in two. By January 8, Prieto's army successfully took Teruel and proved that they could effectively carry out an attack.

Although the Republican troops had succeeded in capturing Teruel, the offensive had not proved as advantageous as expected because of devastating Nationalist counterattacks which resulted in heavy losses for the Loyalists not only in men but in territory. When the Republican assault bogged down in February, 1938, the Nationalists launched their own offensive along the Ebro River near the border of Catalonia and pushed steadily along both shores, inflicting costly defeat after costly defeat on the Republican army. On March 22, 1938, the Nationalists temporarily broke through the Republican lines and pushed a salient deep into Loyalist territory. These continued reverses for the Loyalists had their effect on the frail working balance of Negrín's cabinet.

The strain of the defeats had two main consequences. First, the serious military reversals called for either a radical change in policy or a victim to act as a scapegoat for the failures. The army had done its best and no one could offer a program which could hope for greater success. The only solution, therefore, seemed to be to sacrifice Negrín's cabinet or some member of it as an atonement for the continued losses. To involve the entire cabinet would have discredited the majority of the political forces in the country, leaving only the Anarchists and left Socialists untouched. The logical choice of a sacrifice, therefore, was Prieto—as Minister of War and head of the defenses.

The second consequence of the military reverses was to divide the moderate camp of the Loyalists regarding the policy which should be followed from this point on. Almost two years of civil war had begun to show its strain. The lassitude of the people and leaders was now marked. Food was increasingly short, particularly in Catalonia which had always been deficient in food, and with the large influx of refugees during the war starvation became prevalent.[1] Furthermore, it was impossible to build a modern efficient army with the latest arms out of a backward, shrinking economy with only the help of the far distant Soviet Union. Yet this was necessary in order to fight the well-supplied rebel troops. In the previous year the most strenuous and vigorous efforts had been put forth to create an army of some competence, and even though a disciplined force had been organized, it stood little chance against the forces of Franco backed by the industrial and military might of Italy and Germany. After its first meager success at Teruel, the army had been forced to retreat. It appeared to some of the Loyalist leaders that Spain was fighting alone against the world. The Fascist powers were actively and openly helping Franco while the democracies stood on the side lines and watched the Loyalists being sacrificed without making the slightest effort to help them. England and France were even considering recognizing the belligerency of Franco in order to protect their own interests in Spain and to insure that they would not become involved. Only the Soviet Union lent support, but it was able to offer little assurance and hope. Russia was far away and sent only a small quantity of supplies compared to the Fascists. Furthermore, the price she charged in both influence and gold was high. Thus the revolutionary enthusiasm that had met the first days of the Civil War was replaced by widespread despondency. Victory was now only an illusion shouted in Communist propaganda.

Several of the government leaders, after the failure of the Teruel offensive, concluded that the Loyalist cause was defeated and that the possibility of the democracies coming to their aid was over. They became anxious, therefore, to end the war as soon as possible and come out of it as best they could. By concluding the war they hoped to stop further property losses, to end the heavy and devastating financial burden, to lessen the terrorism which followed after Franco's army, and perhaps to moderate the rule of the Right. They hoped too for a negotiated peace which would salvage at least something of their former position.

Against this despairing group were the Communists who opposed any attempt to shorten the war through negotiation. They still spoke of victory though the word had become increasingly hollow. The Communists were willing to go to any lengths to continue the resistance.

In between these two groups was the mass of the people. They were exhausted and hurt by the hardships of war. Their revolutionary enthusiasm had been replaced by helplessness and dejection; yet they were not anxious to go back to the old days which held nothing for them but a type of semislave existence. In a negotiated peace they could hope for nothing. Their aims of revolution and a better life for themselves would never be considered at the negotiators' table. Unlike the bourgeoisie, they had nothing to save or recover; their struggle had been for a more promising future and their dreams were rapidly fading into the aura of impossibility. Consequently, over the masses was descending a deep despair without the shadow of hope or faith. Yet, as long as there was even the slightest chance for success in the Loyalist cause they fought, though with decreasing ardor. Perhaps they felt it was better to die fighting than to go back to the past.

As a result the Communists, in their demand for resistance, had at least the enervated assistance of the masses. In the government itself the Communists were supported by Negrín and a number of the moderate Socialists. In opposition, on the side of a negotiated peace, stood Prieto as the leader. In his support were the vast majority of the Republicans and right Socialists, including Azaña. They saw no sense in the continued depletion of Spain for a forlorn hope.

From his character it was logical that Prieto should have headed the opposition to continuation of the war. Although he had shown himself a man of excellent capabilities in the organization of the army, there was another side to Prieto—that of the pessimist. Zugazagoitia describes this melancholic aspect of Prieto at the time of the collapse of the northern provinces:

> ... Of all, the most inconsolable was Prieto. His anguish inspired respect.... He said to the Government Council of Vasco:
>
> "I have had some hours so bitter and judged so severely what I considered to be my responsibility that, apart from having sent to the head of the Government a letter of resignation, I thought of suicide. This idea became an obsession and I was on the point of getting a pistol. This seemed to me the only solution."[2]

Zugazagoitia is not an unprejudiced observer but his report is substantiated from other quarters. Being a pessimist, Prieto was soon discouraged by the travails of war. As early as May, 1937, during the Barcelona uprising, he became so fearful of a revolution or a rapid Franco victory because of the internal dissensions of the Republic that he secretly began negotiations for a peace with Franco.[3] Even at that time he felt that the Loyalists could not prevent Franco's victory. Prieto, backed by some of the Republican groups, continued during the summer and fall of 1937 to try through various agencies, including one of his secretaries, Ángel Baza, to see if some basis for a negotiated peace could be found. Franco, however, was too close to military success to desire a negotiated peace. Also, having a continuous supply of war material from his Fascist allies, he saw no reason to give up the campaign short of imposing unconditional surrender. The failure to get any favorable response from Franco, nevertheless, did not deter Prieto's efforts, and his secretary continued to maintain contact through the Commander at Irún.[4]

Another explanation for the discouragement of the Republicans and Prieto for the Loyalist cause is that they felt themselves caught between a Fascist and a Communist dictatorship. Indalecio Prieto and Colonel

S. Casado alluded to this in their explanations for the defeat.[5] Such men as Azaña, and especially Prieto, actively disliked the Communists and perhaps feared them. It was, however, by no means a universal feeling even among the Republicans. Prieto's protegé, Julian Zugazagoitia, for example, did not appear troubled by this fear, nor does he mention it in his history of the Civil War. It is perhaps significant that this explanation for seeking a negotiated peace only appeared later when the various leaders sought to free themselves from blame for the collapse of the Republic. Fear of a Communist dictatorship as the cause of pessimism for men like Prieto also overlooks other facts which are well established. Prieto, as has been indicated, was fundamentally pessimistic in his outlook. Furthermore, the war situation had become hopeless for the Loyalists unless they could secure more aid from abroad and such a possibility seemed remote. In such a case pessimism about the cause was not surprising nor does it seem unjustifiable. The very men who appeared to have feared a Soviet dictatorship were those who had allied with the Communists to overthrow Caballero. Prieto, in fact, had begun his negotiations with Franco not when the danger of Communism was at its height, but when the extreme Left tried to uphold their revolution against encroachment by the central government during May, 1937. Finally the retreat of the Communists before the anti-Communist moves of Prieto must have allayed the fears of many of the Republicans. It would appear, in conclusion, that the Republicans, although not trusting the Communists, did not fear them. They considered the popularity of Communism to be temporary, based mostly on Russian aid. The major reason, therefor, for the pessimism of the moderate groups was the rapidly disintegrating military position of the Republic.

ANOTHER CABINET CRISIS

In view of the two different outlooks of the future on the part of Prieto and the Communists it is not surprising that after the defeats of February and March, 1938, sharp disagreements should have become prevalent. The Communists, following their usual pattern against their opponents, soon began a campaign of defamation against Prieto. Although the main objection to Prieto was his gloomy outlook in respect to the course of the war, personal antagonism toward him on the part of the Communists and their desire for an expiation for the defeats also contributed to the Communist desire to be rid of him. As early as March 1, 1938, Prieto reports that he sent a note to Negrin complaining of attacks on him by the Communists:

I invite you if you have not read them to look at the speeches given at a public function of the Communists which was celebrated day before yesterday in Barcelona and whose literal texts have been published by the press friendly to that party.

* * *

In them and particularly in that of Valdés, (in that of the "Pasionaria" appear paragraphs which should have been cut out by the censor with whom I am not acquainted) are very clear allusions to my ministerial actions which in context constitute an attack. This along with the manifesto which was published by the Regional Committee of the Communist Party of Cartagena, describing me as being none the less than the enemy of the people—a document which I already brought to your attention—signifies the displeasure of the Communist Party is a thing of public knowledge, as I had foreseen and about which as you know Dolores Ibárruri notified me officially, in connection with my official duties in the Ministry of National Defense. (In respect to this I must tell you I received a visit from the "Pasionaria" who came to tell me that the Politbureau of the Communist Party was not in agreement with my actions). . . .[6]

The real frontal attack on Prieto by the Communists came at the end of March when two articles appeared in the Communist press signed by "Juan Ventura," who was actually Jesús Hernández, the Communist Minister of Public Instruction. The articles dealt primarily, as the one title "Pessimist Impenitent" indicates, with Prieto's lack of courage and his despondency which, the article declared, was spreading through the army and was causing a significant lowering of morale. The last article even suggested his elimination from the government. Such an attack by one minister of the government against another was a serious matter and was contrary to the idea of collective responsibility for the acts of the government.[7] Negrín's reaction was to side with Prieto as he considered Jesús Hernández' action reprehensible. Negrín, however, as Prime Minister had to move cautiously. He dared not move rashly against Hernández. Negrín, in the interest of stability in the government at a time when its troops were being forced to retreat before Franco's offensive on the Ebro, had to try to maintain the *status quo* in the cabinet at least until the rebel offensive could be stopped.

Negrín felt that he could not arbitrarily dismiss Jesús Hernández because he feared alienation of the Communists. More than ever the Communists held the whip hand with their control over Soviet aid, which was needed desperately to resist the growing strength and efficiency of the rebel troops. Prieto, himself, admitted this dilemma which the crisis put before Negrín.[8]

Negrín felt that Jesús Hernández had gone too far in making a personal attack on Prieto, but at the same time he agreed with the Communists that Prieto had become a demoralizing influence. Two incidents occurred which alarmed Negrín over the effects of Prieto's despair. In a letter written to Prieto subsequently, when both men were in exile, Negrín explained his concern over Prieto's reaction to the military situation. In respect to its effect on the cabinet he had this to say:

... During the night of 29 and 30 of March there surged within me a very painful and violent struggle. It was the consequence of the meeting of the Ministers on the night of March 29 (cited from memory) in which you, with your suggestive eloquence, your habitual *pathos* and the authority of your position and person demoralized completely our colleagues in the Government by altering the successes with tinges of somber despair and presenting as false, the conclusions which were maintained by the Council of War held the day before together with the Military Staff. Far from encouraging and comforting them concerning the burden of the tasks and events you overwhelmed them with depression by the pessimistic tone of your opinions, your skepticism before all favorable prospects, your sinister forecasts and your lack of faith and enthusiasm.[9]

Even more serious was the effect Prieto's defeatism had on the French Ambassador. In the same letter to Prieto, Negrín describes this incident:

... I was also impressed by a conversation held on Sunday, the 27th of March, with M. Labonne, the French Ambassador, at the moment when we were arranging the rapid dispatch by France of material, which had been offered in principle. When I traveled in that country at the beginning of March, I had succeeded in opening the frontier. When I pressed for speedy implementation of the agreement, the French Ambassador asked me if I did not know that the Minister of Defense, Sr. Prieto, had given up the war as lost. This was the information he had—I never said, nor did he say that he had heard it directly—which as the French representative in Spain he had transmitted though he still advised acquiescence to our demands.[10]

Prieto's so-called pessimism on the military situation at that time was, it would seem, nothing more than an honest and good analysis of the deteriorating military situation during this period. But its expression, even in official circles, was imprudent.

Negrín and Prieto had always been very good friends, which made it difficult for Negrín to take action.[11] Another complicating factor was the fact that Prieto had a very strong personal following among the Socialists who would go into opposition to the government if he were dismissed. The most important consideration, however, was the military situation. As Negrín later described it, "The front was broken; it scarcely existed; a large part of our army was being routed; panic was widespread; the morale of our rear was collapsing...."[12] Such a situation was not the time for a government crisis, which would only further spread chaos. Thus Negrín had no desire to eliminate Prieto from the cabinet altogether, but he was of the opinion that it was necessary to reshuffle the cabinet and give Prieto another job where his pessimism would not have such a disastrous effect. This would also have pleased the Communists who wanted to be sure that the government would persist in its war efforts in spite of the odds and defeats.

Julian Zugazagoitia says, "Negrín struggled sincerely with these two alternatives: to separate Prieto from the Defense Department and keep him in the Government."[13] Negrín's first step was to open negotiations with the Communists to see what could be done to compensate for the indiscretion committed by Jesús Hernández. The Communists agreed that they would not put any difficulty in the way of the dismissal of their comrade from the cabinet. Negrín then tried to form a new cabinet with Prieto either as Minister of Public Works and Railroads or as Minister Without Portfolio. To soothe the feelings of the Communists over the dismissal of Jesús Hernández he also planned to replace José Giral as Foreign Minister with Álvarez del Vayo. The resistance of Azaña to Álvarez del Vayo and the refusal of Prieto to accept either post ended this attempt of Negrín to find a compromise. Prieto later quoted his response to Negrín's proposals as he gave them to Zugazagoitia who served as intermediary:

But Negrín knows that I have advocated all communications should come under the authority of National Defense....

Negrín on previous occasions has dismissed Ministers by naming them Ministers Without Portfolio. This would be a solution to satisfy his wishes—ha!—but I would not be a Minister Without Portfolio simply to be furnished with an automobile and an elegant driver and run out to Councils to dispatch each time thirty or forty cases of death penalties....[14]

Since Prieto refused to hold any other position than Minister of Defense, considering it a demotion and a humiliation which he could not accept,[15] all further attempts at a cabinet solution including Prieto were hopeless and Negrín was forced to form a cabinet without him. He continued to insist, however, on Álvarez del Vayo as Foreign Minister against the objections of Azaña, who in the end could do nothing against Negrín's insistence. As a close friend of Prieto, Zugazagoitia had also resigned from the cabinet. The new cabinet thus included Negrín as Minister of Defense, Gonzales Peña as Minister of Justice, Gómez Sainz of the Socialist party as Minister of Interior, and Álvarez del Vayo as Minister of Foreign Affairs. The party strength was four Socialists, two members of the *CNT*, and one each from the Communists, Basque Nationalists, Catalonian Esquerra, the Union Republicans, and Left Republicans.

Once Prieto had been removed from office the Communists stopped their campaign against him. Unlike their bitter indictment of Largo Caballero after his defeat, the Communists rarely mentioned Prieto in their propaganda. Even when he lashed out against Communist control in the government no counterattack was made against him. The Communists probably felt that it was not the time to make more enemies, especially of such an influential leader as Prieto. Furthermore, such an attack could have been used to accuse them of splitting the Loyalist camp during the final struggle of the Republic for existence.

CHAPTER XXI

THE LAST DAYS

THE POLICIES OF THE NEW NEGRÍN CABINET

FROM THE FIRST glance at Negrín's new cabinet it would seem that the Communists, by the dismissal of Jesús Hernández, had lost half their strength in the government. This does not reflect the true state of affairs. In the first place Álvarez del Vayo, whom the Communists favored, received the very important post of Minister of Foreign Affairs to replace Hernández' loss of the Ministry of Public Instruction, a post of much less importance. Furthermore, the elimination of Prieto, who was the strongest anti-Communist in the cabinet, brought an end to discriminations against the Communists. Left to oppose them were only Azaña and his Republican supporters whose counteractions were not very effective against the Communists in the armed services. The head of the Defense Ministry was now Negrín, who was friendly to the Communists. As a result the hostility to the Communists' strong position in the army was ended, and the campaign to unseat the Communists was reversed. One of the first acts of the new government was to restore the broad powers of the political commissars. Jesús Hernández was appointed chief commissar for central and southern Spain to compensate him for the loss of his cabinet post. In the General Staff, General Rojo was replaced by the strong Communist supporter, Colonel Modesto. Thus it appeared that by the elimination of Prieto the Communists were preparing to seize power. The military situation, however, deterred the Communists from any such idea. The splitting of the Loyalist territory by the successful offensive of Franco along the Ebro River made the situation of the Republic hopeless, barring some radical change on the international scene. Seizure of power by the Communists at this time would have meant taking over control for the inglorious role of leading the Republic into defeat. Furthermore, Soviet aid came to a stop a few months later, which was a strong indication that the Soviet leadership was writing off the Spanish adventure as hopeless. The Communists' reason for strengthening their position after Prieto resigned was probably only to eliminate those leaders who despaired of the Loyalist cause and to build up the forces of resistance.

The policy of the new cabinet followed that of the previous one and was expressed by Negrín on May 1, in the form of thirteen points. This declaration was mainly another attempt to gain adherents among the democracies by expressing democratic and liberal slogans. Also it was to serve as propaganda among the rebels by promising general amnesty. The points were summed up as follows:

The maintenance of the independence and integrity of Spain and its deliverance from invasion and economic penetration; the determination of the legal and social form of the new Republic by the national will expressed in a free plebiscite with full guarantees against reprisals, which would be held as soon as hostilities were at an end; respect for regional liberties, in accordance with law and historical tradition, insofar as these liberties did not impair the unity and integrity of Spain; a guarantee by the state to all citizens of "full civil and social rights, including freedom of conscience," and an assurance of "the free exercise of religious beliefs"; a guarantee by the state of the right to hold lawfully acquired property, within limits determined by the supreme interests of the nation; exploitation would be prevented, but individual enterprise would be allowed and small property-owners would be encouraged, the property of foreigners who had not assisted the Nationalists would be respected, and compensation would be paid for damage done to it as a result of the war; agrarian reform and the creation of a rural democracy owning the land that it worked; adoption of a foreign policy renouncing war, supporting the League of Nations and Collective Security, and claiming a place for Spain in the Concert of Nations as a Mediterranean Power fully capable of defending herself; and amnesty for all Spaniards willing to take part in the reconstruction and liberation of their country.[1]

Although professing liberal principles in his thirteen points, Negrín found it necessary to take more stringent action against "uncontrollables" which soon verged on a reign of terror. It is difficult to say how much of this increased coercion was due to increased Communist influence and how much to the necessities of the situation. It would seem that the two motives were actually closely intertwined. The Communists were not interested in terror *per se*, but when propaganda and persuasion would no longer bring results, the Communists quickly resorted to forceful methods. The defeats of March and April, 1938, and the resignation of Prieto had had serious results on the prosecution of the war. In the first place, among the bourgeoisie these happenings had crystallized the desire to negotiate a peace with Franco before it was too late. There were frequent rumors, often involving Republican cabinet ministers, concerning attempts to come to terms with Franco. Secondly, there was growing despondency among the people who were no longer affected by propaganda and occasionally needed additional persuasion to carry on. Additionally, there was chaos caused by the defeats and the disintegrating prestige of government authority. At such times it is not uncommon for people to lose their respect for the government which is on the way out. Such a trend results in extensive lawlessness which requires additional repression to keep the people in order. Finally the weakening of the Republic made the rebel sympathizers much bolder in their acts against the Loyalists. These factors made the government and the Communists conclude that the only way to deal with the situation was to make use of repressive measures. Therefore, the activities of the *SIM* (*Servicio de Investigación Militar*) were redoubled. Sometimes it spread terror and murder indiscriminately.[2]

Along with the increased use of the secret police the government strengthened its control over industry and assumed more of the powers of the Catalonian Generalitat which it felt was not capable of handling the situation. During August the cabinet approved three decrees: the militarization of industries, the militarization of the special tribunals, and the creation of a Special Chamber in Barcelona directly dependent on the Minister of Justice of the Republic and designed to prevent smuggling and the flight of capital abroad. These decrees were an attempt to establish a system of semimartial law throughout the country in an effort to mobilize forces for the last effort against Franco. In protest against this attempt by the government, Manuel Irujo, Basque Nationalist Minister Without Portfolio, and Jaime Ayguadé, Minister of Labor and member of the Catalan Esquerra, resigned from the cabinet.[3] To take the vacant posts a member of the United Socialist Party of Catalonia (*PSUC*) and a Socialist were appointed. The addition of a member of the *PSUC*, which was Communist-dominated, increased Communist strength in the cabinet.

Though a system of martial law was gradually being imposed on the remaining territory of the Republic, the terrorism carried on by the secret police during the summer of 1938 was relaxed. In August the government tried to prepare the way for a general amnesty by proposing that each side should suspend the execution of death sentences on military prisoners for a month. Though no agreement was reached on this point, both Nationalists and Republicans seem to have considerably reduced the number of executions of civil as well as military prisoners during the rest of the year.

Since the remaining government leaders were more or less of one mind to resist, and since the final stand and evacuation allowed little time for internal politics, the Negrín government remained fairly stable until the last days. On the outside, however, Prieto had begun to attack Negrín more and more openly and was gathering around him all the dissident elements. On August 9, Prieto, before the National Committee of the Socialist Party, openly attacked Negrín for the Russian "intrigues" in the government and for dismissing him.[4] At the same time a group of the

Catalonian bourgeoisie was openly proposing secession and a separate peace with the Burgos government.

THE FALL OF CATALONIA

During the serious setback of the spring of 1938 there had been constant rumors that Franco would continue to push his advantage and would seize Valencia and Barcelona and the war would be over by summer. The government, however, was able to rally its forces and put an end to Franco's advances. His advance along the coast toward Castellon and Valencia was brought to a standstill, and the Loyalist forces were even able to take the offensive along the Ebro at the end of July. As a result, the Republicans recovered some of the previously lost territory but did not have the strength to push their advantage and were stopped by the superior rebel forces. In spite of Franco's superior arms and aircraft, the Republicans continued to hold tenaciously to their positions and to the territory remaining to them.

Throughout the summer and fall Franco assembled troops and provisions for an all-out offensive against Catalonia, the heart of the war industry of the Republic. He felt that once he had eliminated Catalonia the rest of the campaign would merely be mopping-up operations. The offensive began on December 23, and rapidly overran the carefully planned defenses of the Republic. The Nationalist forces were helped by three important factors. First, the Munich agreement, which sacrificed Czechoslovakia to Germany, made the Republicans lose heart.[5] This was final proof that no matter how extensive the invasion of Spain by Italian and German troops the democracies would never come to their aid. The Czechoslovakian crisis marked the final realization by the Loyalists that the democracies had never intended to help them. They had long suspected this but there had always been a faint hope which kept them going and kept them appealing to the humanitarianism of the democratic peoples. Their cause after September, 1938, had become absolutely hopeless against the might of the Fascist powers.[6] A second factor which helped Franco was the growing food scarcity in Catalonia. Although the bombing tactics of the Rebel air force, which were intended to terrorize the people, had failed, the same end was accomplished by the shortage of food. Without food, the people had no heart to fight. As a result, when the Nationalists finally entered Barcelona they were greeted with relief and almost with cheers because it meant the end of starvation. Finally, the Nationalist assault was aided by the end of the flow of foreign aid to the Republic. After the Loyalists' July offensive the International

Brigade was removed and completely disbanded in September, 1938. Furthermore, after the Munich crisis and the immediate threat to Russia's western frontier, it appears from the evidence available that the Soviet Union concluded she could no longer spare war materials for Spain and, consequently, after the summer of 1938 there is no evidence of the Soviet Union sending any more aid. This is also confirmed by the frequent reports of observers on the Republican front that there was a growing shortage of ammunition and weapons. On January 26, 1939, the Nationalist troops entered Barcelona and the remaining Republican forces in the province fought a rearguard action in a retreat across the French border.

The collapse of Catalonia again brought forth the crucial question for the government of whether or not to resist. After the fall of Prieto, Azaña had continued within the government the cause for a negotiated peace.[7] His efforts, however, were frustrated because as President his powers were limited and because his intermediaries were able to get no encouragement from Franco who held out for unconditional surrender.[8] After Catalonia was overrun Azaña saw no point in resisting any longer even without a negotiated peace. After escaping from Catalonia into France, he refused to go back to Spain. On February 28, 1939, his resignation was announced. Into exile with him went President Companys of the Catalonian Generalitat, President Aguirre of the Basque government, and Martínez Barrio, Speaker of the Cortes. All the persuasion of Negrín and Álvarez del Vayo could not influence them to return to that part of Spain still remaining to the Republic.

The Overthrow of Negrín and the Communists

Actually, what remained to the Republic was still a large section of central Spain, including Madrid and several hundred thousand troops, but little war industry. Negrín, accompanied by Álvarez del Vayo and the Communist leaders, returned to Spain to take up the continued defense of the Republic. On his return Negrín was faced with a crisis among the army commanders and within the government. The leaders of all the Popular Front parties, including the Anarchists and the non-Communist military commanders, had concluded that further resistance was fruitless. Colonel Casado, backed by most of the non-Communist commanders, reasoned the military situation over the previous six months as follows:

... when in a counter-offensive the Republican forces of Catalonia occupied an important bridge-head to the south of the Ebro line, all the tacticians in Spain thought they could see in it a starting point for the French Army. And when the Nationalists began their offensive to recapture it, it seemed that this effort came not so much for fear that the Republican forces would begin a whole offensive of reconquest, as from the possibility that France would decide to intervene at last, and make it impossible that, with the Balearics and the Eastern Pyrenees lost, she would be cut off from her Colonial Empire, amputated in such a way that international balance would be disturbed. For this reason all efforts for peace were perfectly justified after the Nationalists had re-conquered Teruel, but when this opportunity was lost, circumstances made it necessary for us to continue the struggle in the hope that France would decide. But once the rich and important region of Catalonia was lost and consequently the Pyrenean frontier was closed, to continue the struggle was to be blind to all reason, and ... It would have meant leading the people to the most barbarous and inhuman sacrifice in history.[9]

The leaders of the various parties also agreed that it was a useless sacrifice to ask the people to go on fighting in such a hopeless cause. Colonel Casado reports that Negrín called a meeting of all the top commanders of the army and navy on February 26, 1939, to confer on the possibility of continued resistance. He reports that the top commanders, except General Miaja, agreed that the situation was hopeless.[10] Nevertheless Negrín decided to carry on even against these odds.

Behind him Negrín had the solid backing of the Communists. Also large sections of the rank and file troops appear to have supported him.[11] The common soldier had been strongly influenced by the Communist propaganda and the Communist political commissars. Furthermore, in resisting they had little to lose and their hate for the regime of the Right, which Franco would impose, kept them fighting even in the desperate situation of February, 1939.

What Negrín's motives were in calling for continued resistance is by no means clear. Colonel Casado reports that Negrín had been trying to negotiate a peace with Franco for almost a year but had been unsuccessful. Similarly both England and France had been seeking a compromise in the war but had failed to get anywhere against Franco's obstinacy, backed by Germany and Italy. It is impossible to conclude whether Negrín's decision to continue resistance was a matter of personal stubbornness or whether he had some plan. Perhaps he hoped that Franco, not wanting to campaign through the next summer, would agree to a limited compromise.[12] Such a hope does not seem justified in the light of two and a half years of Franco's continued refusal to consider negotiations with the "Red" government. The desperateness of these last days, however, led the Loyalists to cling to forlorn hopes. Another possibility was that Negrín was trying to hold out until the international situation broke and a general war was declared. In this case he felt sure that the democracies would be forced to come to the Republic's aid in order to chase the Fascist powers out of the Iberian peninsula. As it turned out, this was a reasonable assumption. Perhaps if the Loyalists could have held out even in central Spain until the following fall their cause would have been taken up by England and France. The possibility, however, of holding out another six months against overwhelming odds was slim. Furthermore, at the time, no one knew that it would be only a matter of six months.

It is not easy to analyze the motivation of the Communists in supporting Negrín and the resistance. Final consideration of this problem must await a thorough discussion of Soviet foreign policy in relation to Spain at this time. Only possible motives will be mentioned here. Like Negrín, the Communists may have supported a resistance in the hope that negotiations with Franco would be successful or that a general war would start in Western Europe.[13] Most likely, however, their motive was tied up with the policies of the Soviet Union at this time. One answer is that the Soviet Union was interested in keeping the Fascist powers engaged in Spain as long as possible in order to keep them from aggressive action in other quarters. They wanted to hold out in Spain long enough for France to wake up to her own interests. Or, they might already have been moving toward their alliance with Hitler. Luis Araquistain and Julian Gorkin think this was the real Communist motive. Julian Gorkin reasons the moves of the Communists during the final three months as follows:

... Here is my hypothesis which I believe has sufficient foundation. Hitler, in secret negotiations with Stalin, knew that Catalonia would be sacrificed, that Russian arms would not arrive in time for its defense, that the Stalinist commanders of the Central Zone would sabotage the strategic diversion of Motril and the sending of re-enforcements and arms to the Catalan front, that the lines held by the Communists would not put up the least resistance.... [*sic*] And knowing this Hitler would not fail to make it known to Franco. The conquest of Catalonia was because of this a military parade.

After the evacuation of Catalonia and before leaving for the Central Zone, with the aim of carrying out a *coup d'état* and putting all the commands dictatorially in the hands of the Stalinists, which provoked the counter coup of Casado-Besteiro, Álvarez del Vayo, still in the position of Foreign Minister, declared according to his information: "The situation calls for resisting for a couple of months. During this time war will without doubt result between France and Italy." This was the voice of Moscow. ...[14]

It need only be said here that Gorkin is hard put to explain the sacrifice of Catalonia by the Communists in negotiations with Hitler, followed immediately by their desire to resist in the central zone. To put all the blame on the Communists for the crises and misfortunes requires some strenuous mental gymnastics.

Another explanation of the resistance, assuming as above that Stalin wanted to open negotiations with Hitler, is that by holding out in Spain the Communists had a strong bargaining point in negotiating a pact. Also, it would show Hitler that Russia was a power to be reckoned with and was capable of upsetting Hitler's plans even in Western Europe.

In order to counteract the influence of the defeatist commanders, Negrín began rapidly replacing them with Communist commanders. To forestall this move to supersede them the non-Communist commanders on March 5 revolted against Negrín. The revolt was lead by Colonel Casado and had the support of General Miaja, who had by this time wavered from his support of the Communists. Colonel Casado, however, failed to get President Azaña to return to Spain and sanction this new government of the National Defense Council and make it appear legal. Behind the National Defense Council, nevertheless, were not only most of the non-Communist military commanders but most of the leaders of the Socialist, Anarchist, and Republican groups. General Miaja was made President and Colonel Casado, Defense Minister. On the Council the Left Republicans, Anarchists, and Socialists each had two representatives.

The success of the coup forced Negrín and his government to flee the country by air to Algiers. This did not end the struggle, however, because about half the army still supported Negrín and his policy of resistance. Consequently, the Communist party led an armed attack against the new government around Madrid. During the second week of March, 1939, Madrid was fiercely besieged before the Communist counterinsurrection was quelled. After the revolt, drastic action was taken against the Communists. Several were put to death and thousands were placed in prison. After securing its position the National Defense Council attempted to open direct negotiations with Franco. It succeeded, but the negotiations were soon undermined by a new Nationalist offensive. In the final analysis the negotiations amounted to nothing and had no effect whatsoever in stopping the reign of Nationalist terror which followed the surrender on March 29, 1939.

CHAPTER XXII

CONCLUSIONS

Communist Responsibility

THE NATIONALISTS and their supporters claimed that their insurrection was to prevent an international Communist plot. The evidence, however, fails to substantiate this contention. From a study of Spanish history before the Civil War we are led to the conclusion that the origins of the revolution lay in domestic questions. Once the fighting began, however, international conflicts were rapidly superimposed on the Spanish issues.

In another context Loyalist supporters have also accused the Communists. Many Spanish *émigré* groups alleged that it was the policies of the Communists in Spain which destroyed both the spirit of revolution and the morale of the Spanish people and resulted in the defeat of the masses. The supporters of this thesis are many, including Luis Araquistain, Largo Caballero, Colonel Casado, the dissident Communist groups, and the Anarchists.[1]

There is no question that the attacks by the Communists perpetrated by the *Cheka* or *GPU* against the revolutionary parties—the *POUM*, Anarchists, and Caballero Socialists—undermined the revolutionary accomplishments the workers had made in industrial and agricultural collectivization and workers' ownership and control. It was the Communists' professed intention to end the Libertarian and Socialist revolutions started by the Anarchists and Socialists. It is also true that their demand for discipline in the army and on the home front provoked the strong individualism of the Spanish people. No doubt, too, their methods of terror and coercion aroused antagonism and hatred for the government sometimes stronger than that against the rebels. Their repressions certainly tended to break the fighting spirit of the people, who were already confused and antagonized. The clearest example of this was during the May crisis when several of the Anarchist columns started to leave the front to aid their associates in Barcelona. It may also be argued that the increasing Communist domination in the government alienated such leaders as Prieto, who concluded that a compromise with Franco was better than a Communist dictatorship.

Though these factors may be valid, they are not the whole story. To attribute the declining morale of the people merely to the activities of the Communists overlooks a multitude of other factors: the growing shortage of food; the length and cruelty of the war with its heavy casualties; the material devastation; the continuous defeats by the Nationalist armies; and the general fatigue from the exertion of two and half years of war effort. In these conditions despair was inevitable.

In support of Communist terror it can be argued that the use of forceful methods against certain elements among the people was necessary for several reasons: to eliminate Nationalist sympathizers; to gain the coöperation and submission of certain groups to the unity and war program of the government; and to force the people, if by nothing more than fear of terror, to greater efforts and sacrifices for the war. Few armies in defeat have not had to use terror to keep the soldiers and people fighting —the Spanish Civil War was no exception. It might be further argued that the vast difference in the factions which made up the Loyalist side required the use of force to maintain a united front against the forces of the Right. Franco, on his side, used force as a major element of cohesion among the Nationalists.

Furthermore, it should be remembered that the Communists in attacking the revolutionaries generally had the support of the middle classes, who perhaps would have gone over to Franco if the revolution had been allowed to go on in the Libertarian or Socialist pattern. They backed the Communist move to remove Caballero from the government and reduce the influence of the Anarchists during the spring and summer of 1937. The Anarchist leaders and the Caballero Socialists, by voluntarily sacrificing their revolutionary aims of collectivization and destruction of the bourgeoisie, showed that they realized the danger of losing the support of the middle class. Likewise, the terroristic tactics and methods of the Communists were sanctioned, at least in part, by the middle-class parties. During the reign of terror against the *POUM*ists and the Anarchists in 1937, the Republican groups stood on the side lines and made ineffectual protests.

Most observers would agree that the discipline forced on the government and the people by the Communists with the help of such leaders as Largo Caballero and Indalecio Prieto, in particular, was the very thing which saved the Republican army from an early defeat by the Italian- and German-trained rebel troops. The defeats of the superior forces of Franco at Guadalajara and Teruel showed the value of Communist-inspired discipline. Communist authoritarianism was not so much the undoer of the Loyalist cause as its temporary savior.

Finally, to attribute to the Communists the Loyalist defeat, as do many of the *émigrés*, passes over the most important, single reason for the defeat of the Loyalist cause—the overwhelming military superiority

of the Nationalist troops supported by the Fascist powers. Lacking the
help of the democracies and without more help from Russia, which she
was not willing or able to give, the Republicans did not stand a chance
against the combined forces of Franco, Mussolini, and Hitler.

THE LESSONS OF SPAIN

Spain offered the first opportunity to the Communist International to
give the United Front program, adopted in 1935, a full test. This new
strategy, which the Communist parties were to follow in establishing the
dictatorship of the proletariat under their leadership, provided for several
stages of development: first, a United Front of the proletariat; second, a
People's Front of all anti-Fascists; third, a United Front or People's
Front government to fight the reactionary bourgeoisie; and fourth, trade-
union unity and a single party of the proletariat. In Spain the Communist party progressed with few deviations through the various steps up
to the last one of establishing one party and one trade-union of the proletariat. A Popular Front of the Left was formed in January, 1936, and
won the election of February. The Communists then tried to establish a
United Front of the Socialist and Communist parties but failed. They
did, however, in the interim before the Nationalist revolt in July, 1936,
double their following and were able to persuade Largo Caballero to unify
the Communist and Socialist youth into the *JSU*, as the first step in the
unity of all the proletariat. Likewise, immediately after the outbreak of
war the Communists were successful in bringing about the unity of the
Communist and Socialist parties of Catalonia into the *PSUC*. In both
unifications the Communists assumed immediate control. A Popular
Front government was formed in September, 1936, and followed closely
in its policies the prerequisites demanded by the Comintern for the formation of such a government. There then remained only the final unification of the Socialist and Communist parties and the creation of one
single trade-union of the proletariat. The Communists, however, had
alienated the Socialists and aroused their suspicion toward any further
coöperation and unification by seizing immediate control of the united
youth and United Socialist Party of Catalonia. The Communists tried
every method to bring about further unity. They played the right faction
of the Socialists against the left, trying to isolate and divide them so that
the right Socialists of Indalecio Prieto might be willing to unite with the
Communists against Largo Caballero. They launched a reign of terror
against the *POUM* and those elements of the Anarchists who opposed
coöperation with the Communists. They infiltrated into the command

positions of the armed forces. But neither force, persuasion, nor intrigue brought the desired results and the United Front program in Spain remained incomplete.

In spite of their failure to achieve final unification of the proletariat, however, the Communists still accomplished other purposes within Spain itself. From an insignificant revolutionary group of about a thousand in 1931, the Communists had attracted by the end of the war almost a half million adherents and had secured a dominant position in the most important ministry of the government, the Defense Ministry, controlling all the armed forces of the country. From the evidence it seems clear that the party was in a position to seize absolute power in the Loyalist government when and if it wanted to. How much of this success, however, was due to the United Front tactic and how much to pressure and influence of Soviet military aid is difficult to ascertain. As the evidence in this study has emphasized, both were responsible. The United Front program was easily coördinated into the political situation and had a broad appeal as the best way to victory. The idea of the Popular Front of all the parties of the Left had already been broached after the reaction of 1933, independently of the Communists' development of their United Front program in 1934.

It is certainly doubtful that the Communists would have gained so many members and such important positions in the government if the Soviet Union had not given military aid. The succor from the Soviet Union at the crucial time of the siege of Madrid allowed the Communists to secure important positions in the military forces and increase the prestige of the party. Perhaps the Spanish adventure was a lesson to the Communists that the best way to carry out the United Front program was through the presence of Soviet military support—a lesson which Russia applied after World War II in the "People's Democracies."

The fulfillment of the United Front program in Spain was not, however, the main aim of the Soviet leaders in entering the Spanish conflict. In fact, as discussed previously, they appeared to have deliberately refrained from allowing the Communists in Spain to seize power in the name of the United Front or of the dictatorship of the proletariat when the opportunities presented themselves during the May crisis of 1937, and the cabinet crisis of March, 1938, when Prieto resigned from the Defense Ministry. The primary purpose of the Communist Party of Spain at the time was rather to put up as strong a resistance against Franco and his allies as possible in order to support Russia's foreign policy of defense against fascism.

How specifically aid to Spain fitted into Russian foreign policy at this time is outside the scope of this study and is reserved for the next volume. This discussion has pointed out, however, the importance of the defensive motive rather than the offensive motive in the Soviet Union's intervention in Spain. She was not interested in a satellite in Spain at this time but only in a tool to stop the aggression of the Fascist states against herself.

Although the ultimate goal of the United Front policy—the dictatorship of the proletariat under the leadership of the Communist hierarchy—was at variance with the Communist policy of aligning all non-Fascist forces against Franco and his allies, the preparatory stages of both policies followed the same pattern and were mutually helpful. The need for unity, discipline, and Communist control of the vital services was useful for either purpose.

On the surface the Communist program and aims for the war period in Spain appeared to be similar to that of the Social-Democratic and liberal parties of Spain and Western Europe. The insistence on a regular, disciplined army, a unified command, and economic mobilization under centralized control, followed the program of the Republican parties. Likewise, in their public demands the Communists aspired for the moment to nothing more than the establishment of a democracy on the English or North American pattern preserving individual enterprise in small industries and agriculture. On closer analysis, however, the activities of the Communists revealed that this democratic program was not to be an end in itself but merely the means to another end—the protection of the Soviet Union. Furthermore, the methods of coercion and terror used by the Communists showed the fundamental difference between the Western type of democracy and the "new type of democracy" or "people's democracy" as developed by the Communists.

NOTES

NOTES TO CHAPTER I

[1] Below are books which discuss in some detail the economic, social, and political background of the Civil War:

E. Allison Peers, *The Spanish Tragedy, 1930–1936; Dictatorship, Republic, Chaos* (3d ed.; London: Methuen and Co. Ltd., 1936). A conservative British scholar.

———, *The Spanish Dilemma* (London: Methuen and Co. Ltd., 1940).

Gerald Brenan, *The Spanish Labyrinth* (2d ed.; London: Cambridge University Press, 1950). An objective analysis from a liberal point of view.

Salvador de Madariaga, *Spain* (London: Jonathan Cape, 1946). A history of Spain by a moderate Spanish Republican.

Richard Pattee, *This Is Spain* (Milwaukee: The Bruce Publishing Co., 1951). Gives a Catholic interpretation.

Franz Borkenau, *The Spanish Cockpit* (London: Faber and Faber Ltd., 1937). An excellent summary by a liberal correspondent who went to Spain during the Civil War.

Henri Rabasseire, *L'Espagne creuset politique* (Paris: Éditions Fustier, n.d.). A liberal French author.

Joaquín Maurín, *Hacia la segunda revolución* (Paris: Éditions Rieder, 1937). A dissident Spanish Communist.

N. Gorozhankina, *Rabochii klass Ispanii v gody revolyutsii* [The Working Class of Spain in the Year of Revolution] (Moscow: Gos. Sotsial'no-Ekonomicheskoe Izdat., 1936). A Communist analysis of the causes.

[2] The landowners kept their control through a system of caciques. This was a system of nothing more than local bosses appointed by the landowners in every town and village. By means of favoritism, bribery, and threats, combined with violence, they were able to control elections to local posts and to the Cortes. The caciques completely dominated the local administration and used it for their own ends. Very often they had a band of thugs in their employ to whom they gave police protection.

[3] In the 1920's there had begun to develop among higher Church circles a minority that felt the Church needed reform and a policy closer to the people.

[4] In Navarre and the Basque country the Church remained close to the masses. Particularly in the Basque region it assumed a program like that of the Catholic Church in Germany, for example, helping the workers to organize unions, and generally looking after the social as well as the religious welfare of the people. The result of this program showed clearly in the Civil War when the Basque Church sided with the Republicans.

[5] The idea of nationalism, which was so influential in the rest of Europe during the nineteenth and twentieth centuries, never struck very deep roots in Spain.

[6] Communism before the Civil War in 1936 had only a few adherents. For a discussion of the growth of communism see pp. 20-21, 31-34.

[7] Indalecio Prieto, a Basque industrialist and a Socialist leader, headed a minority group among the Socialists who still supported evolutionary and democratic means toward their goal of socialism. Prieto's strength came primarily from the Basque Socialists, who were less revolutionary and more conservative than those in the rest of Spain.

[8] Gerald Brenan in his book, *The Spanish Labyrinth*, p. 184, estimates the strength of the *FAI*, whose organization was secret, as about 10,000 between 1934–1936.

[9] Gerald Brenan has also suggested that anarchism, like Carlism, was an expression of the nostalgia of the masses to go back to the bliss and contentment of centuries past. The Anarchists, unlike the Carlists, however, did not shun the material advantages of modern science but did not consider them of prime importance and were willing to sacrifice them for their aim of *comunismo libertario*. Socialism, at the other extreme, stresses the advantages of industrialization and depends upon it to create the abundance of its projected world (*Ibid.*, p. 195).

NOTES TO CHAPTER II

[1] Actually the final results of the municipal elections were never announced. The Home Office in April showed 22,150 councillors to be Monarchist and 5,875 to be Republican. These figures are undoubtedly false, or only certain districts were used to make up the figures. Salvador de Madariaga in his book, *Spain*, states there were 39,248 antimonarchist councillors to 41,224 Monarchist, but does not mention where he obtained these figures. There is, however, little doubt from the evidence available that the Right was still strong in the country in respect to the number of ballots they could command.

[2] For sources, see p. 16n.

[3] For sources, see p. 16n. These figures do not include all parties.

[4] See Diego Martínez Barrio, *Páginas para la historia del Frente Popular* (Madrid and Valencia: Ediciones Españolas, 1937) and Carlos Prieto, *Spanish Front* (London: Thomas Nelson and Sons Ltd., 1936).

[5] No two authorities give the exact same results for the election. The independents and small parties make it difficult to divide the Cortes into clear-cut groups. Authors vary in the placement of the independent deputies and deputies from the smaller parties. For example:

Popular Front	256[a]	257[b]	268[c]	295[d]	267[e]	277[f]	256[g]
Center	55	62	48		64	32	52
Right	143	152	139	177	142	132	165

[a] Carlos Prieto, *Spanish Front*, p. 56.

[b] Louis Fischer, *The War in Spain* (published by the *Nation*, 1937), p. 7.

[c] Anna Louise Strong, *Spain in Arms* (New York: Henry Holt and Co., 1937), p. vi.

[d] Arnold Lunn, *Spanish Rehearsal* (New York: Sheed and Ward, 1937), p. 168.

[e] Felipe Beltrán Güell, *Momentos interesantes de la historia de España en este siglo, Preparación y desarrollo de alzamiento nacional* (Valladolid: Libreria Santaren, 1939), p. 28.

[f] Salvador de Madariaga, *Spain*, p. 340n.

[g] E. Allison Peers, *The Spanish Tragedy*, p. 190.

[6] Claude Bowers, former United States Ambassador to Spain, says in his book, *My Mission to Spain, Watching the Rehearsal for World War II* (New York: Simon and Schuster, 1954), that the anarchy in this period has been overexaggerated.

[7] Henri Rabasseire, *L'Espagne creuset politique*, p. 22.

[8] The government shock troops (*Guardias de Asalto*) were founded by the Republicans in 1931 and continued to remain loyal to the Republican parties of the Left even through the reaction of 1933–1936.

NOTES TO CHAPTER III

[1] Winston Churchill, *Step by Step 1936–1939* (London: T. Butterworth Ltd., 1939), p. 35.

[2] Winston Churchill, *The Gathering Storm* (Boston: Houghton Mifflin Co., 1948), pp. 212–213. Richard Pattee, *This is Spain*, from a Catholic view gives much the same interpretation to events (pp. 196–199).

[3] The Spanish government under Primo de Rivera had persistently refused to recognize the Soviet government. With the overthrow of Primo de Rivera and the proclaiming of the Second Republic in Spain, however, the new government considered it time to recognize the Soviet regime as the government of Russia. During the last Azaña government, just before the reaction of 1933 and almost simultaneously with the United States, Spain and the Soviet Union exchanged notes of recognition *de jure* and *de facto*. The notes provided for the exchange of ambassadors: Julio

Álvarez del Vayo, formerly Ambassador to Mexico, as Ambassador to Moscow; and M. Lunacharsky as Soviet Ambassador to Madrid. The victory of the Right in November and December, 1933, however, forestalled the exchange of ambassadors though the government of the Right did not attempt to withdraw Spanish recognition of the Soviet regime. Exchange of ambassadors did not occur until after the beginning of the Civil War.

⁴ Kol'tsov, *Pravda*'s correspondent in Spain, put the figure at eight hundred. Mikhail Efimovich Kol'tsov, *Ispanskii Dnevnik* [Spanish Diary] (Moscow: Khudozhestvennaia literatura, 1938), p. 84.

⁵ Jesús Hernández in the *Communist International*, XIII, no. 7 (Aug., 1936), gives the figure of 83,000, which differs from other Communist authorities. Most likely the difference can be explained by the inclusion in the figure of about 50,000 Komsomols— not strictly members of the party.

⁶ See p. 33.

⁷ Bill Lawrence, a Communist political commissar of the military base at Albacete, puts the size of the party before February, 1936, at only 20,000. Earl Browder and Bill Lawrence, *Next Steps to Win the War in Spain* (New York: Workers Library Publisher, 1938).

⁸ "The Spanish Communist Party and the Revolutionary Situation," *Communist International*, VIII, nos. 11–12 (July 1, 1931), 324.

Below are some other articles that discuss the prospects of revolution in Spain which appeared in the *Communist International* during the period 1931–1934:

"The Violet Republic and the Bourgeois Democratic Revolution in Spain," VIII, nos. 11–12 (July 1, 1931), 331.

"The Bolshevization of the Communist Party in Spain," VIII, no. 16 (Sept. 15, 1931), 458.

"The Unfulfilled Tasks of the Spanish Revolution (Preparatory to the IV Congress of the C.P. of Spain)," IX, no. 3 (Feb. 15, 1932), 83.

"Examples of Bolshevik Work and Revolutionary Struggle," X, no. 2 (Feb. 1, 1933), 49.

A. Brones, "The Intensification of the Revolutionary Crisis in Spain, and the Tasks of the C.P.S.," X, no. 23 (Dec. 1, 1933), 868; continued in no. 24 (Dec. 15, 1933), 912.

"Fifteen Years of the Comintern," XI, no. 4 (Feb. 20, 1934), 143.

"How the Revolution in Spain Can Be Victorious," XI, no. 18 (Sept. 20, 1934), 591.

"The Struggle Against Fascism, the Struggle for Power, for the Workers' and Peasants' Republic in Spain," XI, no. 23 (Dec. 5, 1934), 803.

⁹ For a detailed discussion see: Kermit E. McKenzie, "Soviet Union: The Comintern and World Revolution," *Political Science Quarterly*, 65, no. 2 (June, 1950), 214–237.

¹⁰ "The Spanish Communist Party and the Revolutionary Situation," *Communist International*, VIII, nos. 11–12 (July 1, 1931), 329.

¹¹ Georgi Dimitroff, *The United Front* (New York: International Publishers, 1938), p. 19. See also Wilhelm Pieck, *Freedom, Peace, and Bread!, Report of the Activities of the Executive Committee of the Communist International at the Seventh World Congress of the Communist International* (New York: Workers Library Publisher, 1935), p. 94.

¹² *Ibid.*, p. 105.

¹³ Wilhelm Pieck, in the report of the Executive Committee of the Comintern, declared: "If, thanks to the struggle for peace of the Soviet Union and the toilers of all capitalist countries, war can be delayed even for a certain time, this also will better enable the proletariat to strengthen its position in the capitalist countries, to strengthen the power of the Soviet Union and to create more favorable conditions for transforming

the war among the imperialists, or a war of the imperialists against the Soviet Union, into a successful and victorious revolution." (*Freedom, Peace and Bread!*, p. 89.)

¹⁴ M. Ercoli, *The Fight for Peace, Report on the Preparations for Imperialist War and the Tasks of the Communist International, Delivered August 13, 1935* (New York: Workers Library Publisher, 1935), p. 81.

¹⁵ Maurice Thorez and others, *The People's Front in France, Speeches Delivered at the Seventh World Congress of the Communist International* (New York: Workers Library Publisher, 1935), pp. 55–56.

¹⁶ In the resolution on the report of Georgi Dimitrov the pattern was laid down: ". . . the Communists, in order to render the road to unity of action easier for the workers, must *strive to secure joint action with the Social-Democratic Parties, reformist trade unions and other organizations of the toilers against the class enemies of the proletariat, on the basis of short or long-term agreement*. At the same time attention must be directed mainly to the development of mass action in the various localities, conducted by the lower *organizations* through local agreements." (*Resolutions, Seventh Congress of the Communist International* [New York: Workers Library Publisher, 1935], p. 27.)

¹⁷ Georgi Dimitroff, *The United Front*, p. 32.

¹⁸ M. Ercoli, *The Fight for Peace*, p. 83.

¹⁹ Georgi Dimitroff, *The United Front*, pp. 36–37.

²⁰ *Resolutions, Seventh Congress of the Communist International*, p. 28.

²¹ Manuilsky gave over his entire speech before the Congress to an attack on the Socialists. The tenor of the speech followed the line that ". . . the leaders and ideologists of the Second International *are not the continuers of the work of Engels, but the work of his enemies*." (*VII Congress of the Communist International, Abridged Stenographic Report of Proceedings* [Moscow: Foreign Languages Publishing House, 1939], p. 234.)

²² M. Ercoli, *The Fight for Peace*, p. 63.

²³ *Resolutions, Seventh Congress of the Communist International*, p. 30.

²⁴ Georgi Dimitroff, *The United Front*, p. 101.

²⁵ *Ibid.*, p. 110.

²⁶ Harry Pollitt, the British delegate to the Congress, declared: "*The Communist Party does not believe that socialism can be achieved through Parliament*, and will always state this standpoint in its agitation and propaganda and will always maintain its international connections with working class parties in other countries which maintain the revolutionary point of view. In fact the establishment of fascism in Germany, and in other countries, together with the victory of socialism in the Soviet Union, is convincing more and more workers in Britain that the revolutionary way is the only correct one." (Harry Pollitt, "Discussion of Comrade Dimitrov's Report," *VII Congress of the Communist International*, p. 234.)

²⁷ Georgi Dimitroff, *The United Front*, pp. 75, 107.

²⁸ *Resolutions, Seventh Congress of the Communist International*, p. 30.

²⁹ *Ibid.*, p. 31.

³⁰ Georgi Dimitroff, *The United Front*, p. 88.

³¹ Ventura, the Spanish representative to the Congress, in his speech prescribed the tasks before the Communist Party of Spain for the fulfillment of the United Front program: "We declare that we are ready to work out the terms of an agreement for united action with all those who want to fight against fascism in Spain; that we are ready to draw up an agreement that will include all sections of the country—from top to bottom, from the principal cities to the most remote hamlet—all the oppressed nationalities and all sectors of the labour movement; that, with this broad proletarian united front as a basis, we are ready to rally the large masses around an anti-fascist People's Front, and to work for the inclusion of all Left Republicans. The present is a particularly momentous juncture. The great experience of the victory of the anti-fascist People's Front in France with its tremendous reverberations in all sections

of the working people of our country shows us the way. Hence, the conclusions that we draw at the present Congress, and that fully correspond to the requirements of the struggle in our country, consist in the following:

"1. The entire political activity of our Party must revolve around the task of organizing Workers' and Peasants' Alliances. We must give these Alliances a revolutionary program, turn them in practice into the mainspring of the entire united front movement of the workers and peasants, as well as of all the other exploited masses, draw into them our Anarchist comrades, and transform these Alliances into live organs of the struggle for the immediate demands of the labouring masses and for preparing the seizure of power.

"2. This is to furnish a basis for bringing about the proletarian united front and the unity of all anti-fascists, and at the same time for the organization and consolidation of the anti-fascist People's Front which should draw support from the common aims— such as, for instance, the expropriation of the large landowners, transference of the land to the peasants, democratic liberties, emancipation of the oppressed nationalities, amnesty, the dissolution and disarming of the fascist organizations, etc.—and could thus serve as a basis for the formation of an anti-fascist people's government. Such a government, relying for support on the Workers' and Peasants' Alliances, would smash the resistance of fascism and the offensive of capital and thereby open up new possibilities and perspectives for the further development of the revolution.

"3. In the sphere of trade union work we must overcome the sectarian tendencies and proceed boldly to amalgamate the dual trade unions in each locality, to build up single trade unions along industrial lines, and to form a single trade union centre on the platform of the class struggle. Simultaneously we must unhesitatingly raise the question of a single revolutionary party of the proletariat, while at the same time overcoming the last doubts of the brave Socialist workers and fighters in the October uprising, striving for organisational unity, and safeguarding the necessary guarantees of revolutionary principles. With regard to our youth and the Socialist youth, we must strive for their early amalgamation in a single organisation embracing the entire anti-fascist youth." (*VII Congress of the Communist International*, pp. 328–329.)

[32] As early as the Congress of the Comintern in August, 1935, the Communists had looked toward a United Front or Popular Front government in Spain. The Spanish delegate to the Congress, Ventura, declared: "All the prerequisites exist for bringing up the question of a government of the united front or the anti-fascist People's Front of which Comrade Dimitrov has spoken." (*VII Congress of the Communist International*, p. 328.)

[33] José Díaz, *Nuestra bandera del Frente Popular*, Speech given at the Monumental Cinema in Madrid on June 2, 1935 (Madrid and Barcelona: Ediciones Europa-America, 1936), p. 27.

[34] *Ibid.*, Speech given at Colesium Pardiñas in Madrid on November 3, 1935, p. 57.

[35] See José Díaz, *Tres años de lucha, por el Frente Popular, por la libertad, por la independencia* (Paris, Mexico, New York: Ediciones Europa-America, 1939), pp. 179f.

[36] José Díaz declared, for example, on February 11, 1936: ". . . There is one man today who has put all his intelligence and all his energy to the service of the United Front in our country, so that when the time comes it will triumph: Comrade Largo Caballero. (Extensive applauding and cries of long live Largo Caballero, the Communist Party and the Socialist Party.) Comrade Largo Caballero is very old in the direction of the working class movement, we could recount the history of the international movement of the proletariat and see that in the era of Largo Caballero it is very difficult to find another case of evolution such as his, especially with regard to everything that has occurred in these last days. There is a considerable mass who follow him with a very clear vision, because they have hopes of what will follow as a result of the revolutionary position that he has embraced. When the comrade who

opened the meeting spoke of Largo Caballero as being the indisputable president of the Socialist Party, he spoke well. . . ." (*Tres años de lucha*, Discurso pronunciado en el Teatro de la Zarzuela, de Madrid, el 11 de febrero de 1936, pp. 106–107.)

[37] Communist sources give the Socialist Youth only 65,000 or even less, which is at great variance with all other sources. Such a low figure would not have been in keeping with the general strength of the Socialists at this time. Most likely the Communists made up this figure so that the number would be close to the membership of their own youth group.

[38] Communist sources do not agree on the number of Komsomols. E. Varga in his book, *Ispaniia i revoliutsiia* (Moscow: Partizdat. TsK VKP(b), 1937, p. 89), gives the figure 51,000, whereas in the Communist pamphlet, *Siete temas de educación política* (*J.S.U.*, Comisión de Educación del Soldado, n.d.), the figure 60,000 is given.

NOTES TO CHAPTER IV

[1] Louis Fischer, a Communist supporter at that time, and Salvador de Madariaga, a moderate, give the Popular Front only about 4,200,000.

[2] In the parliamentary elections in England in 1945, Labor received less than the absolute majority of the popular vote, yet won 64 per cent of the seats in the House of Commons. Likewise, in the 1951 elections, the Conservatives received 48 per cent of the popular vote and 52 per cent of the seats.

[3] Gil Robles' own explanation of his defeat was: "(1) the people voted Left out of sentiment, thinking only of the release of the political prisoners; (2) the sudden inrush of *C.N.T.* voters at the last minute; (3) the abstention of many Right voters, deceived by the calm before the elections and supposing the victory over the revolution was assured; (4) the *C.E.D.A.* had no martyrs." (*Le Petit Parisien* [Feb. 22, 1936], cited by Frank Jellinek, *The Civil War in Spain* [London: V. Gollancz Ltd., 1938], pp. 216–217.)

[4] Diego Martínez Barrio, and others, *Halte aux incendiaires!*, *Discours prononcés le 8 avril 1937* (Paris: Éditions du Comité Mondial Contre la Guerre et la Fascisme, n.d.), p. 13.

[5] H. A. Gwynne and A. Ramos Oliveira, *Controversy on Spain* (London: United Editorial Ltd., 1937), p. 8. H. A. Gwynne goes on to say: "The career of Prieto shows him to be at heart a revolutionary; as for the 'left Socialist' Caballero, he boasted to the American correspondent, H. E. Knoblaugh: 'Lenin declared Spain would be the second Soviet Republic in Europe. Lenin's prophecy will come true. I shall be the second Lenin who shall make it come true.' "

[6] *Communist Operations in Spain* (London: Burns, Oates and Washburn Ltd., 1937) and *Conflict in Spain 1920–1939* (London: Burns, Oates and Washburn Ltd., 1939).

[7] Gertrude M. Godden also quotes a statement by the Minister for Home Affairs in Spain from the newspaper *La Voz*, in which he claimed that £150,000 had been sent to Spain on January 9, 1936, "as a subsidy for the revolt." (*Conflict in Spain*, p. 25.) There is no mention of the Comintern in the statement though the author assumes them to be the culprits. Information, however, given out by the Home Minister was by no means reliable and was almost always for propaganda purposes only. Other information given out had several times been proven to be in gross error.

[8] See pp. 23 ff.

[9] Joaquín Maurín, *Hacia la segunda revolución, El fracaso de la República y la insurrección de octubre* (2d ed.; Madrid: Libreria Enrique Prieto, [1935]), pp. 97–98.

[10] Jacques Bardoux in his book, *Le chaos espagnol éviterons-nous la contagion?* (Paris: Ernest Flammarion, 1937), p. 28, gives as his authority "an English source."

[11] Jacques Bardoux gives as his source to prove the landing of war material by the Russian ships *Neva* and *Jevik* at Seville and at Algeciras "a diplomatic document."

[12] See p. 39n.

[13] See, for example, *The Truth About Spain, Speech Delivered at the National Socialist Party Congress, Nürnberg, 1937,* by Dr. Joseph Goebbels (Berlin: M. Müller and Sohn, 1937), pp. 6–7.

[14] See *Document No. N.I.S. (36) 111,* "International Committee for the Application of the Agreement Regarding Non-Intervention in Spain." (Unpublished.)

[15] For the text of the agreement of March 31, 1934, see microfilmed *Captured Italian Documents,* National Archives, Washington, D. C., Container 1062, 063027-8.

[16] Memorandum by the German Ambassador in Spain, Doc. no. 455 in Department of State, *Documents on German Foreign Policy 1918–1945,* Ser. D, Vol. III, *Germany and the Spanish Civil War 1936–1939* (Washington: Government Printing Office, 1950), hereafter referred to as *Documents on German Foreign Policy 1918–1945,* Ser. D, Vol. III.

The Republican forces claimed to have found four thousand documents in the Falangist headquarters in Barcelona proving German complicity through the Nazi party. The Nazi party was said to have supplied the Falange with money, arms, and propaganda as early as 1930. See *The Nazi Conspiracy in Spain,* trans. by Emile Burns (London: V. Gollancz Ltd., 1937).

[17] Department of State, *Documents on German Foreign Policy 1918–1945,* Ser. D, Vol. III, pp. 1–2.

[18] For German and Italian interest in the events in Spain see: Benito Mussolini, *My Autobiography* (London: Hutchinson, 1939), p. 340; Department of State, *Documents on German Foreign Policy 1918–1945,* Ser. D, Vol. III, p. 932; *Ciano's Diplomatic Papers,* ed. Malcolm Muggeridge (London: Odhams Press Ltd., 1948), pp. 20–21, 36–37, 57, 111; International Military Tribunal, *The Trial of the Major War Criminals before the International Military Tribunal* (Nuremberg: 1947–1949), II, 271; IX, 280–281; *Dokumenty Ministerstva Inostrannykh Del Germanii,* Vol. III, *Germanskaia Politika i Ispaniia (1936–1943gg.)* [Documents of the Ministry of Foreign Affairs of Germany, German Politics and Spain (1936–1943)] (Moscow: 1946), pp. 7–10.

NOTES TO CHAPTER V

[1] José Díaz, a Communist deputy to the Cortes and Secretary-General of the Communist party, also discussed the plot being planned by the Right. (José Díaz, Discurso pronunciado en la sesión de la diputación permanent de las Cortes, el 15 de julio de 1936, *Tres años de lucha,* p. 249.)

[2] E. Varga, "Economy and Economic Policy of the First Quarter of 1936," *Inprecorr (International Press Correspondence),* vol. 16, no. 26, Special Number (June 4, 1936), p. 694.

[3] As early as February the Communists had demanded not only the government's submission to the wishes of the masses, but had expressed the immediate and urgent need of disarming and dissolving the Fascist and reactionary organizations against a possible coup of the Right. José Díaz, "¡En pie y vigilantes!", Discurso pronunciado en el Teatro Bardieri de Madrid, el 23 de febrero de 1936, *Nuestra bandera de Frente Popular,* p. 106.

[4] *Mundo Obrero,* June 8, 13, and 16, 1936.

José Díaz further declared on July 5, 1936: "We must not forget that although defeated on February 16th the enemy is still strong because in their hands are the factories, mines and fields, because they have in their control the courts, command positions in the army and in the ministries, and because they have control over international financial capital.

"Unfortunately the government under control of the People's Front has done almost nothing about striking against this strength of the enemy. The Government thinks that by political concessions it can hold the reactionaries in obedience. We say that this is politically dangerous. There is only one way to deal with the reactionaries that is to put their leaders into prison...." (José Díaz, "Fascism is preparing a revolt. In prison with the reactionary and Fascist leaders!" Speech delivered at a meeting in Oviedo on July 5, 1936, *Ispanskaya Kompartiya boretsya za pobedu* [The Spanish Communist Party's Struggle for Victory] [Moscow: Gos. Sotsial'no-Ekonomicheskoe Izdatelstvo, 1938], p. 6.)

⁵ Martínez Barrio, President of the Cortes, had first attempted to form a cabinet with General Mola as Minister of War, in an effort to bring about a compromise between the Army and the government to end the revolt. He was unsuccessful. He is reported to have said following this attempt, "I have talked with all the generals. Now, let us govern." (Clara Campoamor, *La révolution espagnole vue par une républicaine* [Paris: Plon, 1937], p. 41.)

⁶ Jean Raynaud, *En Espagne "rouge"* (Paris: Les Editions de Cerf, 1937), p. 65.

⁷ At the beginning of the Civil War there was no one leader of the revolt. The army had instigated the insurrection but the Falangists, Monarchists, Clericals, and Traditionalists wanted to take part in any new government which was established. The army, however, already in control of the most important military strength, was able to maintain control by means of playing the Right factions of their following against the Falangists on the Left. Within the army itself, at the beginning, there was no one recognized leader among the revolting generals. General Mola was probably the most able, but his sudden death in June, 1937, left the role of leader open to General Franco, who soon became the acknowledged head of the Nationalists.

⁸ Franz Borkenau declared in respect to the aviators: "Why had the aviators, in contrast with all the other troops, remained faithful to the Government? Pilots after some years of service in the ordinary regiments, were individually selected for aviation training, and thus the links of regimental *comaraderie* which have been the basis of so many compact risings of the Spanish military against various governments, were severed. Moreover, as one of the pilots emphasized, they were selected for technical ability, and that often seems to go hand in hand with a tendency of the Left. After all, modern industrialism does not go well with the Spanish type of Catholic education, and machine-mindedness in Spain, especially among the routine-ridden Spanish officers, must still be something almost revolutionary." (Franz Borkenau, *The Spanish Cockpit*, p. 99.)

⁹ Arnold J. Toynbee, assisted by V. M. Boulter, *Survey of International Affairs 1937*, Vol. II, *The International Repercussions of the War in Spain (1936–1937)* (London: Oxford University Press, Issued under the auspices of the Royal Institute of International Affairs, 1938), pp. 42ff.

¹⁰ See p. 75.

¹¹ Doc. nos. 455 and 586 in Department of State, *Documents on German Foreign Policy 1918–1945*, Ser. D, Vol. III. See also the German Ambassador's Report of July 25, 1936, Document No. 11, in which he declares: ". . . The members of the Red Militia are filled with a fanatic combat fervor and fight with exceptional valor, with corresponding losses. These, however, are easily replaced from the masses of the population, while the rebels, who have only their troops at their disposal, are generally lacking such reserves."

¹² Gerald Brenan, *The Spanish Labyrinth*, pp. 308f. The German documents also make no mention of the Falange taking part in the planning of the insurrection.

¹³ *Pravda's* article on Spain, July 23, 1936, p. 5. The reporting in the Russian newspapers on Spain during the first days was straightforward with little bias except for frequent references to Monarcho-Fascists.

¹⁴ A. Komjat, "Help for Spain!," *Inprecorr*, vol. 16, no. 35 (Aug. 1, 1936), p. 929.

¹⁵ In this review the following sources have been used: G. Dashevskii, *Fashistskaya*

pyataya kolonna v Ispanii [The Fascist Fifth Column in Spain] (Moscow: Voenizdat, 1938), pp. 6–29; M. Ercoli (Member of the Executive Committee of the Communist International), *The Spanish Revolution* (New York: Workers Library Publisher, December, 1936); *Ispanskii narod pobedit* [The Spanish People Will be Victorious] (Moscow: Partizdat, TsK VKP(b), 1937); *Geroiskaya Ispaniya* [Heroic Spain] (Moscow: Partizdat, TsK VKP(b), October, 1936); Mikhail Efimovich Kol'tsov, *Ispanskii dnevnik;* N. Gorozhankina, *Rabochii klass Ispanii v gody revolyutsii;* E. Varga, "Economy and Economic Policy in the First Quarter of 1936," *Inprecorr*, vol. 16, no. 26, Special Number, pp. 691–695; Cesar Falcon, "How the Revolution Was Prepared," *Inprecorr*, vol. 16, no. 38 (Aug. 22, 1936), p. 1015; Speech by N. Shvernik reported in *Pravda*, Aug. 4, 1936, p. 1.

[16] E. Varga, "Economy and Economic Policy in the First Quarter of 1936," *Inprecorr*, vol. 16, no. 26, Special Number, p. 687. This analogy proved embarrassing to the Communists and was soon abandoned. It was turned into good propaganda for those who wanted to prove that Spain was becoming a Soviet Republic modeled after Russia.

[17] Later, as will be described in the following chapters, the attitude of the Communists changed toward the bourgeoisie and they drew a distinction between financial and industrial bourgeoisie.

[18] *Ibid.*, p. 693. See also pp. 59ff.

[19] *Ispanskii narod pobedit*, p. 39.

[20] M. Ercoli, *The Spanish Revolution*, p. 9.

[21] E. Varga, *op. cit.*, pp. 694–695.

[22] *VII Congress of the Communist International*, pp. 327–328.

NOTES TO CHAPTER VI

[1] See pp. 23ff.

[2] Georgi Dimitroff, "Main Report Delivered at the Seventh World Congress of the Communist International, August 2, 1935," *The United Front*, pp. 21–22.

[3] In Georgi Dimitrov's report to the Seventh Congress of the Comintern in 1935 only a few paragraphs had dealt with the People's Front. Georgi Dimitroff, *The United Front*, pp. 39–41.

[4] For example see José Díaz, *Nuestra bandera del Frente Popular*, pp. 139, 141.

[5] See for example their common programs on agriculture and industry, pp. 61ff.

[6] *Inprecorr*, vol. 16, no. 43, (Sept. 19, 1936), p. 1181.

[7] See p. 28.

[8] For example: "The heroic struggle of the Spanish people has once again placed on the order of the day all the questions of revolutionary strategy and tactics which were solved at various periods of the Russian Revolution. It has set them in a new fashion, corresponding with the special features of Spanish conditions and the peculiar features of the present world situation. It is solving them on the basis of its own experience, frequently groping in the dark, and at the expense of mistakes which at times cost it dearly.

* * *

"The assertation repeated year after year by the opponents of Bolshevism that the Communists allegedly preach the 'copying' in all countries of Russian Bolshevik patterns, and 'slavish imitations,' etc., was a slander against Bolshevism. Nobody more than they stressed the particular features of the specific process of development of the Russian revolution, the 'originality' of definite and decisive situations." ("The Nineteenth Anniversary of the October Revolution," *The Communist International* [November, 1936], p. 1415.)

[9] Mikhail Efimovich Kol'tsov, *Ispanskii dnevnik*, p. 178. See also: Maurice Thorez, *Pour la paix avec l'Espagne républicaine, Interpellation de Gabriel Péri prononcée la*

4 décembre 1936, Discours de Maurice Thorez prononcé le 5 décembre 1936, Explication de vote de Jacques Duclos prononcée de 5 décembre 1936 (Paris: Éditions du Comité Populaire de Propaganda, n.d.), p. 17; Garcia Pradas, *Rusia y España* (Paris: Ediciones Tierra y Libertad, 1948), pp. 83–84; "The Struggle Against the Fascist Putsch," *Communist International* (Sept., 1936), p. 1191; Dolores Ibarruri, "What is Happening in Spain?", *Communist International* (Oct., 1936), p. 1309.

[10] *Ispanskii narod pobedit!*, p. 27.

[11] M. Ercoli, *The Spanish Revolution*, pp. 10–11.

[12] From a speech by Antonio Mije, member of the Politbureau of the Communist Party of Spain, quoted in *Inprecorr*, vol. 16, no. 43 (Sept. 19, 1936), p. 1182.

[13] Dolores Ibarruri, member of the Spanish Politbureau of the Communist Party, declared: "The bourgeois-democratic revolution which took place in *other countries* such as France more than 100 years ago is taking place in our country only now, and we Communists are the vanguard fighters in this struggle against obscurantism, and the dark forces of the past." (Dolores Ibarruri, "What is Happening in Spain?", *Communist International* [Oct., 1936], p. 1309.)

[14] M. Ercoli, *The Spanish Revolution*, p. 7.

[15] Louis Fischer, *War in Spain*, p. 34.

[16] José Díaz, Conferencia pronunciada en el Teatro Olympia de Valencia, el 2 de febrero de 1937, *Tres años de lucha*, pp. 342–343.

[17] N. Gorozhankina, *Rabochi klass Ispanii v gody revolyutsii*, pp. vii, 15f.

Kolarov, at the Seventh Congress of the Comintern in 1935, discussed the policy which should be followed in respect to the peasants in such countries as Spain: "In many countries, in which the survivals of feudalism are still alive, the peasants are directly interested in the overthrow of the power of the landlords. In those countries in which the bourgeois revolution released the peasants from feudal dependence, new exploiter classes have taken the place of the old, and the peasantry has fallen into the clutches of the banks, trusts and cartels. The peasantry fights against these with no less determination than formerly against the feudal lords, and thereby it objectively supports the fight of the proletariat against capitalism." (Kolarov, "Discussion of Comrade Dimitrov's Report," *VII Congress of the Communist International*, p. 343.)

[18] The Spanish Communists stressed that the two cases were not analogous. José Díaz, Discurso pronunciado en la asamblea de Activistas de P.C. celebrado en Madrid el 26 de enero de 1937, *Tres años de lucha*, p. 329.

[19] Vicente Uribe (Minister of Agriculture), *Los campesinos y la República, Conferencia pronunciada el día 22 de enero en el Teatro Apolo, de Valencia* (Valencia: n.d.), pp. 17–18.

[20] Quoted by Julio Mateu, *Por qué se constituyó la Federación Provincial Campesina* (Valencia: Ediciones del Partido Comunista [Comisión Provincial de Agit.-Prop.] n.d.), p. 10.

[21] Vicente Uribe, *La política agraria del Partido Comunista, Conferencia pronunciada el domingo 4 de julio de 1937 en el cine Olympia, de Valencia* (Ediciones del Partido Comunista de España [Comisión Nacional de Agit.-Prop.], 1937), p. 21.

[22] *Ispanskii narod pobedit!*, p. 36.

[23] The Communist party claimed that under Uribe's administration of assuring the small farmer against collectivization the area of tillage increased by ten per cent. This figure is impossible to check but certainly within the realm of reason. There is no question that the small farmer was greatly encouraged by the Communist and government policy and was persuaded not to cut down his harvest for fear of having it collectivized. In 1937 it was very easy to increase the area of tillage by ten per cent or even more, because during the depression the farmers, particularly the big farmers, had cut down their tilled area when they could no longer sell the extra produce at a profit. The price boom of the war alone would have induced the peasants to increase their production.

²⁴ The Anarchists claimed that in Aragon, where the Anarchist forces had set up collectives, production had increased twenty per cent from 1936 to 1937, whereas in Catalonia, where they had been unsuccessful in setting up collectives on a wide scale there was a decrease in output by twenty-one per cent. *¡Campo Libre!* Año I, no. 9 (Sept. 18, 1937), p. 7.

Again, as in the case of the government's statistics, the figures cannot be checked, but it is impossible to see how the Anarchists could have measured production and arrived at these figures under the adverse conditions of the Civil War. Agricultural statistics in Spain in general have never proved complete or reliable. Furthermore, the Anarchist figures, by their very extremes, make them appear even less reliable.

²⁵ Federico Melchor, *El frente de la producción, una industria grande y fuerte para ganar la guerra* (Valencia: Ediciones Alianza Nacional de la Juventud, n.d.), p. 13.

²⁶ Manuel Delicado, *Los problemas de la producción, la función de los sindicatos y la unidad sindical, Informe pronunciado ante el Pleno del C.C. del Partido Comunista, celebrado en Valencia, en los días del 18 al 21 de junio de 1937* (Madrid: Ediciones del Partido Comunista de España, 1937), p. 22.

²⁷ *Ibid.*, p. 8, and Juan Peiró, *De la fábrica de vidrio de mataró al Ministerio de Industria, Conferencia pronunciada el 3 de junio de 1937 en el Gran Teatro, Valencia* (Valencia: Ediciones de la Comisión de Propaganda y Prensa del Comité Nacional de la C.N.T., n.d.), p. 14.

²⁸ José Díaz, "Lo que el pueblo espera del Bloque Popular," Discurso pronunciado en el cine Europa, de Madrid, el 11 de abril de 1936, *Nuestra bandera del Frente Popular*, p. 118.

²⁹ Hugh Slater, "Report from Valencia," *Inprecorr*, vol. 16, no. 40 (Sept. 5, 1936), p. 1078.

³⁰ José Antonio de Aguirre, *Discours prononcé par s. Ex. Le Président du Gouvernement Basque aux postes de radio de Catalogne, le 21 décembre 1938* (Librairie Bloud et Gay, n.d.), p. 13.

³¹ Albert Duval, "In Unity Lies the Strength of the Spanish People," *Communist International* (Aug., 1938), p. 768.

³² Such Communist statements as this were common: "We have affirmed categorically that *we are the first and most authentic defenders of the Statute of Catalonia, which we defend because we feel that it is a thing of the highest revolutionary value which is bound in a close manner with the solution of the problems which today affect us.*" Juan Comorera (Secretary-General of the PSUC), *Tres condiciones de la victoria, informe en el Pleno del C.C. del P.S.U. de Cataluña celebrado en Lérida los días 8 y 9 de enero de 1938* (Barcelona: Editat del Departamento d'Agitación y Propaganda del P.S.U., 1938), p. 18.

³³ See p. 148.

NOTES TO CHAPTER VII

¹ Julian Zugazagoitia, a Socialist minister in Caballero's cabinet, says that at one time Caballero offered Prieto the job of Minister of War, but that he refused, giving as his reason that if Madrid had been abandoned the blame would have fallen on him, whereas if Madrid's defense was successful the credit would go to the trade-unions and not to him. Julian Zugazagoitia, *Historia de la guerra en España* (Buenos Aires: Editorial La Vanguardia, 1940), p. 161.

² M. Ercoli, *The Spanish Revolution*, p. 16.

³ Some authorities have claimed that one condition of Soviet aid to the Republic was the entrance of the Anarchists into the government. The new government which was formed on November 4, 1936, was composed of four Anarchists, six Socialists, two Communists and six representatives of the other Popular Front parties. The four Anarchist ministers were: Señora Montseny, Health; Señor Peiró, Industry; Señor Lopez, Commerce; and Señor Oliver, Justice.

⁴ Upon accepting the posts the *CNT* explained its position: "The situation created by the incomprehension of certain sections and by our firm conviction decided us not to postpone our entry into the Government, although we, as the largest anti-fascist force, might have maintained an intransigent position. We desired equal representation of the Marxist parties and the *C.N.T.*, but we were willing to reduce the number of our representatives to four. . . . The main reason why we made this sacrifice is the difficult situation on certain fronts, especially in the Centre, where the enemy is at the gates of Madrid." (Cited in Frank Jellinek, *The Civil War in Spain*, pp. 496–497.)

⁵ Luis Araquistain, "On Labor Unity in Spain," *Socialist Review*, VI, no. 6 (May-June, 1938), 17.

⁶ Caballero, by March, 1937, had completely reversed his position on collectivization and supported the spread of private management of farms.

⁷ Juan Peiró, Anarchist Minister of Industry, related how Caballero deplored the injustice of leaving the foreign firms unnationalized but realized that to nationalize them would shut the door absolutely to any aid from the western democracies. Juan Peiró, *De la fábrica de vidrio de mataró al Ministerio de Industria*, p. 16.

⁸ "Pravda Madrid Correspondent Interviews Comrade Caballero," *Inprecorr*, vol. 16, no. 42, (Sept. 12, 1936), p. 1170.

⁹ See pp. 53ff.

NOTES TO CHAPTER VIII

¹ Gerald Brenan, *The Spanish Labyrinth*, p. 284n. See also Claude Bowers, *My Mission to Spain*, p. 97.

² The *Pravda* reporter, Kol'tsov, reports that going through Asturias he was frequently thanked for the help given in 1934. M. E. Kol'tsov, *Ispanskii dnevnik*, p. 193.

³ This is confirmed by evidence found in the German Foreign Office archives. Franco's government itself admitted that these last figures seemed "exaggerated, since the numbers appear to exceed the capacity of one nation to provide assistance." Director of Political Department to Italian Embassy, Aug. 4, 1937, Doc. no. 407 in Department of State, *Documents on German Foreign Policy 1918–1945*, Ser. D, vol. III.

⁴ Joseph Goebbels, *The Truth About Spain*, p. 12. Another example: ". . . In February, 1938, General Franco's headquarters stated that the figures of foreign prisoners in the Nationalist prison camps were 5,475 French, 3,200 Russians, 2,763 Czechs, 880 Belgians, 275 Americans, 236 British prisoners." (Arthur F. Loveday, *World War in Spain* [London: John Murray, 1939], p. 134.) If the term "Russian" was replaced by "other," the figures would follow very closely the facts found by authorities in Republican Spain. There is no evidence that more than a small handful of Russian technicians ever entered the line of fire in Spain. Russian troops in Spain consisted solely of advisers who kept well behind the lines. See pp. 82f.

⁵ *Pravda*, Aug. 6, 1936.

⁶ Communist literature at this time both in Russia and abroad stressed the danger of fascism in Spain to French security.

⁷ In *Ispanskii narod pobedit!* Communist aid in the various countries is reviewed, pp. 167f.

⁸ Quoted in *Financial News*, Oct. 9, 1937, and *Daily Telegraph*, Oct. 30, 1937.

⁹ The Spanish government likewise maintained official silence. Señor Juan Negrín, President of the Council of Ministers, in acknowledging Soviet help referred only to diplomatic support: "Gentlemen, whenever the U.S.S.R., a country to whom we are at the present moment joined by bonds of cordial friendship, has diplomatically and morally supported the justice of our cause, she has never at any time demanded any

quid pro quo. And from this disinterestedness springs our friendship, and our gratitude to Russia." (Speech given at the Banquet of the Association of Journalists, Aug. 14, 1937, *The Italo-German Aggression Against Spain, Three Speeches of Señor Juan Negrín* [Paris: Coopérative Étoile, (1937)], p. 7.)

¹⁰ *Doc. no. N.I.S. (36) 81,* "International Committee for the Application of the Agreement Regarding Non-Intervention in Spain." (Unpublished.)

¹¹ José Díaz, *Para aplastar a Franco, más unidos que nunca dentro del Frente Popular, Texto integro del informe pronunciado en el Pleno de Comité Central de Partido Comunista de España, celebrado en Valencia el 13 de noviembre de 1937* (Madrid and Barcelona: Ediciones del P.C. de España, 1937), pp. 17–18.

¹² See the works of Louis Fischer and Ramón Sender at this time.

¹³ Constancia de la Mora, *In Place of Splendor, The Autobiography of a Spanish Woman* (New York: Harcourt, Brace and Co., 1939), pp. 274–275.

A Nationalist communiqué reported Russian tanks used first on October 29, which may very well be true. Cited by Arnold J. Toynbee, assisted by V. M. Boulter, *Survey of International Affairs 1937,* Vol. II, *The International Repercussions of the War in Spain (1936–1937),* p. 58.

¹⁴ José Martin Blazquez, *I Helped to Build an Army* (London: Secker and Warburg, 1939), p. 7.

¹⁵ Louis Fischer says that the decision was made by Russia during the first week of October. This seems too late for materials to be transported from Russia to Spain by the end of October. Louis Fischer, *Men and Politics, An Autobiography* (New York: Duell, Sloan and Pearce, 1941), p. 370.

¹⁶ For Krivitsky's discussion of organizing supplies for Spain see Walter Krivitsky, *In Stalin's Secret Service* (New York and London: Harper and Bros., 1939), pp. 78–87.

¹⁷ It might be argued that, since the Soviet Union had repudiated the Non-Intervention Pact in the London Committee in October, 1936, because of Italian and German intervention in Spain, she was not violating a treaty agreement and, therefore, international law, by sending aid. This argument, however, overlooks the important fact that even after the Soviet Union denounced the pact as a fraud she still officially adhered to it by keeping her seat on the Non-Intervention Committee in London.

¹⁸ Note from the Ambassador in the Soviet Union to the Foreign Ministry, Oct. 26, 1936, Doc. no. 107; Telegram from the Ambassador in Italy to the Foreign Ministry, Oct. 28, 1936, Doc. no. 110; Telegram from the Ambassador in Turkey to the Foreign Ministry, Nov. 6, 1936, Doc. no. 115; Telegram from the Chargé d'Affaires in the Soviet Union to the Foreign Ministry, Nov. 13, 1936, Doc. no. 118; Note from the Consul at Odessa to the Embassy in the Soviet Union, Nov. 16, 1936, Doc. no. 120 in Department of State, *Documents on German Foreign Policy 1918–1945,* Ser. D, Vol. III.

¹⁹ Walter Krivitsky, *In Stalin's Secret Service,* pp. 86–87.

²⁰ Segismundo Casado, *The Last Days of Madrid* (London: Peter Davies, 1939), p. 54.

²¹ José Martin Blazquez, *I Helped to Build an Army,* p. 289.

²² Indalecio Prieto, *Cómo y por qué salí del Ministerio de Defensa Nacional, Intrigas de los Rusos en España, Texto taquigráfico del informe pronunciado el 9 de agosto de 1938 ante el Comité Nacional del Partido Socialista Obrero Español* (Mexico: Impresos y Papeles, 1940), p. 94.

²³ The magnitude of German and Italian supplies is revealed by a report of Hitler's discussion with Count Ciano, the Italian Foreign Minister, on September 28, 1940. Hitler reported that: "When the Civil War broke out in Spain, Germany supported Franco on what was for her situation at the time a very extensive scale. This support, moreover, had not been without risk. It had not been confined merely to the delivery of matériel, but volunteers had also been provided and many Germans and Italians had fallen in Spain. He did not wish to reckon this sacrifice of blood in economic terms but regarded it as an absolute gift to Spain.

228 *Notes*

"Economically, Germany had expended many hundreds of millions for Spain. . . ."
Ciano replied that: "Italy had not forgotten the experiences of the Spanish Civil
War either. Franco had declared at that time, that, if he received 12 transport or
bombing planes, he would win the war in a few days. These 12 planes had grown into
more than 1,000 planes, 6,000 dead, and 14 billion lire. . . ." (Department of State,
Documents on German Foreign Policy 1918–1945, Ser. D, Vol. III, pp. 932–933.)

[24] Louis Fischer describes, in his discussion with Comintern agent Uritzky, the
difficulties of hiding shipments of war material to Spain: ". . . The Italians, he declared, had their spies at Constantinople and watched every ship that came out of the
Black Sea. Moscow had a big bureau which did nothing else but devise means of dis-
guising war munitions and the vessels that carried them. They sometimes rebuilt
freighters, giving them a false deck, and placed arms between the decks. Tanks were
immersed in the oil tankers, and so on. But airplanes could scarcely be hidden. I
wondered whether big bombers might not fly from the nearest Soviet point to the
nearest Loyalist airfield. He said it was physically impossible. Nor could they land in
Czechoslovakia. The Czechs would not allow it for fear of antagonizing Germany. No
Soviet airplanes flew from Russia to Spain at any time during the Spanish war.
Uritzky explained that if a Soviet machine made one forced landing anywhere in
Europe the whole world would squeal and 'Litvinov wouldn't like that.' This made it
clear to me that Soviet aid to the Loyalists would remain within the limited legal-
illegal bounds of Non-Intervention." (Louis Fischer, *Men and Politics*, pp. 405–406.)

[25] See p. 77.

[26] The German Ambassador in Italy reported to the Foreign Ministry on August
5, 1937: "With regard to the subject matter [of Franco's request to use the Italian
fleet to prevent Russian assistance via the Mediterranean], Ciano declared that, although the estimates regarding Russian transports might be somewhat exaggerated,
the Duce was in principle still inclined to do everything he could to put a stop to them
—not with surface vessels, to be sure, but only with submarines, in Sicilian waters; in
case the submarines had to surface, they would display the Spanish flag." (Doc. no.
408 in Department of State, *Documents on German Foreign Policy 1918–1945*, Ser.
D, Vol. III.)

And the German Embassy at Salamanca reported to the Foreign Ministry on
August 13, 1937: "Chief of the Diplomatic Cabinet Sangroniz just informed me that
Mussolini had declared that he was prepared to carry out the measures requested by
Franco for preventing the transit of Russian war matériel through the straits south
of Italy. Whether this action will be undertaken under the Italian or the Spanish flag
was still uncertain." (Doc. no. 409, *ibid.*)

[27] The German Ambassador in Italy reported on December 23, 1936, that: "Soviet
deliveries had greatly diminished as a result of measures taken at sea." (Doc. no. 161,
ibid.)

The Soviets themselves confirmed the effect of the piracy on their shipping. The
Russian representative on the Non-Intervention Committee claimed that from October 30, 1936, through April, 1937, eighty-four Russian ships had been interfered
with. (*Doc. no. N.I.S. (36)* 20th Meeting, Stenographic notes of the Twentieth Meeting of the Committee held on Wednesday, May 5, 1937, "International Committee
for the Application of the Agreement Regarding Non-Intervention in Spain." [Un-
published.])

[28] *Doc. no. N.I.S. (36)* 787 and 788, *ibid.*

[29] William Foss and Cecil Gerahty, *The Spanish Arena* (London: John Gifford,
Ltd., 1938), pp. 383–384.

[30] A memorandum (Department of State, Doc. 852.24/456 [unpublished]) from
Valencia on March 25, 1937, stated that it was reported that the government had in
its air force 460 airplanes of all classes divided as follows: 200 Russian pursuit of both

the biplane and monoplane types; 150 Russian bombers of the bimotor Martin type; 70 Russian observation planes equipped for ground attack; 8 French Bloch-210 bombers; 32 miscellaneous types.

[31] Pierre Hericourt, *Pourquoi mentir?, L'aide franco-sovietique à l'Espagne rouge* (Paris: Éditions Baudinière, 1937), p. 102. See also his later work, *Les Soviets et la France, fournisseurs de la révolution espagnole* (Paris: Éditions Baudinière, 1938), p. 28.

[32] It is not known whether the Russian planes were actually manufactured in Spain or merely assembled there. The latter supposition is probably correct since the fabrication of airplanes requires a well-developed industrial system probably not available in Spain.

[33] Mexico was one of the few countries openly sympathetic to the Loyalist cause and not being a party to the Non-Intervention Agreement was able to send material legitimately to the Spanish government. On January 2, 1937, President Lázaro Cárdenas of Mexico reported that his government had sent $1,500,000 in armaments to the Loyalists. The difficulty was that in order to do so Mexico had had to deplete its own war stores and as a result could offer very little additional material since she had no armament industry of any size of her own. (New York *Times*, Jan. 2, 1937, p. 2.)

[34] Telegram from the Ambassador in Italy to the Foreign Ministry, Mar. 17, 1937, Doc. no. 230; Telegram from the Director of the Political Department to the Embassy in Italy, Aug. 4, 1937, Doc. no. 407; Memorandum by the Ambassador to Spain, Apr. 22, 1938, Doc. no. 573 in Department of State, *Documents on German Foreign Policy 1918–1945*, Ser. D, Vol. III.

[35] See P. A. M. van der Esch, *Prelude to War, The International Repercussions of the Spanish Civil War (1936–1939)*, (The Hague: Martinus Nijhoff, 1951), pp. 72f.

[36] Memorandum by the Ambassador in Spain, Apr. 22, 1938, Doc. no. 573 in *Documents on German Foreign Policy 1918–1945*, Ser. D, Vol. III.

[37] See pp. 192f.

[38] "India and Spain," *Inprecorr*, vol. 17, no. 16 (Apr. 17, 1937), p. 419.

[39] See William Foss and Cecil Gerahty, *The Spanish Arena*, pp. 372–376, and A. Barrister, *I Accuse France*, reprinted from the *Catholic Herald*, n.d.

[40] Louis Fischer says the French in respect to airplanes sent a total of one hundred, seventy of which went to Spain in 1936. Louis Fischer, *Men and Politics*, p. 375.

[41] Louis Fischer says that the reserves amounted to 2,446,000,000 pesetas or about $600,000,000 gold. *Ibid.*, pp. 364–365. The New York *Times* on August 7, 1936, reported that at the beginning of the war Spain's gold reserve was $718,000,000.

[42] Indalecio Prieto, *Cómo y por qué salí del Ministerio de Defensa Nacional*, p. 17.

[43] *Ibid.*, pp. 14–16, and Julian Zugazagoitia, *Historia de la guerra en España*, pp. 287–289.

[44] Álvarez del Vayo claims, on the other hand, that Prieto was fully informed about the plan to send the gold to Russia. Julio Álvarez del Vayo, *The Last Optimist* (London: Putnam and Co., Ltd., 1950), p. 285.

[45] In the beginning some gold was sent to Paris, but apparently subsequent transfers were considered inadvisable.

[46] Julian Zugazagoitia, *Historia de la guerra en España*, p. 289.

[47] Louis Fischer, *Men and Politics*, p. 365.

[48] Note from the Ambassador in Spain to the Foreign Ministry, Apr. 21, 1937, Doc. no. 247; Note from the Chargé d'Affaires in Great Britain to the Foreign Ministry, Feb. 4, 1938, Doc. no. 519 in *Documents on German Foreign Policy 1918–1945*, Ser. D, Vol. III.

[49] Claude Bowers in his book, *My Mission to Spain* (pp. 316, 399) states that the number of Russians in Spain never reached more than five hundred.

[50] Louis Fischer also points out that the antimilitary policy of the Comintern had kept most Communists from getting military training so they were of little use to the brigade. Louis Fischer, *Men and Politics*, p. 405.

[51] William Rust, an English Communist in the brigade, describes the recruiting of members in England:"... Scotland Yard detectives fussed around the London office where the recruits were enrolled; they shadowed men; they threatened and blarneyed, and sometimes found a pretext for turning men back at the ports. But, if stopped at one port, the men merely presented themselves at another. It was in any case difficult to stop British subjects from leaving for Paris on a weekend ticket, which permits exit from Britain and entry into France without a passport. And if obviously poor subjects of His Majesty, travelling without pajamas, and clean shirts, were asked to explain the purpose of their weekend trip, they could always bashfully answer, that unexpected luck in the football pools now permitted the fulfilment of a long cherished dream of spending some hectic days in the gay city. After a political and medical examination in London, recruits went on to Paris, where they were again examined and sent on the final stages of their journey, which became more and more exciting after the closing of the frontier. Most of them had a nerve-wracking night climb over the Pyrenees before they arrived on the welcome soil of Spain and paraded before the Republican authorities in an old fortress at Figueras. Others made the journey by sea, sometimes in small open boats which shipped a lot of water before the safety of the Spanish harbours was reached. One big boat, the *City of Barcelona*, which was torpedoed on its way from Marseilles to Barcelona, was carrying several hundred volunteers, many of whom were drowned, including three British." (William Rust, *Britons in Spain, The History of the British Battalion of the XVth International Brigade* [London: Lawrence and Wishart Ltd., 1939], pp. 9–10.)

[52] Telegram from the Ambassador in Spain to the Foreign Ministry, June 27, 1937, Doc. no. 363 in Department of State, *Documents on German Foreign Policy 1918–1945*, Ser. D, Vol. III.

[53] Franco used this figure in his conversation with the German Ambassador to justify his failure to take Madrid and, therefore, would have had a tendency to exaggerate its strength.

[54] Tom Wintringham, a non-Communist officer in the International Brigade, estimated the casualties at fifteen per cent a month or one hundred and eighty per cent a year. Tom Wintringham, *English Captain* (London: Faber and Faber, 1939), pp. 328–329.

[55] Tom Wintringham estimated that the total foreigners fighting in Spain was about 50,000 of which 40,000 were in the International Brigade. He concludes, however, that there were never more than 15,000 brigade combatants on the front lines at one time. *Ibid.*, p. 327.

NOTES TO CHAPTER IX

[1] See pp. 88ff.

[2] Dolores Ibarruri, "Forward to Victory," Radio Broadcast, Madrid, Jan. 3, 1937, *Speeches and Articles 1936–1938* (London: Lawrence and Wishart Ltd., 1938), pp. 50–51.

[3] José Martin Blazquez, *I Helped to Build an Army*, p. 128.

[4] *Ibid.*, p. 205. Still a further anecdote: "Whenever I started arguing with some militiamen who wanted, say, five wireless sets, two sewing machines, eight typewriters, and a vast quantity of rations, and someone stepped out of the queue and supported me, he was sure to be a Communist. There could be no mistake about that." (*Ibid.*, p. 125.)

[5] "Manifesto of the C.P. of Spain," *Inprecorr*, vol. 16, no. 39 (Aug. 29, 1939), p. 1048.

[6] José Díaz, *Por la unidad, hacia la victoria, Discurso pronunciado en el Pleno del C.C. ampliado del Partido Comunista de España, celebrado en Valencia los días 5, 6, 7 y 8 de marzo de 1937,* por el camarada José Díaz, Secretario General del Partido Comunista, sobre el primer punto del orden del día: Frente Popular y union de todos los Españoles y de los pueblos de España para ganar la guerra (Ediciones del Partido Comunista de España Comisión Nacional de Agit.-Prop., 1937), p. 21.

The Communists judged the weaknesses in the defense during the first days as follows:

1. The absence of reserves
2. The absence of unity in war operations and connected fronts and the absence of a unified command and unified strategic plan of war
3. The complete absence of war discipline
4. Weakness of the war command
5. Absence of war training
6. Weakness of political work among the people's militia.

(*Ispanskii narod pobedit!,* pp. 89–95.)

[7] Jesús Hernández, *El Partido Comunista antés, durante y después de la crisis del Gobierno Largo Caballero, Texto íntegro del discurso pronunciado en el cine Olympia de Valencia el 28 de mayo de 1937* (Ediciones del Partido Comunista de España, n.d.), p. 26.

[8] André Marty, "The War of Independence of the Spanish People," *The Communist International,* no. 7 (July, 1937), p. 453.

Most of the articles in the *Communist International* during the Civil War were translations of speeches and reports by Spanish Communists or were articles by Georgi Dimitrov and other leaders of the Comintern which appeared simultaneously in *Pravda* and *Izvestiia* and/or in pamphlets.

[9] See pp. 113ff.

[10] José Martin Blazquez, *I Helped to Build an Army,* Introduction by F. Borkenau, p. x.

[11] A Soviet staff study on the conduct of the Spanish Civil War in 1939 concluded as follows:

"During the length of the whole war in Spain the problems of organizing the high command and administering the armed forces was very acute. At the outset of the war there occurred a series of substantial changes but until the end of the war the problems had not completely been resolved. Frictions among the parties of the People's Front, the criminal activities of the Trotskyites, and their complicity, finally, with the secret agents of the rebels in the central administrative machinery—all these hindered the work of the command and war planning." (General'nyi Shtab R.K.K.A. *Upravlenie voiskami i rabota shtabov v Ispanskoi Respublikanskoi Armii* [The administration of the troops and the work of the staff in the Spanish Republican Army], Moscow: Voenizdat, 1939, p. 5.)

[12] The Communists were not unjustified in claiming that they had led the Spanish people to a system of central organization and discipline. *Geroiskiya Ispaniya,* pp. 65f.

[13] Juan Comorera, *El camino del Frente Popular anti-fascista es el camino de la victoria, Informe presentado en el Primera Conferencia Nacional del Partido Socialista Unificado de Catalunya I.C., 24 julio de 1937* (Ediciones del Secretariado de Agitació i Propaganda del P.S.U., n.d.), p. 21. [In Catalan.]

[14] *Ibid.,* pp. 25–26. See also Antonio Mije, *El papel de los sindicatos en los momentos actuales, Conferencia pronunciada en el cine Capitol de Valencia, el día 1 de enero de 1937* (Ediciones del Partido Comunista de España, n.d.), pp. 9–10.

[15] Since before the Civil War Spain produced neither armaments nor planes, it is impossible to compare output. The loss of territory, especially the northern provinces, also greatly affected the output. Furthermore, it is difficult to check for accuracy the few figures available.

[16] *De Companys a Indalecio Prieto, Documentación sobre las industrias de guerra en Cataluña* (Buenos Aires: Ediciones del Servicio de Propaganda España, August, 1939), p. 9.

[17] Pedro Checa, *Tareas de organización y trabajo práctico del Partido, Texto del informe pronunciado en el Pleno del Comité Central del Partido Comunista de España, celebrado en Valencia el 13 de noviembre de 1937* (Madrid and Barcelona: Ediciones del Partido Comunista de España, 1938), pp. 14–15, 25.

[18] Juan Comorera, *Tres condiciones de la victoria: ¡Unidad proletaria! Frente Popular! Unión de los pueblos de la República!, Informe en el Pleno del C.C. del P.S.U. de Cataluña, celebrado en Lérida los días 8 y 9 de enero de 1938* (Barcelona: Editat del Department d'Agitación y Propaganda del P.S.U., 1938), p. 23.

[19] Georgi Dimitroff, "The Supreme Demand of the Present Moment," June, 1937, *The United Front*, p. 236.

[20] Dolores Ibarruri, *For the Independence of Spain, for Liberty, for the Republic, Union of all Spaniards, Complete text of the report to the plenary session of the Central Committee of the Communist Party of Spain, at Madrid on May 23, 1938* (Madrid and Barcelona: Communist Party of Spain, 1938), p. 28.

[21] See pp. 27f.

[22] F. Furini, "The Policy of the Democratic Countries," *Inprecorr*, vol. 16, no. 42, (Sept. 12, 1936), p. 1146.

[23] M. Ercoli, *The Spanish Revolution*, p. 8.

[24] José Díaz, *Lessons of the Spanish War 1936–1939* (London: Modern Books, 1940), p. 12.

[25] José Díaz, *Por la unidad, hacia la victoria*, pp. 13–15. This report was quoted frequently in Communist literature.

[26] Juan Comorera, "Catalonia, an Example of Unity," *Communist International* (Apr., 1938), p. 376.

[27] The Communists give a figure of 70,000. "The Plenum of the Central Committee of the United Socialist Party of Catalonia," *Communist International*, nos. 3–4 (Mar.-Apr., 1937), p. 199.

[28] Anna Louise Strong, *Spain in Arms* (New York: Henry Holt and Co., 1937), p. 72.

[29] By September, 1937, the Communists claimed almost 600,000 members in the *UGT* in Catalonia. Because of forced unionization in Catalonia, this increase was possible as the *CNT* was the only other sizable trade-union, and most of the petty bourgeoisie and governmental employees refused to join an Anarchist trade-union.

[30] José Díaz, *Por la unidad, hacia la victoria*, p. 51.

[31] José Martin Blazquez, *I Helped to Build an Army*, p. 205.

[32] A. Brones, "The Intensification of the Revolutionary Crisis in Spain, and the Tasks of the C.P.S.," *Communist International*, Vol. X, no. 23 (Dec. 1, 1933), p. 868.

[33] Wilhelm Pieck, *Freedom, Peace and Bread!*, p. 95.

[34] See for example: Colonel Segismundo Casado, *The Last Days of Madrid;* Indalecio Prieto, *Cómo y por qué salí del Ministerio de Defensa Nacional;* Walter Krivitsky, *In Stalin's Secret Service*, pp. 91f; Louis Fischer, *Men and Politics*.

NOTES TO CHAPTER X

[1] Felix Morrow, *Revolution and Counter-Revolution in Spain* (New York: Pioneer Publishers, 1938), p. 160.

[2] See p. 167.

[3] Francisco Anton, *Madrid, orgullo de la España antifascista, Discurso pronunciado en el Pleno del C.C. del Partido Comunista, celebrado en Valencia los días 5, 6, 7 y 8 de marzo de 1937*, por Francisco Anton, Secretario del Comité Provincia de Madrid (Ediciones del P.C. de España, 1937), pp. 5–6. See also A. Samarin. *Bor'ba za Madrid*

[Struggle for Madrid], Period from September, 1936 to March, 1937 (Voenizdat, n.d.), p. 3.

⁴ Colonel S. Casado, *The Last Days of Madrid*, pp. 80–81.

⁵ Luis Araquistain makes the same indictment: "Our propaganda abroad sang the praises of Negrín, Álvarez del Vayo and their friends the Communists." (Quoted in Reginald Dingle, *Russia's Work in Spain* [London: Spanish Press services Ltd., n.d.], p. 20. Also as an article in the New York *Times*, May 21, 1939, p. 31.)

⁶ *Ibid.*, p. 20.

⁷ Constancia de la Mora, *In Place of Splendor*, pp. 339f.

⁸ Reginald Dingle, *Russia's Work in Spain*, p. 20.

⁹ Luis Araquistain, *La verdad sobre la intervención y la no intervención en España* (Madrid: 1938), p. 13. For criticism of the various disfavored ministers see pp. 154, 196.

¹⁰ Walter Krivitsky, *In Stalin's Secret Service*, p. 101.

¹¹ Julian Zugazagoitia, *Historia de la guerra en España*, pp. 408f, 424. In an interview Luis Araquistain told the author that Negrín had never been a Communist but had tried to use the Communist party for his own benefit. Negrín told Araquistain after he came back from a Conference of Physiology in Russia that he had no use for Communism and Russia would be a terrible country to live in. He did, on the other hand, like dictatorships—the efficiency of strong-man rule.

¹² See p. 207.

¹³ Indalecio Prieto, *Cómo y por qué salí del Ministerio de Defensa Nacional*, pp. 80–93.

¹⁴ See p. 202.

¹⁵ Colonel S. Casado, *The Last Days of Madrid*, p. 52.

¹⁶ *Ibid.*, p. 57.

¹⁷ *Ibid.*, pp. 60–62, 75.

¹⁸ Colonel Luis Romero, *Impresiones de un militar republicano* (Barcelona: Oficinas de Propaganda, C.N.T.-F.A.I., 1937), p. 11. See also Julian Gorkin, *Canibales politicos, Hitler y Stalin en España* (Mexico: Ediciones Guetzal, 1941), p. 156.

¹⁹ Jesús Hernández on May 28, 1937, gave the Communist case: "The fall of Málaga was the result of incompetence and treachery of the Minister of War, who, in spite of knowing the gravity of the situation—as he did know it through various channels, not only the Communist, but also Socialist and Republican—could not or would not take the necessary measures for reorganising this front. . . ." (Jesús Hernández and Juan Comorera, *Spain Organises for Victory* [London: Communist Party of Great Britain, n.d.], pp. 20–21.)

²⁰ Walter Krivitsky, *In Stalin's Secret Service*, p. 91. For Anarchist evidence see Diego Abad de Santillán, *Por qué perdimos la guerra*, (Buenos Aires: Ediciones Iman, 1940), pp. 118–119.

²¹ Fenner Brockway, *The Truth about Barcelona* (London: Independent Labour Party, n.d.), pp. 6–7.

²² "A Letter from Barcelona," *Vanguard*, III, no. 6 (Feb.-Mar., 1937), 5, and William Krehm, *Revolution and Counter-Revolution* (Toronto: League for a Revolutionary Workers' Party, n.d.), pp. 31–32.

²³ Katia Landau, *Le Stalinisme en Espagne* (Paris: Spartacus-Cahiers Mensuels, Nouvelle Série, no. 11, 1938), p. 6. See also: William Krehm, *Revolution and Counter-Revolution*, p. 35; Johan Matteo, *Democracy or Revolution in Spain* (London: Independent Labour Party, n.d.), p. 6; Garcia Pradas, *Rusia y España* (Paris: Ediciones Tierra y Libertad, 1948.)

²⁴ Diego Abad de Santillán, *Por qué perdimos la guerra*, pp. 106–108.

²⁵ F.A.I., *Memoria del Pleno Peninsular de Regionales, celebrado los días 21, 22 y 23 de febrero de 1937* (Barcelona: Ediciones de la Sección de Prensa y Propaganda del Comité Peninsular de la F.A.I., 1937), p. 5.

Note that the government is blamed and not the Communists, though they undoubtedly had the most say as to distribution of the Soviet supplies.

[26] For a detailed discussion of this change see pp. 153ff.

[27] Prieto, in a letter to Negrín dated July 3, 1939, admonished him for claiming not to be aware of Communist domination: "You pretend to be ignorant of the predominance attained by the Communists and as proof you cite your failure to submit the name of any Communist for high positions in the Presidential Staff, the Council, and the Ministry of Finance. Without checking to see if the Communist Party had men qualified to occupy administrative posts in the Ministry of Finance, which require a very special technical knowledge—in the Presidential Staff I know of no other post more influential than that of Assistant Secretary—it is appropriate to point out that the sole interest of this party was to control the Army, because with control over the armed forces it held the power in a compact manner in its hands if victory was gained." (Indalecio Prieto, *Epistolario Prieto y Negrín, Puntos de vista sobre el desarrollo y consecuencias de la guerra civil española* [Paris: Imprimerie Nouvelle, 1939], p. 93.)

[28] Colonel S. Casado, *Last Days of Madrid*, p. 53.

[29] *Ibid.*, p. 110.

[30] Indalecio Prieto, *Epistolario Prieto y Negrín*, Letter dated July 3, 1939, p. 95.

[31] See: Articles by Luis Araquistain in the New York *Times*, May 19, 1939, and June 4, 1939; Diego Abad de Santillán, *Por qué perdimos la guerra*, pp. 194, 222–223, 241–242; J. Garcia Pradas, *La traición de Stalin, como terminó la guerra de España* (New York: Ediciones de Cultura Proletaria, 1939), pp. 58–59.

[32] Jesús Hernández, *El Partido Comunista antes, durante, y después de la crisis del Gobierno Largo Caballero*, pp. 27–28. The Soviet staff study of the Civil War in 1939 declared: "On the basis of party the staff officers of the Levant Army were as follows: Socialists 22%, Communists 36%, Left Republican 12%, Anarchists 14% and without any party affiliations 16%." (General'nyi Shtab R.K.K.A., *Upravlenie voiskami i rabota shtabov v Ispanskoi Respublikanskoi Armii* [The administration of the troops and the work of the staff in the Spanish Republican Army], p. 44.)

[33] They assumed the army as their special domain. Pedros Checa, member of the Central Committee of the party, declared: ". . . If there are organizations whose work in the Army is against the policy of the Popular Front, against the unity and the discipline in the Popular Front, we will be the first in opposing this work of disintegration." Checa went on to discuss in detail how the Communists were helping to build a regular army. Pedro Checa, *A un gran partido, un gran organización, Discurso pronunciado en el Pleno del C.C. ampliado del Partido Comunista de España, celebrado en Valencia los días 5, 6, 7 y 8 de marzo de 1937* (Ediciones del Partido Comunista de España [Comisión Nacional de Agit.-Prop.], 1937), pp. 5ff.

[34] *Largo Caballero denuncia, la traición del Partido Comunista Español, Texto del discurso pronunciado en Madrid el 17 de octubre de 1937* (Buenos Aires: Ediciones de Servicio de Propaganda España, 1937), p. 16.

[35] *Siete temas de educación política* (J.S.U., Comisión de Educación del Soldado, n.d.), pp. 11–13.

[36] Antonio Mije, *6 artículos del Subcomisario Antonio Mije acerca de la experiencias de la conferencia de Comisarios de Albacete* (Valencia: Editado por el Subcomisariado de Propaganda del Comisariado General de Guerra, n.d.), p. 12.

[37] *Ibid.*, p. 7.

[38] Dolores Ibarruri, *Speeches and Articles 1936–1938*, p. 86.

[39] General V. Rojo, *¡Alerta los pueblos! Estudio político-militar del período final de la guerra española* (Buenos Aires: Aniceto López, ed., 1939), p. 24.

[40] John McGovern, *Terror in Spain, How the Communist International has destroyed working class unity, undermined the fight against Franco, and suppressed the social revolution* (London: Independent Labour Party, n.d.), p. 11.

[41] Following is a partial list of the evidence to be found: Katia Landau, *Stalinisme*

en Espagne; John McGovern, *Terror in Spain; La dominacion roja en España,* Causa General—Avance de la Información instruda por el Ministerio Publico (Ministerio de Justicia, 1943), pp. 66, 201–206; Walter Krivitsky, *In Stalin's Secret Service,* pp. 99–102; Franz Borkenau, *The Spanish Cockpit,* p. 239f; Lazarillo de Tormes, *España cuna de la libertad* (Valencia: Ediciones Ebro, n.d.), pp. 106–113, 182–183.

⁴² The Ambassador in Spain to the Foreign Ministry, May 1, 1937, Doc. no. 248 in Department of State, *Documents on German Foreign Policy 1918–1945,* Ser. D, Vol. III.

⁴³ Largo Caballero did, however, refuse to participate in the complete liquidation of the *POUM* as the Communists demanded, but Indalecio Prieto and the right Socialists and the Republican parties coöperated in its annihilation. See pp. 153, 156.

⁴⁴ The most outstanding foreign revolutionary eliminated in this was the Italian Anarchist, Camillo Berneri. See pp. 133f.

NOTES TO CHAPTER XI

¹ Franz Borkenau, *The Spanish Cockpit,* p. 196, and Walter Krivitsky, *In Stalin's Secret Service,* p. 101. Both authors report that the Communists had lost confidence in Caballero by January, 1937. Luis Araquistain writes in the same vein: "From my post of observation as Ambassador in Paris, I noticed with surprise that as early as the first months of 1937, some liberal newspapers in London which allowed themselves to be more or less consciously inspired by Communists or sympathizers with Communism, were beginning to publish, without apparent reason, photographs and articles in praise of Dr. Negrín, who was then Minister of Finance. The hidden reason·was that Moscow had chosen him to succeed Largo Caballero. . . . He was not known, however, either in political or scientific circles, for he had never been a speaker or writer on politics. International opinion, therefore, had to be prepared and a name as a statesman had to be rapidly created for him. The Communists are past masters in the art of setting up figure-heads." (Luis Araquistain, article in the New York *Times,* May 21, 1939.)

² Julian Gorkin, *Canibales politicos, Hitler y Stalin en España,* p. 64.

³ José Díaz, *Lo que el Partido Comunista considera indispensable hacer para ganar la guerra, Resolución del Pleno ampliado del C.C. del P.C. de España, sobre el informe hecho por el Comarada Díaz, el 5 de marzo de 1937* (Ediciones del P.C. de España, 1937), p. 10.

⁴ Santiago Carrillo, *En marcha hacia la victoria, Conferencia Nacional de Juventudes, enero de 1937,* p. 14.

⁵ Hugh Slater, "For the Unity of the Spanish Proletariat," *Inprecorr,* vol. 17, no. 4, (Jan. 23, 1937), p. 70.

⁶ Antonio Mije, *Por una potente industria de guerra, Discurso pronunciado en el Pleno ampliado del C.C. del P. C. de España, celebrado en Valencia los días 5, 6, 7 y 8 de marzo de 1937* (Barcelona: Ediciones del P.C. de España, 1937), p. 11.

⁷ André Marty, *Heroic Spain* (New York: Workers Library Publisher, 1937), p. 35.

⁸ See pp. 173ff.

⁹ M. E. Kol'tsov, *Ispanskii dnevnik,* p. 18.

¹⁰ *Ispanskii narod pobedit!,* pp. 117–118, and Louis Fischer, *The War in Spain,* pp. 40–41.

¹¹ "Spain, the struggle against fascism" *Communist International* (Nov., 1936), p. 1429.

¹² H. E. Kaminski, *Ceux de Barcelone* (Paris: Les Editions Denoël, 1937), pp. 271–273.

¹³ "In Memory of Buenaventura Durruti," *Communist International* (Dec., 1936), pp. 1596–1597.

[14] José Díaz, *Por la unidad, hacia la victoria*, p. 43, and Hugh Slater, "For the Unity of the Spanish Proletariat," *Inprecorr*, vol. 17, no. 4, (Jan. 23, 1937), p. 70.

[15] *Mundo Obrero*, Jan. 4, 1937.

[16] Hugh Slater, "On the Death of the Spanish Anarchist Durruti," *Inprecorr*, vol. 16, no. 54 (Dec. 5, 1936), p. 1438.

[17] José Díaz, *Lo que el Partido Comunista considera indispensable hacer para ganar la guerra*, p. 11.

[18] José Díaz, "Los obreros unidos," Discurso pronunciado en el Teatro de la Zarauela, de Madrid, el 11 de febrero de 1936, *Nuestra bandera del Frente Popular*, pp. 88–89.

[19] Pascual Tomás, *La U.G.T., columna y base de la victoria, Discurso pronunciado por el compañero Pascual Tomás, Vice-Secretaria de la Comisión Ejecutive de la Unión General de Trabajadores, en el Congreso Provincial del Secretariado de Valencia* (n.d.), p. 23.

[20] *Boletín de Información*, C.N.T., A.I.T., F.A.I., no. 246 (Barcelona: Apr. 30, 1937), p. 1.

[21] F.A.I., *Memoria del Pleno Peninsular de Regionales, celebrado los días 21, 22 y 23 de febrero de 1937*, pp. 36–37.

NOTES TO CHAPTER XII

[1] For example, Hugh Slater, correspondent for the *International Press Correspondence*, reported in December, 1936: "In Madrid it is generally agreed that the International Column is responsible, to a large extent, for the successful defense of the capital during these last four precarious weeks. . . ." (Hugh Slater, "The International Column," *Inprecorr*, vol. 16, no. 57 [Dec. 19, 1936], p. 1498.)

Tom Wintringham, a captain in the brigade, declared, however: "Don't let us exaggerate. Our Brigade did not save Madrid. Madrid would have saved itself without us. But without us Franco would have got further into Madrid; he would have crossed the Casa del Campo and forced his way into the streets of the city itself. . . ." (Tom Wintringham, *English Captain*, p. 135.)

[2] Julian Zugazagoitia, *Historia de la guerra en España*, pp. 198–199.

[3] Walter Krivitsky claims that Kleber was not a Canadian as he was "presented" to the world: "This picture was compounded at the Ogpu headquarters in Moscow, which supplied Kleber with his false Canadian passport. Kleber played his part under Ogpu dictation. His interviews were outlined for him by the agents of the Kremlin.

"I had known Kleber and his wife and children and brother for many years. His real name was Stern. He was a native of Bukovina, then in Austria and now in Rumania. During the World War, he served as an officer, was taken prisoner by the Czar's troops, and sent to a camp in Krasnoyarsk, Siberia. After the Soviet revolution he joined the Bolshevik Party and the Red Army, and fought throughout the Russian Civil War on the Soviet side. Then he attended the Frunze Military Academy, from which he was graduated in 1924. For a while we worked together in the Intelligence Department of the General Staff. In 1927, Kleber was assigned to the military section of the Comintern and acted as an instructor in its military schools. He went to China for the Comintern on confidential missions.

"Kleber had never been to Canada and never associated with the White Guards. This bit of fiction was used to cover up the fact of his being a staff officer of the Red Army. It made his role as leader of the International Brigade more plausible. . . ." (Walter Krivitsky, *In Stalin's Secret Service*, pp. 97–98.)

This is the story Krivitsky told. But it is not true that the Communists hid his true identity as he claims. In the *International Press Correspondence* on December 19, 1936, there was the following description of General Kleber: ". . . General Kleber is a man of few words, but an excellent linguist. He is a born general with long experience of wars and civil wars. When he was a prisoner of war in Russia he was released by the revolution and offered his services to the Soviet Government. While in command of important units he first became well known for his victories over Kolchak and the French General, Janin. After having participated in the organization of the Hamburg insurrection he became one of the military leaders of the anti-imperialist struggle in China." (Hugh Slater, "The International Column," *Inprecorr*, vol. 16, no. 57 [December 19, 1936], pp. 1498–1499.)

NOTES TO CHAPTER XIII

[1] This renewed antagonism against the Anarchists was never expressed in the open —the censor took care of that. It was a struggle of the backstair, back-alley variety. See Franz Borkenau, *The Spanish Cockpit*, pp. 233–235.

[2] See Ramón Sender, *The War in Spain* (London: Faber and Faber, 1937), p. 175. The United States edition was called *Counter-Attack in Spain* (New York: Houghton Mifflin Co., 1937).

[3] A.I.T., *Boletín de Información*, Service d'Information Français de l'A.I.T., Édition Speciale du 11 mai 1937, p. 4. (Mimeographed.)

[4] José Díaz, "Organising for the Victory of the Spanish People," *Communist International*, no. 5 (May, 1937), p. 325.

[5] Professor Camillo Berneri, "El estado y las clases," *Tiempos Nuevos*, Ano IV, num. 1 (Enero de 1937), p. 13.

[6] Camillo Berneri, *Guerre de classes en Espagne*, Les Cahiers de "Terre Libre," Année III, nos. 4–5 (Avril-mai, 1938), pp. 23–24.

[7] Franz Borkenau, *The Spanish Cockpit*, p. 228. Martin Blazquez reports how in the early days the Communists had even deterred action against the Anarchists: "During the darkest days . . . we considered the idea of a surprise attack on the well-armed Anarchist strongholds, and dreamt of being able to send reinforcements to the front armed with munitions from the Anarchist hoard. So tempting was the idea that we actually discussed it seriously with leading members of the Communist Party, who, however, always dissuaded us. . . ." The author does go on to mention, however, that the Communists planned to get rid of the Anarchist leaders as soon as the rank and file had been won over to the government. José Martin Blazquez, *I Helped to Build an Army*, p. 215.

[8] See for example Manuel Azaña, *Discours prononcé par S.E.M. Manuel Azaña, Président de la République espagnole à Valence, 21 janvier 1937* (Switzerland: n.d.), pp. 24–25.

[9] Jacinto Toryho, *La independencia de España, Tres etapas de nuestra historia* (Barcelona: Editorial Tierra y Libertad, 1938), pp. 224ff.

[10] Canovas Cervantes, *Durruti y Ascaso, La C.N.T. y la revolución de julio* (Historia de la revolución española), (Toulouse: Ediciones Páginas libres, n.d.), p. 15, and F.A.I., *El Anarquismo en España, Informe del Comité Peninsular de la Federación Anarquista Iberica al Movimiento Libertario Internacional, 6 de junio de 1937* (El Comité Nacional de la C.N.T., n.d.), pp. 14ff.

[11] The Communist analysis of the *POUM* in the early days of the war was as follows: "The *P.O.U.M.*, a Trotsky organization, plays a provocative and demoralizing role. It was created instantly after the rebellion from two groups, from the Trotskyist group of Nin and the organization of Maurín in the Bukharin sense of Right renegades expelled from the Communist Party. Maurín, himself, was seized somewhere in the fascist territory—the leadership of the United Spanish Trotskyists-Bukharinists has come under Nin. The *POUM*ists have their own newspaper, ingratiate themselves with the Anarchists, they set upon the Communist worker, demanding immediate carrying out of the socialist revolution in Spain, come forward with the most disgust-

238 *Notes*

ing demagoguery against the Soviet Union. In practical activities they seized the most aristocratic hotels of Barcelona, control the streets of restaurants and amusement places...." (M. E. Kol'tsov, *Ispanskii dnevnik*, p. 19.)

¹² Zugazagoitia points out: "The influence which the members of the *P.O.U.M.* declared they had over the working masses of Catalonia did not exist. The predominating groups were the Syndicalists and the *C.N.T.* who sheltered and protected the Workers' Party of United Marxists (*P.O.U.M.*) because of the antipathy of both organizations for official Communism." (Julian Zugazagoitia, *Historia de la guerra en España*, p. 259.)

¹³ *Ibid.*, p. 259.

The *POUM*, which the Communists characterized as Trotskyite, was actually not supported by Trotsky who criticized it. He declared: "Despite its intention, the *P.O.U.M.* proved to be, in the final analysis the chief obstacle on the road to the creation of a revolutionary Party." (Leon Trotsky, *The Lessons of Spain—The Last Warning* [London: Workers' International Press, n.d. (written on December 17, 1937)], p. 23.)

¹⁴ José Díaz, *Por la unidad, hacia la victoria*, p. 46.

¹⁵ Michael Koltsov, "The Trotskyist Criminals in Spain," *Inprecorr*, vol. 17, no. 5 (Jan. 30, 1937), p. 112.

¹⁶ Georgi Dimitroff, "The Second International and the Trial of the Terrorists October 1936," *The United Front*, p. 189.

¹⁷ *Pravda*, Mar. 22, 1937.

¹⁸ José Díaz, *Tres años de lucha*, pp. 427–428.

¹⁹ Manuel Azaña, *Discours prononcé par S.E.M. Manuel Azaña, Président de la République espagnole à Valence, 21 janvier 1937*, p. 20.

²⁰Jesús Hernández and Juan Comorera, *Spain Organises for Victory*, "Position in Catalonia," by Juan Comorera, June 1, 1937 (London: Communist Party of Great Britain, n.d.), pp. 52–53.

²¹ *Ispanskii narod pobedit!*, p. 116.

²² Doc. no. 105 in Department of State, *Documents on German Foreign Policy 1918–1945*, Ser. D, Vol. III. During the Czech crisis the German Ambassador to Nationalist Spain also reported to the German Foreign Ministry that the French government was thinking of intervening in Catalonia and protecting her territorial integrity. Doc. no. 658, *Ibid.*

²³ On April 5, 1938, Franco actually annulled the Autonomy Statute of Catalonia.

NOTES TO CHAPTER XIV

¹ Marcel Ollivier, *Les journées sanglantes de Barcelone (3 au 9 mai 1937)* (Paris: Spartacus-Cahiers mensuels, Nouvelle Série, no. 7, June, 1937), p. 16.

² *Ibid.*, pp. 15–16.

³ The armistice stipulated that all parties should leave the barricades. Patrols and guards were to retire to their headquarters, unions, and fortified positions. Both parties were to release their prisoners and the police patrols were to resume their functions.

⁴ "We manifest our surprise at seeing certain tracts which are being circulated in the city, signed by a group with the name of 'Friends of Durruti.' Their contents are absolutely unacceptable and contrary to the principles of the Libertarian movement; we are obliged to disavow them entirely and publicly....

The Regional Committee of the *C.N.T.*
and the Regional Committee of the *F.A.I.*"

(Quoted in Max Rieger, *Espionnage en Espagne, faits et documents recueillis par un officier de l'armée espagnole* [Paris: Les Éditions Denoël, 1938], p. 181.)

⁵ Lazarillo de Tormes, *España cuna de la libertad, la revolución española y sus con-*

flictos (Valencia: Ediciones Ebro [1937]), pp. 108–109, 215–218, 222; *Los sucesos de mayo en Barcelona* (Relato Autentico) (New York: Editado por la Federación Local de Grupos Libertarios, July, 1937), pp. 16–17; R. Louzon, *La contra-revolución en España* (Buenos Aires: 1938), pp. 6–7; *El Anarquismo en España* [Printed in May, 1937], pp. 11–13. (Mimeographed.)

⁶ Augustin Souchy, *The Tragic Week in May* (Barcelona: 1937), pp. 7–8.

Many articles appeared such as the one below condemning the government and the Communists as provocateurs: "Beyond a doubt what has happened is due to a preconceived plan of provocation, unequalled in labor history. This is proved by the fact that 15 days before, it was already being talked about in European diplomatic circles, and by ambassadors very close to Catalonia. It was being prophesied that, once the *C.N.T.* and the *F.A.I.* were displaced from leadership of the masses in Valencia and Madrid, the definitive struggle against the Anarcho-Syndicalists' movement in Catalonia would be launched. These prophesies were being made in the diplomatic circles and cafes of Paris by people close to the Catalan Government. ... The arrival of foreign warships a few hours after the struggle began, proves its premeditated character. These boats were on their way to Barcelona long before the first shot was fired. ... Discipline was the backbone of the movement since all comrades obeyed the directives given by their organizations. Thanks to this it was possible to prevent more bloodshed, for our militias, even in the face of fire, resisted without shooting back...." (*Solidaridad Obrero*, Barcelona *C.N.T.* organ, May 13, 1937.)

⁷ *El Anarquismo en España*, p. 10.

⁸ The United Socialist party, in a statement issued after the uprising, admitted that they had been preparing energetic measures to end the activities of the "uncontrollables": "... The working class and the whole population demanded that an end should be put to the provocations. They demanded that the agents provocateurs should be disarmed and then destroyed and the Trotskyist criminals brought to justice.

"The Government was preparing energetic measures, and the Trotskyists, 'uncontrollables' and other agents provocateurs thought to forestall them by an armed rising...." ("The Truth About the Events in Barcelona—a Statement of the United Socialist Party of Catalonia," *Inprecorr*, vol. 17, no. 22 [May 22, 1937], p. 516.)

⁹ *La C.N.T. parle au monde, le discours de Valence de Mariano Vasquez, Secrétaire Général de la C.N.T.* (Paris: n.d.), p. 58.

¹⁰ Jesús Hernández and Juan Comorera, *Spain Organises for Victory*, p. 52.

¹¹ *Ibid.*, pp. 58–59.

¹² André Marty, *Heroic Spain*, p. 19.

¹³ Doc. no. 254 in Department of State, *Documents on German Foreign Policy 1918–1945*, Ser. D, Vol. III.

¹⁴Constancia de la Mora, *In Place of Splendor*, pp. 319–320.

¹⁵ Quoted in Général Duval, *Les leçons de la guerre d'Espagne* (Paris: Librairie Plon, 1938), pp. 187–189.

¹⁶ A.I.T., "Manifeste des Comités de la C.N.T. et de la F.A.I.," *Boletín de Información*, Service d'Information Français de l'A.I.T., Édition speciale du 11 mai 1937, p. 8.

¹⁷ *El Anarquismo en España*, p. 16.

¹⁸ *Ibid.*, p. 17.

¹⁹ Dolores Ibarruri, "The Heroic Struggle of the Spanish People," Abridged report of a speech delivered at a Plenary Meeting of the Central Committee of the Spanish Communist Party held in Madrid May 23–25, 1938, *Speeches and Articles 1936–1938*, pp. 248–249.

²⁰ Juan Comorera, *El camino del Frente Popular anti-fascista es el camino de la victoria*, pp. 15–16.

²¹ Georgi Dimitroff, "Fascism is War," Aug., 1937, *The United Front*, p. 265.

NOTES TO CHAPTER XV

[1] José Díaz, "Organising the Victory of the Spanish People," Abridged stenogram of the report of the Secretary-General of the Central Committee of the Communist Party of Spain at the enlarged Plenum of the Central Committee, March 5, 1937, *Communist International* (May, 1937), pp. 320–321.

[2] Several military estimates have concluded that the leadership of the Republican forces was of very low caliber and that very often the troops were sacrificed unnecessarily or not used to their maximum efficiency. See for example: Katherine Duff, Part II, "The Course of the War in Spain," *Survey of International Affairs 1937*, Vol. II, *The International Repercussions of the War in Spain (1936–1937)*, Arnold J. Toynbee, assisted by V. M. Boulter, pp. 48–80; and Général Duval, *Les leçons de la guerre d'Espagne*, pp. 227f.

[3] On February 19, 1937, after the fall of Málaga, Dolores Ibarruri declared: "We demand a cleaning of the army and the creation of a powerful, strong republican army. For our children and our mothers we cannot permit—no one can permit—the existence of generals who were sitting comfortably drinking in cafés and similar places at the time when in Málaga there reigned a terrible fascist terror, when the road leading from Málaga was flooded with homeless children and women being killed from planes by German-Italian interventionists. We cannot and do not want to give our sons to the command of generals who are not in sympathy with the affairs of the people and who are not sick at heart from them." (Dolores Ibarruri, "The Way of Victory," Speech at a meeting in the Olympia Theatre in Valencia on February 19, 1937, *Ispanskaya Kompartiya boretsya za pobedu*, pp. 29–30.) See also: "Mandos fieles a la Republica y al Pueblo!, Declaración del C.C. del P.C. de E. ante la caída de Málaga," *El Partido Comunista por la libertad y la independencia de España*, pp. 155–158.

[4] Julian Zugazagoitia, *Historia de la Guerra en España*, p. 227.

[5] José Martin Blazquez, *I Helped to Build an Army*, p. 327.

[6] Francisco Largo Caballero, "The Crisis in Spanish Socialism," *Socialist Review*, vol. 6, no. 9 (Jan.-Feb., 1939), p. 1.

[7] See pp. 113f.

[8] Largo Caballero, *op. cit.*, p. 2.

[9] Colonel S. Casado, *The Last Days of Madrid*, p. 73, and Luis Araquistain, Article in the New York *Times*, May 21, 1939, p. 31.

[10] In this connection Araquistain declared: ". . . This state of mind was expressed by Simeon Vidarte, a Socialist Deputy, who belonged to Señor Prieto's group, with these candid and criminal words: 'If Largo Caballero is successful in that offensive, nobody will be able to throw him out of the government.' " (*Ibid.*, p. 31.)

[11] See Caballero's own discussion of the crisis below.

[12] André Marty, *Heroic Spain*, p. 26.

[13] Luis Araquistain, Article in the New York *Times*, May 21, 1939, p. 31, and *La Batalla*, Barcelona *POUM* organ, May 21, 1937.

[14] Caballero in a speech on October 17, 1937, discussed the crisis as follows: ". . . I must point out to you that this crisis was provoked by the representatives of the Communist Party in the government. The day before the precipitation of the crisis, several Madrid newspapers were already announcing political changes within the Council of Ministers. In it the Communist representation instigated the scandal, as we may well call it, by demanding a change of policy both in the war and in the maintenance of public order. This was a pretext, because, so far as the war was concerned, the Communist Party knew as well as I what was happening, since it had representation in the Superior War Council. And, as for the question of public order, with regard to Catalonia, we, as a central government had no jurisdiction.

"It was a pretext. In that meeting it was asked of me, that the government dissolve a political organization not in agreement with the Communist Party. I, who together with the organizations to which I belonged and to which I still belong have been persecuted by reactionary elements in our country, answered I would not dissolve any organization, political or trade-union. I had not come to the government to serve the political interest of any one of the factions which were contained in it; that whoever felt the necessity of denouncing criminal acts or misdemeanors, however they may be called, should do so and the courts would take charge and would dissolve the organization or not as they saw fit, but that Largo Caballero, the President of the Council of Ministers, would not dissolve any of these organizations." (*Largo Caballero denuncia*, pp. 12–13.)

[15] Luis Araquistain, New York *Times*, May 21, 1939.

Julian Gorkin has this to say about the same episode: "The President of the Republic had entrusted to Largo Caballero the formation of a new Government without the Communists. . . . Negrín and Álvarez del Vayo, Ministers of Treasury and State respectively, who although appearing as Socialists, were two docile instruments of Stalinism, refused their assistance to Caballero. . . ." (Julian Gorkin, *Canibales Politicos*, pp. 86–87.)

Gorkin in his discussion, however, fails to mention the resistance of Prieto to a cabinet without Communists. It is very doubtful that the refusal alone of Negrín and Álvarez del Vayo without any large personal following in the country or in the Socialist party would have prevented Caballero from forming a government free from Communists.

[16] Jesús Hernández, *El Partido Comunista antes, durante, y después de la crisis del Gobierno Largo Caballero*, p. 50.

[17] *Largo Caballero denuncia*, pp. 17–18.

[18] Juan Garcia Oliver, *Mi gestión al frente del Ministerio de Justicia, Conferencia pronunciada en el teatro "Apolo," de Valencia, 21–30 de mayo de 1937* (Valencia: Ediciones de la Comisión de Propaganda y Prensa del Comité Nacional de la C.N.T., n.d.), pp. 22–23.

[19] *El Anarquismo en España*, p. 9.

[20] Louis Fischer, *Men and Politics*, p. 418.

[21] Louis Fischer adds: ". . . Azaña and Prieto were opposed to del Vayo. They suspected that he was too sympathetic to the Communists. Moreover, Negrín wanted to be his own Foreign Minister, and to achieve this he had to have somebody who knew nothing about foreign affairs." (*Ibid.*, p. 417.)

[22] See p. 186.

[23] See pp. 130f.

[24] See p. 67.

NOTES TO CHAPTER XVI

[1] The answer of the *CNT* was: "The *C.N.T.* will not collaborate, directly or indirectly, in the Government which might be constituted by Comrade Negrín. It has nothing to do with opposition to the Minister of Finance who has resigned. This is the line of conduct outlined. We did not provoke the crisis, unwise, inopportune and harmful for the war and the antifascist bloc. In conforming to the loyal work of the President and Minister of War of the Cabinet of Largo Caballero we cannot take a partisan position which would prove the lack of nobility and the defectiveness of collaboration. The *C.N.T.*, powerful and disciplined, is confident that reflection may stop the errors which can only aggravate more the difficult situation provoked by folly." (Quoted in D. Abad de Santillán, *Por qué perdimos la guerra*, p. 140.)

[2] On the day of the formation of Negrín's cabinet, May 17, the Communists issued a manifesto declaring in part: ". . . Our wish is to go hand in hand as united brothers with our comrades of the *C.N.T.* and together with them struggle for victory. The

happiness of the people will certainly be sufficiently protected at all times." (Manifesto of the Central Committee of the Communist Party of Spain, Valencia, May 17, 1937. *Ispanskaya Kompartiya boretsya za pobedu*, p. 75.)

³ *Carta del Comité Central del Partido Comunista al C. Nacional de la C.N.T.*, signed by Pedro Checa.

⁴ *El Anarquismo en España*, p. 9.

⁵ "The *C.N.T.* from the first moment intervened in order to curtail the struggles in the streets. This committee, together with the National Executive of the *U.G.T.* rushed to Barcelona and applied superhuman efforts to liquidate the conflict. We looked for a solution. It was accepted by all, but the Communists refused to put it into action immediately. They allowed the solution to slip by, in hope that the Valencia Government, which could not permit the situation to continue any longer, would proceed to take over and establish public order: and thus it occurred. . . ." (Quoted in Lazarillo de Tormes, *España cuna de la libertad*, pp. 110–111.)

⁶ *Ibid.*, pp. 113–114.

⁷ Jesús Hernández, *El Partido Comunista antes, durante, y después de la crisis del Gobierno Largo Caballero*, pp. 8–9.

⁸ M. E. Kol'tsov, *Ispanskii dnevnik*, p. 265.

⁹ This is a condensed review of Jesús Hernández, *El Partido Comunista antes, durante, y después de la crisis del Gobierno Largo Caballero*.

NOTES TO CHAPTER XVII

¹ See p. 103.

Such men as Julian Besteiro, a prominent leader of the moderate Socialists, and Colonel Casado, who led the final revolt against Negrín (see pp. 204ff), declared, "He is an agent of Moscow." Zugazagoitia says, however, that while "all appearances seem to strengthen the thesis of Besteiro," this is not a true analysis of Negrín's character. He describes Negrín's motives as follows:

(Quoting Negrín) "If any organization gives me what I ask, it is the Communists. Always it is under the conditions of carrying it through with spirit in the roughest sections of the fight.

"Negrín ended by leaning on them. It was the line of least resistance for his plans, plans which I doubt very much owe anything to the Soviet Advisory Council. It is clear to me that in the exercise of power Negrín had undergone a radical transformation as if it brought to the fore the value of his personality before ignored. He had confidence in himself."

Zugazagoitia concludes, however, that Negrín was very positive in his judgment and had great respect for strong-man rule:

"His judgments on international policies, instituted as absolutes, he emanated as definitives. On various occasions he praised Mussolini, in comparison to Hitler whom he thought inferior. On Stalin I do not remember that he gave an opinion in my presence. In the democracies he found no men of ability. . . ." (Julian Zugazagoitia, *Historia de la guerra en España*, pp. 479–480.)

General Vicente Rojo also agrees with Zugazagoitia's analysis of Negrín as a patriotic Spaniard. V. Rojo, *¡Alerta los pueblos!*, pp. 221–222.

² Indalecio Prieto, *Cómo y por qué salí del Ministerio de Defensa Nacional*, pp. 48–49.

³ An unusual combination of Anarchists and bourgeoisie were allied in Catalonia in an effort to save their industry from Valencia's domination. For example, President Companys of the Esquerra, the bourgeois autonomist party of Catalonia wholeheartedly endorsed by the Anarchists, sent an open letter on December 13, 1937, to Indalecio Prieto attacking him and the United Socialist party for alleging that Catalonia was not pulling its weight in supplying armaments and needed more centralized control. *De Companys a Indalecio Prieto, Documentación sobre las industrias de guerra*

en Cataluña (Buenos Aires: Ediciones del Servicio de Propaganda España, Agosto de 1939), p. 9.

⁴ Manuel Delicado, *Los problemas de la producción, la función de los sindicatos y la unidad sindical, Informe pronunciado ante el Pleno del C.C. del Partido Comunista, celebrado en Valencia, en los días del 18 al 21 de junio de 1937*, pp. 37–38.

⁵ All news about Caballero had to be smuggled out of the country. One interview slipped over the border and, as originally reported in the *Independent of Perpignan*, quoted Caballero as saying: "I cannot approve of the erroneous military policy or the discriminatory social attitude of the present Valencia regime. . . . I am a spectator of events. When I was obliged to resign people said that the Government would then win the war. Although this victory will come, it is not yet here. . . . My support for a victorious war does not necessarily mean unconditional support of the Government. I feel, furthermore, that it was unwise to remove from power those who had since the beginning given heart, and even blood, to fight fascism. . . ." (Quoted in the New York *Times*, Aug. 9, 1937, p. 7.)

⁶ *Boletín de Información*, C.N.T., A.I.T., F.A.I., May 25, 1937, no. 266, p. 1.

⁷ *Largo Caballero denuncia*, p. 20.

⁸ An interview with Prieto quoted from *La Flêche*, August 18, 1937, gives his viewpoint. Prieto declared: "What is serious is that arrest of the leaders of the *P.O.U.M.* was not decided by the Government and that the police proceeded with these arrests on their own authority.

"Those responsible, he continued [*sic*], are not the directors of the police but their entourage who have been swamped by the Communists in pursuing their ordinary operations." (Quoted in Paul Lapeyre, *Revolution et contre-revolution en Espagne*, [Paris: Spartacus-Cahiers Mensuels (Nouvelle Série, no. 9, février, 1938], p. 28.)

⁹ For the conclusions of the second mission headed by James Maxton, Independent Labour party deputy to the House of Commons, see Lazarillo de Tormes, *España cuna de la libertad*, pp. 182–185.

¹⁰ Manuil'skii, "Concerning the Capitalist encirclement and the Trotsky reserve," *O mezhdunarodnom polozhenii* [About International Relations] (Moscow: Partizdat Tsk VKP(b), 1937), pp. 25–26.

¹¹ *El P.O.U.M. en el banquillo, ¡El proceso de alta traición contra la República!* "Escrito de calificación del fiscal de la República en el proceso contra el *P.O.U.M.*" (Ediciones del Partido Comunista de España, n.d.), pp. 11–13.

¹² Francisco Anton, *El Trotskismo, encarnizado enemigo del Frente Popular, Texto íntegro del informe pronunciado en el Pleno del Comité Central de Partido Comunista de España, celebrado en Valencia el 13 de noviembre de 1937* (Madrid and Barcelona: Ediciones del Partido Comunista de España, 1938).

¹³ See pp. 122ff.

¹⁴ Manuel Delicado, *Los problemas de la producción, la función de los sindicatos y la unidad sindical*, pp. 46–48.

¹⁵ Quoted in Sam Baron, "Behind the Scenes in Spain," *Socialist Review*, vol. 6, no. 4 (Jan.-Feb., 1938), p. 5.

¹⁶ *Ibid.*, p. 6.

¹⁷ Caballero was careful in his attacks to distinguish that he was not against the government but against the leadership of Negrín: "Among the accusations which have been leveled against the *U.G.T.* is that it has not aided the Government. This we must state, as we have previously, is untrue. Let them present us with one case, only one case, in which the Government demanded aid of the *U.G.T.* and did not receive this support. . . ." (*Largo Caballero denuncia*, pp. 24–25.)

¹⁸ Francisco Anton, *El Trotskismo, encarnizado enemigo del Frente Popular*, p. 24.

¹⁹ José Díaz, *Para aplastar a Franco*, pp. 8, 11, 48–49.

²⁰ Juan Comorera, *Tres condiciones de la victoria*, p. 8.

²¹ Francisco Largo Caballero, "The Crisis in Spanish Socialism," *Socialist Review*, vol. 6, no. 9, (Jan.-Feb., 1939), pp. 1–3. In his turn Largo Caballero after his dismissal as Secretary-General of the *UGT* began to demand the convocation of a representative convention of the *UGT* to clear up his name and show the true tenor of the working classes. Caballero declared: "As a result of this campaign [by the Communists and followers of Prieto and Negrín], unquestionably certain groups of the organised working class have been incited to a feeling of hostility against me that will not disappear as long as things are not clarified at a convention—a convention which I desire as much as life itself—at which justice can be done when the truth, now hidden, is made known!" (*Ibid.*, p. 3.)

²² A. Volkov, *Za chto boretsya ispanskoe krest'yanstvo* [What the Spanish Peasantry Struggles for] (Moscow: Gos. Izdat. Kolhoznoi i Sovhoznoi Literaturi "Selkhozgiz," 1938), p. 73.

NOTES TO CHAPTER XVIII

¹ Dolores Ibarruri, *Es hora ya de crear el gran partido único del proletariado, Informe pronunciado ante el Pleno del C.C. del Partido Comunista, celebrado en Valencia, en los días del 18 al 20 de junio de 1937* (Madrid: Stajanov, 1937), p. 52.

² See "Letter of the Political Bureau of the C.P. of Spain to the Executive of the S.P. of Spain," *Inprecorr*, vol. 17, no. 30 (July 17, 1937), p. 672.

³ Dolores Ibarruri, *Es hora ya de crear el gran partido único del proletariado*.

⁴ Comité Nacional de Enlace de los Partidos Socialista y Comunista, *Programa de acción común* (Valencia: n.d.), p. 1.

⁵ *Ibid.*, pp. 14–15.

⁶ Dolores Ibarruri, in a speech on August 10, 1937, described how in Albacete the merger was proceeding without the sanction of the national organs of the parties: "... The striving for unity is so great among the rank and file of the Socialist Party that certain organizations, as for example, in Albacete, have already established not liaison committees but merger committees, and now jointly discuss all problems directed towards the defense of the interests of the proletariat." (Dolores Ibarruri, "Reply to the Enemies, Slanderers, and Wavering Elements," Abridged stenogram of the speech by Comrade Dolores Ibarruri at a meeting in Valencia on August 10, 1937, *Communist International*, Nov., 1937, p. 813.)

⁷ Comité Nacional de Enlace de los Partidos Socialista y Comunista, *Programa de acción común*, pp. 11–12.

⁸ Santiago Carrillo and Amaro del Rosal, *Por la unidad de la J.S.U.* (Ediciones de la J.S.U. de España, n.d.), p. 9.

⁹ Arnold J. Toynbee, assisted by V. M. Boulter, *Survey of International Affairs 1937*, Vol. II, *The International Repercussions of the War in Spain (1936-7)*, p. 114.

¹⁰ José Díaz, Jesús Hernández, and Francisco F. Monteil, *Como fortalecer nuestra democracia? Con una consulta al pueblo, Texto de los discursos pronunciados en el Pleno del C.C. del P.C. de España, celebrado en Valencia el 13 de noviembre de 1937* (Madrid and Barcelona: Ediciones del Partido Comunista de España, 1938), pp. 4–5.

¹¹ The Communists occasionally reopened the question of holding new elections as something desirable but never again carried on a campaign for them. See for example, José Díaz, Articulo publicado en la revista "Nuestra Bandera," en febrero de 1938, *Tres años de lucha*, pp. 597, 603.

¹² For example in the Manifesto of the Communist Party of Spain on the evacuation of Teruel published by the Politbureau on February 23, 1938, number one item on the list of proposals was: "The unity of the Communist and Social-Democratic Party is to be strengthened, so that the United Party of the Proletariat may be created in the shortest possible time—a Party which would represent the progressive interests of the masses and, within the People's Front, would be the decisive driving force of

the democratic development of the Spanish Republic." (Manifesto of the Communist Party of Spain on the evacuation of Teruel published by the Politbureau on February 23, 1938, *Inprecorr*, vol. 18, no. 9 [Mar. 5, 1938], p. 177.)

NOTES TO CHAPTER XIX

[1] Dolores Ibarruri, "Heroic Aragon," *Frente Rojo*, Sept. 8, 1937, p. 149. Even when attacking Caballero bitterly the Communists exclaimed, "Our policy continues to be in support of the most close collaboration with the Anarchists in the Army and the economic organizations." The quote is from a speech by José Díaz in which he berates Caballero. José Díaz, *Para aplastar a Franco*, p. 53.

[2] For example, during February, 1937, the Communists asked for a national convention of all youth to establish a single organ of youth. José Díaz, Conferencia pronunciada en el Teatro Olympia de Valencia, el 2 de febrero de 1937, and Declaraciones publicadas en "Frente Rojo" el 16 de febrero de 1937, *Tres años de lucha*, pp. 358, 377.

[3] "Alianza Juvenil Antifascista, Resolución aprobada por el Consejo Nacional de la Alianza Juvenil Antifascista y por las Direcciones Nacionales de la Organizaciones participantes de la misma, en reunión conjunta celebrado en Barcelona los días 22 y 23 de enero de 1938," *Boletín de la Federación Nacional de las J.S.U.*, febrero de 1938, p. 1.

[4] *Boletín de Información*, no. 51, p. 13.

[5] Dolores Ibarruri, *Speeches and Articles 1936–1938*, p. 156.

[6] "It is the concern of the Communists in the unions, the strongest defenders of the unity of action between the two great central unions, to give more attention to the Committees of Coördination between the *U.G.T.-C.N.T.* which will facilitate the creation of one central union, and enlighten all the workers to the necessity that this be realized in the shortest time and of the benefits which this unity will give to the cause of the war and the revolution." (Pedro Checa, *Tareas de organización y trabajo práctico del Partido*, p. 37.)

[7] "Program of Joint Action of the Spanish Trade Unions," *Communist International*, May, 1938, pp. 455–456.

[8] Some of the more important clauses of the accord are as follows:

1. The Sub-Secretary of Armament will assume sole direction of the industries of war, in agreement with the National Council of War Industries which will be created with the participation of the *C.N.T.* and *U.G.T.*

2. Coördination of all factories and work shops which will permit such adaption to the necessities of the war industries.

3. Centralization of all raw materials, principally those which supply the war industries.

4. Transport, which by its characteristic is needed for the purpose of war, will be put at the disposition of the Government, centralized and militarized. While respecting that which is absolutely necessary it will not be allowed to extort from production and commerce in the rear.

5. The syndicalist organizations, the *U.G.T.* and *C.N.T.*, will coöperate in the rapid creation of a powerful war industry. The unions must try, as the most urgent and pressing task, to create among the workers a serious spirit of vigilance against all kinds of sabotage and slowdown in the work and at the same time with strenuous efforts work toward the increase and betterment of production.

6. Immediate action must be taken in respect to the nationalization of the mines, railroads, heavy industry, air transport, banks, and those industries considered necessary for the national reconstruction after nationalization has been approved by competent organs of the State. The nationalized industries must be centralized and their development coördinated.

7. In order to put into action the plan of industrial nationalization as well as for the organization and general planning of production, the *U.G.T.* and the *C.N.T.* propose the formation immediately of a Superior Council of Economy under the State and with the participation of the trade-union organizations.

The Superior Council of Economy will prepare the national economic plan through the National Councils of Industry—on which the unions also will participate—will regulate, especially in the nationalized industries, production, credit distribution, prices and profits, the importation and exportation of goods, the forms of compensation, commerce, and the utilization of all services which are needed for the proper carrying out of these functions.

The Government will legislate in respect to economic matters in accord with the National Council of Economy [*sic*].

The National Council of Economy will establish a labor inspection service of overall production.

* * *

Collectives

1. The *U.G.T.* and the *C.N.T.* judge the need to enact laws regulating collectives and to determine which of those will be allowed to continue their existence, rules for their constitution and functions, as well as the intervention of the state in them. The collectives which are not subject to this legislation must be disbanded.

2. The State will aid the collectives which adhere to this legislation and whose economic profitableness is recognized.

Workers' Control

1. The Government must pass a law on Workers' Control which will fix the rights of the workers in respect to control of production and protection of its income, intervention into the administration and profits, conditions of work for the laborers and defense of social legislation.

* * *

Agriculture

The *U.G.T.* and the *C.N.T.* favor the rapid nationalization of the land which ought preferably be turned over in usufruct to the agricultural collectives and coöperatives, within them, especially those constituted by the *U.G.T.* and *C.N.T.* The wishes of the peasants who prefer individual cultivation must be respected, and the state should carry out a policy of support for the existing collectives with preference to those of the *U.G.T.* and *C.N.T.* and those which voluntarily constitute the organized farm workers in accordance with the law. (Condensed from *Programa de unidad de acción entre U.G.T.-C.N.T.* [Barcelona: Ediciones Españolas, Mar., 1938].)

⁹ Dolores Ibarruri, *For the Independence of Spain, For Liberty, For the Republic, Union of All Spaniards*, p. 65.

NOTES TO CHAPTER XX

¹ Even the ever optimistic Communists admitted the great shortage of food. The "Pasionaria" was interviewed in Paris on November 30, 1937:

"And *food supplies* in Spain?

"Well, we have had difficulties which we don't wish to hide. We are forced to mobilise considerable numbers of men who otherwise would have been to work. In addition to this, the normal population of those regions under Republican control has been swollen by millions of fugitives from the rebels; and finally, the import of certain products is absolutely necessary. We have huge quantities of oranges, but we lack flour; gallons of oil but potatoes are lacking; wine, but no milk." (*Inprecorr*, vol. 17, no. 52 [Dec. 4, 1937], p. 1274.)

² Julian Zugazagoitia, *Historia de la guerra en España*, pp. 299–300.

[3] The Ambassador in Spain to the Foreign Ministry, May 23, 1937, Doc. no. 264 in Department of State, *Documents on German Foreign Policy 1918–1945*, Ser. D, Vol. III.

[4] It would appear from the German documents that Ángel Baza, Prieto's secretary, acted not only as a go-between but as an agent for Franco in that he forwarded to the Commander at Irún reports of the internal conditions of the Republic. See Ambassador in Spain to the Foreign Ministry, Dec. 3, 1937, Doc. no. 476, *ibid.*

[5] See Indalecio Prieto, *Cómo y por qué salí del Ministerio de Defensa Nacional;* Colonel S. Casado, *The Last Days of Madrid*, pp. 80f.; and *Epistolario Prieto y Negrín.*

[6] Indalecio Prieto, *Cómo y por qué salí del Ministerio de Defensa Nacional*, pp. 40, 44–45. The Cartagena Manifesto was issued after an explosion on board the cruiser *Jaime I* in which several sailors were killed. The manifesto, issued by the Communists, blamed the Minister of Defense for the catastrophe. It further declared, "The enemies of the political commissars are the enemies of the people."

[7] The Communists' defense was that a minister had the right to divulge his thoughts. They also claimed that the article did not in the least reflect favorably or unfavorably on the Minister of Defense. Julian Zugazagoitia, *Historia de la guerra en España*, p. 381.

[8] Indalecio Prieto, *op. cit.*, pp. 48–49.

[9] *Epistolario Prieto y Negrín*, p. 23. Álvarez del Vayo also reports that at the meeting of the War Council on the day before Prieto was excessively pessimistic: ". . . Prieto's statement—the only one he uttered at that meeting—was shattering to the morale of everyone present. The military chiefs, exhausted by days of endless fighting, he treated curtly and with an incredible lack of consideration, posing obviously insoluble problems and putting on them responsibilities which were his as Commander-in-Chief of the Army. In the end Negrín intervened. He defined and affirmed the responsibility of the Ministry of Defense, and he assured the military chiefs that as long as they held their posts they would have the confidence of the Government and its support in whatever they did, whether their actions resulted in success or failure. . . ." (Álvarez del Vayo, *The Last Optimist,* p. 303.)

[10] *Epistolario Prieto y Negrín*, p. 24.

[11] Zugazagoitia speaks of this relationship: "The two natures were distinct but not incompatible. Prieto held sort of a cordial indulgence for what he termed the "bohemian" nature of Negrín, who declared that he was envious of Prieto's smooth oratory. Negrín felt that Prieto was necessary as a contradictor. Their personal relations at this time were good. . . . The strength of their friendship was such that one time, when the Government was still in Valencia, Prieto was asked by Azaña to pacify Negrín. . . ." (Julian Zugazagoitia, *Historia de la guerra en España*, p. 337.)

[12] Dr. Juan Negrín, *Discours prononcé devant les Cortès de la République espagnole réunies au Monastère de Saint Cugat del Vallès, le 30 septembre 1938* (Paris: Edité par le Comité Franco-Espagnol, n.d.), p. 4.

[13] Julian Zugazagoitia, *Historia de la guerra en España*, p. 385.

[14] Indalecio Prieto, *Cómo y por qué salí del Ministerio de Defensa Nacional*, pp. 59–60.

[15] *Ibid.*, pp. 61–62.

NOTES TO CHAPTER XXI

[1] Arnold J. Toynbee, assisted by V. M. Boulter, *Survey of International Affairs 1937*, Vol. II, *The International Repercussions of the War in Spain (1936–1937)*, p. 281.

[2] *Ibid.*, pp. 284–285.

[3] Negrín, defending the decrees against attacks, claimed that they did not violate any of the clauses of the Constitution. He explained: "It is a difference in conception which is held on the one hand by certain Catalonian parties, and on the other by the Government of the Republic concerning the manner in which collaboration of the

Catalonian Government and the central Government ought to be carried out. For my part, I have always thought and upheld that it is the central Government, uniquely and exclusively, which has the direction of the policies of the State and the full authority over it." (Dr. Juan Negrín, *Discours prononcé devant les Cortès de la République espagnole réunies au Monastère de Saint Cugat del Vallès le 30 septembre 1938*, p. 9.)

[4] Zugazagoitia commented on the speech as follows: "The reception that the public gave the orator was ardent. The comments on the speech were extremely favorable. Nevertheless, the speech turned out badly. It is supposed that Prieto, as he frequently did, abandoned himself to his inclination of improvising and was obliged to supplement his resources with too much polemics. I copy from my notes of that day: 'Prieto did not give the speech which he had agreed to and much less did it correspond to the occasion being commemorated by the party. Was this not being equivocal in his point of view, of orientation and of tone. . . .' " (Julian Zugazagoitia, *Historia de la guerra en España*, pp. 467–468.)

[5] General Rojo declared: "We lost the war definitely in the international field during the last ten days of September when the diplomats concocted the pact of Munich. . . ." (General V. Rojo, *¡Alerta los pueblos!*, p. 28.)

[6] Even the usually optimistic Communists admitted the tragedy of the Czech crisis for their cause in Spain. José Díaz wrote on October 5, 1938: "Let us have no illusions nor close our eyes in the face of reality. That which occurred in Czechoslovakia is *a defeat for the international proletariat*, a defeat for the forces of democracy and peace. Fascism has won a victory. . . ." (José Díaz, Artículo publicado en "Frente Rojo," el 5 de octubre de 1938, *Tres años de lucha*, p. 637.)

[7] The difference in outlooks of Negrín and Azaña is seen very clearly even in the titles of their speeches which they gave during July, 1938. Azaña's was called: "Peace, charity and pardon"; Negrín's: "Resist, resist, resist."

[8] Louis Fischer, *Men and Politics*, pp. 420–421.

[9] Colonel S. Casado, *The Last Days of Madrid*, pp. 98–99.

[10] *Ibid.*, pp. 117–125.

[11] Colonel Casado himself admitted that in planning his coup he had to figure that large sections of the army would not follow him. *Ibid.*, pp. 168–169.

[12] General Rojo supports this thesis: "We had visualized the end of the war in another manner. We had felt that it should have been the legal government which should have carried it out, as was its duty, because our war was, more than any other, eminently political and it was politics which should have dispelled the lost contest. We wanted above all to avoid shedding blood, now useless, once it was realized that we were unable to continue the struggle of liberation of our people against three states. We had also wanted to avoid the chaos which we foresaw if the decision to end the war had been made public, and therefore, we had to proceed in a manner in which the decision by the Government would be a surprise to all, to the commands, to the troops, and to the political organizations. Finally we desired to save those who, in discharging their duty and led by their ideology, had fought the war nobly. But all this was only possible under the direction of a government which was in legal command of its rights and it was further necessary that its resolution not be charged with treason. . . ." (General V. Rojo, *¡Alerta los pueblos!*, pp. 249–250.)

[13] A Communist manifesto issued at this time mentioned the possibility of a general conflagration. See Julian Zugazagoitia, *Historia de la guerra en España*, pp. 534–535.

[14] Julian Gorkin, *Canibales politicos*, p. 54.

NOTES TO CHAPTER XXII

[1] See for example: Luis Araquistain's article in the New York *Times*, May 21, 1939, p. 31; D. Abad de Santillán, *Por qué perdimos la guerra;* Julian Gorkin, *Canibales politicos;* Colonel S. Casado, *The Last Days of Madrid*.

BIBLIOGRAPHY

BIBLIOGRAPHY

PRIMARY SOURCES

DOCUMENTS

Anti-Comintern Archives, Hoover Library.

Ciano's Diplomatic Papers. Edited by Malcolm Muggeridge; translated by Stuart Hood. London: Odhams Press Ltd., 1948.

"Documents of the International Committee for the Application of the Agreement Regarding Non-Intervention in Spain." (Unpublished.)

International Military Tribunal. *The Trial of the Major War Criminals Before the International Military Tribunal.* Nuremberg: 1947–49. 37 vols.

Russia. *Dokumenty Ministerstva Inostrannykh del Germanii* [Documents of the Ministry of Foreign Affairs of Germany], Vol. III, *Germanskaia politika i Ispaniia (1936–1943gg.)* [German politics and Spain (1936–1943).] Moscow: 1946.

VII Congress of the Communist International, Abridged Stenographic Report of Proceedings. Moscow: Foreign Languages Publishing House, 1939.

Spain. Ministerio de Estado. *La agresión italiana, documentos occupados a las unidades italiano en la acción de Guadalajara.* Valencia: 1937.

———. Ministerio de Justicia. *La dominación roja en España, Avance de la información instruda por el Ministerio de Justicia.* Madrid: December, 1943.

United States. Department of State. *Documents on German Foreign Policy 1918–1945, Ser. D, Vol. III, Germany and the Spanish Civil War 1936–1939.* Washington: Government Printing Office, 1950.

———. ———. "Documents." (Unpublished.)

———. National Archives. *Documents of the Italian Foreign Office.* Washington. (Microfilmed.)

BOOKS

Abad de Santillán, Diego. *Por qué perdimos la guerra.* Buenos Aires: Ediciones Iman, 1940.

Álvarez del Vayo, Julio. *Freedom's Battle.* London: William Heinemann, 1940.

———. *The Last Optimist.* London: Putnam and Co., Ltd., 1950.

de Baraibar, Carlos. *La guerra de España en el plano internacional.* Barcelona: Ediciones Tierra y Libertad, 1938.

Beltrán Güell, Felipe. *Momentos interesantes de la historia de España en este siglo, Preparación y desarrollo de alzamiento nacional.* Valladolid: Libreria Santaren, 1939.

Berneri, Camillo. *Mussolini à la conquête des Baléares.* Paris: Bureau d'Information et de Presse, 1938.

Bowers, Claude G. *My Mission to Spain. Watching the Rehearsal for World War II.* New York: Simon and Schuster, 1954.

Browder, Earl, and Bill Lawrence. *Next Steps to Win the War in Spain.* New York: Workers Library Publisher, January, 1938.

Campoamor, Clara. *La révolution espagnole vue par une républicaine.* Paris: Plon, 1937.

Canovas Cervantes, S. *Durruti y Ascaso, Le C.N.T. y la revolución de julio, historia de la revolución española.* Toulouse: Ediciones Páginas libres, [1948].

———. *De Franco a Negrín pasanda por el Partido Comunista, historia de la revolución española.* Toulouse: Ediciones "Páginas libres," n.d.

Casado, Segismundo. *The Last Days of Madrid.* Translated by Rupert Croft-Cooke. London: Peter Davies, 1939.

Communist Atrocities, Second and Third Report. Preface by Arthur Bryant. London: 1937.

Cordonie Canella, Rafail. *Madrid bajo el Marxismo, estampas.* Madrid: Libreria General de Victoriano Suarez, 1939.

Dashevskii, G. *Fashistskaya pyataya kolonna v Ispanii* [The Fascist Fifth Column in Spain]. Moscow: Voenizdat, 1938.

Dautun, Yues. *Valence sous la botte rouge, histoire vécue.* Paris: Édition Baudinière, 1937.

Delo Ispanii ne chastnoe delo Espantsev [The affair in Spain is not just a private affair of the Spaniards]. Partizdat Tsk VKP(b), 1937.

Díaz, José, *Lessons of the Spanish War 1936–1939.* London: Modern Books, 1940.

———. *Nuestra bandera del Frente Popular.* Madrid and Barcelona: Ediciones Europa-America, 1936.

———. *Tres años de lucha.* Paris, Mexico, and New York: Ediciones Europa-America, 1939.

Díaz, José, and Dolores Ibarruri. *España y la guerra imperialista.* Mexico City: Editorial Popular, 1939.

Díaz, Santiago Montero. *La política social en la zona marxista.* Bilbao, Spain: Ediciones Libertad, julio, 1938.

Dimitroff, Georgi. *The United Front.* New York: International Publishers, 1938.

Domínguez, Edmundo. *Los vencedores de Negrín.* Mexico: Editorial Nuestro Pueblo, 1940.

Dzelepy, E. N. *The Spanish Plot.* Preface by Pertinax; Translated by Edward Fitzgerald and Frank Budgen. London: P. S. King and Son, Ltd., 1937.

Ehrenburg, Il'ia Grigor'evich. *No pasarán! (Sie kommen nicht durch!).* London: Malik Verlag, 1937.

Epistolario Prieto y Negrín, Puntos de vista sobre el desarrollo y consecuencias de la guerra civil española. Paris: Imprimerie Nouvelle, 1939.

Ercoli, M. *The Spanish Revolution.* New York: Workers Library Publisher, December, 1936.

Erenburg, Ilya. *Estampas de España.* Ediciones S.R.I., 1937.

F.A.I. *Memoria del Pleno Peninsular de Regionales, celebrado en Valencia los días 4, 5, 6 y 7 de julio de 1937.* Valencia: Ediciones de la Sección de Prensa y Propaganda del Comité Peninsular de F.A.I., 1937.

———. *Memoria del Pleno Peninsular de Regionales, celebrado los días 21, 22 y 23 de febrero de 1937.* Barcelona: Ediciones de la Sección de Prensa y Propaganda del Comité Peninsular de la F.A.I., 1937.

———. *Memoria del Pleno Regional de Grupos Anarquistas de Levante, celebrado en Alicante durante los días 11, 12, 13, 14 y 15 de abril de 1937.* El Comité National de la C.N.T., n.d.

Gannes, Harry. *How the Soviet Union Helps Spain.* New York: Workers Library Publisher, November, 1936.

———. *Soviets in Spain.* New York: Workers Library Publisher, January, 1935.

Gannes, Harry, and Theodore Repard. *Spain in Revolt.* New York and London: Alfred A. Knopf, 1936.

Garcia Pradas, J. *Rusia y España.* Paris: Ediciones Tierra y Libertad, 1948.

————. *La traición de Stalin, como terminó la guerra de España.* New York: Ediciones de Cultura Proletaria, 1939.

General'nyi Shtab R.K.K.A. *Upravlenie voiskami i rabota shtabov v ispanskoi respublikanskoi armii* [The administration of the troops and the work of the staff in the Spanish Republican Army]. Moscow: Voenizdat, 1939.

Geroiskaya Ispaniya [Heroic Spain]. Moscow: Partizdat TsK VKP(b), October, 1936.

Gorkin, Julian. *Canibales politicos, Hitler y Stalin en España.* Mexico City: Ediciones "Guetzal," 1941.

Gorozhankina, N. *Rabochii klass Ispanii v gody revolyutsii* [The working class of Spain in a year of revolution]. Pod redaktsiei L. Gellera. Moscow: Gos. Sotsial'no-Ekonomicheskoe Izdat., 1936.

Guzman, Eduardo de. *Madrid rojo y negro, milicias confederales.* Buenos Aires: Ediciones de C. de A. y D. por C.N.T.-F.A.I., 1939.

Hernández, Jesús. *Negro y rojo, los Anarquistas en la revolución española.* Mexico: La España contemporanea, 1946.

Hispanicus. *Foreign Intervention in Spain.* London: United Editorial Ltd., 1938.

Ibarruri, Dolores. *Speeches and Articles 1936–1938.* London: Lawrence and Wishart Ltd., 1938.

Ignotus, *pseud.* [i. e., Manuel Villar]. *La represión de octubre.* Barcelona: Ediciones "Tierra y Libertad," 1936.

Ispaniya v borbe protiv fashizma, sbornik statei i materialov [The struggle of Spain against fascism, a collection of articles and materials]. Moscow [?]: Partizdat TsK VKP(b), 1936.

Ispanskaya Kompartiya boretsya za pobedu, sbornik materialov [The Spanish Communist Party struggles for victory, a collection of materials]. Moscow: Gos. Sotsial'no-Ekonomicheskoe Izdat., 1938.

Ispanskii narod pobedit [The Spanish people will be victorious]. Moscow: Partizdat TsK VKP(b), 1937.

Kaminski, H.-E. *Ceux de Barcelone.* Paris: Les Éditions Denoël, 1937.

Klotz, Helmut. *Uroki grazhdanskoi voini v Ispanii* [The lessons of the Civil War in Spain]. Moscow: Gos. Voennoe Izdat. Parkomata Oboroni Soyuza SSR, 1938.

Kol'tsov, Mikhail Efimovich. *Ispanskii dnevnik* [Spanish diary]. Moscow: "Khudozhestvennaia literatura," 1938.

Korok'kov, Yur. *Ispaniya v ogne, desyat dnei v Respublikanskoi Ispanii* [Spain on fire, ten days in Republican Spain]. Leningrad: Izdat. TsK VKP(b) Molodaya Gvardiya, 1937.

Krivitsky, Walter. *In Stalin's Secret Service.* New York: Harper and Bros., 1939.

Louzon, R. *La contra-revolución en España.* Buenos Aires: 1938.

Low, Mary and Brea. *Red Spanish Notebook.* London: Secker and Warburg, 1937.

Martin Blazquez, José. *I Helped to Build an Army.* London: Secker and Warburg, 1939.

Marty, André. *Heoric Spain.* New York: Workers Library Publisher, 1937.

Maurín, Joaquín [Morrow, Felix]. *Hacia la segunda revolución, El fracaso de la República y la insurrección de octubre.* Paris: Éditions Rieder, 1937; 2d ed., Madrid: Libreria Enrique Prieto, [1935].

————*Révolution et contre-révolution en Espagne.* Paris: Éditions Rieder, 1937.

Minlos, [Bruno Robertovich]. *Paysans d'Espagne en lutte pour la terre et la liberté.* Paris: Bureau d'Éditions, 1937.

Mora, Constancia de la. *Fière Espagne*. Translated by Cl. Delsace and L. Viñes. Paris: Éditions Hier et Aujourd'hui, 1948.

———. *In Place of Splendor, the Autobiography of a Spanish Woman*. New York: Harcourt, Brace and Co., 1939.

Morrow, Felix [Maurín, Joaquín]. *The Civil War in Spain, Towards Socialism or Fascism?* New York: Pioneer Publishers, 1936.

———. *Revolution and Counter-Revolution in Spain*. New York: Pioneer Publishers, 1938.

Mussolini, Benito. *My Autobiography*. London: Hutchinson, 1939.

The Nazi Conspiracy in Spain. Translated by Emile Burns. London: Victor Gollancz Ltd., 1937.

O mezhdunarodnom polozhenii, sbornik [About international relations, collection]. Moscow: Partizdat. TsK VKP(b), 1937.

Orwell, George. *Homage to Catalonia*. London: Secker and Warburg, 1938.

Palacio, Solano. *La tragedia del norte (Asturias mártir)*. 2d ed., Barcelona: Ediciones "Tierra y Libertad," 1938.

Partido Comunista de España, Comité Central. *Pleno Ampliado del C.C. del Partido Comunista de España*. (Collections of speeches given in March and November, 1937.)

———. *El Partido Comunista por la libertad y la independencia de España (llamamientos y discursos)*. Valencia: Ediciones del P.C. de E. (S.E. de I.C.), marzo, 1937.

Peirats, José. *La C.N.T. en la revolución española*. Vol. I. Toulouse: Ediciones C.N.T., 1951.

Perez Salas, Coronel Jesús. *Guerra en España 1936 a 1939*. Mexico: 1947.

Pitcairn, Frank. *Reporter in Spain*. Moscow: Co-operative Publishing Society of Foreign Workers in the U.S.S.R., 1937.

Podorolskii, N. (ed.). *Kryl'ya Ispanii, ocherki i rasskazy o letchikakh respublikanskoi Ispanii* [Spanish wings, essays and stories about pilots of Republican Spain]. Moscow: Izdat. Molodaya Gvardiya TsK VKP(b), 1938.

Ramos Oliveira, Antonio. *Controversy on Spain between H. A. Gwynne and A. Ramos Oliveira*. London: United Editorial Ltd., 1937.

Rieger, Max. *Espionnage en Espagne, faits et documents recueillis par un officier de l'armée espagnole*. Paris: Les Éditions Denoël, 1938.

Rojo, General Vicente. *¡Alerta los pueblos! Estudio político-militar del período final de la guerra española*. Buenos Aires: Editor Aniceto López, 1939.

Romero, Luis. *Impresiones de un militar republicano*. Barcelona: Oficinas de Propaganda C.N.T.-F.A.I., 1937.

Rotbuch über Spanien, Bilder, Dokumente, Zeugenaussagen, Gesammelt und Herausgegeben von der Anti Komintern. Berlin and Leipzig: 1937.

Samarin, A. *Bor'ba za Madrid, period sentyabr' 1936g do mart 1937g*. [The struggle for Madrid, the period from September 1936 to March 1937]. Voenizdat., n.d.

Somoza Silva, Lázaro. *El General Miaja, biografía de un héroe*. Mexico: Ediciones "Tyris," 1944.

Souchy, A. *(Avant—Propos de), Collectivisations, l'oeuvre constructive de la révolution espagnole, recueil de documents*. Édité par les Officines de Propaganda Extérieure, C.N.T.-F.A.I., April, 1937.

S.S.S.R. i fashistskaia agressiia v Ispanii, sbornik dokumentov [The U.S.S.R. and Fascist aggression in Spain, a collection of documents]. Moscow: Gos. Sotsial'no-Ekonomicheskoe Izdatelstvo, 1937.

Strong, Anna Louise. *Spain in Arms.* New York: Henry Holt and Co., 1937.
Three Years Struggle in Spain 1936-1939. Libertarian Movement C.N.T., F.A.I., F.I.J.I. London: Freedom Press, 1939.
Tormes, Lazarillo de. *España cuna de la libertad, la revolución española y sus conflictos.* Valencia: Ediciones Ebro, [1937].
Toryho, Jacinto. *La independencia de España, tres etapas de nuestra historia.* Barcelona: Ediciones Tierra y Libertad, 1938.
El trabajo en el campo, emisiones radiadas por el Ministerio de Agricultura. Subsecretaria de Propaganda, 1938.
Unidad proletaria U.G.T.-C.N.T., los dos poderosas sindicales españolas, colección España. Vol. 5. Mexico: Ediciones de la Sociedad de Amigos de España, 1938.
Varga, Eugen. *Ispaniia i revolyutsiia* [Spain and revolution]. Moscow: Partizdat. TsK VKP(b), 1937.
Vilaplana, Antonio Ruiz. *Sous la foi du serment, une année en Espagne nationaliste.* Paris: Jean Flory, 1937.
Volkov, A. *Za chto boretsya ispanskoe krest'yanstvo* [What the Spanish peasantry struggles for]. Moscow: Gos. Izdat. Kolkhoznoi i Sovkhoznoi Literaturi Selkhozgiz, 1938.
Zugazagoitia, Julian. *Historia de la guerra en España.* Buenos Aires: Editorial la Vanguardia, 1940.

PAMPHLETS

L'action des Communistes en Espagne. Bruxelles: Imprimerie Coopérative Lucifer [1939?].
Acuerdos del Pleno Economico Nacional Ampliado, El primer Congreso Nacional de carácter constructive, celebrado en la España antifascista desde el 19 de julio, cuyas sesiones han tenido lugar desde el 15 al 23 de enero de 1938. Barcelona: Artes Graficas C.N.T., n.d.
Aguirre, José Antonio de. *Discours prononcé par s. Ex. Le Président du Gouvernement Basque aux postes de radio de Catalogne le 21 décembre 1938.* Librairie Bloud et Gay, n.d.
———. *Speech, December 22, 1936.* Bilbao: La Editorial Vizcaina, n.d.
Aidez l'Espagne!, Conférence Internationale de Paris 16-17 janvier 1937 pour l'aide aux blessés, aux veuves, aux orphelins, aux réfugiés de l'Espagne Républicaine, Commission Exécutive Élargie du Comité de coordination tenue a Londres le 12 mars 1937. Paris: Edité par le Comité International de Coordination et d'Information pour l'Aide a l'Espagne Républicaine, n.d.
Alvarez, Santiago. *El pueblo de Galicia contra el fascismo, discurso pronunciado en el Pleno ampliado de C.C. del Partido Comunista de España, celebrado en Valencia los días 5, 6, 7 y 8 de marzo de 1937.* Barcelona: Ediciones del Partido Comunista de España, 1937.
Alvarez, Segis. *La juventud y los campesinos, Conferencia Nacional de Juventudes.* Enero de 1937.
El Anarquismo en España. [May, 1937]. (Mimeographed.)
Anton, Francisco. *Madrid, orgullo de la España antifascista, Discurso pronunciado en el Pleno del C.C. del P.C., celebrado en Valencia los días 5, 6, 7 y 8 de marzo de 1937.* Barcelona: Ediciones del P.C. de España, 1937.

————. *El Trotskismo, encarnizado enemigo del Frente Popular, Texto íntegro del informe pronunciado en el Pleno del Comité Central de Partido Comunista de España, celebrado en Valencia el 13 de noviembre de 1937.* Barcelona: Ediciones del Partido Comunista de España, 1938.

Araquistain, Luis. *Mis tratos con los Comunistas.* Toulouse: Ediciones de la Secretaria de Propaganda del P.S.O.E. en Francia, n.d.

————. *La verdad sobre la intervención y la no intervención en España.* Madrid: 1938.

Aristeguieta, Silva. *España moscovita y sus consecuencias.* Octubre, 1938.

L'assassinat de Andrés Nin, ses causes, ses auteurs, la Guépéou en Espagne. Paris: Spartacus-Cahiers Mensuels, Nouvelle Série, no. 19, juin, 1939.

"Autour du procès du P.O.U.M., des revolutionnaires en danger de mort, Julian Gorkin, Juan Andrade, Geronella, José Rovira, Jordi Arquer, Daniel Rebeull, Pedro Bonet, José Escuder." *Independent News*, 1938.

Azaña, Don Manuel. *Discours prononcé par s. Ex. M. Azaña, Président de la République espagnole, à Valence, 21 janvier 1937.* Switzerland: n.d.

————. *Madrid, Speech made in Madrid on November 13, 1937.* London: Friends of Spain, 1937.

————. *Speech Delivered by His Excellency Don Manuel Azaña in the Barcelona City Hall, July 18, 1938.* Spanish Editions, 1938.

Barrio, Diego Martínez and Camille Huysmans, Paul Langevin, Victor Basch, Jacques Duclos, Jules Prudhommeaux, Gaston Prache. *Halte aux incendiares!, Discours prononcés le 8 avril 1937.* Paris: Éditions du Comité Mondial Contre la Guerre et la Fascisme, n.d.

Barrio, Diego Martínez. *Páginas para la historia del Frente Popular.* Madrid and Valencia: Ediciones Españolas, 1937.

Barrio, Josep del. *La tasca dels militants del P.S.U. en el sindicat de cara a la guerra, Intervenció del comarada Josep del Barrio, del C. C., en la Primera Conferència Nacional del Partit Socialista Unificat de Catalunya (I.C.), celebrado durant els dies 24 a 26 de julio del 1937.* [In Catalan.]

Barrister, A. *I Accuse France.* Reprinted from the *Catholic Herald*, n.d.

Berneri, Camillo. *Guerre de classes en Espagne.* Année III, nos. 4–5, Avril-mai, 1938. Les Cahiers de Terre Libre.

Burger, Jean, and Marius Lacroix, Camille Maumey, Louis Rabardel, André Servant. *Grandeur et Martyre de l'Espagne Republicaine.* Preface d'André Ribard. Paris: Éditions de Paix et Liberté (Amsterdam: Pleyel), n.d.

Caballero de Ronte. *Santander rojo.* Valencia: Imprenta, Libreria y Papeleria Merino, 1936.

Cachin, Marcel, and Maurice Thorez, André Marty. *The People's Front in France, Speeches before the Seventh World Congress of the Communist International.* New York: Workers Library Publisher, 1935.

Campbell, J. R. *Spain's "Left" Critics.* London: The Communist Party of Great Britain, March 16, 1937.

Carrillo, Santiago. *En marcha hacia la victoria, Conferencia Nacional de Juventudes.* Enero de 1937.

————. *¡Fuera el invasor de nuestra patria!, Discurso pronunciado en el cine Capitol de Valencia, el 2 de mayo de 1938.* Valencia: Ediciones Alianza, 1938.

————. *J.S.U., Nuestra lucha por la unidad.* Ediciones de la J.S.U. de España, n.d.

————. *La juventud, factor de la victoria, Discurso pronunciado en el Pleno ampliado del C.C. del Partido Comunista de España, celebrado en Valencia los días 5, 6, 7 y 8 de marzo de 1937.* Barcelona: Ediciones del Partido Comunista de España (Comisión Nacional de Agit-Prop.), 1937.

————. *Para resistir a los invasores, Discurso pronunciado por Carrillo, Secretario General de la Comisión Ejecutiva, el día 15 de mayo de 1938, ante el activo de los Clubs de Educación de la J.S.U. de Ejército del Centro.* Barcelona: Sociedad General de Publicaciones (E.C.), 1938.

————. *Por una juventud victoriosa, Experiencia de un año de guerra y revolución popular, Intervención en el Pleno ampliado del C.N., celebrado en Madrid durante los días 24, 25 y 26 de septiembre de 1937.* Editorial Alianza de la Juventud, n.d.

————. *La unidad juvenil arma de combate de nuestro pueblo, Discurso pronunciado en el Monumental Cinema el 4 septiembre de 1938.*

Carrillo, Santiago, and Amaro del Rosal. *Por la unidad de la J.S.U.* Ediciones de la J.S.U. de España, n.d.

Carta del Comité Central del Partido Comunista al C. Nacional de la C.N.T. Signed by Pedro Checa, n.d.

Castro, Enrique. *Balance y perspectivas de nuestra guerra, Discurso pronunciado en el Pleno ampliado de C.C. del P.C. de España, celebrado en Valencia los días 5, 6, 7 y 8 de marzo de 1937.* Barcelona: Ediciones del P.C. de España, 1937.

Checa, Pedro. *A un gran partido, un gran organización, Discurso pronunciado en el Pleno del C.C. ampliado del Partido Comunista de España, celebrado en Valencia los días 5, 6, 7 y 8 de marzo de 1937.* Ediciones del Partido Comunista de España (Comisión Nacional de Agit.-Prop.), 1937.

————. *Tareas de organización y trabajo práctico del Partido, Texto del informe pronunciado en el Pleno del Comité Central del Partido Comunista de España, celebrado en Valencia el 13 de noviembre de 1937.* Madrid and Barcelona: Ediciones del Partido Comunista de España, 1938.

La chute de Bilbao, Une information objective. Bruxelles: Imprimerie Coopérative Lucifer, n.d.

Clavego, P. *El trabajo de los comisarios políticos.* Madrid and Barcelona: Ediciones Europa-America, n.d.

C.N.T. Memoria del Congreso de Comités Españoles de Acción Antifascista en Francia celebrado en Nimes el 21 y 22 de agosto de 1937. Paris: Éditions de la Delegation Permanente du Comité National de la C.N.T., n.d.

Code, Joseph B. *The Spanish War and Lying Propaganda.* New York: The Paulist Press, July 21, 1938.

Comité International d'Aide au Peuple Espagnol. *Notre bilan de solidarité septembre, 1936–juillet, 1938.* No. 8, n.d.

Comité Nacional de Enlace de los Partidos Socialista y Comunista. *Programa de acción común.* Valencia: n.d.

Cómo fortalecer nuestra democracia? Con una consulta al pueblo, Texto de los discursos pronunciados en el Pleno del Comité Central del Partido Comunista de España, celebrado en Valencia el 13 de noviembre de 1937, sobre "La consulta electoral al pueblo." Barcelona: Ediciones del Partido Comunista de España, 1938.

Cómo piensa el Partido Sindicalista en este momento histórica de vida española, Tres manifiestos del Comité Nacional, con nueve reproducciones de los carteles de propaganda anti-fascista. Editados por esta Partido [March, 1937].

Comorera, Juan. *El camino del Frente Popular anti-fascista es el camino de la victoria, Informe presentado en el Primera Conferencia Nacional del Partido Socialista Unificado de Catalunya I.C., 24 julio de 1937.* Ediciones del Secretariado de Agitació i Propaganda del P.S.U., n.d. [In Catalan.]

————. *Tres condiciones de la victoria: ¡Unidad proletaria! Frente Popular! Unión de los pueblos de la República!, Informe en el Pleno del C.C. del P.S.U. de Cataluña, celebrado en Lérida los días 8 y 9 de enero de 1938.* Barcelona: Editat del Department d'Agitación y Propaganda del P.S.U., 1938.

De Companys a Indalecio Prieto, Documentación sobre las industrias de guerra en Cataluña. Buenos Aires: Ediciones del Servicio de Propaganda España, August, 1939.

Contreras, Carlos J. *Nuestra gran ejército popular, Discurso de saludo pronunciado en el Pleno del C.C. ampliado del P.C. de España, celebrado en Valencia los días 5, 6, 7 y 8 de marzo de 1937.* Barcelona: Ediciones del P.C. de España, 1937.

Delicado, Manuel. *Cómo se luchó en Sevilla; Discurso pronunciado en el Pleno ampliado del C.C. del P.C. de España, celebrado en Valencia los días 5, 6, 7 y 8 de marzo de 1937.* Barcelona: Ediciones del P.C. de España, 1937.

————. *Le peuple de France aux cotés de l'Espagne republicaine, Extraits des rapports et interventions, Discours de Camarade Delicado, Membre du Bureau Politique de Parti Communiste Espagnol, 9e Congrès National du Parti Communiste Français 25 au 29 decembre 1937.* Paris: Éditiones du Comité Populaire de Propagande, n.d.

————. *Los problemas de la producción, la función de los sindicatos y la unidad sindical, Informe pronunciado ante el Pleno del C.C. del Partido Comunista, celebrado en Valencia, en los días del 18 al 21 de junio de 1937.* Madrid: Ediciones del Partido Comunista de España, 1937.

Díaz, José. *Frente Popular y unión de todos los Españoles y de los pueblos de España para ganar la guerra, Discurso pronunciado en el Pleno del C.C. ampliado del Partido Comunista de España, celebrado en Valencia los días 5, 6, 7 y 8 de marzo de 1937.* Ediciones del Partido Comunista de España (Comisión Nacional de Agit.-Prop.), 1937.

————. *Para aplastar a Franco, más unidos que nunca dentro del Frente Popular, Texto integro del informe pronunciado en el Pleno de Comité Central de Partido Comunista de España, celebrado en Valencia el 13 de noviembre de 1937.* Madrid and Barcelona: Ediciones del P.C. de España, 1937.

————. *Por la unidad, hacia la victoria, Discurso pronunciado en el Pleno del C.C. ampliado del Partido Comunista de España, celebrado en Valencia los días 5, 6, 7 y 8 de marzo de 1937.* Ediciones del Partido Comunista de España (Comisión Nacional de Agit.-Prop.), 1937.

————. *El que Espanya ensenya a Europe i a America, Conferencia pronunciado el dia 29 de novembre de 1938 a la Unió Ibero-Americana, Sala Studium, Barcelona.* Agitació i Propaganda del P.S.U., n.d. [In Catalan.]

————. *Lo que el Partido Comunista considera indispensable hacer para ganar la guerra, Resolución del Pleno ampliado del C.C. del P.C. de España, sobre el informe hecho por el Comarada Díaz, el 5 de marzo de 1937.* Barcelona: Ediciones del P.C. de España, 1937.

————. *Qué somos y qué queremos los Comunistas, Texto integro del discurso pronunciado el 9 de mayo de 1937 en el cine Capitol de Valencia.* Ediciones del Partido Comunista de España, 1937.

Díaz, José, Jesús Hernández, and Francisco F. Monteil. *Texto de los discursos pronunciados en el Pleno del C.C. del P.C. de España, celebrado en Valencia el 13 de noviembre de 1937, sobre "La consulta electoral al pueblo."* Madrid and Barcelona: Ediciones del P.C. de España, 1938.

Díaz, Santiago Montero. *La revolutión nacional-sindicalista y los trabajadores.* Ediciones Libertad, 1939.

Dimitrov, Georgi. *Fascism is War.* New York: Workers Library Publisher, 1937.

———. *Spain and the People's Front.* New York: Workers Library Publisher, 1937.

———. *Spain's Year of War.* New York: Workers Library Publisher, 1937.

———. *Two Years of Heroic Struggle of the Spanish People.* New York: Workers Library Publisher, August, 1938.

Ercoli, M. *The Fight for Peace, Report on the Preparations for Imperialist War, the Tasks of the Communist International, delivered August 13, 1935.* New York: Workers Library Publisher, 1935.

L'Espagne et la paix, Discours prononcés a la séance plénière de conference internationale d'aide a l'Espagne républicaine le 21 novembre 1937 à la Maison de la Chimie. Paris: Edité par le comité internal de coordination et d'information pour l'aide a l'Espagne républicaine.

"Les événements de Catalogne," *A.I.T. Boletin de Información.* Édition spéciale du 11 mai 1937. Sub-Secretariado de Barcelona, Service d'Information Française de l'A.I.T. (Mimeographed.)

Exposición del plan secreto para establecer un "Soviet" en España. Bilbao: 1939.

Fabregas, Juan P. *Los factores económicos de la revolutión española, Conferencia pronunciado en el cine Coliseum de Barcelona el día 14 de marzo de 1937.* Oficinas de Propaganda C.N.T.-F.A.I., n.d.

F.A.I. *El Anarquismo en España, Informe del Comité Peninsular de la Federación Anarquista Iberica al Movimiento Libertario Internacional, Valencia, 6 de junio de 1937.* El Comité Nacional de la C.N.T., n.d.

Gallego, Ignacio. *El problem campesino en Andalusia, Conferencia Nacional de Juventudes.* Enero de 1937.

Gilabert, Alejandro G. *Los escritores al servicio de la verdad, carta abierta a Ramón J. Sender.* F.A.I. Secretaria de Propaganda del Comité Peninsular, n.d.

Goebbels, Joseph. *The Truth About Spain, Speech delivered at the National Socialist Party Congress, Nürnberg, 1937.* Berlin: M. Müller and Sohn, 1937.

Gorkin, J. G., and Andrés Nin. *El P.O.U.M. ante la revolución española, Texto taquigráfico de los discursos pronunciados en el Gran Price de Barcelona, el día 6 de septiembre de 1937.* Barcelona: Editorial Marxista, n.d.

Hernández, Jesús. *¡Atrás los invasores! El pueblo entero tiene que movilizarse al llamamiento de la patria, Texto íntegro del discurso pronunciado el día 14 de marzo de 1938.* Ediciones del P.C. de España, 1938.

———. *La gran democracia Soviética está con nosotros, Discurso pronunciado en el Pleno de C.C. del P.C. de España, celebrado en Valencia los días 12 a 15 de noviembre de 1937.* Madrid and Barcelona: Ediciones del P.C. de España, 1937.

———. *A los intelectuales de España, Discurso pronunciado en el Pleno ampliado del C.C. de P.C. de España, celebrado en Valencia los días 5, 6, 7 y 8 de marzo de 1937.* Barcelona: Ediciones del P.C. de España, 1937.

———. *El Partido Comunista antes, durante, y después de la crisis del Gobierno Largo Caballero, Texto íntegro del discurso pronunciado en el cine Olympia de Valancia el 28 de mayo de 1937.* Ediciones del P.C. de España, n.d.

————. *Todo dento del Frente Popular, Discurso pronunciado el 7 de marzo en el cine Terys, de Valencia en el mitin de clausura de Pleno ampliado del C.C.* Barcelona: Ediciones del P.C. de España, 1937.

Hernández, Jesús, and Juan Comorera. *Spain Organises for Victory.* London: Communist Party of Great Britain, n.d.

Ibañez, F. Martí. *Granderas y miserias de la revolución social española, Conferencia pronunciada en el cine Coliseum de Barcelona el día 7 de marzo de 1937.* Oficinas de Propaganda, C.N.T.-F.A.I., n.d.

Ibarruri, Dolores. *Ejército popular unido, ejército de la victoria, Texto del informe pronunciado en el Pleno del Comité Central del Partido Comunista de España, celebrado en Valencia el día 13 de noviembre de 1937.* Madrid and Barcelona: Ediciones del P.C. de España, 1938.

————. *Es hora ya de crear el gran partido único del proletariado, Informe pronunciado ante el Pleno del C.C. del Partido Comunista, celebrado en Valencia, en los días del 18 al 20 de junio de 1937.* Madrid: Stajanov, 1937.

————. *For the Independence of Spain, for Liberty, for the Republic, Union of All Spaniards, Complete text of the report to the plenary session of the Central Committee of the Communist Party of Spain, at Madrid on May 23, 1938.* Madrid and Barcelona: Communist Party of Spain, 1938.

————. *Los heroicas mujeres de España, Discursos pronunciados en el homenaje del pueblo argentino a PASIONARIA el día 28 de marzo de 1937.* Valencia: Editorial Nuestro Pueblo, 1937.

————. *No hay más posibilidad de gobernar ni de victoria que a través del Frente Popular, Texto íntegro del discurso pronunciado ante el micrófono, el día 16 de febrero de 1938, en Barcelona.* Ediciones del Partido Comunista de España, 1938.

————. *Un pleno histórico, Discurso de apertura del Pleno ampliado del C.C. de P.C. de España, celebrado en Valencia los días 5, 6, 7 y 8 de marzo de 1937.* Barcelona: Ediciones del P.C. de España, 1937.

I.F.T.U., L.S.I. International Solidarity Fund. *Aid for Spain (Two Years Aid for Spain).* Paris: n.d.

Instituto de Reforma Agraria. *Por una cooperative en cada pueblo, dentro del Instituto de Reforma Agraria.* Valencia: Ministerio de Agricultural, mayo, 1937.

————. *La reforma agraria en España, sus motivos, su esencia, su acción.* Valencia: Ministerio de Agricultura, mayo, 1937.

Intellectuals and the Spanish Military Rebellion. London: The Press Department of the Spanish Embassy in London, [1936].

La Internacional Obrera Socialista y España. Brussels: Secretariado de la Internacional Obrera Socialista, 1937.

Jimenez, Lourdes. *La joventut en la lluita por la unitat, Discursos pronunciados en el IV conferencia de Barcelona de J.S.U.C.* Barcelona: Ediciones Nova Joventut, n.d. [In Catalan.]

De julio a julio, un año de lucha, Texto de los trabajos contenidos en el extraordinario de Fragua Social, de Valencia, del 19 de julio de 1937. Barcelona: Ediciones Tierra y Libertad, n.d.

Lain, José. *Por un ejército regular disciplinado y fuerte, Conferencia Nacional de Juventudes, enero, 1937.* Valencia, n.d.

Lapeyre, Paul. *Revolution et contre-revolution en Espagne.* Paris: Cahiers Mensuels, *Nouvelle Série*, no. 9, février, 1938.

Largo Caballero denuncia, la traición del Partido Comunista Español, Texto del discurso pronunciado en Madrid el 17 de octubre de 1937. Buenos Aires: Ediciones de Servicio de Propaganda España, deciembre de 1937.

Larrañaga, Jesús. *¡Por la libertad de Euskadi, dentro de las libertades de España!, Discurso pronunciado en el mitin de clausura del Pleno ampliado del C.C. del P.C. de España, celebrado en el cine Tyres, de Valencia, el 7 de marzo de 1937.* Barcelona: Ediciones del P.C. de España, 1937.

A Lead to World Socialism on Spain, War, Fascism, Imperialism, Report of Revolutionary Socialist Congress, Brussels, October 31st—November 2nd 1936. London: The Spanish Workers' Party of Marxist Unity (P.O.U.M.), n.d.

Libro de oro de la revolución española 1936-1946. Toulouse: Editado por el M.L.E.-C.N.T. en Francia, n.d.

López, Juan. *Concepto de federalismo en la guerra y en la revolución, Conferencia pronunciado en el cine Coliseum de Barcelona, el día 7 de febrero de 1937.* Oficinas de Propaganda C.N.T.-F.A.I., n.d.

——. *6 meses en el Ministerio de Comercio, Canferencia pronunciada el 27 de mayo de 1937 en el Gran Teatro—Valencia.* Valencia: Ediciones de la Comisión de Propaganda y Prensa del Comité Nacional de la C.N.T., n.d.

Marañon, G. *The Background of the Spanish Civil War.* London: Spanish Press Services, n.d.

Mateu, Julio. *La obra de la Federación Provincial Campesina, Discurso pronunciado en el Pleno ampliado del C.C. del P.C. de España, celebrado en Valencia los días 5, 6, 7 y 8 de marzo de 1937.* Barcelona: Ediciones del P.C. de España, 1937.

——. *El Partido Comunista en el campo, Conferencia pronunciada en el salón de actos del Comité Provincial del P.C.* Valencia: Ediciones de la Comisión Provincial de Agit.-Prop., n.d.

——. *Por qué se constituyó la Federación Provincial Campesina.* Valencia: Ediciones del Partido Comunista (Comisión Provincial de Agit.-Prop.), n.d.

Matteo, Johan. *Democracy or Revolution in Spain, Speech as Fraternal Delegate from the P.O.U.M. to the I.L.P. Annual Conference, March 28, 1937.* London: Independent Labour Party, n.d.

Melchor, Federico. *El frente de la producción, una industria grande y fuerte para ganar la guerra.* Valencia: Ediciones Alianza Nacional de la Juventud, n.d.

Merry de Val, Marquis. *Spain's Fight for Civilization, Throwing Light upon the Origin of Spain's Plight.* The Paulist Press, [1936?].

de Miguel, Alfonso. *La guerra de España ante la situación de Europe, Conferencia pronunciada el 15 de abril de 1937.* Valencia: Ediciones de la Comisión de Propaganda y Prensa del Comité Nacional de la C.N.T., n.d.

Mije, Antonio. *El papel de los sindicatos en los momentos actuales, Conferencia pronunciada en el cine Capitol de Valencia, el día 1 de enero de 1937.* Ediciones del Partido Comunista de España, n.d.

——. *Por una potente industria de guerra, Discurso pronunciado en el Pleno ampliado del C.C. del P.C. de España, celebrado en Valencia los días 5, 6, 7 y 8 de marzo de 1937.* Barcelona: Ediciones del P.C. de España, 1937.

——. *6 artículos del Subcomisario Antonio Mije acerca de la experiencias de la conferencia de Comisarios de Albacete.* Editado por el Subcomisariado de Propaganda del Comisariado General de Guerra. Valencia: n.d.

Montel, Francisco Feliz. *Por qué el ingresado en el Partido Comunista, Discurso pronunciado en el Pleno del C.C. ampliado del P.C. de España, celebrado en Valencia los días 5, 6, 7 y 8 de marzo de 1937.* Barcelona: Ediciones del P.C. de España, 1937.

Montseny, Federica. *El Anarquismo militante y la realidad española, Conferencia pronunciada en el cine Coliseum de Barcelona el día 3 de enero de 1937.* Oficinas de Propaganda C.N.T F.A.I., n.d.

———. *La commune de Paris y la revolución española, Conferencia pronunciada en el cine Coliseum de Valencia el día 14 de marzo de 1937.* Valencia: Imp. y lit. Ortega, n.d.

———. *Mi experiencia en el Ministerio de Sanidad y Asistencia Social, Conferencia pronunciada el 6 de junio de 1937 en el teatro Apolo—Valencia.* Valencia: Ediciones de la Comisión de Propaganda y Prensa del Comité Nacional de la C.N.T., n.d.

Negrín y Prieto culpables de alta traición, Informe sobre las comisiones de Compras, la Subsecretaria de Armamento y el despilfarro escandaloso de las finanzas de la República. Buenos Aires: Ediciones del Servicio de Propaganda España, junio de 1939.

Negrín, Juan. *L'adieu de Président Negrín aux combattants internationaux, Discours prononcé par le Dr. Juan Negrín le 9 octobre 1938, a Barcelone, a l'occasion du départ d'Espagne des volontaires étrangers.* Paris: Délégation de Propagande, n.d.

———. *Allocution prononcée par le Dr. Juan Negrín, a l'occasion de Noël, 24 decembre 1938.* Paris: n.d.

———. *Discours du Dr. Juan Negrín, Président du Conseil des Ministres d'Espagne (Madrid, 18 juin 1938).* Paris: Edité par le Comité International d'Aide au Peuple Espagnol, n.d.

———. *Discours prononcé devant les Cortès de la République espagnole réunies au Monastère de Saint Cugat del Vallès le 30 septembre 1938.* Paris: Edité par le Comité Franco-Espagnol, n.d.

———. *Habla el Gobierno del Frente Popular, Discurso pronunciado el día 26 de febrero de 1938.* Barcelona: Ediciones Españolas, n.d.

———. *The Italo-German Aggression Against Spain, Three Speeches of Sr. Juan Negrín, Geneva, September 1937.* Paris: Coopérative Étoile, n.d.

———. *Speech by Dr. Negrin, Barcelona, 14th October 1938.* Spanish editions, 1938.

Nuestra lucha por la unidad. Valencia: Ediciones Alianza Nacional de la Juventud, n.d.

Oehler, Hugo. *Barricades in Barcelona, The First Revolt of the Proletariat Against the Capitalist People's Front, Eyewitness Account—Barcelona, May 15, 1937.* Chicago: Demos Press, 1937.

Oliver, Juan Garcia. *El fascismo internacional y la guerra anti-fascista española, Conferencia pronunciada en el cine Coliseum de Barcelona, enero de 1937.* Oficinas de Propaganda C.N.T.-F.A.I., n.d.

———. *Mi gestión al frente del Ministerio de Justicia, Conferencia pronunciada en el teatro "Apolo," de Valencia, 21–30 de mayo de 1937.* Valencia: Ediciones de la Comisión de Propaganda y Prensa del Comité Nacional de la C.N.T., n.d.

Ollivier, Marcel. *Les journées sanglantes de Barcelone (3 au 9 mai 1937).* Paris: Spartacus, Cahiers Mensuels, Nouvelle Série, no. 7, juin, 1937.

L'onze de septembre. Barcelona: Casal Nacional de la Joventut, 1938. [In Catalan.]

Ossorio y Gallardo, Angel. *Discours prononcé le 10 octobre, 1936 à la conférence européene pour l'aide à l'Espagne républicaine.* Paris: Edité par la Comité international de coordination et d'information pour l'aide à l'Espagne républicaine, n.d.

———. *L'avenir de l'Espagne, Discours prononcé le 22 febrier 1939 à la Maison de la Chimie, Paris.* Paris: Edité par le Comité international de coordination et d'information pour l'aide à l'Espagne républicaine, n.d.

———. *Texto integro de los discursos pronunciados ante los microfonos del Ministerio de la Guerra y del Partido Comunista, los días 25 de agosto y 6 de septiembre respectivemente.* Socorro Rojo Internacional, n.d.

Partido Comunista de España. *Nuestro Programa y el de la C.N.T.* Valencia: Ediciones del Partido Comunista, n.d.

Peiró, Juan. *De la fábrica de vidrio de mataró al Ministerio de Industria, Conferencia pronunciada el 3 de junio de 1937 en el Gran Teatro, Valencia.* Valencia: Ediciones de la Comisión de Propaganda y Prensa del Comité Nacional de la C.N.T., n.d.

Peña, Roman Gonzales. *Discurso pronunciado en el cine Bilbao de Madrid, el 1 de agosto de 1937.* Madrid: Partido Socialista Obrero Español, n.d.

Le peuple de France aux côtes de l'Espagne républicaine, Extracts des rapports et interventions IX congress du Parti Comuniste Français, Arles, 25–29 decembre 1937. Paris: Editions du Comité Populaire de Propaganda, n.d.

Pieck, Wilhelm. *Freedom, Peace and Bread!, The Report of the Activities of the Executive Committee of the Communist International at the Seventh World Congress of the Communist International.* New York: Workers Library Publisher, 1935.

Pollitt, Harry. *Arms for Spain.* London: Communist Party of Great Britain, October 30, 1936.

———. *Pollitt Visits Spain, Harry Pollitt's Story of his Visit to Spain in December 1937.* London: International Brigade Wounded and Dependents' Aid Fund, February, 1938.

———. *Spain and the T.U.C.* London: Communist Party of Great Britain, September 17, 1936.

Pope Pius XI. *To the Spanish Refugees, address delivered on September 14, 1936, to the 600 Spanish refugees, bishops, priests and laymen whom he received in audience at Castel Grandolfo.* New York: The America Press, 1937.

El P.O.U.M. en el banquillo, ¡El proceso de alta traición contra la República!, Escrito de calificación del fiscal de la República en el proceso contra el P.O.U.M. Ediciones del Partido Comunista de España, n.d.

El Comité Ejecutivo del P.O.U.M. *Qué es y qué quiere el Partido Obrero de Unificación Marxista.* Barcelona: Ediciones La Batalla, 1936.

Pour la paix avec l'Espagne républicaine, Interpellation de Gabriel Péri prononcée de 4 décembre 1936, Discours de Maurice Thorez prononcé le 5 decembre 1936, Explication de vote de Jacques Duclos prononcée le 5 decembre 1936. Paris: Éditions de Comité Populaire de Propaganda, n.d.

Prieto, Indalecio. *Cómo y por qué salí del Ministerio de Defensa Nacional, Intrigas de los Rusos en España, Texto taquigráfico del informe pronunciado el 9 de agosto de 1938 ante el Comité Nacional del Partido Socialista Obrero Español.* Mexico: Impresos y Papeles, S. de R.I., 1940.

———. *Discurso pronunciado el día 1 de mayo de 1936 en el Teatro Cervantes, de Cuenca.* Ediróne La Motorizada, n.d.

Programa de unidad de acción entre U.G.T.-C.N.T. Barcelona: Ediciones Españolas, March, 1938.

Report on Spain. Washington, D.C.: Spanish Embassy, Office of Cultural Relations, October, 1946.

264 *Bibliography*

Los representantes de la Confederación Nacional del Trabajo (C.N.T.) de Espagna. *Ante el gobierno de Valencia, exponen al pueblo su actuación pública 1937.* Valparaiso: Imp. Gutemburg, n.d. [In Catalan.]

La République Espagnole et l'Amérique, Quatre discours (Dr. Juan Negrín, Julio Álvarez del Vayo, Indalecio Prieto, José Díaz). Paris: Archives Espagnoles, 1939.

Resolución política del Pleno del Comité Central del P.S.U., celebrado en Barcelona los días 28 y 29 de septiembre de 1938. Agitación y Propaganda del P.S.U., n.d.

Resolutions, Seventh Congress of the Communist International. New York; Workers Library Publisher, 1935.

Rossell, Mariano Cardona. *Aspectos económicos de nuestra revolución, Conferencia pronunciada en el cine Colesium de Barcelona el día 31 de enero de 1937.* Barcelona: Oficinas de Propaganda C.N.T.-F.A.I., n.d.

Rudiger, H. *El Anarcosindicalismo en la revolución española.* Barcelona: Editado por el Comité Nacional del la Confederación Nacional del Trabajo de España, 1938.

Siete temas de educación política. J.S.U., Comisión de Educación del Soldado, n.d.

Silva, José. *La revolución popular en el campo colectividades agricolas.* Barcelona: Ediciones del P. S. de España, n.d.

Socorro Rojo Internacional, Sección Española. *Seis meses de solidaridad antifascista.* Ediciones S.R.I., n.d.

Souchy, Augustin [probably the translator]. *The Tragic Week in May.* Barcelona: 1937.

Spain, The Elections of February 16, 1936. Published by the Press Department of the Spanish Embassy in London, n.d.

Los sucesos de Barcelona, Relación documental de las trágicas jornadas de la 1ª semana de mayo 1937. Valencia: El Comité Nacional de la C.N.T., junio de 1937.

Los sucesos de mayo en Barcelona (Relato auténtico). New York: Editado por la Federación Local de Grupos Libertarios, 1937.

Thorez, Maurice. *Des avions pour l'Espagne!, Contre l'encerclement de la France!* Paris: Éditions du Comité Populaire de Propaganda, 1936.

———. *Main dans la main por la ronde de la paix.* La Brochure Populaire, Année 2, no. 8, mars, 1938.

———. *The People's Front in France, Speeches Delivered at the Seventh World Congress of the Communist International.* New York: Workers Library Publisher, 1935.

———. "La sécurité française et l'Espagne." *La Brochure Populaire,* Année 3, no. 4, January, 1939.

Tomás, Pascual. *La U.G.T., columna y base de la victoria, Discurso pronunciado por el compañero Pascual Tomás en el Congreso Provincial del Secretariado de Valencia.* Valencia: n.d.

———. *U.G.T. sindicatos; Movilizad nuestros hombres, ante el objetivo supremo; ¡Ganar la guerra!, Discurso pronunciado en el "Gran Price" de Barcelona, el día 17 de enero de 1937.* Barcelona: Union General de Trabajadore (Secretariado de Cataluña), n.d.

Tresaco, I. *En l'aplicació de la linia de la III Conferencia, IV Conferencia J.S.U.C.* Barcelona: Ediciones Nova Joventut, n.d. [In Catalan.]

Trotsky, Leon. *The Lessons of Spain, the Last Warning.* London: Workers' International Press, n.d. [Written on December 17, 1937.]

Uribe, Vicente. *A los campesinos de España, Conferencia pronunciada en Algemesi el 29 de noviembre de 1936.* Ediciones del Partido Comunista de España (S.E. de la I.C.), n.d.

——. *Los campesinos y la República, Conferencia pronunciada el día 22 enero en el Teatro Apolo, de Valencia.* Valencia: n.d.

——. *La política agraria del Partido Comunista, Conferencia pronunciada el domingo 4 de julio de 1937 en el cine Olympia, de Valencia.* Ediciones del Partido Comunista de España (Comisión Nacional de Agit.–Prop.), 1937.

——. *Todos unidos por la reconquista de la República, Discurso pronunciado en el gran mitin de unidad republicana, celebrado en Mejico el 29 de enero de 1945.* Ediciones España Popular, [1945.]

Valdes, Miguel, and Dolores Ibarruri. *Tot el poble decidit a guanyar la guerra, Gran Assemblea d'Informació del Partit Socialista Unificat (Internacional Comunista), Informes i Resolució Política, Barcelona, 27 febrero 1938.* Partit Socialista Unificat, Department d'Agitació i Propaganda, del C.C. Barcelona: n.d. [In Catalan.]

Vasquez, Mariano. *La C.N.T. parle au monde, le discours de Valence de Mariano Vasquez, Secrétaire Général de la C.N.T.* Paris: n.d.

La victoria exije el partido unico del proletariado, Carta del Buro del C.C. del Partido Comunista de España a la Comisión Ejecutiva del Partido Socialista Obrero España. Ediciones del Partido Comunista de España, n.d.

SECONDARY SOURCES

Books

Altmaier, J. *Sur le front de la liberté, un reportage en Espagne républicaine.* Articles parus dans "Le Populaire" de Paris. 1938.

Atholl, Duchess of. *Searchlight on Spain.* London: Penguin Books Ltd., 1938.

Bardoux, Jacques. *Lechaos espagnol, éviterons-nous la contagion?* Paris: Ernest Flammarion, 1937.

Belforte, Francesco. *La guerra civile in Spagna, gli interventi stranieri nella Spagna rossa.* 4 vols. Milan: Instituto per Gli Studi di Politica Internazionale, 1938.

Block, J. R. *Espagne, Espagne!* Paris: Éditions Sociales Internationales, 1936.

Borkenau, Franz. *The Spanish Cockpit.* London: Faber and Faber Ltd., 1937.

Brasillach, Robert, and Maurice Bardèche. Histoire de la guerre d'Espagne. Paris: Librairie Plon, 1939.

Brenan, Gerald. *The Spanish Labyrinth.* 2d ed. London: Cambridge University Press, 1950.

Britain in Spain by "An Unknown Diplomat." London: H. Hamilton, 1939.

Cantalupo, Roberto. *Fu la Spagna.* Milan: A. Mondadori Editori, 1948.

Churchill, Winston Spencer. *The Gathering Storm.* Boston: Houghton Mifflin Co., 1948.

——. *Step by Step 1936–1939.* London: T. Butterworth, 1939.

Duval, Général. *Les espagnols et la guerre d'Espagne.* Paris: Librairie Plon, 1939.

——. *Les leçons de la guerre d'Espagne.* Paris: Librairie Plon, 1938.

Esch, P. A. M. van der. *Prelude to War, The International Repercussions of the Spanish Civil War (1935–1939).* The Hague: Martinus Nijhoff, 1951.

Fischer, Louis. *Men and Politics, an Autobiography.* New York: Duell, Sloan and Pearce, 1941.

——. *Why Spain Fights On.* London: Union of Democratic Control, n.d.

Foltz, C. *Masquerade in Spain.* Boston: Houghton Mifflin Co., 1948.

Foss, William, and Cecil Gerahty. *The Spanish Arena.* London: John Gifford Ltd., 1938.

Gerahty, Cecil. *The Road to Madrid.* London: Hutchinson and Co., 1937.

Godden, Gertude M. *Communist Operations in Spain.* London: Burns, Oates and Washbourne Ltd., 1937.

———. *Conflict in Spain, 1920–1939.* London: Burns, Oates and Washbourne Ltd., 1937.

Hericourt, Pierre. *Arms for Red Spain.* London: Burns, Oates and Washbourne Ltd., 1937.

———. *Pourquoi mentir?, L'aide franco-sovietique à l'Espagne rouge.* Paris: Éditions Baudinière, 1937.

———. *Pourquoi Franco a vaincu.* Paris: Éditions Baudinière, 1939.

———. *Les Soviets et la France, fournisseurs de la révolution espagnole.* Paris: Éditions Baudinière, 1938.

Jellinek, Frank. *The Civil War in Spain.* London: V. Gollancz Ltd., 1938.

Kamiski, H. E. *Ceux de Barcelone.* Paris: Les Éditions Denoël, 1937.

Knoblaugh, H. Edward. *Correspondent in Spain.* New York: Sheed and Ward, 1937.

Langdon Davies, J. *Behind the Barricades.* London: Secker and Warburg Ltd., 1936.

Loveday, Arthur F. *World War in Spain.* London: John Murray, 1939.

Lunn, Arnold. *Spanish Rehearsal.* New York: Sheed and Ward, 1937.

Madariaga, Salvador de. *Spain.* London: Jonathan Cape, 1946.

Pattee, Richard. *This is Spain.* Milwaukee: The Bruce Publishing Co., 1951.

Peers, E. Allison. *Catalonia Infelix.* London: Methuen and Co. Ltd., 1937.

———. *The Spanish Dilemma.* London: Methuen and Co. Ltd., 1940.

———. *The Spanish Tragedy, 1930–1936, Dictatorship, Republic, Chaos.* 3d ed. London: Methuen and Co. Ltd., 1936.

Poncins, Léon de. *Histoire secrète de la révolucion espagnole.* Paris: Gabriel Beauchesne et ses fils, 1938.

Prieto, Carlos. *Spanish Front.* London: Thomas Nelson and Sons Ltd., November, 1936.

Rabasseire, Henri. *l'Espagne creuset politique.* Paris: Éditions Fustier, 1938.

Raynaud, Jean. *En Espagne "rouge."* Paris: Éditions de Cerf, 1937.

Rocker, Rudolph. *The Tragedy of Spain.* New York: Freie Arbeiter Stimme, 1937.

Rust, William. *Britons in Spain, The History of the British Battalion of the XVth International Brigade.* London: Lawrence and Wishart, Ltd., 1939.

Sender, Ramón. *The War in Spain.* London: Faber and Faber, 1937. U.S. edition: *Counter-Attack in Spain.* New York: Houghton Mifflin Co., 1937.

Toynbee, Arnold J., assisted by V. M. Boulter. *Survey of International Affairs 1937,* Vol. II, *The International Repercussions of the War in Spain (1936–1937).* London: Oxford University Press, Issued under the auspices of the Royal Institute of International Affairs, 1938.

Wintringham, Tom. *English Captain.* London: Faber and Faber, 1939.

PAMPHLETS

Brockway, Fenner. *The Truth About Barcelona.* London: Independent Labour Party, [1937?].

Dingle, Reginald. *Russia's Work in Spain.* London: Spanish Press Services Ltd., n.d.

Echeverría, Frederico de. *Spain in Flames.* The Paulist Press, December, 1936.

Fischer, Louis. *The War in Spain.* Published by the *Nation,* 1937.

Joubert, H. *L'Espagne de Franco, Synthèse de trois conférences donnés du 17 janvier au 10 février 1938.* Soulot: Les Amis de l'Espagne Nouvelle, 1938.

Krehm, William. *Revolution and Counter-Revolution.* Toronto: League for a Revolutionary Workers' Party, n.d.

Lambda. *The Truth About the Barcelona Events.* New York: Workers Age Publishers, 1937.

Landau, Katia. *Le Stalinisme en Espagne, Documents recueillis par Katia Landau, témoignages de militants révolutionnaires sauvés des prisons staliniennes.* Série Nouvelle, no. 11. Paris: Spartacus-Cahier Mensuel, 1938.

McGovern, John. *Terror in Spain, How the Communist International has destroyed working class unity, undermined the fight against Franco, and suppressed the social revolution.* London: Independent Labour Party, n.d.

Norden, Henri. *L'Espagne trahie et la guerre qui vient, bilan d'un mois de "Non-Intervention."* Bruxelles: Imprimerie Cooperative Lucifer, n.d.

One Year of War 1936–1937. New York: The Paulist Press, n.d.

Rocker, Rudolph. *The Truth About Spain.* New York: Freie Arbeiter Stimme, n.d.

Spain 1938, Report of Trade Union and Labour Party Members Delegation to Spain, February, 1938. London: International Brigade Wounded and Dependents' Aid Committee, 1938.

"Wayfarer." *The International Brigade.* Reprinted from the *Weekly Review* [1939].

Wolfe, Bertram. *Civil War in Spain.* New York: Workers Age Publishers, 1937.

BULLETINS

Boletín de Información C.N.T., A.I.T., F.A.I.
Boletín de la Federación Nacional de las J.S.U.
Spanish Boletín de Information [sic], London, Glasgow (mimeographed)
Spanish Labor Bulletin, New York
The Spanish Revolution, Weekly English language bulletin of the P.O.U.M., Barcelona

NEWSPAPERS

SPANISH

Adelante
Batalla
Campo Libre, C.N.T., A.I.T., Organ de la Federacion Regional de Campesinos del Centro
Front Rojo
Mundo Obrero
Solidarido Obrero

RUSSIAN

Izvestiia
Journal de Moscow
Pravda

OTHERS

Daily Telegraph
Financial News
Journal de Genève
Journal des Nations
London *Times*
Manchester Guardian
New York *Times*
Le Temps

INDEX

INDEX

Action de Secours pour l'Espagne, 80
Adelante, 156, 171
Africa, danger to French communications with, 76
Agent provocateur, in Barcelona uprising, 146–7. *See also* Foreign agents
Agrarian reform. *See* Agriculture
Agrarian Reform, Institute of, 61
Agricultural workers in Communist party, 94
Agriculture, 2; Communist attitude toward, 30, 85, 92; production reduced, 72; reforms in, 3, 12, 16, 58, 91
Agriculture, Minister of, 66, 111, 159
Aguirre, President, goes into exile, 204
Air and Navy, Minister of. *See* Prieto, Indalecio
Air Force (Italian), patrols Málaga road, 107
Air Force (Loyalist), 222 n. 8, 228 n. 30, 229 n. 40; control of, 74, 75; foreign planes in, 77; Soviet interference in, 104–5
Airplane production, 78, 231 n. 15
Air, Undersecretary of, Communist, 112
AJA, membership and policies of, 187, 245 n. 2
Albacete, 113, 184, 244 n. 6
Alcalá Zamora, Niceto: accused of fraud in 1936 elections, 36–7; deposed, 17; dissolves Cortes, 15; and government crisis (1934), 14; President of the Republic, 13; voted out of Presidency, 37–8
Alfonso XIII, 8, 9
Algiers, Negrín flees to, 207
Alianza de Intelectuales Antifascistas, 115
Alicante, 73, 108, 113
Alliance of Anti-Fascist Youth. See *AJA*
Almería, 133, 169, 184
Álvarez del Vayo, Julio: 233 n. 5, 247 n. 9; as Ambassador to Mexico and the USSR, 217 n. 3; appoints commissars, 154; and cabinet crisis, 156; and the Communists, 33, 102, 111, 200; continues defense of Republic, 204–7; as General Commissar, 113–4; as Largo Caballero's aide, 32–3; as Minister of Foreign Affairs, 66; Negrín tries to make Foreign Minister, 198; and overthrow of Largo Caballero's government, 241 n. 15; as representative to

League of Nations, 159; resigns as Chief Political Commissar, 184; and Russian gold removal, 81, 229 n. 44; supports unified party, 179
Amigos de la Unión Soviética, 115
Amnesty: to political prisoners, 15, 30; propaganda for, among rebels, 201, 202
Anarchism compared to Carlism, 215 n. 9
Anarchist movement, 6–7; and Azaña, 91; in Barcelona revolt, 164–5; and church burnings, 63; and collectivization, 60, 109; and Communists, 50, 170, 187–90, 245 n. 1; entering government changes policy of, 125–7; and Largo Caballero, 132, 158, 170; militias, 47, 67, 87; and Negrín government, 183; newspapers suppressed, 134, 136, 149; and Popular Front, 15; and *POUM*, 127, 136; recruiting of, 132–3; and sabotage in Catalonia, 99; and Socialists, 66–7; and Soviet aid in Catalonia, 107–11; strength of, 95; and terror, 7, 98; uprising of in Almería, 169. See also *CNT*
Anarchist youth movement, 133, 141, 187. See also *CNT*
Andalusia, 107, 139, 155
Ángel Baza, 194, 247 n. 4
Anticlericalism, 4, 51
Anton, Francisco, 101
Aragon: Anarchist revolt in, 13; collectivization in, 60, 189, 225 n. 24
Aragon front, 110–11, 150, 165
Araquistain, Luis: 233 nn. 5 and 11, 235 n. 1, 240 n. 10; and Anarchist-Socialist coöperation, 66–7; and Caballero's military strategy, 155; on the cabinet crisis (May, 1937), 156; and Communist activities in Spain, 102, 112–3, 206, 208
Arms: given to workers, 47; Largo Caballero-Communist disagreement over, 153–5; ordered surrendered by workers, 149; Spanish production of, 231 n. 15
Army: and Caballero, 120, 167; called out against Cullera, 67; and Catalonia, 68, 169; Communist campaign for discipline in, 84; Communist domination in, 113, 185, 234 nn. 27, 32, and 33; Communist purge of, 89–90; and the *coup* of February, 1939, 248 n. 11; and the generals' insurrection (July,

Army—*Continued*
1936), 222 nn. 5 and 7; need for reform in, 240 n. 3; and 19th-century *coups*, 7, 8; occupies Ceuta and Melilla, 47; Prieto· creates new, 191–2, 247 n. 9; Soviet analysis of, 231 n. 11; USSR advisors to, 103, 105
Army, Undersecretary of, 112, 153–4
Asensio, General, 153–4, 166
Assassinations: of Anarchists, 133, 135; in February-June, 1936, 17; in Catalonia, 146–7, 164–5; of Communists, 141; reported by German Ambassador, 48
Assault Guards. See *Guardias de Asalto*
Asturias: 98, 226 n. 2; and Anarchism, 7; Loyalists cut off from, 49; *UGT* in, 174
Asturias revolt: and the Communists, 21–2, 29, 69; and elections of 1936, 16; as result of *CEDA*'s entering cabinet, 14
Atrocities, "red," Nationalist account of, 48
Autonomy: in Catalonia and Basque region, 5, 12, 14, 64, 139, 140, 148, 225 n. 32, 238 n. 23; Communist party program of, 30, 182, 219 n. 31
Ayguadé, Jaime: Anarchists accuse, 149; illegal actions of, 144, 148; in Negrín government, 159; resigns, 202
Azaña, Manuel: and Álvarez del Vayo, 198, 241 n. 21; asks Prieto to pacify Negrín, 247 n. 11; and cabinet crisis, 156; calls on Negrín for new government, 158–9; and Communists, 86, 160, 200; election of as President, 17; and Franco conservatives, 91; and governmental changes, 18; for negotiated peace, 204; opposed to Anarchists, 91, 135; overshadowed by Left, 65; policies of, 138, 248 n. 7; and Popular Front program, 16; recognition by USSR of government of, 216 n. 3; refuses to return to Spain, 207

Badajos, 155
Bakunin, Mikhail A., 67, 124
Balearic Islands, 44, 205
Bank of Spain: gold reserve in, 80; nationalization of, 92
Barcelona: and Anarchism, 7; Anarchist arms in, 134; bombing of, 139; city police of, shoot Berneri, 134; collectivi-

zation of industries in, 62; Comintern has no following in, 93; decree for militias in, 47; Franco and, 203; industrial revolution in, 2; *POUM* influence in, 238 n. 11; *POUM* under *CNT* protection in, 136; rebellion in (1934), 14, 29; semi-civil war in early 20th century in, 8; and Soviet aid, 108; Special Chamber of, put under Minister of Justice, 202; USSR Consul in, 103. *See also* Catalonia
Barcelona revolt: 208, 242 n. 5; and Anarchists, 164–5; Armistice, 238 nn. 3 and 4; Caballero-Communist disagreement over, 155–6; and cabinet crisis, 156; Communists charge *POUM* instigated, 173; foreign warships in, 239 n. 6; Prieto fears revolution during, 194
Barcelona uprising (1934), and United Front program, 29
Basque Nationalists (party): in Caballero government, 66; in Negrín government, 159
Basque provinces: 109, 167; aid of Catalonia to, 139; autonomy in, 12, 14; the Church in, 63, 215 n. 4; Communist strength in, 32; industrial revolution in, 2; modern aspects of, 5
Basque Socialists, 215 n. 7
Batalla, suppression of, 136
Berneri, Professor Camillo: 235 n. 44; murder of, 133–4; on Bolshevism, 134
Bernhardt, Johannes, asks Hitler's aid, 44
Berzin, General, and Soviet military advisors, 103
Besteiro, Julian, 206, 242 n. 1; countercoup of, with Casado, 206
Bilbao, Franco offensive against, 110
Biscay: Loyalists cut off from, 49; *UGT* in, 174
Black Sea, 228 n. 24
Blockade, Franco's naval, hinders reception of aid, 89
Blum government, Communists refuse to enter, 55
Blum, Léon, proposes Non-Intervention Agreement, 80
Borkenau, Franz, 87, 135, 222 n. 8
Borodin, General Mikhail, supposedly Comintern agent in Spain, 40
Bourgeois democracy, transitional stage between socialism and, 92, 93

Bourgeois-democratic revolution: 224 nn. 13 and 17; Communist view of, in Spain, 50–1; united party essential to, 120
Bourgeoisie: and Communists, 98, 223 n. 17; in unified party pact, 182
Bowers, Claude, 216 n. 6, 229 n. 49
Brenan, Gerald, 69, 215 n. 9
Bukharin, Nikolai, 146, 237 n. 11

Caballero government: cabinet of, 65–6; called "counterrevolutionary," 67; and collectives, 61; and Communists, 55–6, 84, 156–8; and nationalization of industry, 67; opposition of Republicans to, 135; overthrow of, 240 n. 14; rumor of Communist *coup d'etat* against, 130–1. *See also* Largo Caballero
Caciques, 6, 8, 37, 215 n. 2
Calvo Sotelo, José, assassination of, 18
Campesino, El, Communist general, 185
Campo Libre, 61, 225 n. 24
Carlists, 7–8, 48, 215 n. 9
Carrillo, Santiago, 122, 154
Cartagena: Communist Party of, 196; gold sent to, 81; naval base at has Communist chief, 113; Ruiz in command of, 104; Soviet aid in, 110
Cartagena Manifesto, 247 n. 6
Casado, Colonel Segismundo: accused of negotiations with Franco, 105; accuses Communists, 208; and Álvarez del Vayo, 33; and army, 248 n. 11; and Caballero's military strategy, 155; on Communist propaganda, 101; and Communists in Defense Ministry, 112–3; countercoup of, with Besteiro, 206; on end of the war, 204–5; and Negrín, 242 n. 1; overthrows Negrín, 207; and Russian interference, 104–5; and use of Soviet aid, 74
Casa Viejas, uprising in, 12
Castellon, 203
Castile and autonomy movements, 5
Castille Libre, suspended, 134
Castillo, Lieutenant, murder of, 18
Casualties: 208; in Barcelona uprising, 143–4; of International Brigade, 83
Catalan-French border, Communists want control of, 140
Catalan language, Communist propaganda in, 64
Catalonia: 67, 167, 206–7; agricultural reform law of revoked, 14; Anarchists

in, 99, 132, 164–5; arming of workers in, 47, 49–50; bourgeoisie in, propose separate peace, 202–3; collectivization in, 60, 62, 68, 189, 225 n. 24; Communists and, 32, 93, 123, 126, 138–140, 161; Council of Food Supplies of, 109; food shortage in 192; French intervention in, plans for, 238 n. 22; industrial production of, 89; Largo Caballero in, 132; mobilization of against Franco, 139; modern aspects of, 5; *POUM* and, 127, 135–6, 173, 238 n. 12; *PSUC* and *UGT* in, 94; public order in, 240 n. 14; relations of with Negrín government, 247 n. 3; retreat to, 100; rivalry of with Madrid, 109; and Russian aid, 107–11; and separate peace with Franco, 139; Socialist youth and parties in, 93, 98; suppression of, 169–71; *UGT* in, 95, 96, 174, 232 n. 29; USSR advisors in, 103; war effort of, 242 n. 3. *See also* Autonomy, Catalonia; Barcelona revolt; Esquerra party (Catalonia)
Cazorla, Commissioner of Public Order, 117
CEDA (*Confederación Española de Derechos Autónomos*): 13; and government crisis (1934), 14; growth of, 15; reasons for failure of, in 1936 elections, 220 n. 3
Censorship: Communist control of, 101, 102; of press and radio, 149; and propaganda, department of, Communists strong in, 112
Centre party, 185
Ceuta occupied by army, 47
Chapaprieta, Joaquín, and financial reforms, 15
Chatos airplanes assembled in Spain, 78
Checa, Pedros, 234 n. 33
Cheka. See GPU
Church, the: 4, 8; and Basque provinces 215 n. 4; burnings of, 63; Communist party program on, 31, 57, 58, 92; and the Constitution, 11; lands, 3, 4; legislation against subsidy of, 11; in Navarre, 215 n. 4; and the Popular Front program, 16, 19; reforms of, in 1920's, 215 n. 3; village priests support Republicans against, 11
Churchill, Sir Winston, and Communist plot in Spain, 19
Ciano, Count, 227 n. 23, 228 n. 26

Ciscar incident, 103–4
City of Barcelona, 230 n. 51
Claridad: seizure of, 171; used by Communists, 179
Clericals, coup of, 222 n. 7
CNT (Confederación Nacional del Trabajo): agreement with *UGT*, 126; Anarchist trade-union, 6; arrests of members, 142; in Asturias uprising, 29; in Barcelona rebellion (1934), 14; in Barcelona revolt, 236 n. 6, 238 n. 4, 242 n. 5; Barcelona revolt manifesto, 164–5; in Caballero government, 66; Caballero pact with, to form a government, 157; and Communists, 124, 128, 165, 170, 241 n. 2; compared with *UGT*, 232 n. 29; control in Catalonia, 238 n. 12; controls industry in Catalonia, 169–70; and elections of 1936, 220 n. 3; and elections to Cortes (1931), 10–11; enters the Generalitat, 68; entry into the government, 226 n. 4; and food supplies in Catalonia, 109–10; and healing of breach with Communists and government, 188; membership (1936), 21; middle-class fear of, 95–6; militias and Soviet aid, 110; and Negrín's government, 190, 241 n. 1; strength in 1931, 7; and *UGT*, 14, 127–8, 170, 171, 188–9, 245 nn. 6 and 8; in unified party pact, 182; and United Front, 24; weakness of, 174. *See also* Anarchist movement
CNT (newspaper), suppressed, 117
C.N.T. del Norte, seized, 134
Collective security, new Russian policy of, 43
Collectivization: of agriculture, 68, 126, 208, 224 n. 23, 226 n. 6, 246 n. 8; and Anarchists, 60, 109, 170; in Aragon, 225 n. 24; in Barcelona, 62; in Catalonia, 224 n. 24; and Communists 30, 58, 60, 62; decree suspended, 67; of industry, 61–2, 68, 125, 126, 208, 246 n. 8; reduces production, 72; *UGT-CNT* provisions for, 189
Colonies, Spanish, 2
Comintern: agents, 40, 42, 74, 78, 97, 228 n. 24; and the bourgeosie, 27; and Communist party in Spain, 96–7; and defense of Madrid, 100; and dictatorship of the proletariat, 25; and International Brigade, 82–3; and intrigue in Spain, 220 n. 7; and Nazism and fascism, 59;

Nin and Maurín split off from, 93; and parliamentarianism, 218 n. 26; and peasants in Spain, 224 n. 17; policies of, 22, 23, 24, 25, 28, 121, 160–1, 230 n. 50; program of, 23–9; proof of involvement in Spain, 39–40; and propaganda, 58, 101–2; *PSUC* affiliates with, 94; relations with Spain before July, 1936, 20; revolutionary prospects in Spain (1931–34), 217 n. 8; and Russia, 53, 162; and the Second International in the unified party pact, 182; Seventh Congress of, 23–9, 90, 96, 121, 218 n. 16; and Socialists, 218 n. 21; Spanish section of, 22–3; and *UGT*, 6; and United Front, 27–8, 218 n. 16; and world revolution, 25
Comité International d'Aide au Peuple Espagnol, 71
Commerce, Minister of, 225 n. 3
Commissar, El, 113
Commissar, General, 113–4
Commissariat of Army, Navy and Air, creation of, 113
Commissariat of War, Communist idea of functions of, 157
Commissars, political. *See* Political commissars
Commissioner of Public Order, responsible for *GPU* organizations, 117
Committee of Coordination, 245 n. 6
Committee for Internal Security (Catalonia), 68
Communist Federation of Trade Unions (*CUGT*), 122–3
Communist party (Spanish): as agent of foreign power, 99; agricultural workers in, 94; careerists in, 95; joins Popular Front, 15; joins *PSUC*, 93–4; in Madrid, 95; militia of, 86; for new parliamentary elections, 185–6; reputation among peasants and bourgeoisie, 98; social composition, 94–5; sources for membership figures, 21–3; strength, 211; strength (1931), 20–1, 217 n. 4; strength (1934), 21; strength (1936), 21, 31–2, 217 nn. 5 and 7; strengthened by anticipated Soviet aid, 86–7; telegram of condolence for Durruti, 127; trade-unionists in, 45; workers in, 94
Communist party program: on agriculture, 60, 61; on autonomy, 30, 182, 219 n. 31; criticism of, 208–10; for the

dictatorship of the proletariat, 40; on entering government, 57; inconsistency of, 30–1; for industry, 88; in June, 1935, 30; on militarism, 85, 92, 154–5; modified after Sept., 1936, 84; motivation for, 84; in new type democratic republic, 92–3, 212; organizations, 115; postelection 1936, 31; and protection of Soviet Union, 212; of resistance against Franco, 186; and winning war, 58–9; and workers' control, 62, 92

Communists, foreign, in *GPU*, 116

Communists (French), refuse to enter Blum government, 55

Communists (Spanish): accused, 208; analyze Spanish situation, 52; and Anarchists, 50, 164, 187–90, 237 n. 7; attack Caballero, 159; attack Giral cabinet, 66; attack Minister of War, 247 n. 7; in Barcelona revolt, 242 n. 5; blamed for defeat of Loyalists, 99; blame Republican government for revolt, 50; build-up of Negrín, 235 n. 1; in Caballero's government, 66; and *CNT* and Negrín's government, 241 n. 2; conditions for victory, 85; considered foreign agents, 93; control censorship, 102; in defense of Madrid, 100, 101; demand workers' control, 85; disagree with Caballero over military, 153–5; dominate *PSUC*, 94; domination of, 234 nn. 27, 32, and 33; emphasize People's Front, 54; enter government, 55–6; feared by Prieto, 208; idea of trade-union tasks, 88; in International Brigade, 106; left, united in *POUM*, 93; limited by moral factors, 98–9; manifesto of, on the evacuation of Teruel, 244 n. 12; maximum demands of, 58; military governors, 113; military policy of, 85, 87; and the Munich crisis, 248 n. 6; in Negrín government, 159; oppose Anarchist equalitarianism, 62; and overthrow of Caballero government, 240 n. 14; and percentage of Cortes seats, 54; play up arming of workers, 49–50; plot of, 208; and *POUM*, 237 n. 11; promote *UGT-CNT* unification, 127–8, 188–9; protection of foreign capital by, 62; reaction of to insurrection, 49; recruiting of after 1936 elections, 31–2; seek unification of youth, 121–2; and Socialists, 32, 50; Spaniards dislike foreign control of, 121; sponsor world organizations for aid, 71; strength of in *UGT* 174; strengthened by Soviet aid, 84; strong in department of censorship and propaganda, 112; support Negrín in resistance of Nationalists, 206–7; sympathy of, for Álvarez del Vayo and Negrín, 241 nn. 15 and 21; terroristic policies of, in Spain, 170, 208, 209, 210; trade-unions controlled by, 122–3; undermine discipline of government, 104; Undersecretary of Air is, 112; uprising of, Nationalist documents on, 41, 42; urge trade-union unification, 188–9; want support of trade-unionists, 165; warn of Right plot, 46

Communist and Socialist party unification: Caballero refuses, 121; Central Committee meeting of Communist party decides on, 179; resisted by Negrín, 169; United Youth provision in pact of, 184

Communist Youth: experience of, and unified party, 122; strength, 33, 217 n. 5, 220 n. 38; unification with Socialist youth, 33, 55, 219 n. 31

Comorera, Juan: accuses *FAI* in Barcelona revolt, 145–6; on Catalonia's mobilization for war, 139; meetings of, with fascists, 144

Companys, Luís: asks aid of Anarchists, 47; attacks Prieto, 242 n. 3; on Catalonian industry, 89; goes into exile, 204; letter of to Prieto, 89

Communismo libertario: Anarchists carry out, 57–8; and autonomy, 64; Communist antagonism toward, 124, 125, 208, 209; modern science not important to, 215 n. 9; and program for collectives, 60. *See also* Anarchists; *CNT; FAI*

Condor Legion in Spain, 82

Confederación Española de Derechos Autónomos. See *CEDA*

Confederación Nacional del Trabajo. See *CNT*

Confiscation of land. *See* Agriculture, reforms in; Expropriation; Nationalization

Conservatives in 19th century, 7–8

Consorcio de Fábricas Militares and arms supply, 69

Constantinople, 228 n. 24
Constitution, the: and dissolution of Cortes, 38; of 1931, 11
Coöperatives, Department of, 61
Coöperative, volunteer, encouraged by Communists, 60–1
Córdoba, 154
Cortes: Communist seats in, 31; dissolution of, 15, 38; elections to, 1933, 13; minority groups expelled from, 36; reconvened, 183, 185; role of after 1936 elections, 16–7
Council for Catalonia, negotiations for, 141. *See also* Generalitat
Council of Food Supplies of Catalonia, 109
Council of Industrial and Economic Coordination, Communist demand for, 85
Council of Industry, Communist plan for, 88
Councilor for the Interior (Catalonia), 68
Councilor of Public Security (Barcelona). *See* Director of Public Security
Courts and militarization of special tribunals, 202
CUGT. *See* Communist Federation of Trade Unions
Cullera, army called out against, 67
Czechoslovakia, 74, 203, 228 n. 24. *See also* Munich crisis

Defense industry in Catalonia, 139
Defense Junta. *See* Junta of Madrid
Defense, Minister of. *See* War, Minister of
Defense, Ministry of (Catalonia). *See* War, Ministry of (Catalonia)
Defense, weakness of, according to Communists, 231 n. 6
Delbos, visit to Moscow, 39
Delegations, international, investigate POUM, 172
Delicado, Manuel, on Communist reform of UGT, 175
Democratic centralism, in unified party, 28, 180
Department of State. *See* U.S., Department of State
Depots under Russian or Communist control, 74
Deviationists and the Communist party, 20

Díaz, José: Anarchists and "uncontrollables," 133; on the Church, 63; and Communist party program, 30; condolence telegram for Durruti, 127; on democratic revolution, 56; explains omission of dictatorship of proletariat, 58; and importance of Soviet aid, 72–3; on Munich crisis, 248 n. 6; and "new type democracy," 91, 92; on peasants, 60; on Peoples' Front and the generals' insurrection, 221 n. 4; praises Largo Caballero, 219 n. 36; on Republicans, 137–8; shows inconsistency of party program, 30–1; speaks against Caballero government, 153; stigmatizes Caballero group, 178; on UGT-CNT unity, 128; on UGT reform, 175; on unified army command, 87; warns of military coup, 221 nn. 1, 3, and 4
Dictatorship, Communist: Berneri on, 134; Loyalist fear of, 194–5
Dictatorship of the proletariat: 121, 211; aim of Communists in Spain, 40; Communists play down, 33; denied as aim of Communists, 54, 56, 57; new type democracy a transitional stage to, 92; omitted in propaganda, 58, 59; and revolutionary movement in Spain, 91; and unified proletarian party, 28; and United Front program, 25
Dimitrov, Georgi: attack on Socialists, 53; on purges in Spain, 137; report to Seventh Congress of Comintern, 24; on role of Peoples' Front, 27, 223 n. 3; and United Front formation, 218 n. 16; on United Front government, 27
Diplomatic relations, Soviet-Spanish, before July, 1936, 20
Dirección General de Seguridad (Security Police), and Communist strength, 21
Director General of Security, Communist, 112
Director of Public Security (Barcelona), 142, 144
Discipline: 208, 209, 231 n. 12, 234 n. 33; of Anarchists, 150, 171, 239 n. 6; Communist campaign for army, industrial and home front, 84–7; Communists and Republicans on, 138; Communists undermine government, 104
Domenech, 109
Durán, dismissed, 191

Durruti, Buenaventura: asked to aid Generalitat, 47; Communist telegram of condolence, 126–7; deputation to government, 110; and *UGT-CNT* unification, 127

Durruti, Friends of. *See* Friends of Durruti

Ebro, army of the, commanded by Communist, 113

Ebro River: Nationalist offensive along, 72, 192, 200; offensive of Loyalists, 203

Echevarrieta, Horacio, orders arms supply, 69

Economic Council (Catalonia), merged into Generalitat, 68

Education, Minister of, 159

Elections: British 1945 and 1951, 220 n. 2; Communist campaign for new parliamentary, 185–6, 244 n. 11; Communist vote in 1933, 21; to Cortes, 1931, 10–11; to Cortes, Nov. and Dec., 1933, 12–13; to Cortes, Feb., 1936, 16, 31, 35–7; to Cortes, supplementary, Mar. 1, 1936, 16; municipal, April, 1931, 216 n. 1; 19th century, 8; reason for failure of *CEDA* in, 220 n. 3; sources for returns of, 216 n. 5; of *UGT* Executive Committee, 123–4

Equalitarianism of Anarchists in industry, 62

Ercoli, M.: describes new type democracy, 91; states demands of Communists, 58

Esquerra party (Catalonia): 142, 242 n. 3; alliance with *PSUC*, 140; Anarchists blame for terror, 135; and Barcelona revolt, 164; in Caballero's government, 66; interests of, 139; in Negrín government, 159

Estremadura, Loyalists hold, 49

Euzkadi autonomy and Communist party program, 30

Euzkadi government, Teruel attack to relieve, 146

Evacuation of government from Madrid, Caballero's role in, 167

Executive Committee of the *UGT*, election of, 123–4

Expropriation: and Negrín government, 169; and United Front, 219 n. 31. *See* Agriculture, reforms; Nationalization

FAI (*Federación Anarquista Ibérica*): in the Barcelona revolt, 238 n. 4, 239 n. 6; Communists attack, 165, 170; conference, Feb., 1937, 110; and elections to Cortes, 1931, 10–11; manifesto on Barcelona revolt, 164; representation in Caballero government, 66; and Soviet aid, 110, 233 n. 25; strength, 215 n. 8; supports Caballero and *UGT*, 158; on trade-union unity, 128; unifying factor of Anarchist movement, 6; youth group retaliates against *GPU*, 141. *See also* Anarchist movement; *CNT*

Falange Española: connection with insurrection, 49; founding, 49; protection of, 117; relations with Nazis, 221 n. 16; responsibility for generals' insurrection, 222 nn. 7 and 12; strength, 17, 45, 48

Fascism, *POUM* connection with, 173

Federación Anarquista Ibérica. See FAI

Federation of Land Workers, strength, 123

Federation of Metal Workers' Union, supports Caballero, 175

"Fifth Column," 89–90, 116, 172–3. *See also* Anarchist movement; *POUM*

Fifth Regiment: Communist militia, 86, 100; merged into regular army, 131; USSR aid to, 130

Finance, Minister of, Negrín, 66. *See also* Negrín, Juan

Fischer, Louis: on antimilitary policy of Comintern, 230 n. 50; on cabinet crisis of May, 1937, 241 n. 21; on French aid, 229 n. 40; on Loyalists' debt to Soviet Union, 82; on Soviet aid, 227 n. 15, 228 n. 24; on Spanish gold reserves, 229 n. 41; on strength of Popular Front, 220 n. 1; stresses bourgeois aspects of Communist policies, 58

Food shortage, 72, 192, 203, 208, 246 n. 1

Foreign Affairs, Minister of: 159, 200; Álvarez del Vayo, 66, 198, 241 n. 15

Foreign Affairs, Ministry of: Communists strong in, 112; controlled censorship, 102

Foreign agents, 93, 239 nn. 6 and 8

Foreign Anarchists and *GPU*, 133

Foreign Communists: carry out important function in Spain, 97; in *GPU*, 11

Foreign equipment captured by Nationalists, 78, 79

Foreigners, Spanish antipathy toward, 131

Foreign interference in Barcelona revolt, 145

Foreign Legion: Loyalist army withstands, 87; strength, 48; used in Asturian uprising, 14

Foreign non-Communist revolutionaries, 118, 235 n. 44

Foreign observers' estimates of Soviet aid, 75, 76

Foreign trade, Spanish, 72, 77, 80. *See also* USSR, aid of, to Loyalists

France: 91, 205, 206; arms to Loyalist Spain sent by, 78, 80, 229 n. 40; attitude of USSR towards, 226 n. 6; Comintern purchases in, 74; Communists in refuse to enter government, 55; considers recognizing belligerency of Franco, 193; effect of Prieto's pessimism on Ambassador, of 197; menaced by Italian aid, 76; and planes sent to Spain, 77; plans of for intervention into Catalonia, 238 n. 22; and Popular Front, 218 n. 31; and recognition of Catalonia, 139–40; revolution delayed in, 25; Russians refuse photographs of German planes to, 104; smuggling over border of, 80; and Socialist-Communist alliance, 32; and Soviet aid, 71; and Soviet foreign policy, 71

Franco, General Francisco: 102, 120, 131, 135, 138, 150, 161, 162, 163, 166, 169, 170, 179, 181, 186, 187, 189, 193, 227 n. 23, 228 n. 26; agents of, 247 n. 4; Anarchists fall under, 95; armies of, 105; attack on Madrid by, 236 n. 1; attempts to justify uprising by Communist plot, 43; attitude of on autonomy, 140; Casado accused of negotiating with, 105; Catalonia and defeat by, 139–40, 203–4; declares Left government illegal, 35; defeat of Loyalists by, 99; ends Catalonian autonomy, 238 n. 23; England's intervention on behalf of, 62; and the generals' insurrection, 222 n. 7; and German and Italian aid, 48, 79; Kleber suggests offensive against, 130; Loyalist army withstands, 87; moved from Madrid, 46; National Defense Council negotiations with, 207; naval blockade of, hinders reception of aid, 89, 108; need for centralization to fight against, 89; negotiations

for peace with, 194, 195, 201, 205, 207, 208; offensive against Bilbao, 110; offensive along Ebro, 79, 200; *POUM's* connection with, 173; Prieto attempts to negotiate with, 208; reports on war prisoners, 226 n. 4; speech of Goebbels supporting, 70; suppresses opposition, 117; and use of force, 209; use of foreign troops, 82; uses *agent provocateur* in Barcelona, 146–7. *See also* Nationalists

Franco conservatives, division between Azaña and, 91

Franco, Nicolás, and agents in Barcelona, 146

Franco supporters: block Spanish funds in France, 81; Communists advocate expropriation of estates of, 60

French-Catalan border, Communists want control of, 140

Friends of Durruti: in Barcelona revolt, 142–3, 238 n. 4; retaliate against *GPU*, 141

Gaikis, M., replaces Rosenberg as Ambassador, 131

Galacian autonomy and Communist party program, 30

Galarza, Communists request dismissal of, 155–6, 157

Gandhi, and aid to Spain, 80

Garcia Oliver, Juan: in Barcelona revolt, 143; Minister of Justice, 225 n. 3; supports Caballero, 158

Generalitat (Catalan): and agricultural reform law, 14; Anarchists included in, 126; in Barcelona revolt, 144; Communist struggle with, 92–3; Communists want *PSUC* to control, 161; composition of, 67–8; Decree of Collectivization by, 62; expulsion of *POUM* from, 136; militiamen requested in Barcelona by, 47; not to be eliminated, 151; passes law workers must join union, 95; *POUM* not to participate in, 109; reorganizes Department of Public Order, 134; *UGT* members resign from, 141; Valencia government takes control from, 148, 202

Gerahty, Cecil, alleged Anarcho-Syndicalist uprising, 41

German planes, Russians refuse French photographing of, 104

Germany: aid of, to Franco, 48, 71, 75, 79, 193, 227 n. 23; Ambassador of, in Spain, reports, 117, 228 n. 26; Foreign Office documents, 79, 226 n. 3; implication in starting Civil War, 43–4; propaganda of, on Soviet aid, 70; Soviet fear of war with, 73–4; supports Portugal in Non-Intervention Committee, 41; and training of rebel troops, 209; troops of, in Spain, 82, 87, 105, 185, 227 n. 23; and USSR foreign policy, 23, 59, 162; violations by, of Non-Intervention Agreement, 75, 227 n. 17

Gerona, uprising in, 142

Gijón and Asturian uprising, 1934, 14

Gil Robles, José María: conditions under government of, 15; leader of Right faction, 13; and precipitation of government crisis, 1934, 14; and reason for *CEDA* failure in 1936 elections, 220 n. 3; reports on destruction, 17

Giral, José: cabinet of, attacked by Communists, 66; forms government, 47, 65; in Negrín government, 159; Negrín's attempt to replace, 198

Godden, Gertrude M., on Communist activities in Spain, 39, 220 n. 1

Goebbels, Dr. Joseph, speech of, on Soviet aid, 70

Gold reserves in Spain, 80–2, 229 nn. 41 and 44

Gorkin, Julian, 206–7, 241 n. 15

GPU: 129, 208; activities in Spain, 106, 191; attacks alarm Left, 141; and Barcelona revolt, 149; and disappearance of Nin, 172; and General Kleber, 236 n. 3; and Soviet aid, 74; used against Anarchists, 133–4; used against *POUM*, 137, 152

Great Britain: 91; considers recognizing belligerency of Franco, 193; document on Communist uprising revealed to, 42; elections 1945 and 1951, 220 n. 2; intervention of, in Spain, 62; and newspaper reports, 235 n. 1; nonmilitary trade of, with Spain, 80

Greek ships, 76

Guadalajara, 87, 105, 209

Guardia Civil, strength of, 48

Guardias de Asalto: 216 n. 8; sent to Barcelona, 148; strength, 48

Guipúzcoa, Loyalists cut off from, 49

Hamburg, Comintern purchases in, 74

Health, Minister of, 225 n. 3

Hericourt, Pierre, and foreign arms, 78

Hernández, Jesús: 54, 113, 165, 166–7, 233 n. 19; attacks Prieto, 196; dismissed, 200; in Negrín government, 159; and strength of Communist party and Komsomols, 217 n. 5

Hitler, Adolph: 91, 146, 161, 162, 227 n. 23; and aid to rebels, 82, 210; Negrín's opinion of, 242 n. 1; receives Germans from Morocco, 44; and use of "Red Menace" propaganda, 38; USSR negotiations with, 206–7

Holland, Comintern purchases in, 74

Home Affairs, Minister of. *See* Interior, Minister of

Ibarruri, Dolores: 240 n. 3, 244 n. 6, 246 n. 1; on Álvarez del Vayo's support of unified party, 179; attacks Prieto, 196; Communist party leader, 96; conditions of victory, 84–5; describes unified party, 179–80; hopes for *CNT* to join government, 188; lists casualties among commissars, 114–5; on necessity to win the war, 90

Iglesias, Pablo, 6

India and aid to Spain, 80

Individualism of Spanish people, 208

Industry: and Anarchism, 215 n. 9; in Catalonia, 109, 242 n. 3; central control of, in *UGT-CNT* pact, 188–9; Communists demand workers' control in, 85; control of Catalonian, passed to central government, 151, 169–70; equalitarianism in, 62; increase in production of, 89; militarized, 202; Socialist program for, 63; in unified party pact, 182; war, and Caballero, 167; war mobilization of, 245 n. 8; workers' committees in, 88

Industry, Minister of, 62, 225 n. 3, 226 n. 7

Inestal, González, and Communists in armed forces, 113

Institute of Agrarian Reform. *See* Agricultural Reform, Institute of

Interior, Councilor for the (Catalonia), 68, 149

Interior, Minister of: Communists request dismissal of, 155–6; orders arrest of *POUM* Central Committee, 172

Interior, Ministry of: 159, 220 n. 7; *GPU* in, 116

Internal issues and the Civil War, 19

International Brigade: backs Communists, 98; casualties, 230 n. 54; in defense of Madrid, 100, 131, 236 n. 1; disbanded, 79, 203–4; General Kleber and, 130–1, 236 n. 3; and *GPU*, 118; recruiting for, 230 n. 51; and Soviet advisors, 106; strength of, 83, 230 n. 55; and USSR aid, 130

International delegations of leftists investigate *POUM*, 172

International law and Soviet aid, 73

Iron Column, Anarcho-Syndicalist. *See* Anarchist movement

Irrigation, necessity for, 3

Irujo, Manuel: backs Prieto against Communists, 191; efforts to normalize religious life, 63; in Negrín government, 159; and *POUM* trial, 185; resigns, 202; speech of, to Cortes, 17–8

Irún, Commander at, and peace negotiations, 194, 247 n. 4

Italy: and aid to Nationalists, 48, 71, 75, 76, 79, 193; Air Force of, patrols Málaga road, 107; Army of, at Guadalajara, 105; implication of, in starting Civil War, 43–4; intervention of, 227 nn. 17 and 23; Navy of, 228 n. 26; Russian fear of war with, 74; supports Portugal in Non-Intervention Committee, 41; and training of rebel troops, 105, 209; troops of, 73, 82, 87, 162, 185, 227 n. 23; troops of, assault Madrid, 101; and USSR foreign policy, 162; and violations of Non-Intervention Agreement, 75

Jaén, Socialist youth organization in, 184

Jaime I, 247 n. 6

Japanese aggression, USSR fear of, 161

Jevik, 220 n. 11

Jouhaux, Leon, called upon to heal *UGT* schism, 177

JSU (Juventudes Socialistas Unificadas): Communist control of, 33, 183; Communist example, 122; Communists in, 112; role in defense of Madrid, 101; Socialist Youth organs refuse to join, 184; strength, 33, 220 n. 37; in unified party pact, 182; used to obtain *AJA*, 187

Junta of Madrid. *See* Madrid, defense of

Justice, Minister of, 159, 202, 225 n. 3

Juventudes Sociaistasl Unificadas. See *JSU*

Kleber, General, 106, 160, 236 n. 3

Knoblaugh, H. E., interview of, with Largo Caballero, 40–1, 220 n. 5

Kolarov, report of, to Comintern Congress, 224 n. 17

Kol'tsov, M. E.: on Communist party strength (1931), 217 n. 4; reports from Asturias, 226 n. 2

Komsomol, sinking of, 77

Komsomols. *See* Communist Youth

Krivitsky, Walter: Comintern agent in Spain, 40, 74; and General Kleber, 236 n. 3; on Soviet aid to Catalonia, 108; on Soviet decision to send aid and its organization, 73; and USSR advisors, 103

Kun, Béla, Comintern agent in Spain, 40

Labonne, French Ambassador, 197

Labor, Minister of, 159

Labour party of Great Britain and money for Spain, 80

Lagenheim, Adolph, Moroccan Nazi leader asks Hitler's aid, 44

Landau, Katia, and Soviet aid, 110

Largo Caballero, Francisco: accuses the Communists, 208; asks arms distribution to workers, 18, 46; attempts to form new government, 241 n. 15; and attitude of Socialists, 6; backs Miaja against Kleber, 132; becomes popular hero, 17; builds a strong army, 209; calls for a new Convention of *UGT*, 244 n. 21; *CNT* attitude on overthrow of, 241 n. 1; and collectivization of agriculture, 226 n. 6; and Communist aims, 68, 160–1; Communist influence over, 33; Communists condemn, 100, 111, 159, 166–8, 235 n. 1, 245 n. 1; Communists criticize military policies of, 167; Communists hope to eliminate, 140; and Communists in Defense Ministry, 112–4; Communists want as figurehead, 165, 219 n. 36; defeat of, has severe consequence for the *POUM*, 172; defends government, 240 n. 14;

and defense of Málaga, 107, 233 n. 19;
and disposition of gold, 80, 81, 103;
does not stop assassinations, 135; and
elections to *UGT* Executive Committee, 124; and elimination of Communists from *UGT*, 174–8; government
actions against, 171; interviewed by
H. E. Knoblaugh, 40–1; and *JSU*, 122,
210; leader of Socialists, 32; lessened
threat of, 183; and liquidation of
POUM, 235 n. 43; moderate Socialists'
and Republicans' fear of, 180–1; and
nationalization, 226 n. 7; and Negrín's
government, 243 nn. 5 and 17; over-
shadows Azaña, 65; planned offensive
of, 240 n. 10; as Prime Minister and
Minister of War, 65; rallies Socialists
and Anarchists, 170–1, 181; relations
with Prieto, 225 n. 1; resigns, 156, 179,
195, 209; sanctions actions against Anarchists, 147; "Spanish Lenin," 220
n. 5; suspends collectivization decree,
67; under house arrest, 243 n. 5; unions
supporting, 123; uses force against revolutionary groups, 67
Largo Caballero, government of. *See* Caballero government
Law, electoral, of Cortes, 13
Lawrence, Bill, 217 n. 7
Lázaro Cárdenas, President of Mexico,
229 n. 33
League of Nations: Loyalist representative to, 159; Soviet Union enters, 23
Left Republicans, join Popular Front, 15
Lenin, V. I.: 134, 180; on alliance with
peasants, 59; April Thesis of, 58; Spain
to be second Soviet Republic according
to, 40–1, 220 n. 5; on trade unions,
66–7; views on Russia by, apply to
Spain, 51
Lérida, 143
Lerroux, Alejandro, 156, 185
Liberals in 19th century, 3, 7–8
Libertarian revolution. See *Comunismo
libertario*
Lister, General, Communist troop com-
mander, 150, 185
Litvinov, Maxim, 228 n. 24
Llobregat Valley uprising, 12
Localism: of Anarchists, 171; strength of,
67
Loyalist debt to Soviet Union, 82

Lunacharsky, M., Ambassador to Madrid, 217 n. 3

Madariaga, Salvador de: and the Con-
stitution, 11; and the municipal elec-
tions (1931), 216 n. 1
Madrid: Catalonia in defense of, 139;
Communist party in, 94; Communist
trade-unions in, 122; defense of, 107,
108, 130–1, 166, 236 n. 1; front, 165;
military Junta of, 100, 103, 130, 131;
uprising (1934), 14
Málaga: Communist deputy of, to Cortes, 21; fall of, 106–7, 139, 153, 167,
233 n. 19, 240 n. 3
Mancha, Loyalist hold, 49
Maniulsky, 218 n. 21
Maroto, imprisoned by *GPU*, 133
Marseilles, 108
Marti, Antonio, murder of, 141
Martial law established, 202
Martin Blazquez, José: arrival of Russian
aid, 73; on Communists deterring ac-
tion against Anarchists, 237 n. 7; on
control of Air Force, 75; describes
Communist help in army, 85; on move-
ment to join Communist party, 95
Martínez, Alfredo, leader of Anarchist
youth movement, 133
Martínez Barrio, Diego: attempts to form
a government, 222 n. 5; attitude of,
138; and dissolution of Cortes, 38; goes
into exile, 204; and Soviet aid, 72
Martín Luna, Lt. Col., and bombing of
Valladolid, 104
Marty, André, 87
Marx, Karl, 66–7, 124
Maurín, Joaquín: and Comintern agents
in Spain, 40; Communists accuse, of
being Right renegade, 237 n. 11; Communists in Catalonia under, 93; on
importance of Madrid to Communists,
100; leader of Communist party, 20;
leaves Communist party, 20
Mediterranean: Italians requested to prevent Russian assistance via the, 228
n. 26; Mussolini interested in Balearic
Islands in, 44; piracy in, 76–7; submarines in, 75. *See also* Piracy; Submarines
Melilla occupied by army, 47
Merida, 154, 155

Mexico, aid to Spain of, 80, 229 n. 33

Miaja, General José: Caballero jealous of, 167; and Caballero's planned military offensive, 155; Communist supported general, 185; jealous of Kleber, 130, 131; overthrows Negrín, 207; says military situation not hopeless, 205; selected by Russians, 103

Middle class in Communist party, 94, 95–6

Mije, Antonio: on elections to *UGT* Executive Committee, 123–4; states reasons Communists enter government, 55

Milicias de la Cultura, 115

Militarism, Communist program on, 92. *See also* Communists

Military: Caballero-Communist disagreement over, 153–5; USSR advisors to, 103. *See also* USSR aid

Military aid, Soviet Union and acknowledgment of, 72. *See also* USSR aid

Military coup and the government, 18

Military governors, Communist, 113

Military Junta of Madrid. *See* Madrid, military Junta of

Military leadership, Loyalist, 240 n. 2

Military policy: Caballero's, Communist criticism of, 167: of Communists, 87; Soviet analysis of, 231 n. 11

Military service, compulsory, Communists favor, 85

Military situation at beginning of Civil War, 49

Military strategy, Communist-Caballero disagreement over, 154–5. *See also* Communists; Largo Caballero

Military strength of Nationalists and Loyalists, 48, 209–10

Military weakness of Loyalists, 49

Militia Committee merged into Generalitat, 68

Militia, Communist, offer to disband, 86, 100. *See also* Fifth Regiment

Militias: Anarchist, 87, 148, 208; Catalonian, 68, 109, 110, 169; of *CNT* in Barcelona revolt, 239 n. 6; coördinating committees of, 47; for the Defense of the Republic, decree establishing, 47; report of German Ambassador on "Red," 222 n. 11; separate, 85, 86; and Soviet aid, 108, 110

Modesto, General: Communist general, 185; replaces Rojo, 200

Mola, General Emilio, 116, 222 nn. 5 and 7

Monarchists: coup of, 222 n. 7; strength of, in municipal elections (1931), 216 n. 1

Montseny, Federica, 143, 225 n. 3

Mora, Constancia de la, and Communist control of censorship, 102

Moroccan Germans ask Hitler's aid, 44

Moroccan troops: Loyalist army withstands, 87; strength, 48; use in Asturian uprising, 14

Moroccan War, conclusion of, 9

Morocco: Communist program on, 57; revolt of troops (1936), 18

Morrow, Felix. *See* Maurín, Joaquín

"Moscow agents" in Spain, 69

Motril, 206

Mujeres Antifascistas, 115

Mundo Obrero, Communist newspaper, admonished by Anarchist *Solidaridad Obrero*, 145

Munich crisis, 79, 203, 204, 238 n. 22, 248 nn. 5 and 6

Murcia, Communist military governor at, 113

Mussolini, Benito: aids rebels, 210; aims to split Catalonia from Spain, 151; army divisions of, 105; is prepared to use submarines against Russian ships, 228 n. 26; and Italian troops in Spain, 82; Negrín's opinion of, 242 n. 1; prestige of, 162; promises aid to Monarchists (1934), 44; strategic interest in Spain, 44; supports Franco, 161; threats of, 91; and use of "Red Menace" propaganda, 38

National Confederation of Labour. See *CNT*

National Council of Economy, 246 n. 8

National Council of Industry, 246 n. 8

National Defense Council, 207

National Federation of Socialist Youth. *See* Socialist Youth

Nationalism, Communist view of, 51

Nationalist regime: documents on alleged Communist uprising, 41–2; documents on instructions to Red agents in Spain, 42; foreign prisoners held by, 226 n. 4; offensive along Ebro River, 192, 196; reports of Soviet aid, 70, 77, 78; sympathizers, 209; troops assault Madrid, 101. *See also* Franco, General Francisco; Germany; Italy

Nationalization: of Bank of Spain, 92; of banks in *UGT-CNT* agreement, 126; and Caballero government, 67; and Communist party program, 30, 58, 85, 88, 89, 92; of foreign-owned industries, 226 n. 7; and Popular Front program (1936), 16; in *UGT-CNT* program, 245 n. 8

Navarre: population of supports Nationalists, 48; status of the Church in, 215 n. 4; statute of autonomy, 12

Navy, Minister of, Russian orders to, 103-4

Navy, Undersecretary of, Communist, 112

Nazi party: close contact of, with Spain, 44; relations to Falange, 221 n. 16

Negrín, Juan: and attacks on Largo Caballero, 244 n. 21; attempts to restore Anarchists to cabinet, 164; and cabinet crisis of May, 1937, 156, 241 n. 15; and Catalonia, 247 n. 3; characterization of, 242 n. 1; and the Communists, 103, 111, 169, 233 n. 5, 234 n. 27, 235 n. 1, 242 n. 1; and Conference of Physiology in Russia, 233 n. 11; continues defense of Republic, 204-7; controls Socialists, 180; ends discussion of unified party, 186; favors unified party, 181; forms new cabinet, 198; Minister of Finance, 66; and negotiations with Franco, 248 n. 12; opinion of, on Hitler, Stalin, and Mussolini, 242 n. 1; policies of, 248 n. 7; Prieto complains of Communists to, 195-6; and Prieto's dismissal, 247 n. 9; reconvenes Cortes, 185; and relations with Prieto, 247 n. 11; and religious life, 63; and removal of gold, 80-1; report of Casado on Communists to, 112; sides with Prieto against Hernández, 196-8; and Soviet aid, 226 n. 9

Negrín government: attitude of *CNT* toward, 241 nn. 1 and 2; Communists consider Caballero dangerous to, 168; Communists hope for Anarchists in, 188; effect of military reverses on, 192, 194, 195, 197; hostile toward Communists, 191; Largo Caballero prevents *UGT* support of, 174, 175; Largo Caballero's attitude toward, 243 n. 17; less hostility of Anarchists toward, 183;

opposition of *UGT-CNT* toward, 170; refuses new parliamentary elections, 186; *UGT* agrees to support, 176

Neva, 220 n. 11

New Castile, Loyalists hold, 49

Newspapers, seizure and censorship of, 171. *See also* Anarchist movement, newspapers suppressed

"New type of democracy," 90-3, 212

Nin, Andrés: anti-Communist, 136; disappears, 172; Gestapo agent letter to, 173; leader of Communist party, 20, 93; leaves Communist party, 20; Trotskyite, 237 n. 11

Non-Intervention Agreement: adherence of Soviet Union to and Soviet aid, 71; German and Italian fulfillment of, 75; hinders reception of aid, 89; legal cargo under, 76; Mexican nonadherence to, 80, 229 n. 33; Soviet violation of, 72, 73, 75, 227 n. 17, 228 n. 24; western democracies support, 65

Non-Intervention Committee: Control Scheme establishment reduces Russian shipments, 76, 77; democracies' procrastination in, 79; Naval Control Scheme of hinders International Brigade, 83; and piracy against Soviet ships, 228 n. 27; Portugal accuses Soviet Union in, 41; Secretary of estimates Soviet shipping, 76

Nosotros, suspended, 134

No votad, Anarchist, in election compaign (1933), 13

Odessa, port for Soviet aid, 74

OGPU. See GPU

Orlov, chief *GPU* agent, 106, 116

Oulansky, Captain, head of *GPU* in Spain, 74

Oviedo and Asturian uprising (1934), 14

Ovseenko, Antonov: admired Catalan Anarcho-Syndicalists, 126; Russian Consul in Barcelona, 103

Parliamentarianism, Comintern hostility toward, 27, 218 n. 26

Partido Obrero de Unificación Marxista. See POUM

Partido Socialista Unificado de Cataluña. See PSUC

Pasionairia, La. See Ibarruri, Dolores

Peace negotiations: Azaña for, 204; Cata-

Peace negotiations—*Continued*
Ionian bourgeoisie propose, 202–3; hopes for, 193; Prieto for, 194, 195

Peasants: and the Church, 4; and collectivization, 67, 246 n. 8; and Communist agricultural program, 30, 57, 60, 61, 92, 224 n. 17; Communist alliance with, 51, 59–60; in Communist party, 94, 96; Communist party has favorable reputation among, 98; conditions of, 2–3; need of for land, 3; resistance of, to Anarchists, 109–10; seize land, 4; uprisings of, 3

Peiró, Juan, Anarchist Minister of Industry, 225 n. 3, 226 n. 7

Peña, Gonzales: head of new Executive Committee of *UGT*, 176, 177; Minister of Justice, 198; signs reservation in unified party pact, 181–2

Penarroya, 154

People's Army: in Catalonia, 151; Communist commands in, 112; and Communist party program, 31, 57; creation of, 85; and political commissars, 114; *UGT-CNT* agreement on, 126

People's Courts in Catalonia, integrated with all Spain, 141

People's Democracies, 211, 212. *See also* "New type of democracy"

People's Executive Committee controls Valencia, 65. *See also* Revolutionary committees

People's Front. *See* Popular Front

Piracy, 76–7, 228 n. 27. *See also* Submarines

Poland, Comintern purchases in, 74

Police, secret: Communists in, 116; developed to purge the rear, 116. See also *GPU*

Political commissars: activities restricted, 184–5; Álvarez del Vayo head of, 159; Caballero reduces Communist influence over, 154; creation of, 87; Communist domination of, 87, 113–5; Communist influence on soldiers through, 205; in International Brigade, 106; and Negrín, 169; power restored to, 200; and Prieto, 247 n. 6

Pollit, Harry, 218 n. 26

Popular Front (French), 218 n. 31

Popular Front (Spanish): 53, 184, 185, 218 n. 31; Anarchists in, 124; in Asturias revolt (1934), 211; Caballero

group opposed to, 178; Church condemnation of, 19; and Communist program, 84, 234 n. 33; Communists' claim to inauguration of, 30; Communists emphasize, 54; Communists tend to disrupt, 84; composition and role, 26–7; danger of split in, 150; Dimitrov discusses, 223 n. 3; and dissolution of Cortes, 38; formed Jan. 15, 1936, 15, 210; and generals' insurrection, 221 n. 4; and Left coöperation, 98–9; and need of United Workers party, 244 n. 12; *POUM* campaign against, 173; program (1936), 16; Right alleges Russia behind, 39–43; and secret police, 116; strength, 220 n. 1; in unified party pact, 182

Popular Front government in France, sympathy for Loyalists, 80

Popular Front government in Spain: Azaña wants, 65; to be followed by unified party, 121; Communist party program on, 31; Communist prerequisites for formation of, 219 n. 32; Communist support by members of, 90; Communists enter, 55–6; Communists maintain on surface, 111; conditions for formation, 55–6; and documents concerning uprising, 42; formation of, a step against revolutionary armies, 86, 225 n. 3; and *UGT-CNT* pact, 219 n. 31

Portela Valladares, Manuel, 185

Portugal, accuses Soviet Union of plotting in Spain, 41

POUM (*Partido Obrero de Unificación Marxista*): 124, 125; Anarchist approval for removal of, from Catalan government, 127; Communist analysis of, 237 n. 11; Communist scapegoat, 118–9; Communists attack, 102, 208, 210; Communists demand outlawing of, 140, 156; enters Generalitat, 68; influence in Catalonia, 238 n. 12; joins Popular Front, 15; and Largo Caballero, 132, 153, 235 n. 43, 240 n. 14; Left Communists unite in, 93; members prevented from becoming commissars, 115; militiamen requested in Barcelona, 47; and proletarian revolution, 90; purge of, 182, 243 n. 8; retaliate against *GPU* actions, 141; and Soviet aid, 109, 110, 111; strength, 93;

trial is setback for Communists, 185; and Trotsky, 238 n. 13

Presidential Staff, 234 n. 27

Priests, village, 4

Prieto, Indalecio: accounts of Soviet aid, 75; aids Azaña, 65; and Álvarez del Vayo, 33, 241 n. 21; and arrests of *POUM*, 172, 235 n. 43, 243 n. 8; associate of Peña, 176; attacked by Communists, 208; attacked by President Companys, 242 n. 3; and attacks on Largo Caballero, 244 n. 21; a Basque Socialist, 215 n. 7; blamed by Anarchists for terror, 135; builds a strong army, 209; and cabinet crisis (May, 1937), 156; and Communist domination, 181, 234 n. 27; and Communist program, 68; and Communists in Defense Ministry, 112–3; Communists use split between Caballero and, 111, 120, 132, 210; controls Socialists, 180; criticizes removal of gold, 81, 229 n. 44; friend of Echevarrieta, 69; and Largo Caballero, 225 n. 1, 240 n. 10; letter from Companys to, 89; of little help to United Front program, 161; Minister of Air and Navy, 65–6; moderate Socialists under, 186; on Negrín and Communists, 169; in Negrín government, 158–9, 160; and overthrow of Caballero's government, 156, 241 n. 15; pessimism of, 247 n. 9; reactions to speech of, Aug., 1938, 248 n. 4; relations with Negrín, 202, 247 n. 11; resignation of, as Minister of War, 200, 211; a "revolutionary," 220 n. 5; sanctions actions against Anarchists, 147–8; says Russians countermanded orders, 103–4

Primo de Rivera, General Miguel: 3; and the army, 9; and public improvement projects, 4; and recognition of USSR, 216 n. 3; Red threat helped to power, 38; resignation, 9

Primo de Rivera, José Antonio, founds *Falange Española*, 49

Prisoners, foreign, 226 n. 4

Proletarian dictatorship. *See* Dictatorship of the proletariat

Proletarian party, unified. *See* United Front; Unification of Socialist and Communist parties

Proletarian revolution: Communists deny nearness of, 56; Communists stress less and less, 90. *See also* Dictatorship of the Proletariat

Propaganda, Anarchist, 170

Propaganda and censorship, department of, Communists strong in, 112

Propaganda, Communist: abroad, 101–2; against Caballero, 167–8, 177, 178; against *FAI*, 170; against *POUM*, 135, 172, 173; against Prieto, 195, 199; for control over Valencia government, 101; influences soldiers, 205; for unified party, 180; use of Catalan language for, 64

Propaganda, Fascist: of Communist dictatorship, 185; of "Red Menace," 162

Propaganda, Loyalist: among rebels, 201; in praise of Negrín, 233 n. 5

Propaganda, Nationalist: abroad, 101; of Communist church burnings, 63; reference of, to Revolutionary Museum in Moscow, 39; on Soviet aid, 69–70; use of "Red Menace" in, 38

Propaganda of political commissars, 114

PSUC (*Partido Socialista Unificado de Cataluña*): 122, 142, 180, 183; attacked by President Companys, 242 n. 3; and Barcelona revolt, 164, 239 n. 8; Communist leadership in, 94, 112, 210; Communists want in control of Generalitat, 140, 161; controls *UGT* in Catalonia, 94; and Council of Food Supplies, 109; enters Generalitat, 68; formed, 93–4; makes Socialists wary of unified party, 181; member of appointed to cabinet, 202; petty bourgeois party, 96; strength, 94, 232 n. 27

Public Aid and Communications, Minister of, 159

Public Instruction, Minister of, 66, 111, 200

Puigcerdá, 141

Purge, Communist, of army, 89–90

Purge of officers, Communists want, 153

Purge of the rear, secret police developed to make, 116,

Purge of revolutionary Left in unified party pact, 182

Purges in USSR, 21, 172, 173

Quiroga, Casares, 18, 46, 47

Radical party, 65, 185
Raynaud, Jean, describes workers' arming in Catalonia, 47
Recognition of USSR by Spain, 216 n. 3
Red International. *See* Comintern
"Red Menace," Fascist propaganda of, 162
Regionalism: omitted in Communist program, 92; statutes of local autonomy (1931), 11–12. *See also* Autonomy
Relief funds for Spain, 70, 80. *See also* USSR aid
Republicans: and aid to Aragon front, 110; coöperate in terror against Anarchists, 135; criticize Caballero, 154; Left, in Giral government, 65; in Negrín government, 159
Republican Union in Giral government, 65
Revolutionary committees: and Caballero government, 66; control Valencia, 65; end of, 67
Revolutionary Museum in Moscow, visit of M. Delbos to, 39
Revolutionary program and United Front, 219 n. 31
Revolutionary prospects in Spain 1931–34, according to Communists, 217 n. 8
Ríos, Fernando de los, Prieto letter to, 147
Rios, Giner de los, in Negrín government, 159
Rodríguez Salas: illegal actions of, 144, 148; tries to relieve *CNT* of Telephone Exchange Building, 142
Rojo, General Vicente, 200, 242 n. 1, 248 nn. 5 and 12
Roldán Cortada, murder of, 141, 142
Rosenberg, Marcel: recalled, 131; Soviet Ambassador to Spain, 103
Ruiz, Antonio, Russians want relieved of command, 104
Russia. *See* Soviet; USSR
Russia in 1917, Spain in same state as, 51
Russian Revolution: 65, 223 n. 8; appeal in Spain, 22; less emphasized, 56; similarity of Soviets and militia committees, 47; used in Communist propaganda, 101
Rust, William, 230 n. 51

Sainz, Gómez, Minister of Interior, 198
Salamanca, 104

Santander, Loyalists cut off from, 49
Satellite in Spain. *See* Soviet Republic in Spain; USSR, foreign policy of
Scandinavian ships, 76
Schools: religious, legislation against, 11; state need of, 11
Second International, 101, 137
Second and Third Internationals, in unified party pact, 182
Servicio de Investigación Militar (SIM): increased activities of, 202; Prieto attacks, 191
Seventh Congress of the Comintern. *See* Comintern, Seventh Congress
Seville, 154
Ships. *See* specific country
Shock troops. See *Guardias de Asalta*
Shvernik, Secretary of All-Union Central Soviet of Trade Unions, 70
SIM. See *Servicio de Investigación Militar*
Skoda works, purchases made from, 74
Slater, Hugh, 236 n. 1
Smuggling over French border, 80
Socialism, transitional stage between bourgeois democracy and, 92
Socialist-Anarchist coöperation, 66–7
Socialist-Communist pact, United Youth provision in, 184
Socialist and Communist youth, 55
Socialist League joins *PSUC*, 93–4
Socialist parties in Catalonia, 98
Socialists: and aid to Aragon front, 110; Caballero refuses unification of, 121; in Caballero's government, 66; Communist influence over, 32; Communists cease criticism of, 50; coöperate in terror against Anarchists, 135; criticize Caballero, 154; criticize war on *POUM*, 136; join Popular Front, 15; members appointed to cabinet by, 202; membership (1936), 21; proclaim general strike (1934), 14; program of for industry, 63; refuse United Front pact, 54; relations with *UGT*, 6; strength in *UGT*, 174; support terror against Anarchists, 135; unification with Communists resisted by Negrín, 169
Socialists, Basque, 215 n. 7
Socialists, moderate, in Negrín government, 159
Socialist youth: 15, 98, 122, 219 n. 31; strength, 33; unification with Communist youth, 33

Socorro Rojo Internacional, Communist organization, 115–6

Solidaridad Obrero, Anarchist newspaper, admonishes Communist *Mundo Obrero,* 145

Soviet aid. *See* USSR, aid of, to Loyalists

Soviet advisers: dole out supplies, 74; put pressure on industry, 89

Soviet Advisory Council, 242 n. 1

Soviet arms. *See* USSR, aid of, to Loyalists

Soviet Consul at Barcelona, 103, 126

Soviet control of supply depots, 74

Soviet "intrigues," Prieto attacks Negrín for, 202

Soviet money. *See* USSR, aid of, to Loyalists

Soviet novels and movies in Spain, 22

Soviet press. *See* USSR press

Soviet Republic in Spain, 19, 59, 161–3, 212, 223 n. 16

Soviets: emulated in Spain, 22; formation urged, 24; similarity of militia committees to, 47

Soviet troops. *See* USSR troops

Special Information Section of the State, *GPU* section of Loyalist secret police, 116

Staff officers, composition of, 234 n. 32

Stalin, Joseph: 180; attempt of to control Loyalists, 108; negotiations of with Hitler, 206–7; Negrín's opinion of, 242 n. 1; on victory of revolutionary party, 25; warns Russians in Spain, 73

Stalinism: basis of unified party, 181; Berneri on, 134

Stashevsky, Arthur, Soviet advisor in Spain, 103

State Department. *See* U. S. Department of State

Stern (General Kleber), 236 n. 3. *See also* Kleber, General

Strategy, military. *See* Military strategy

Strategy and tactics, revolutionary, 223 n. 8

Strike, general (1934), 14

Submarines, Nationalist and Italian, 75, 76–7, 228 n. 26

Superior Council of Economy, 246 n. 8

Superior Council of War, 112, 157, 240 n. 14, 247 n. 9

Supply and Transport, Director General of a Communist, 112

Tank Corps, control of, 74

Tanks, USSR, 227 n. 13

Tarragona, uprising in, 142

Telephone Exchange Building (Barcelona), 142–5

Terror: against Anarchists, 187, 188; against "uncontrollables," 201–2; and the Anarchists, 98; Communist, 170, 208, 209, 210; of *GPU,* 133; of *GPU,* Nationalists, Anarchists, Socialists, and Republicans, 117–8

Teruel: attack on by Loyalists, 146; defeat of Franco at, 209; evacuation of, 244 n. 12; fall of, 189, 205; front and Anarcho-Syndicalist Iron Column, 67; Loyalist offensive toward, 79; offensive against, 192, 193

Third International. *See* Comintern

Thorez, Maurice, on revolution delayed in France, 25

Togliatti. *See* Ercoli, M.

Toledo, fall of, 100

Tomás, Pascual, on *UGT* attitude toward unification, 128

Trade of Russia and Spain, 72

Trade-unions: Communist campaign for influence in, 122–4; Communist idea of tasks of, 88; Communists want support of members of, 165; members of, in Communist party, 95

Trade-union unification, 55, 182, 188–9, 210, 219 n. 31, 245 n. 6. *See also CNT; UGT*

Traditionalists, coup of, 222 n. 7

Transport, war mobilization of, 245 n. 8

Trotsky, Leon, 136, 146, 238 n. 13

Trotskyism, 118

Trotskyites: agents of Mussolini, 151; and Caballero, 177; Fascists use organizations of, 152; hinder war effort, 231 n. 11; in Russia and Spain, 172–3. *See also POUM*

UGT (Unión General de Trabajadores): and agreement with *CNT,* 123, 170, 171; allied with *CNT* against Right, 14; and Asturias uprising, 29; and Barcelona revolt, 242 n. 5; becomes more radical, 66; Communist campaign for influence in, 122–4; Communists want to remove Caballero from, 132; controlled in Catalonia by *PSUC,* 94;

UGT—Continued
and disguised Communists, 112; elections of Executive Committee of, 123–4; Executive Committee of, refuses support of non-Communist government, 158; *FAI* supports Caballero and, 158; and joint action with *CNT*, 245 n. 8; membership, 5, 21, 95; members resign from Generalitat, 141; middle class joins, 95–6; militiamen requested in Barcelona, 47; and Negrín government, 243 n. 17; petty bourgeois union in Catalonia, 96, 232 n. 29; removal of Largo Caballero as Secretary General of, 244 n. 21; Socialists allow Communists in new Executive Committee of. 183; strength in Catalonia, 94; strongholds in Catalonia, 170; in unified party pact, 182; united with *CNT*, 127–8, 188–9, 245 n. 6
"Uncontrollables": 239 n. 8; campaign against, 67; in *CNT*, 165; Communist campaign against, 132–3, 135, 136, 165; Communist support of bourgeois parties against, 137; and the *GPU*, 106; Negrín action against, 201–2; prevented from becoming commissars, 115. *See also* Anarchist movement; *POUM*
Under-Commissar General of War, 113
Unemployment in 1931, 12
Unification of *CNT* and *UGT*. *See* Trade-union unification; *CNT*; *UGT*
Unification of Socialist and Communist parties: 210, 219 n. 31, 244 nn. 6 and 12; Comintern policy on, 28; and dictatorship of proletariat, 28; end of discussions of, 186; resisted by Negrín, 169; stressed, 55; United Youth provision in, 184
Unification of youth movement. *See* *AJA;* Anarchist youth; Communist youth; *JSU;* Socialist youth
Unión de Madres Jóvenes, 115
Unión de Muchachas, 115
Unión General de Trabajadores. See UGT
Unionization, forced, 232 n. 29
Union Republicans, join Popular Front, 15. *See also* Republican Union in Giral government
United Front: 121, 123, 210, 211; and Asturias revolt, 29; Communist fulfillment of, 179; and Communist program, 26, 84, 218 n. 31; Communists

emphasize People's Front instead of, 54; Communist setback to, 184; and Communist success in adapting to Spain, 33–4; and conditions for unity of action, 26; and coöperation with Socialists, 53; and defense of Soviet Union, 26; Dimitrov reports on, 218 n. 16; early expression of, 24; necessary to combat fascism, 24; and Prieto, 161; refused by Socialists, 54; stressed by Communists, 55; unified party agreement considered belated, 182. *See also* Popular Front
United Front government: and Comintern policy, 27–8; and new type of democracy, 90. *See also* Popular Front government
United Socialist Party of Catalonia. See *PSUC*
United Socialist Youth. See *JSU*
United States, 91
United States, Department of State, reports of Russian planes, 77
Uprising: Anarchist, January, 1932, 12; Madrid, 1934, 14; peasant, 3. *See also* Asturias revolt; Barcelona revolt
Uribe, Vicente: on collectivization, 224 n. 23; on coöperatives, 60–1; in Negrín government, 159
Uritzky, Comintern agent, 228 n. 24
USSR (Union of Soviet Socialist Republics): anti-Stalinists in, 136; attack on press of, 137; behind counterrevolution, 151; collectivization in, 60; and coming imperialist war, 217 n. 13; and Comintern control Communists in Spain, 96–7; Communists model industrial plan after that of, 88; contributions to International Brigade, 83; defense of in unified party pact, 182; demands commands in People's Army, 112; enters League of Nations, 23; fearful of French security, 226 n. 6; fears uncontrollable revolution in Spain, 118; General Kleber in Army of, 236 n. 3; gold sent to, 81, 229 n. 44; and *GPU* purges, 118; Loyalist debt to, 82; Nazi agents in, 146; Politbureau of the Communist party of, decides to intervene in Spain, 73; Portugal accuses, in Non-Intervention Committee, 41; possibility Nin sent to, 172; *POUM* attacks on, 173, 237 n. 11; revolution-

ary aims of, 53; Right alleges, behind Popular Front, 39–43; signs security pact with France, 23; and *Socorro Rojo Internacional*, 115–6; and Spanish Communist party, 23; Spanish press prohibited from criticizing, 102; staff study of Spanish high command by, 231 n. 11; sympathy of Left for, 22; and trade with Spain, 72; United Front and defense of, 26, 180

USSR advisors to military, 103, 229 n. 49

USSR, aid of, to Loyalists: 122, 192, 193; acknowledgment of, 72, 226 n. 9; Anarchists fear end of, 151; to Asturias, 69; and bourgeois-Communist alliance, 159; Caballero fears end of, 121; and cabinet crisis of May, 1937, 157; Communists no longer rely only on, 131; concealment of, 73; conditions of, 225 n. 1; and defense of Madrid, 100, 130; distribution of, 233 n. 25; end of, 79, 200, 204; first use of, 73, 100; form of, 70; and *GPU*, 116; helps Communist party, 95, 98, 111, 196, 211; limit of, 162, 210; to Loyalist Air Force, 228 n. 30, 229 n. 31; methods of sending, 228 n. 24; Mussolini's attempts to stop, 228 n. 26; and Negrín, 169, 181; popularity of communism based on, 195; prior to Civil War, 40; quantity of, 74, 75, 79; reasons for, 70–1; tanks as part of, 227 n. 13; value of, 105

USSR, foreign policy of: 59, 206–7, 211–2; and Communist aims in Spain, 161–3; and Communist plot in Spain, 42–3; and Communist position in Spain, 138; and Communist program, 84, 161–3; and fear of war with Germany and Italy, 73–4; and isolation of France 71; and the Non-Intervention Agreement, 227 n. 17; secret police to aid, 119; and a Soviet Republic in Spain, 59

USSR press: attack on, 137; reports, 222 n. 13

USSR shipping: 220 n. 11, 228 n. 26; quantity of, 76; smuggles money, 69; and Soviet aid, 74, 77; and submarines, 75

USSR troops: number and kind in Spain, 82; Spain as training ground for, 75; use in Spain, 73

Utopia, Anarchists cling to, 93

Valdés attacks Prieto, 196

Valencia: controlled by People's Executive Committee, 65; Franco and, 203; government evacuation to, 100; retreat to, 100; rumor of International Brigade march on, 106; situation in, 135; speech of Hernández in, 113

Valencia government: Communists try to control, 101; and integration of Catalonia, 144; moved to Barcelona, 148; orders arms collected from workers, 134; and People's Courts in Catalonia, 141; takes control from Generalitat, 148

Valladolid, erroneous bombing of, 104

Varga, Eugene: on nationalism, 51; on a Soviet Republic for Spain, 223 n. 16; on Spanish situation, 46; on strength of Communist youth, 220 n. 38

Ventura, Spanish representative to Seventh Congress of Comintern, 52, 218 n. 31, 219 n. 32

Ventura, Juan. *See* Hernández, Jesús

Vidarte, Simeon, 240 n. 10

Violence: Churchill attributes to Communists before Civil War, 19; in Feb.-June, 1936, 17; general, in 1930's, 6

War Council. *See* Superior Council of War

War, Minister of: attacks on, 247 n. 7; in Caballero's government, 225 n. 1; *CNT* will accept only Largo Caballero as, 241 n. 1; Communist idea of functions of, 157; and control of Air Force and Tank Corps, 74; controls all fighting forces, 67; and the fall of Málaga, 233 n. 19; and the *Jaime I* explosion, 247 n. 4; Largo Caballero becomes, 65; Martínez Barrio wants General Mola as, 222 n. 5; Negrín as, 200; Prieto as, 159, 247 n. 9; Prieto's resignation as, 211

War, Minister of (Catalonia), refuses to apply mobilization decree, 141

War, Ministry of: Caballero allows Communists into, 120; Communists in the, 112, 113; is influenced by Russians, 103, 104; Socialists move against Communists in, 184–5, 186

War, Ministry of (Catalonia), absorbed into central government, 148

War mobilization, 245 n. 8

Wintringham, Tom, 230 nn. 54 and 55, 236 n. 1
Workers' committees in industry, 88
Workers' control: Communist demand for, 85; Communist idea of, 62; in industry, 88; omitted in Communist program, 92
Workers in Communist party, 94
Workers, industrial, conditions of, 2
Workers' and peasants' alliances, 219 n. 31
World revolution: emphasis on, changed, 56; and Soviet aid, 71; and the United Front program, 25

Youth: movements, strength of, 33; unification of, 55, 121–2. See also *AJA*; Anarchist youth; Communist youth; *JSU*; Socialist youth

Zinoviev, Gregory R., 146
Zugazagoitia, Julian: backs Prieto against Communists, 191; and Caballero government, 225 n. 1; comments on Prieto's speech, 248 n. 4; criticizes gold removal, 81–2; describes fame of Kleber, 130; describes Prieto's pessimism, 194; describes resignation of Asensio, 153–4; does not fear Communists, 195; explains independence of *GPU*, 116; and Negrín, 242 n. 1; in Negrín government, 159; on Negrín's difficulty with Prieto, 198; orders arrest of *POUM* Central Committee, 172; on relationship of Prieto and Negrín, 247 n. 11; and Trotskyism, 136